Theatre: Collaborative Acts

Theatre
Collaborative Acts

Ronald Wainscott

Indiana University

Kathy Fletcher

Indiana University

PEARSON
A B
and

Boston • New York • San Francisco • Mexico City • Montreal
Toronto • London • Madrid • Munich • Paris • Hong Kong
Singapore • Tokyo • Cape Town • Sydney

Executive Editor: *Karon Bowers*

Series Editor: *Molly Taylor*

Senior Development Editor: *Carol Alper*

Editorial Assistant: *Michael Kish*

Marketing Manager: *Mandee Eckersley*

Senior Production Administrator: *Donna Simons*

Composition and Prepress Buyer: *Linda Cox*

Manufacturing Buyer: *Megan Cochran*

Cover Administrator: *Linda Knowles*

Editorial-Production Service: *Omegatype Typography, Inc.*

Interior Designer: *Carolyn Deacy*

Cover Designer: *Studio Nine*

Photo Researchers: *Ronald Wainscott; Martha Shethar*

Illustrations: *Omegatype Typography, Inc.*

Electronic Composition: *Omegatype Typography, Inc.*

For related titles and support materials, visit our online catalog at www.ablongman.com.

Library of Congress Cataloging-in-Publication Data

Wainscott, Ronald Harold
    Theatre : collaborative acts / Ronald Wainscott, Kathy Fletcher.
      p. cm.
    Includes bibliographical references and index.
    ISBN 0-205-33379-6
     1. Theater and society.   I. Fletcher, Kathy, 1955–   II. Title.

  PN2049.W26 2004
  792—dc21

                          2003044419

Printed in the United States of America

10 9 8 7 6 5 4 3 2   WEB   08 07 06 05 04

Dedication

For Marion and Keith Michael,
who have inspired a passion for theatre in so many students

Brief Contents

Contents

♦♦♦♦♦ **CHAPTER 4** ♦♦♦♦♦

Understanding the Play:
A Theatrical Blueprint 87

Photo Gallery: Theatre of Diversity 164

♦♦♦ ACT II

Collaboration in History 172

♦♦♦♦♦ **CHAPTER 7** ♦♦♦♦♦

Foundations: Classical Theatrical Forms 175

◆◆◆ **ACT III**

Collaboration in Art and Practice 266

◆◆◆◆◆ **CHAPTER 12** ◆◆◆◆◆

The Playwright: Imagination and Expression 327

Preface

Imagine an activity at once physical, emotional, and intellectual. Imagine people creating art out of their own bodies and voices. Imagine an art form in which people can relate to each other directly, vibrantly, without the intervention of technology: no cell phones, no screens, no modems, no satellites. Imagine being able to observe, evaluate, participate in, and comment on this immediate communication. Imagine an activity that reproduces a wealth of human experience—both the best and worst our species has to offer—without physical hardship and pain.

The act of creating theatre is all of this. Theatre is human beings coming together at a particular time and place for no other reason than to practice being human, perhaps with the shared but unspoken hope that some day we will get it right!

How could we possibly describe an experience as rich and vast as the theatre in a book that would be light enough to carry around in a backpack? After spending over twenty years together seeing, producing, and directing plays, teaching classes, conducting research, and writing, we needed to make some difficult choices. The task of writing this book forced us to focus on what we believe is most important to share about the theatre experience at this moment in time: Theatre is *collaboration* in the purest sense of the word—it is co-labor, working together. This co-labor exists on many levels. To participate in theatre, as either audience member or practitioner, means to be at once an individual and part of a larger whole, even part of a continuum stretching far into the past as countless people find remarkably different ways to express the condition of being human. The essence of the theatre is shared experience. As such, it holds great potential for making connections in the twenty-first century.

Organization of This Text

Theatre throughout the ages has brought different answers to the questions: Who am I? Who are we? What belongs to me? What belongs to us? What really matters?

In the first part of this book, Act I, we explore theatre and its audience. We examine the theatre as cultural activity with its many possible social functions and relationship to society in order to provide a window into the way a society views itself. We have drawn on examples from many cultures as well as the Western tradition. We also consider the collaboration of the audience with the other components of theatre-making in experiencing and analyzing plays and productions. Act I concludes with the producing aspect of theatre—bringing the theatrical production and the audience together, another collaborative act.

The three chapters of Act II provide a brief history of theatrical collaboration. Because the past continually collaborates with the present in the theatre, we have included examples from other time periods in the chapters throughout the book. Act II, however, provides a sense of historical continuity and chronology. The discussion in Act II organizes theatrical events in chronological order and depicts the theatre as an ongoing negotiation of the personal and the social, the individual and the communal. Selecting what to include in an overview of 2,500 years of activity is, of course, extremely difficult. In some ways the choice is highly subjective; other theatre historians could give you their own versions, which would no doubt differ from ours. And of course, what we see as important is informed by the time at which we write.

Act III describes in detail the jobs and artistic contributions of theatre practitioners other than the audience—those who collaborate to prepare the theatrical event prior to the arrival of the audience: the playwright, director, actor, and designer.

◆◆◆◆◆◆◆◆◆◆

Special Features

Within each chapter we provide several series of special features to introduce students to the major themes and principles discussed in this book. In each chapter "Exploring Collaboration" boxes include profiles

◆ *Exploring Collaboration*

◆ *Exploring Historical and Cultural Perspectives*

◆ *Artists of the Theatre*

of successful artistic teams and feature a variety of approaches to the collaborative process. "Exploring Historical and Cultural Perspectives" boxes provide windows to specific theatrical events. "Artists of the Theatre" boxes introduce contemporary colorful and influential theatrical figures.

We have collected interrelated visuals as Photo Galleries after Acts I and III. "Theatre of Diversity" demonstrates a range of cultural, racial, stylistic, gender, and topical diversity in theatrical experiences. "Interpreting Space and Design" illuminates ways in which spaces have been redefined by directors and designers, and examines the human figure in space and the dynamics of three-dimensional performance. Following Act II we include "Key Theatrical Events,"

◆ *Photo Gallery: Interpreting*
Space and Design

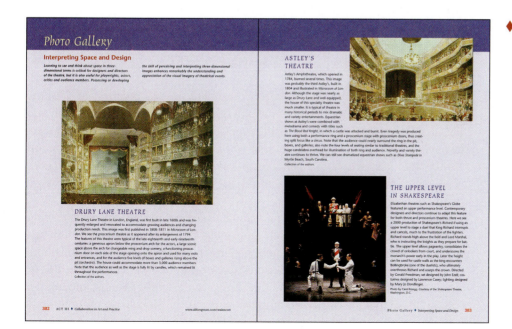

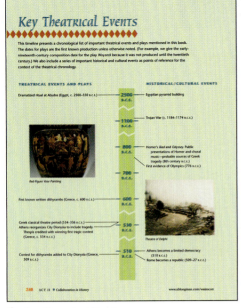

◆ *Key Theatrical Events*

a timeline of selected theatrical, social, and artistic events that allows students to place their explorations in a wider context.

At the end of each chapter we offer a series of study aids. "Questions and Activities" provide springboards for class discussions or outside projects. We arrange "Key Terms and Concepts" by topic followed by page number (the terms appear in boldface within the text). In "For Further Exploration" we suggest articles, books, videos, and web sites as places for students to pursue theatre topics that interest them.

◆ ◆ ◆ ◆ ◆ ◆ ◆ ◆ ◆

Supplemental Resources

We have prepared a package of resources to accompany *Theatre: Collaborative Acts*. The Instructor's Manual/Test Bank provides suggested syllabi, a course outline, and suggestions for using the book in an introduction to theatre course. The test questions include multiple-choice, true/false and short essay questions for each chapter and are available as a computerized test bank in TestGen as well as in printed format. A series of PowerPoint lectures are available online at www.ablongman.com/ppt. A Companion Website, found at www.ablongman.com/wainscott, contains an array of electronic materials for students and instructors including objectives, flashcards, weblinks, and practice tests.

In addition, Allyn and Bacon offers *Explore Theatre: A Backstage Pass*, a peer-to-peer interactive DVD learning tool (available in a package with the text at no additional cost) developed by students for students under the direction of Michael O'Hara, an award-winning teacher of theatre at Ball State University. Seventeen major content areas (director, actor, costume designer, etc.) are covered, with an eye toward introducing students to the people and processes that make theatre happen.

◆ ◆ ◆ ◆ ◆ ◆ ◆ ◆ ◆

Acknowledgments

Many people contributed directly or indirectly to the creation of *Theatre: Collaborative Acts*. This book began with a suggestion from our colleague and friend Michael Connolly to acquisitions editor Karon Bowers. Karon's successor, Molly Taylor, saw the work through the publication process. Our development editor, Carol Alper, encouraged and supported us and managed to remain both patient and good-humored while she organized, explained, critiqued, and asked stimulating questions.

We would like to thank our friend and colleague, Charles Railsback, teacher of introduction to theatre, for sharing ideas and his experiences with the course. Other friends and colleagues generously shared materials or read and responded to portions of the manuscript at various points, including Wes Peters, Robert Shakespeare, Rakesh Solomon, Linda Pisano, David Grindle, and Murray McGibbon at Indiana University, and Rob McKercher at Lincoln Community Playhouse. We thank Sue Vargo at Indiana University for her support and encouragement. Graduate students and colleagues who have taught introduction to theatre and theatre appreciation have shared their problems, ideas, and concerns with us, especially DeAnna Toten Beard, Terry Brino-Dean, Eileen Curley, Heather McMahon, Heather May, Larry Dooley, Laurie Schmeling, Michael Solomonson, and Andrew Hayes. Our many undergraduate students, especially those in our own introduction to theatre courses, have stimulated our thinking through their questions and insights.

We appreciate the help of librarians and photographic assistants, including Ms. Michael Scott, Folger Shakespeare Library, Washington, D.C.; Jeremy Megraw, New York Public Library for the Performing Arts; Kathleen Coleman, Harvard Theatre Collection; and the staff at the Museum of the City of New York.

Many theatre companies and arts organizations have contributed numerous hours in locating and providing photographs, programs, and other materials. We would like to thank the following individuals:

Kyle Shepherd, Actors Theatre of Louisville
Sara Gruber, The Shakespeare Theatre, Washington, D.C.
Ann Marie Czaban, Arena Stage, Washington, D.C.
Megan McKinney and Janet Allen, Indiana Repertory Theatre, Indianapolis
Julie Fogel, Cleveland Play House
Donna Law and Bruce C. Lee, Utah Shakespearean Festival, Cedar City
Cathy Taylor, Steppenwolf Theatre Company, Chicago
Dr. Marianne Tråvén, Sveriges Teatermuseum, Stockholm
Dina Croce and Holly Mosiello, Huntington Theatre Company, Boston
Jon Wolanske, American Conservatory Theatre, San Francisco
Beth Downing, La Jolla Playhouse
Ellen Charendoff, Stratford Festival Archives
Clay Hapaz, The Wooster Group, New York
Christy DeSmith, Theatre de la Jeune Lune, Minneapolis
Carla Steen, Guthrie Theater, Minneapolis
Elizabeth Wehrle, The Public Theater, New York
David LeShay, Theatre Development Fund
Pattie Haubner, League of American Theatres and Producers
Louis Spear, photographer, Baltimore

A number of our colleagues have provided helpful manuscript reviews at each stage of development. We hope this book has benefited from their helpful comments and advice. We wish to thank the following reviewers:

DeAnna Toten Beard, Baylor University
Brook Davis, Wake Forest University
Jerry R. Dickey, University of Arizona
Pamela Fields, Scottsdale Community College
Kathleen Gossman, Furman University
Matthew Gitkin, University of Miami
Michael Gravois, University of Memphis
Susan A. Hagedorn, Virginia Polytechnic Institute and State University
Randi J. Collins Hard, Parkland College
Mark Harvey, University of Minnesota, Duluth
Dennis R. Henneman, Youngstown State University
Leslie Hinderyckx, Northwestern University

Lani B. Johnson, Central Connecticut State University
David M. Jones, Parkland College
Ann Klautsch, Boise State University
Jasmin L. Lambert, The College of William and Mary
Scott McCoy, The University of Mississippi
Ray Miller, Georgia State University
Linda M. Pisano, Iowa State University
Ellis M. Pryce-Jones, University of Nevada, Las Vegas
Tina Redd, University of Washington
Douglas B. Rosentrater, Bucks County Community College
Yvonne Shafer, St. John's University
Terry D. Smith, University of South Carolina

We could not complete such a major project without the understanding, cooperation, and support of those closest to us. Jeremy and Kendra Fletcher Wainscott put up with many hours of parents doing "homework" rather than participating in family activities, and Doris and Chuck Fletcher helped us keep the family functioning while the writing progressed. The book itself is a collaborative act—the product of two authors, many colleagues, friends, and family members. We now leave it in the hands of you, the reader, to complete the collaborative process.

Ronald Wainscott
Kathy Fletcher

Theatre: Collaborative Acts

Theatre and Its Audience

Whereas literature is a private act of the imagination
(for writer and reader), theatre happens in the present
tense (fleetingly) before the eyes of an audience.
In order to be theatre, it must have witnesses.

TRACY C. DAVIS[1]

As a form of art and entertainment, theatre happens when audience and artists collaborate: Actors perform live for people watching, listening, and reacting. There is a certain satisfaction in the immediacy of theatre: It is always in present tense. Unlike the novel, film, poetry, and painting, which are created and then left for our experience, theatre is created anew with each performance. Theatre is malleable—it is formed and shaped by the here and now. It shares this quality with live performance of music and dance. Theatre also shares with dance the use of the human body to create art and with vocal music the use of the human voice. Human beings use their own forms to create meaning for other human beings—an intensely personal act.

Live theatre provides two-way communication. The audience member is not just a passive observer or receiver of a message; each spectator contributes in some measure to the nature of the theatrical event. In the vast majority of cases, theatre is a group activity—a group of theatre artists combines their talents to create an experience for a group of spectators. When individuals make the commitment to attend a performance, they become part of the entity of the audience and, to a great extent, respond as a group. It is difficult to laugh in an empty theatre; it is quite easy and enjoyable to laugh along with a crowd. A sense of unity is created when we recognize that those around us react with the same emotional intensity, whether with happiness, sadness, or anger. In the theatre, we feel that we are not alone.

FRENCH AUDIENCE in 1837 singing with a theatre orchestra.
Hand-tinted lithograph by Pruche. Collection of the authors.

Mr. Barry and Miss Nofsiter,
in the Characters of Romeo and Juliet.
Act 2d. Scene 2d.
Publish'd according to Act of Parliamt. May 19th. 1759

CHAPTER 1

Cultural Collaboration

Theatre and Society

Theatre as Entertainment and Art

The Social Functions of Theatre

- *Theatre and Religion*
- *Theatre and Socialization*
- *Theatre and Politics*
- *Theatre and Subversion*
- *Theatre and Coercion*
- *Theatre and Empowerment*
- *Theatre and Cultural Exploration*

Social Control of Theatre

- *Theatre and the Threat to Morality*
- *Theatre Regulation*
- *Theatre Censorship*

Cultural Context and Personal Experience

ROMEO AND JULIET. Mr. Barry and Miss Nossiter in the balcony scene, London, 1750s.
By permission of the Folger Shakespeare Library.

Human beings can live without theatre; some societies—such as the Sumerian, Mayan, and Aztec cultures—never developed sustained theatrical activity. But in different places all over the world, theatre has been invented and reinvented many times. Theatrical productions are artistic and cultural events that function as an integral part of the community within the society that supports it. The artistic context for theatrical production is an array of arts and humanities, some of which, like literature, dance, music, painting, and architecture, bear a close relationship to theatre art. Theatre may imitate, parody, criticize, or celebrate a society's foibles and greatness and sometimes lead or incrementally alter a society's development and identity. The larger social context is usually reflected in theatre, but the theatre also interacts directly with other aspects of culture.

The span of theatrical activity in the twenty-first century is vast. Folk performances that have continued, little changed, for centuries bring people together in small villages. Tourists enjoy multi-million-dollar productions using state-of-the-art electronic equipment in metropolitan centers. Schoolchildren perform their own interpretations of historical events, and elders find a voice and camaraderie in performance. To be fair, most contemporary society is fragmented, and so is the theatre art that serves and reflects that society. To talk about theatre is to talk about many theatres. In this chapter, we explore the primary purposes of theatre, the various social roles that theatre fulfills, and its position in society.

◆◆◆◆◆◆◆◆◆◆
Theatre as Entertainment and Art

Theatre is a form of entertainment. It provides diversion—a vacation from reality. Like other live entertainment experiences such as concerts, dance performances, and live sporting events, theatre provides an experience that a person chooses for its own sake. Going to the theatre is not about earning money or paying bills. For a while, the audience member focuses on the world within the theatre, the fictional action and events played out by the actors.

Theatre that is meant strictly as entertainment concentrates on this escape from reality and does not usually challenge the beliefs of the majority of its audience or push an audience beyond its comfort zone. In this way theatre serves the important social function of reinforcing values. In the nineteenth century the theatre served as a leisure activity for a mass audience in Europe, Asia, and North America. In the twentieth century that role was largely taken over by film, then radio, television, and the Internet. Many of today's comedies, thrillers, and musical comedies, however, are examples of theatre as popular entertainment. Some of the best-loved American plays fall into this category; *Harvey* (1944) by Mary Chase, *The Odd Couple* (1965) by Neil Simon, and *The Fantasticks* (1960) by Harvey Schmidt and Tom Jones feature exciting action, humor, and poignancy, all the while confirming our basic notions of good and evil. Likewise, many British thrillers continue to engage audiences. New generations feel the mounting tension as suspicion shifts from one eccentric character to another in Agatha Christie's *The Mousetrap* (1952). A lot can be learned about a society by looking

The Lure of Safe Conduct and Invisible Rabbits

EXPLORING HISTORICAL AND CULTURAL PERSPECTIVES

The safe but entertaining domestic comedy has long been important to the success of popular theatre, especially when good fortune at the box office is a major concern of the producers. Such plays were important to the Greeks in the Hellenistic era, to the Roman Republic, and in nearly every major period of professional theatre. Escapist plays are popular during periods of great stress, such as wartime and economic downturns, but are also popular in periods of comparative equanimity. Most notable of all, perhaps, many popular plays of the past continue to grace the stages of high schools, universities, community theatres, resident professional theatres, and commercial houses of major cities. The appeal, while not quite universal, is clearly widespread and far-reaching.

The initial popularity of Neil Simon's mega-hit *The Odd Couple* in 1965 led to a first Broadway run of 996 performances, a feature film (starring Walter Matthau as Oscar, a character he had also created on stage), and a television series (starring Jack Klugman, who followed Matthau in the original run as Oscar). Audiences enjoy the focus on disparate lifestyles and value systems and the quirky, incompatible characters who are in almost constant conflict with one another but ultimately demonstrate compassionate friendship. In 1985 Simon fashioned a new incarnation of *The Odd Couple* with female characters. A seemingly endless number of revivals (with casts of both sexes) continue up to this moment. The play's familiar comic structure and generous supply of funny one-liners create an ideal formula for satisfying the entertainment needs of millions of people.

On the other hand, *Harvey* (1944) by Mary Chase is a much gentler approach to the oddball in society. The eccentricities of the central character, Elwood P. Dowd, lead to many misunderstandings and the suspicion that Elwood is insane. He claims to be in the company of a man-sized rabbit he calls Harvey, who is invisible to everyone else, including the audience. The initial popularity of this play outdistanced that of *The Odd Couple* by running for over seventeen hundred consecutive performances. It has also enjoyed frequent revivals at all levels and a feature film starring the genial Jimmy Stewart as Elwood.

As *Harvey* develops, it becomes clear to the audience that even if Elwood imagines the rabbit, he is much more well-adjusted than any other character—including a psychia-

◆ **SAM STEWART**, *as the leading character Elwood P. Dowd, in* Harvey *by Mary Chase, a perennial American favorite comedy revived by the Utah Shakespearean Festival in 2002.*
Photo by Karl Hugh. By permission of the Utah Shakespearean Festival.

trist who goes off the deep end trying to ferret out Elwood's problem but ends up imagining that he is being pursued by the invisible rabbit. Such a take-down of authority figures is a recurring plot element in many comedies and melodramas. Even though in life many people shun the outsider and the misunderstood soul in their midst, when a character such as Elwood appears onstage, audiences are often drawn to the eccentric. A similar shift of sensibilities occurs with stage villains. Audiences are often intrigued with stage villains, though in life they would likely be terrified of a similar person.

◆ **OEDIPUS THE KING,** *produced by the Shakespeare Theatre, Washington, D.C. Avery Brooks, as Oedipus, enters to the chorus in this production inspired by African culture and art. Notice the large central door, normally a feature traditional to Greek tragedy; but its decoration and all elements of the scenic design by Charles McClennahan are African motifs. The dark tribal costumes of the chorus stand in stark contrast to the majestic, colorful costume of Oedipus in designs by Toni-Leslie James. The staging and design leave no doubt about which character is the ruler of the city of Thebes. The 2001 production of Nicholas Rudall's translation of Sophocles'* The Oedipus Plays *was directed by Michael Kahn.*
Photo by Carol Rosegg. By permission of the Shakespeare Theatre.

at its forms of popular entertainment, since these tend to reinforce currently accepted values. It is often hard to analyze objectively the entertainment of our own society, since it calls on deeply held assumptions and beliefs.

Theatre is also an art form. As such, it often challenges its audience to think harder, look deeper, confront uncomfortable truths, or come to a higher understanding. This is not to say, of course, that theatre as art is not entertaining. While it requires some effort on the part of the audience, such theatre can be exhilarating, enlightening, and life-changing. Like other forms of art, theatre can help an audience member look at life in a different way or provide a focused version of reality.

Some of the world's greatest authors looked to the theatre as the best forum to express specific ideas as well as explore the human condition in general. *Oedipus the King* (c. 430 B.C.E.) by Sophocles, for example, has long stood as a remarkable examination of duty to whatever gods may exist and the necessity of adhering to important rules of conduct. Oedipus is guilty of violating human and divine law, even though he does not realize he has committed crimes until he comes face to face with his own guilt. Although he is looking for a murderer throughout most of the action of the play, he does not recognize until late that he himself is the criminal he seeks. While he has sight, he is figuratively blind. He punishes himself by putting out his own eyes and, now blinded, can at last see clearly. Although the conditions inherent in this play are extreme (Oedipus kills his father, marries his mother, and has children who are also his brothers and sisters), it still leads us to ponder the nature of humanity and our own failure to see our lives clearly. The issues in *Copenhagen* (2000), a play by Michael Frayn, are more contemporary; three friends, two of whom were scientists whose contributions were central to the development of atomic physics and weapons, examine the past, trying to identify reasons for each other's actions. Like *Oedipus*, however, the play asks difficult questions about the perception of reality and personal moral responsibility.

◆◆◆◆◆◆◆◆◆◆

The Social Functions of Theatre

Although providing entertainment and artistic experience are its primary purposes, theatre can serve a number of functions simultaneously. At various times theatre has been part of religious ritual, a civic celebration, a status symbol, a means of educating the young, a way of maintaining or challenging the status quo, a protest against the establishment, a means of sexual titillation, a way of raising morale and expressing solidarity, a propaganda vehicle, a profit-making venue, and a way of sparking discussion. The collaboration of actors and audience has created a powerful force in many different cultures.

THEATRE AND RELIGION

Theatre shares many important connections with religious institutions. The earliest known theatrical presentations appear to have been steeped in religious ritual and dance. In ancient Egypt priests reenacted stories of the gods, probably for an audience. Many other old societies, including those of Native Americans, Africans, and Southeast Asians, performed theatrical rituals led by a priest or shaman. The shaman celebrated the past or invoked the gods by collaborating with both the deities and the audience of believers. The performance was often very interactive in terms of impersonation, song, chant, dance, and spiritual response. Transformation was frequently a part of religious ritual. Performers not only represented another being but also believed that wearing the mask of a god or an ancestor led to a kind of possession—the spirit of the deity or ancestor inhabited the body of the performer. Ritual can be a way of connecting with other worlds and is sometimes meant to effect a change in this world. Some Native American tribes, for example, performed a particular dance ritual when rain was needed or before setting out to hunt or fight.

The traditional view of historians is that Western theatre had its beginnings in religious ritual. Its development was associated with festivals celebrating and praising the Greek god Dionysus. Although it is difficult to say when, the Greeks moved from using theatrical performance as a part of ritual to enjoying the performance for its own sake while still using it to communicate important stories or information. Unaware of the Greek legacy, the medieval Christian church introduced theatrical activity into religious service and then recognized the potential of theatre as a means to familiarize a mainly illiterate public with biblical stories. This tradition

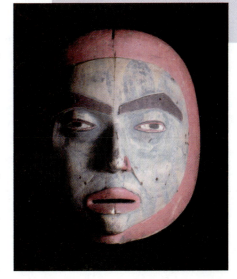

◆ **TLINGIT SHAMAN WOODEN MASK,** *emblematic of the moon, from the nineteenth century. In ritual the mask is often a very powerful adornment of the Shaman, who may be seen to become one with the mask and what the mask represents.* Princeton Museum of Natural History, New Jersey/Bridgeman Art Library.

KATHAKALI PERFORMERS *in extravagant costume and makeup with percussive musicians, simple open stage with cloth backing. During the Middle Ages and the Renaissance in Europe, this would have been called a booth stage.*
Photo by and courtesy of Rakesh Solomon.

continues in dramatizations within houses of worship (the traditional Christmas pageant, for example) as well as in large outdoor spaces. Today in India, Kathakali dance drama still enacts episodes from the great Hindu epics, the *Ramayana* and the *Mahabharata*. Some of our century's most eloquent playwrights recognize the cultural and dramatic importance of religious ritual. Nigerian playwright Wole Soyinka (b. 1934) uses traditional Yoruba ritual to structure many of his plays. Even when recognized primarily as a form of entertainment, the theatre has been used as a vehicle to disseminate and reinforce religious beliefs.

THEATRE AND SOCIALIZATION

The Roman writer Horace defined the function of theatre as to teach and to please. At times the educational potential of theatre has been considered its most important asset, particularly as a way of passing on a society's rules of behavior. Generations of young people absorbed social and moral lessons by watching actors on the stage. Even at a time when attending the theatre was thought inappropriate for proper young ladies, British author Hanna More (1745–1833) wrote plays to be performed at home, specifically designed to teach acceptable feminine values. Nineteenth-century melodramas offered a host of heroes and heroines to emulate as well as villains to despise. Apprentices in eighteenth- and nineteenth-century London were encouraged to attend the theatre on Boxing Day (the day after Christmas) to see a traditional performance of *The London Merchant* (1731), the sad story of a young apprentice who fell into bad company, murdered his master, and suffered dire consequences. Although child- and family-oriented television programs have largely taken over the job of teaching moral standards and behavior to young people, life lessons that are acceptable to the current audience are still embedded in plays. *The Lion King* (1997)—first an animated film and then a popular Broadway musical—demonstrates that the circle of life is sacred and that in disrupting that natural balance, one risks losing everything. But if one accepts the circle of life and nourishes it, one is rewarded.

THEATRE AND POLITICS

Theatre has frequently been used to reinforce the political status quo and build support for the government that is in power. Ruling monarchs were often praised in the plays of the sixteenth and seventeenth centuries. Early American theatres staged the apotheosis of George Washington shortly after his death to honor and celebrate a cultural hero; audiences watched an actor representing the first president ascend to heaven to be welcomed by the angels. In the twentieth century the struggles of the founding fathers and mothers were memorialized in the musical *1776* (1969) as it created a lively, human background for the birth of the Declaration of Independence.

Theatrical performance has often been used to present **propaganda**—material specifically designed to advocate a particular point of view—to both support the status quo and challenge or undermine it. Before the era of newsreels and, later, television news programs, military victories (including naval battles) were reenacted and celebrated in theatres, from ancient Rome to the early twentieth century in the United States and Europe. Besides providing escape from highly stressful reality during times of war, theatre has offered patriotic support. During World War I, for example, the American theatre featured musical reviews (complete with dancing girls) such as *Doing Our Bit* (1917), which encouraged its audience to conserve war materials. *Mother's Liberty Bond* (1918) advocated the purchase of bonds to support the war effort, and ticket sales from the show helped to supply cigarettes for U.S. soldiers. Theatre has also been used to spread a negative image of enemies. *War Brides* (1915) depicted a German government forcing women to have children to populate its army.

♦ **THE CRUCIBLE,** *performed at the University of Nebraska. In this photograph a group of girls pretends to be possessed by witches. The play reveals the duplicity of the girls yet makes their pretended possession seem real to the adult characters and moves the audience as well.* Collection of the authors.

THEATRE AND SUBVERSION

Although the theatre often supports and maintains the dominant culture, it can also be used to subvert the status quo in society. Just as the theatre can provide support for a society's values, it can also offer a public forum for challenge and disagreement. An undercurrent of subversive thought may be introduced even in plays that, as a whole, reinforce traditional standards. In the seventeenth century, British playwright Aphra Behn wrote delightful comedies such as *The Rover* (1677) that pleased her audiences. In the midst of the fun, however, her heroines manage to protest

◆ **THE MERCHANT OF VENICE,** *produced by Augustin Daly in the 1880s. This photograph is a good example of a white actor in blackface. Although the Prince of Morocco is a black character in Shakespeare's play, he is played here (as was the norm in Europe and North America before well into the twentieth century) by a white actor in blackface. The Prince is a suitor to Portia, played by the production's star, Ada Rehan, who is sitting on the chaise and gesturing to the small caskets that hold the fate of the prince.*
By permission of the Folger Shakespeare Library.

the limitations on women's behavior. They speak very clearly about the difficult position of a woman whose entire future rested on the marriage she could make. Sometimes theatre artists have commented on politically sensitive issues by carefully selecting material to send a message yet avoid a direct challenge to the governing powers. Arthur Miller wrote *The Crucible* (1953) at the height of the McCarthy era, when many members of the performance community were being blacklisted for their real or perceived leftist beliefs. A play that is ostensibly about the Salem witch trials of the seventeenth century, *The Crucible* could also be interpreted as a comment on the anticommunist hysteria and injustice at work in the United States after World War II.

At other times, theatre has been used quite obviously as a tool for protest and social change. African Americans have been using the stage to break down stereotypes since the 1950s. In Douglas Turner Ward's *Day of Absence* (1965), black actors play white characters in white makeup—a comment on the theatrical stereotype created by white minstrels playing in blackface. The plays of Athol Fugard carried an antiapartheid message far beyond his native South Africa. *Master Harold . . . and the Boys* (1982) explores the larger issues of black and white relations by concentrating on the interaction between two adult black men and their white employers' son, a lonely schoolboy. Feminist troupes such as Spiderwoman Theatre (formed in 1985) use the stage to explore women's position in society and work for change. Theatre has provided a forum for challenging gay and lesbian stereotypes. *Cloud Nine* (1979) by Caryl Churchill examines twentieth-century assumptions about gender by juxtaposing them to Victorian attitudes about sex. *The Normal Heart* by Larry Kramer (1985) advocates AIDS activism and criticizes the sluggish response to the disease by the general public.

Theatre has been used to protest war. American antiwar plays frequently appeared in the twentieth century beginning in 1915. Dramatic images of horror and violence appear in many plays of the late twentieth century protesting war and racist violence in Bosnia and the Middle East, such as *The Balkan Express* (1994) by Mima Vulović. Playwright Tony Kushner sets most of the action of *Homebody/Kabul* (2001) in Kabul, Afghanistan. Written shortly before September 11, 2001, and the subsequent U.S. invasion of that country, the play is a remarkable study in cultural and linguistic confusion ("chaos" is probably a better word). Kabul becomes a kind of cradle of Cain (the first murderer), a crossroads of international manipulation resembling a biblical Tower of Babel.

Opposition to U.S. involvement in Vietnam formed the centerpiece of the late 1960s counterculture, which found expression in theatrical experiment in the cities of Paris, New York, and San Francisco. The concerns of young people were embodied in productions as disturbing as the Living Theatre's *Paradise Now* (1968), in which audiences were berated from the stage and challenged to join the revolution. Although a relatively safer production, the rock musical *Hair*

♦ *MASTER HAROLD . . . AND THE BOYS,* by Athol Fugard. The two black characters are played here by (left to right) Ramolao Makhene, as Sam, and Alfred Nokwe, as Willie. Directed and costumes by Murray McGibbon; scenic design by Martin Bekker; produced by the Natal Performing Arts Council, Durban, South Africa. Photo by Val Adamson. By permission of the director.

♦ *HOMEBODY/KABUL,* by Tony Kushner, New York Theatre Workshop. Milton Ceiling, played by Dylan Baker, a British man searching for his murdered wife in Afghanistan, interviews an Afghani woman, Mahala, played by Rita Wolf. Directed by Declan Donnellan. Photo by Joan Marcus.

Exploring Historical and Cultural Perspectives

Antiwar Plays

Western theatre has a long history of antiwar plays or, in some cases, plays that can be interpreted as antiwar statements. In the United States antiwar or anti-specific-war plays regularly appeared throughout the twentieth century—usually just as a war was threatening on the horizon or after its horrors were concluded. During wartime (at least when the United States was engaged) antiwar plays were rarely produced, either because of government restrictions or because artists wished to avoid productions that could be interpreted as unpatriotic. The big exception to this pattern is the Vietnam War, which was marked by antiwar demonstrations throughout.

As World War I was beginning in Europe, the United States attempted to remain neutral. Although it was clear which side the United States favored, it still remained out of combat from 1914 (when the war began) until 1917. Early on during the war a number of antiwar plays were professionally produced in New York and on tour, and some were published as books or in periodicals. Many of the plays were written by women. One of the most effective was *Moloch* (1915) by Beulah Dix. The action is set in Europe and focuses on the violence and inhumanity (including senseless killing) practiced on civilians by unfeeling soldiers and government representatives. Such plays not only stood as a warning, but also sparked much debate among critics and audiences. Once the United States declared war on the Central Powers, all that was seen on the stage was patriotic and supportive of the war effort. After the smoke cleared in November 1918, however, the antiwar plays appeared again, this time arguing that such a horrendous global cataclysm must never be allowed to occur again. One of the most effective antiwar plays ever, and one that is frequently revived, is *Aria da Capo* (1919) by Edna St. Vincent Millay. A symbolic portrayal of war is embedded in a silly comedy that both begins and ends the play; at the end the comedy attempts to disguise the fact that the audience just watched two young men kill each other over possessions and petty jealousy. *What Price Glory* (1924) by Maxwell Anderson and Laurence Stallings demonstrated military ineptitude and brought a cynical view of war to the stage. In a very disturbing scene, the dead and wounded yield to terror and deny God in the midst of cacophony and pain. The upshot is that the Great War should never have been fought in the first place.

Just as antiwar plays appeared as a prelude to World War I, dramatic warnings began to appear when European saber-rattling started in the mid-1930s. One of the new efforts was *Bury the Dead* by Irwin Shaw (1936), which forecast World War II but saw it in World War I terms. The play depicts a stalemate in no-man's-land and senseless carnage; the soldiers are pawns of the unfeeling generals. Because the 1930s were a period of labor and political unrest marked by demonstrations and strikes, Shaw has his slain soldiers create a demonstration of their own. As living soldiers are attempting to bury some of the fallen soldiers, the corpses rise up, stand in their graves, and refuse to be buried.

The most unpopular war in American history must be the Vietnam War, which inspired loud protest. The mid- to late-1960s resonated with antiwar chants on the streets as well as in the theatres. Megan Terry's play with music, *Viet Rock* (1966), assaulted the senseless carnage of the war, and the musical *Hair* (1968) by Gerome Ragni (who performed in the first production of *Viet Rock*) and James Rado confronted the audience with many social and cultural issues of the day (especially a youthful counterculture), overshadowed by the ever-present war in Indochina. Many playwrights in the 1970s focused on soldiers returning home from war, trying to readjust to civilian life—always with difficulty and often without success. David Rabe's portrayal was especially effective in *Sticks and Bones* (1971), a disturbing wartime domestic conflict that parodied the TV sitcom *Ozzie and Harriet*. Since World War I, playwrights have explored the readjustment period of soldiers, and many of these have proven to be the most effective antiwar efforts or poignant demonstrations of the lingering effects of warfare.

Interested? Check out

Coming to Terms: American Plays and the Vietnam War, introduction by James Reston, Jr. New York: Theatre Communications Group, 1985.

(1968) questioned the U.S. participation in Vietnam and celebrated social protest and nonconformist behavior.

Specific needs have been the catalyst for theatre troupes with a clearly defined social and political purpose. The Free Southern Theatre was created in 1963 to support the civil rights movement. Luis Valdéz (b. 1940) formed El Teatro Campesino in 1965 to help change the situation of migrant workers in the United States. Believing that traditional theatre reinforces the existing class system, Brazilian Augusto Boal (b. 1931) has developed the "theatre of the oppressed," an alternative way of making performance in communities designed to empower the disenfranchised.

Propaganda has been used to protest as well as support government action and to argue directly for social and political change. Women lobbied for the vote in suffrage plays during the late nineteenth and early twentieth centuries. Beginning in 1961, Bread and Puppet Theatre combined larger-than-life puppets with human actors on the streets as well as in theatres to express impassioned disagreement with foreign and domestic U.S. policy.

THEATRE AND COERCION

Recognizing its potential power, very repressive governments have entirely coopted theatre, along with the other arts, in attempts to win the hearts and minds of the people. In Germany during the 1930s the Nazi regime used highly theatricalized political rallies and forbade the production of any plays that did not seem to support its political position. Many theatrical artists fled Germany during this period.

In China during the period known as the Cultural Revolution (1966–1980) the communist government attempted to suppress or reform all "decadent" traditional forms of theatre, replacing them with works designed to praise and justify the current ideology. To disrupt the artistic legacy, officials ordered renowned artists put to work at menial jobs or hard labor.

Similarly, for many years the only accepted style of art in the Soviet Union was socialist realism, which was judged by those in power to support and reflect the Soviet value system. Artists who insisted on voicing an opposing viewpoint or experimenting with different forms did so at their peril. In 1939 the brilliant and unconventional director Vsevelod Meyerhold (1874–1940) disappeared one night from his Leningrad apartment. After being tortured and beaten, the 66-year-old man signed a confession (later recanted) that he had participated in anti-Soviet activity. He was executed in 1940, and his actress wife was mutilated and murdered. For fifteen years the Soviet Union suppressed any mention of Meyerhold's name.

THEATRE AND EMPOWERMENT

Theatrical performance can be a tool for healing, for individual growth, and for facilitating group process. A visit to the web site "Arts As a Force of Healing, Building, and Empowerment" at www.artslynx.org/heal will give you an idea of the vast number of ways in which theatre is currently being used. The site was created for the Colorado Council on the Arts with funding from the National Endowment for the Arts after the tragic shooting of students at Columbine High School. Creators of the web site recognize the role of the arts in community building and dedicate the site "not only to the healing power of the arts, but to

Exploring Collaboration

Interact Center for the Visual and Performing Arts

Examples of theatre dedicated to both accessibility and empowerment are created at the Interact Center for the Visual and Performing Arts. Located in Minneapolis, Minnesota, the Center describes itself as a place where artists gather because of their abilities, not their disabilities. At Interact artists with disability labels create, perform, earn, and help the community understand that gifts are given to all people and that vision is not lost or even impaired by a disabling condition.

Theatre is made at Interact when artists create and perform their own dialogue, lyrics, music, and dance. Performers include those diagnosed with physical challenges, Down syndrome, schizophrenia—any condition that would put them outside the traditional venues for making art. Interact lists its objectives as follows:

◆ To challenge stereotypes caused by labels that focus on peoples' deficits and to illuminate talents and abilities

◆ To create opportunities for artists in the community to work together in an inclusive, creative, and truly diverse company

◆ To create a conduit for change in the community leading to a more humane and supportive treatment for people with disabilities, the elderly, and the disadvantaged.

Besides providing an opportunity for special performers, the center facilitates the presentation of viewpoints that are usually unavailable to, or at least unrecognized by, most audience members.

Arts that are practiced at Interact include acting, singing, music composition, creative writing, painting, sculpting, ceramics, fiber arts, and bookmaking. Professional artists are employed to help coach and instruct. Interact's performing artists share their work by touring and giving workshops and performances to educate professionals in the social service community. In 2002 the theatre troupe toured Scandinavia to share its creations with an international audience.

Interested? Check out

The Interact Center for the Visual and Performing Arts web site at www.interactcenter.com.

---

providing access to the arts for diverse populations that all humans may be empowered by the arts to be able to realize their full positive potential."[2] Links are provided to theatre organizations dedicated to fighting prejudice, to helping youth at risk, to AIDS prevention, and to special initiatives addressing the September 11, 2001, tragedy as well as those focused on learning disabilities, older adults, and blind and deaf populations.

In the twentieth century accessibility to theatre for all audience members became a serious consideration. For deaf and hearing-impaired audience members many theatres now have sound intensification systems available and offer performances translated into sign language or captioned (with dialogue projected above the stage or in another location). Audio description provides a moment-by-moment narration of what is happening on stage for blind theatre patrons. While watching the show, a describer transmits descriptions over individual headsets. Some theatrical troupes go a step further and actually integrate the cultures of differently abled groups. The National Theatre of the Deaf (founded in 1967) has been a pioneer in this field, combining deaf and hearing performers and visual and aural expression to produce an exciting new language of the theatre.

Some theatrical organizations specialize in interactive performance designed to accomplish a specific goal. Actors develop skits to spark discussion on problems facing young people—drugs, date rape, domestic and street violence—or may help groups of people to tell and then dramatize their own stories. The intended result of such theatrical activity does not end with the performance; the performance is used as a catalyst for individual and group exploration.

The act of creating theatre, along with other arts, can have a therapeutic effect for those involved. Although such effects are useful, they remain a by-product when the focus is on creating art and entertainment. In arts therapy, however, the purpose of theatrical activity changes to individual development rather than audience communication. Drama therapy, as defined by the National Association for Drama Therapy (NADT), has the therapeutic goals of symptom relief, emotional and physical integration, and personal growth.[3] Drama therapy is included in many different settings, including mental health facilities, nursing homes, schools, businesses, and correctional facilities.

THEATRE AND CULTURAL EXPLORATION

The study of theatre as a social institution is a vital method for learning about the goals and aspirations, the prejudices and blind spots—the good and the bad—of different societies. Human beings create theatre in the image of themselves—of how they see themselves or wish themselves to be. As such, the theatre mirrors the personality not only of the author of the play, the leading actor, or the famous director but also of the society in which and for which it was developed. Every theatrical performance is embedded in a particular context—social, political, and historical. No matter how far removed an audience might be from a play or record of its performance, some residue of that context remains.

As with other art forms, theatre can expand our cultural horizons. While watching Caryl Churchill's *Mad Forest* (1990), an English-speaking audience can begin to understand the despair and paranoia that were rampant in Romania during the rule of the dictator Ceaușescu and the subsequent joy and confusion after his fall. Even a play set in the audience's home country can provide a connection to a different cultural experience. Encountering the effects of racism on the south side of Chicago with the Younger family opened the eyes of white audience members who attended Lorraine Hansberry's *A Raisin in the Sun* (1959). Mark Medoff's *Children of a Lesser God* (1980) traced the relationship of a

◆ *PICASSO AT THE LAPIN AGILE,* by Steve Martin. The action of the play takes place in a bar in Paris in 1904, mixing then-unknowns Albert Einstein and Pablo Picasso at a time when their careers were about to explode on the world. Directed by Sullivan Canaday White; scenic design by Tom Burch; costumes designed by Jessica Byrd Watters and Annelise Beeckman.
Photo by Richard C. Trigg.
By permission of Actors Theatre of Louisville.

deaf woman and a hearing man and opened a door for many people who had never experienced deaf culture.

The fact that theatre is usually a live production of a previously written play makes it particularly effective as a means for exploring life in other times. Even though theatre performance lasts only a few hours, play texts may be preserved indefinitely. Plays still exist from ancient Greece, Rome, India, and China, and plays can be studied as literary documents in and of themselves. William Shakespeare wrote most of his scripts in the last decade of the sixteenth century and the first decade of the seventeenth for a troupe of actors (including himself) who were eager to draw an audience and outsell a rival company. Today, Shakespeare's plays are read for quite different reasons; they are examples of English poetry at its most beautiful, of thought about the human condition at its most profound. Because Shakespeare chose to write plays, however, you can watch and hear as well as read them. Although theatrical performance can never be recovered, it is possible today to witness the same play that our ancestors saw 400 years ago—or even 2,400 years ago. Certainly, the actors perform it differently, and the audience brings a very different context to its understanding of the words and the action. The very fact that it is possible to witness a human reenactment of the same story, however, creates the possibility for connection with and greater understanding of the past.

The nature of a theatrical event in society may be quite different today from that in the past. Greek tragedy, for example, developed as a dynamic element of art and competition in a multiple-day festival that was both a civic event and a religious celebration. Even though classical Greek tragedies are still revived, sometimes in surviving outdoor Greek theatres, the productions are no longer associated with the worship of the god Dionysus, and Greek Dionysian priests are no longer in prominent attendance in the front row. Athens long ago ceased to be a cultural, political, and economic power in the world, and its current festivals have little to do with the festivals of 534 B.C.E. Much of that ancient cultural context has disappeared or is only marginally applicable to current European life. Nonetheless, people are still interested in many of the ancient Greek plays. An understanding of the cultural context surrounding their origins and first performances helps us to better understand the possibilities of the work. Surviving plays and other evidence of production such as critical reviews, letters, diaries, and ruins of ancient theatres provide clues to what happened in theatres long ago and might inspire theatre artists in presenting plays for an audience to appreciate now.

The French playwright Molière wrote *The Misanthrope* in 1666. In this comedy, the main character, disgusted by the hypocrisy of his peers, rejects them all and vows to live a solitary life. If you read this play, even in a modern English translation rather than the original French, you will see many reflections of the seventeenth century when it was written and first produced: portraits of wealthy

◆ **THE MISANTHROPE,** *by Molière, in traditional costuming and wigs of the seventeenth century, Stratford Shakespeare Festival. Brian Bedford courts Vivian Pickles as Célimène.*
Photo courtesy of Billy Rose Theatre Collection, the New York Public Library for the Performing Arts, Astor, Lennox and Tilden Foundations.

Parisian society, that society's regard for social duplicity, the power of rich widows, and a host of other conditions, large and small, that are etched into the text overtly or subtly. Unless you completely rewrite the text, much of the world of seventeenth-century French culture remains. You could choose to update the play's sets and costumes to 2004 and change the setting to a public dance floor instead of an ornate room in the house of the heroine. Nonetheless, the seventeenth century still lurks in many corners of the play.

If you produce *The Misanthrope* now, however, you cannot help but infuse it with twenty-first century ideas and interpretations. Even if you slavishly recreate costumes of 1666, imitate the interior of an expensive Parisian house of the time, complete with period furniture and decorations, and teach the actors what we still know of courtly manners and movement, much of the production will smack of the twenty-first century. The cultural assumptions, values, and tastes of the moment of production always combine with the culture of the past that gave birth to the original play. This combination of past and present is one of the exciting but also daunting aspects of producing plays from other periods and cultures. As much as we might like to, we cannot really revisit history or travel to the past. We can, however, reconstruct possibilities of past cultures, somewhat like cultural and artistic anthropologists and archeologists.

The opportunity to make material from the past come alive in the present also raises interesting and sometimes difficult ethical questions. Should a theatre company present a work from the past if it contains material that would be objectionable today? Shakespeare's *The Merchant of Venice* (c. 1596), the story of a shopkeeper who insists on extracting a "pound of flesh" as payment from a

◆ **PUSS IN BOOTS**, *as produced in this children's version by Eric Schmiedl at the Cleveland Play House, with a racially diverse cast. The actors are Nick Koesters, Brandon Lewis, James Mango, and Ebony Wimbs. Directed by William Hoffman.* Photo by Roger Mastroianni. By permission of Cleveland Play House.

young man, depicts Christians more sympathetically than Jews. American plays written before 1960 by white authors sometimes include stereotypical portrayals of people of color. Is producing such work insulting to the modern audience? Or is it important to present such material from the past as a reminder of our history and opportunity for analysis?

While theatre can be a place where different cultures meet, are there some boundaries that should be kept intact? **Nontraditional casting**—casting actors of a different race than the character as written—has slowly become an accepted practice in the theatre since the civil rights movement. Casting an actor of color to play a character written as white is one way of expanding opportunities; because of many years of exclusion, there are fewer roles in plays for actors of color. But should white actors play characters of color? Should playwrights depict cultures that are different from their own? Resurrecting pieces of the past and crossing cultural boundaries offer exciting opportunities but bring significant responsibilities. The road is not always easy to negotiate.

◆ ◆ ◆ ◆ ◆ ◆ ◆ ◆ ◆

Social Control of Theatre

Although theatre's potential for positive contribution is recognized in many societies, such is not always the case. In some cultures and subcultures any kind of theatrical activity has been (and continues to be) thought of as a threat to morality and the entire fabric of society and has been the target of many attempts at official control.

THEATRE AND THE THREAT TO MORALITY

The Greek philosopher Plato found theatre disturbing and potentially dangerous. Because Plato found theatre so effective in performance, he feared that convincing acting and the powerful language of a gifted playwright could harm society if the artists decided to present subversive or morally corrupt ideas. Theatre was not truthful in his view because it was based on imitation of action and character rather than being reality. Early Christian leaders (second to fifth century C.E.) invoked arguments similar to Plato's but went much further in finding the whole nature of performance corrupt, establishing a long history of opposition to theatrical activity in some branches of the church. In seventeenth-century France, it was standard practice for retired actors to renounce their profession in order to be eligible for Christian burial. In some teachings of Islam any theatrical depiction of character is prohibited along with other forms of art that represent life.

Even in societies in which theatrical activity was accepted, a deep suspicion of performers sometimes remained. In Elizabethan England an actor had to carry a document proving that he was under a nobleman's protection. Without such a document he was considered a "rogue" and "vagabond." The moral integrity of actors continued to be questioned until well into the late nineteenth century in Europe and North America. Although they might be recognized for superior artistic achievement, actors were still not welcome in middle- or upper-class social circles. In some cultures the suspicion of public performance was complicated by gender expectations. Public display was often considered inappropriate for women, and women were banned from the stage entirely in some periods. Female characters were played by men or boys in ancient Greek, Elizabethan, and various traditional Asian forms of theatre. At other times acting was one of the few professions open to women, even though it carried the threat of social ostracism for those who practiced it.

Theatre has often provided a haven for those who did not fit the current social mold. On the other hand, it has also lived up to its reputation as a morally dangerous place and has functioned as a vehicle for exploiting the less powerful members of society. Chorus girls were notoriously fair game for idle young men in Victorian England and the Gilded Age (c. 1890–1915) in New York City. Both young male and female actors in the early years of Japanese Kabuki theatre were charged with prostitution, leading to the banishment of young men from the stage temporarily and women from the stage for centuries.

THEATRE REGULATION

Because of the real and imagined dangers of the theatre, many societies have felt it necessary to closely monitor and regulate theatrical activity. The history of the theatre in England is an interesting example. In the seventeenth century the Puritans sought to suppress theatrical performance because of the "lying" nature of character portrayal and disapproval of the theatre's tendency to distract its audience from more devout or useful activities. All London theatres were closed during the Civil War in Britain (1642–1660), when the Puritans controlled Parliament. When theatrical activity was restored in 1660, it was tightly controlled by the government. Charles II issued only two patents, or licenses, for producing theatre in London. In the eighteenth and nineteenth centuries the ballooning London population and passion for theatregoing demanded more performance opportunities, yet the two licenses remained in effect until 1843. Entrepreneurs opened "illegitimate" theatres, and a battle began to clearly distinguish "legitimate" regular (spoken) drama (which rightly belonged to the two "patent houses") from "illegitimate" forms containing music and dance. A few British performers sought new audiences in colonial North America, but in areas settled by strict religious sects, particularly New England, theatrical performance was prohibited. Ingenious actors, however, managed to keep working. It was not unusual, for example, to see a performance of Shakespeare's *Othello* advertised as "a moral dialogue on jealousy."

THEATRE CENSORSHIP

Fear of the power of the theatre as a public forum for dissent has often resulted in strict censorship of dramatic material. In England some form of preproduction censorship was in place beginning with the Elizabethan period, and from 1737 to 1968 all plays had to be issued a license by the Lord Chamberlain before production. The United States has never had a nationwide institutionalized system of censorship, but local authorities have at times halted productions that were deemed offensive to the community. In 1918 federal authorities in Philadelphia closed *The Little Belgian* because of subject matter that was deemed inappropriate during wartime. The New York production of *Sex,* a play by Mae West, ran for 375 performances before it was closed by authorities in 1926. West was performing at the time and was arrested and imprisoned along with the rest of the company.

Governments have frequently used censorship to suppress dissident political statements as well as material that is embarrassing to those in power. The entire work of Václav Havel (b. 1936) was banned in his native Czechoslovakia before the disintegration of the communist bloc. Havel served four years in prison for subversion, but clandestine theatrical performances continued. After the fall of communism, Havel was elected first president of the Czech Republic. Wole Soyinka challenged the Nigerian authorities in many of his plays, essays, and books. He was imprisoned for two years, most of it in solitary confinement, and for many years has lived away from his homeland. In 1986 Soyinka won the Nobel Prize for Literature.

Subject matter that is not overtly political but considered dangerous to the fabric of society has also been restricted by censors. In eighteenth-century Japan the enormous popularity of *The Love Suicides at Sonezaki* (1703) ultimately led to a very specific prohibition. The play, written for a puppet theatre (Bunraku) by Chikamatsu (1653–1725), presented a fictionalized account of the joint suicide of two young lovers. A number of plays on similar subjects and, unfortunately, a rash of actual suicides followed. In 1722 the government banned all such plays from the stage. In the late nineteenth century realism was considered a radical movement in Europe. The plays of Norwegian Henrik Ibsen (1828–1906), for example, dared to publicly discuss social issues such as environmental pollution, gender conflict, and sexually transmitted disease. Since most existing theatres were limited by government censorship, theatrical and social reformers in Germany, France, and England found ways to circumvent the existing rules. Such "independent" theatres evaded censorship regulations by claiming to be private clubs rather than public venues.

Citizen Play Juries

From 1905 until the late 1920s the professional theatre in the city of New York found itself frequently under attack for promoting or depicting immoral or obscene acts on the stage. Many of the objections that were raised in this period would strike most people today as quaint and certainly reactionary, since community standards of morality are much less restrictive than they were in the first quarter of the twentieth century. Although the standards were a bit vague, the threat to artistic expression at the time was quite real, and the result was the unlikely collaboration, beginning in 1922, of law enforcement, the district attorney's office, theatrical producers, Actors Equity (the actors' union), theatre critics, the Dramatists Guild (society of playwrights), and purity leagues, which were common in the period.

◆ **DESIRE UNDER THE ELMS**, by Eugene O'Neill, (a severe reworking of the Greek tragedy Hippolytus) came under attack by would-be censors largely because the protagonist Eben, played by Charles Ellis (upstairs on left), falls in love with his stepmother, Abbie (on right with her husband, played by Walter Huston), played by Mary Morris. In this scene there is a wall between them, but they are imagining being with the object of their affection on the other side of the wall. Produced by Experimental Theatre, Inc., at the Greenwich Village Theatre in 1924. By permission of Theatre Collection, Museum of the City of New York.

Before 1922 the New York police frequently visited and sometimes raided plays and musical revues when they received complaints from members of the public or the district attorney's office that the productions included obscene language or acts. Many of the complaints came from the Society for the Suppression of Vice. A number of productions were closed or threatened with closure, sometimes actors or producers were arrested, and sometimes a trial ensued. Even George Bernard Shaw's *Mrs. Warren's Profession* was raided in 1905; several members of the company were arrested, and the production was closed.

The collaborative solution struck by the theatre, the community, the police, and the district attorney was the creation of Citizen Play Juries made up of adult community members (male and female) who were not professionals in the theatre or members of law enforcement. From a large pool of potential jurors twelve would be selected whenever a formal complaint against a production was made to the office of the district attorney. These twelve would then see the production, meet secretly, and pass judgment on the production in terms of violation of community standards of decency. If at least two thirds of the jury found the play indecent, it would be closed. There was no appeal from either the district attorney (if the jury acquitted) or the production's producer (if the jury condemned).

This jury system was never formulated as municipal law or statute but was an informal agreement made by all the parties involved. For some time no production was condemned by the play juries, and the district attorney's office began to get nervous about the process. In 1926 the first production closed was a musical revue that included nudity. (Nudity appeared from time to time in revues but not in plays or musicals. This barrier was not breached until 1968.) The climate grew increasingly problematic for the authorities, because the district attorney was eager to close down Eugene O'Neill's *Desire under the Elms* in 1924, Mae West's *Sex* in 1926, and *The Captive* (which included a lesbian character) by Edward Bourdet also in 1926. The play juries acquitted all of them. Despite the previous agreement, the district attorney abolished the play juries in early 1927 and promptly raided *Sex, The Captive,* and *The Virgin Man* (also by Mae West) and made many arrests. The shows were closed, and collaboration was over. Nonetheless, for a few years these unlikely bedfellows made the attempt to compromise and work together. Ultimately, the standards were taken out of the hands of the city's government because the New York State Legislature passed the Wales Padlock Law later in 1927. The harsh law mandated that any producer who was convicted of producing an obscene play would have his theatre padlocked for a year. This extreme measure resulted in many producers being unwilling to take risks with sexual material for some time. The censorship standards used by the courts of New York in the 1920s were not overturned until the Supreme Court did so in 1957.

Placing restrictions on theatre has frequently resulted in such uses of subterfuge. The theatrical impulse is remarkably widespread and tenacious. Artists want to create, and audiences want to attend the theatre. Sometimes theatre goes underground, as in Czechoslovakia before the fall of communism. Sometimes the theatre makes a place for itself on the fringes of society. The Globe Theatre, which saw the first productions of many of Shakespeare's magnificent plays, was built on the south side of the Thames River to avoid City of London restrictions. It sat in an entertainment and red-light district next to arenas that held bloody contests in which animals fought to the death.

Cultural Context and Personal Experience

Every theatrical performance is a collaboration, furnishing a place for past, present, and future to merge; for traditions to be celebrated, analyzed, and challenged; for different cultures to interact with one another. Cultural context is also part of personal memory and personal theatrical experiences. In 1963 one of the authors of this book at a young age witnessed a professional production of the musical *West Side Story* (1957) by Arthur Laurents, Leonard Bernstein, and Stephen Sondheim. It was a remarkable experience that had much to do with the author's decision to pursue a life and career in the theatre. Because of its personal importance, the theatrical memory looms large and no doubt has been colored nostalgically with the passage of time. Nonetheless, the memory of that production evokes much about the time in which it was written and composed and when and where it was produced. A 1963 production cannot be duplicated, and in an artistic and cultural sense there is no reason anyone should attempt it. The authors have both witnessed many other productions of *West Side Story* since 1963, some of which were probably more effectively produced, but for one of us that first experience was far more significant because of its personal importance and its position in time and place. It was a cultural event that was transformed into a very personal and influential event. In that recognition lies much of the potential power of the theatre.

QUESTIONS AND ACTIVITIES

1. Scholars disagree about where to draw the line between "theatre" and other activities that have a theatrical component. What do you consider theatre? Discuss the ways in which different public activities are theatrical, for example, parades, pep rallies, sporting events, air shows, political demonstrations, and the like.

2. Defining "art" is a difficult task and is very subjective. What do you expect from an artistic experience? Think about your experiences with theatre, painting, sculpture, dance, music. Which ones would you call art? Why? Do the same with films and television programs.

3. Choose one experience that you consider art and another that you consider strictly entertainment. Write a letter to a friend explaining why.

4. Theatre can be an important tool in crossing cultural boundaries. Are there times when it is important to

keep those boundaries intact? Read about the public debate on nontraditional casting between playwright August Wilson and producer and critic Robert Brustein. You may begin your research at **www. csmonitor.com/durable/1998/05/15/fp54s2-csm. htm** and **www.princetoninfo.com/wilson.html**.

Discuss the following questions.

- Is it acceptable for an actor to play a character of a different race? If the character's race is an important issue in the play, is it still acceptable for an actor of a different race to play the character?

- Is it acceptable for a male playwright to write about women's issues? Is it acceptable for a female playwright to explore male bonding? Is it acceptable for a white playwright to write about the experience of a black character? Is it acceptable for an Asian playwright to create a play about Native Americans?

- Is it acceptable to produce a play that is meant to speak directly to a specific group defined by sex, race, or religion?

5. Plays from former periods often reflect viewpoints that are unacceptable in contemporary society. Should plays from the past be produced when those plays contain material that is objectionable because of racial, religious, or sexual stereotypes? Defend one of the following positions:

- Such plays should not be produced. (Should they be studied?)

- Such plays should be produced only with changes in offensive components.

- Such plays should be produced as written but with commentary (for example, notes in the programs, panel discussions to examine the problematic material in a historical context).

- Such plays should be produced without comment.

6. What are some other functions that theatre can serve that are not mentioned in the chapter?

7. Is censorship necessary? At what points do free speech and protection of citizens collide? What are the potential dangers of censorship?

♦♦♦♦♦♦♦♦♦♦
KEY TERMS AND CONCEPTS

propaganda, p. 9
nontraditional casting, p. 18

♦♦♦♦♦♦♦♦♦♦
FOR FURTHER EXPLORATION

Augusto Boal. *Theater of the Oppressed*. London: Pluto, 1998. For alternative readings of the theatrical experience.

Don Wilmeth and Christopher Bigsby. *The Cambridge History of American Theatre*, vol. 3. New York: Cambridge, 2000. For a history of American theatrical activity and dramatic literature since World War II.

Alan Sinfield. *Out on Stage: Lesbian and Gay Theatre in the Twentieth Century*. New Haven, Conn.: Yale, 1999; and Kaier Curtin. "We Can Always Call Them Bulgarians," in *The Emergence of Lesbians and Gay Men on the American Stage*. Boston: Alyson, 1987.

James Roose-Evans. *Experimental Theatre*. London: Routledge, 1989; and Arthur Sainer. *The New Radical Theatre Notebook*. New York: Applause, 1997. For overviews and pictorial evidence for twentieth-century experimental theatre.

Helen Krich Chinoy and Linda Walsh Jenkins. *Women in American Theatre*. New York: Theatre Communications Group, 1987; and Helene Keyssar. *Feminist Theatre: An Introduction to Plays of Contemporary British and American Women*. Olympic Marketing, 1985.

Errol Hill. *The Theatre of Black Americans*. Englewood Cliffs, N.J.: Prentice-Hall, 1980; and L. C. Sanders. *The Development of Black Theater in America: From Shadows to Selves*. Baton Rouge: Louisiana State University Press, 1988. For a history of black theatre in the United States.

"Censorship" in *The Cambridge Guide to World Theatre*, edited by Martin Banham. Cambridge, England: University Press, Cambridge, 1988, pp. 165–171. For a brief history of censorship in the theatre.

STRATFORD FESTIVAL THEATRE, a thrust stage, viewed from house left.
Photo by Terry Manzo. Courtesy of the Stratford Festival Archives.

Experiencing Theatre

Collaboration of Actor, Audience, and Space

I n his inspirational book *The Empty Space* (1987), director Peter Brook (b. 1925) reminds us that only three elements are necessary for theatre to exist: "I can take an empty space and call it a bare stage. A man walks across the empty space whilst someone else is watching him, and this is all that is needed for an act of theatre to be engaged."[1]

Whenever one person performs and another watches in the same location, theatre is created. Lots of other things *might* be present: lights, costumes, scenery, makeup, seats, a raised platform, music, predetermined words; the event *could* incorporate hundreds of actors, thousands of spectators, and millions of dollars. But the basis of theatre, the essence of the event, is a theatrical collaboration: one person "acting," one person "auding" (listening and/or watching), in the same space at the same time.

Since, by definition, the performer and the spectator (or "seer") share the same time and space, a theatrical performance can happen only once. The same actors may perform the same text with the same movement for two different audiences, but it is *not* the same event if different people are watching. Even if the same people attended both performances and the actors said exactly the same words and played the same action, the events could not be identical. An actor might inflect a word differently; the audience might laugh at a particular line, causing a performer to wait before beginning the next speech.

Every performance is different because human beings are not static. An actress's opening-night performance is not the same as her hundredth; a performer who just experienced a painful breakup plays a love scene differently than he did the night before. Every audience is different. An audience composed mostly of college students reacts differently than one composed primarily of senior citizens; a Tuesday night audience, arriving after a long day at work, is different from a Saturday night audience coming straight from bars and restaurants, ready to have a good time. The audience reaction, in turn, shapes the performance. In the midst of a comedy, actors faced with stony silence might "push"—overemphasize lines, try too hard to be funny, kill the jokes; an audience that is ready to laugh can elicit easy, polished delivery from the performers. Audience members help to shape the theatrical event, depending on what they bring along with them: familiarity with the play, with the actors; a love of action; a commitment to a specific idea; a capacity for caring; a large or small vocabulary; a short or long attention span; an annoying cough or an infectious laugh. The space makes its contribution as well. Watching a performance in an elegant, well-equipped theatre is very different from watching one in a large, empty warehouse or a small, intimate space.

Because most of us will be audience members more times in our lives than we will perform, we begin this exploration of the theatrical collaboration from the audience point of view.

◆◆◆◆◆◆◆◆◆

The Audience

At its most basic level, theatre provides a sensory experience for the audience; it appeals to the human senses as the audience is actively involved in perceiving, processing, reacting to, and storing a vast number of stimuli. In a complex production, you might be

◆ **HAMLET** *at Drury Lane Theatre, London, 1787. Portrait of an actor in the title role.*
By permission of the Folger Shakespeare Library.

Hamlet.

Mr. Wroughton as Hamlet.
Drury Lane 1787.

bombarded with the effects of light, color, form, movement, the human voice, sound effects, music, the smell of the people around you, the temperature of the air, the feel of the seats, the sense of closeness. To experience this wealth of sensory activity is exciting, often pleasant, sometimes unpleasant. But more is at work. You could have an exciting sensory experience at a laser light show. Something else takes place in the theatre.

EMPATHY AND AESTHETIC DISTANCE

When you watch a performance, you experience two phenomena simultaneously: empathy and aesthetic distance. **Empathy** is emotional identification. In everyday life, it

means the ability to put yourself in someone else's shoes. In the theatre, it refers to a sense of participation—an identification with character. It is not the same thing as sympathy, although that also might be at work. Empathy is when you feel along *with* the characters (not just *for* them). In *Aida* (2000) by Elton John and Tim Rice, the title character is a captive Nubian queen, torn between duty to her oppressed people and passion for her white lover. That lover's father, the villain of the musical, is guilty of abusing Aida's people. The audience identifies with Aida's dilemma and feels her conflict and pain. In *The Poor of New York* (1857) by Dion Boucicault, a sea captain, alarmed by a financial panic, brings all of his savings to a bank for safekeeping. The bank's employees are corrupt and decide to steal the money. When the captain begins to suspect foul play, he is stricken by a heart attack, but the employees offer no assistance and do not call for help until it is too late. One simply counts money while the other watches with interest as the captain dies in front of them. The audience might identify with the terror and struggle of the sinking captain as well as feel anger at the corrupt employees.

Marsha Norman's play *'night, Mother* (1983) focuses on the aging Thelma and her daughter Jessie. Because of many physical and emotional problems, Jessie decides, quite rationally, that she would rather be dead than alive and prepares for her suicide as she explains her reasons to her mother. Throughout the play the audience is pulled back and forth between identifying with Jessie (whose arguments make sense) and with Thelma, who desperately tries to change her daughter's mind. At the play's end Jessie exits and locks the door behind her as her mother screams and pleads through the closed door. The answer is a gunshot heard offstage. The audience's emotional participation in those excruciating moments is intense. Emotional involvement in this play is heightened also by its playing without a break in the action; the play has no intermission.

Empathy is a key component in many entertainment forms and is sometimes so strong that feeling spills over into action. Have you ever screamed at the climax of a horror film or found your body trying to run the plays while you watched a football game on television? In the theatre the fact that the actors are

live and sharing the same space with the audience tends to make the identification even stronger than in film. It is not unusual for a child to stand in the theatre and shout to his favorite character, "He's hiding inside that box!" The child's actions are motivated by empathy, taken to the extreme of interference in the fictional world.

Aesthetic distance is psychological separation, or a sense of detachment. It is what keeps the audience (usually) from shouting—from trying to influence the action on stage. You understand that what you are watching is not real. When the lights come back up, the audience members will talk and laugh and go back to their homes, and the actors will take off their costumes, put on their street clothes, and reenter daily life. The term "aesthetic distance" literally means "the distance of art"; the audience members are able to step back and view the events on stage objectively because they realize the action represented is fictional. Aesthetic distance allows you to appreciate the way something is done—to admire the skill with which an actor portrays a character, the beauty of the scenery, or the way lighting changes the mood of the play—because you realize that the effect is being crafted for you.

Another way to think about empathy and aesthetic distance is that the first appeals to the heart and the second to the head. In most theatrical events, both are present; at times audience members' emotions are engaged, and they experience the events of the

◆ **OTHELLO** *by William Shakespeare. In this scene between Othello and Desdemona, played by Johnny Lee Davenport and Allison Krizner, Othello will ultimately murder his wife. Directed by Scott Wentworth; scenic design by Russell Metheny; costume design by Ann Sheffield.*
Courtesy of Indiana Repertory Theatre.

play as if they were truly participating; at other times they figuratively step back, remember where they are, and admire the way the fictional world is created. Both are necessary for a complete experience. Empathy makes the event exciting and personal; aesthetic distance makes analysis possible and allows you to exercise your intellect as well as your feelings.

Much of the success of a theatrical performance depends on how skillfully the people who are creating the fiction are able to manipulate empathy and aesthetic distance. In a production of Shakespeare's *Othello* (c. 1604–05), a husband filled with jealous rage approaches his innocent young wife, who is lying on the bed. If the lights dim slowly and music slips in under the action, the production elements are encouraging the audience to empathize—to surrender emotionally to the suspense of the situation on stage.

On the other hand, the audience members might be asked to step back from the fictional world and remember that they are in a theatre. If an actor looks at the audience and addresses it directly, the audience is encouraged to relate to the actor as an actor, or perhaps a narrator, rather than the fictional character. In Thornton Wilder's *Our Town* (1938), the character of the Stage Manager regularly comments on events happening on stage, all props are mimed, and the actors perform on a bare stage; the audience is reminded constantly that it is witnessing a performance. In *Urinetown: The Musical* (2001) by Mark Hollman and Greg Kotis, the play's narrator, Officer Lockstock, is also a corrupt cop (a villain is our guide through the dramatic action). He and others often address the audience directly and sometimes comment on the structure of the play and how much they hate the play's title.

In any play deliberate decisions are made to shift audience experience at specific moments, and depending on the effect desired, a production might emphasize empathy or aesthetic distance throughout a total performance. In

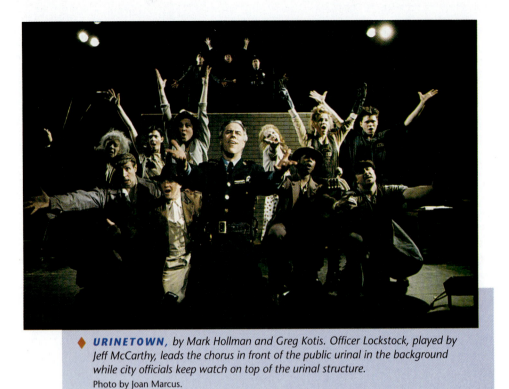

The Conduct of Life (1985) by Maria Irene Fornes, the manipulation of aesthetic distance is closely related to physical distance. The audience observes Latin American power struggles, including torture and rape, at first in a military setting but eventually brought into the domestic life of a family. Four different locations are seen simultaneously, the living room of a home being closest to the audience (see Figure 2.1). The most horrific scenes are at first kept at a distance,

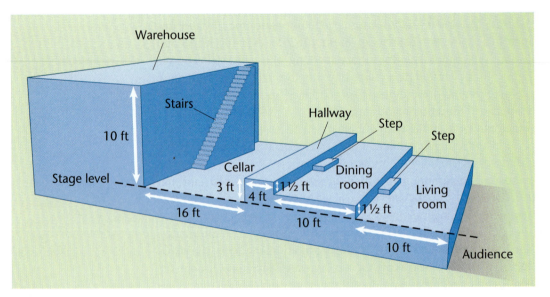

◆ **FIGURE 2.1** *Ground Plan for* **The Conduct of Life** *by Maria Irene Fornes* This is a plan for staging indicated in the play text. The living room is stage level, but the dining room is 1½ feet higher. The hallway rises another 1½ feet above the living room, or 3 feet higher than stage level, and so on. The setting has five distinct playing spaces.

Exploring Collaboration

Impromptu Spatial Collaboration: *Pinocchio*

From time to time audiences are invited to break the actor/audience boundary and collaborate more actively in the space with the actors. In the 1960s and early 1970s this interaction sometimes occurred in environmental productions by the Living Theatre and the Performance Group. In the midst of one production in particular, *Commune* (1970) by the Performance Group, fifteen audience members were asked to leave their seats and sit in a circle onstage to represent the villagers in the Vietnamese village of My Lai (the scene of a massacre). If the number of fifteen was not reached, the performance would stop and the play would not end. Although the audience had to participate in the performance space to finish the play, this condition was preplanned by the theatre company and was related to experimenting with audience participation and exploring the conditions of performer/audience relationships.

More than thirty years earlier a very successful production of *Pinocchio,* a children's theatre play, was performing in New York. It was part of the Federal Theatre Project, a government-sponsored effort that, as part of the Works Progress Administration, was intended to put people back to work across the United States during the Great Depression. This acrobatic and circuslike production about a puppet who becomes a real boy had been performed in California and other parts of the country. In the midst of the very successful New York run of this show, the U.S. Congress cut off funding for the Federal Theatre, which meant that all productions had to shut down. The experiment with public funding for theatre arts was over. Members of the *Pinocchio* company, led by the playwright/director Yasha Frank, decided at the last minute to demonstrate in their final performance. They did so not only by altering the play but also by involving the audience in an onstage demonstration that moved subsequently into the streets. As the production neared its end, the magically animated puppet died. It was time for Pinocchio to come back to life as a real boy, but he remained dead on the stage. The other actors plopped him into a coffin inscribed with "killed by act of Congress." Not only was Pinocchio dead, but so was the Federal Theatre. The company and some of the audience began to tear down the scenery and create a heap on the stage. All then walked out together bearing the coffin into the urban night. The play, the children's theatre, and the Federal Theatre Project remained unfinished.

Interested? Check out

Hallie Flanagan. *Arena: The Story of the Federal Theatre.* New York: Duell, Sloan and Pierce, 1940.

John O'Connor and Lorraine Brown. *Free, Adult and Uncensored: The Living History of the Federal Theatre Project.* Washington, D.C.: New Republic, 1978.

For other productions by the Federal Theatre Project, see 13,000 images of items selected from the Federal Theatre Project Collection at the Library of Congress at "The New Deal Stage: Selections from the Federal Theatre Project 1935–1939" at memory.loc.gov/ammem/fedtp/fthome.html.

---

but as the play progresses, the young rape victim and her military abuser come closer and closer to the audience. By the end of the play the victim of the horrors is sitting in the living room where a murder is about to take place.

Sometimes the consistent manipulation of aesthetic distance can yield surprising results. In the play *Miss Margarida's Way* (1977) by Brazilian Roberto Athayde, the leading character (nearly the only character) is a vocally abusive seventh-grade teacher who treats and berates the audience members as if they are her junior high students. The house lights remain up throughout, and the audience is encouraged to talk back to the teacher. When this play is performed, the audience often acts badly—standing, yelling at the stage, throwing things— actually taking on the role of the delinquent students. The playwright in fact

includes the audience in his list of characters. In *Miss Margarida's Way* the audience is
encouraged to abandon aesthetic distance
to some extent and actually become physically involved in the fictional events.

Despite the best efforts of theatre artists
to control empathy and aesthetic distance,
things can happen in production through
no one's design or intent that have a profound impact on audience response. An
actor's slip of the tongue or a noise backstage might pull an audience out of the fictional world at an inopportune moment. A
person who has experienced an event similar to one depicted on stage might identify
so strongly with a character's sorrow that
sadness overwhelms any possibility of analyzing the performance from an objective
point of view. This audience member has little distance from his or her own sorrowful
experience and therefore can create none
for the performance.

As an audience member, you are probably seldom aware of the swings between
empathy and aesthetic distance. You think
only of integrated experience, and that is as
it should be. Because these two phenomena
are at work, the audience can experience
great emotional intensity in the theatre with complete physical and psychological safety. In this way, the theatre provides vicarious experience; it is possible
for the audience to be present in unlikely, impossible, or undesirable situations.
As the audience members watch Emily in *Our Town,* they discover how it might
feel to die and come back to life for one special day. While viewing *Valparaiso*
(1999) by Don DeLillo, the audience learns what it might be like to become
famous by accident. As television invades the main character's life, the audience
may share his mounting confusion, panic, and paranoia. Theatre allows us
to learn about ourselves and to come to an emotional understanding of the
experience of others.

OVERALL EFFECT ON THE AUDIENCE

For centuries, people have speculated about the desired effect of theatrical performance on the audience, and many theories exist. The Greek philosopher
Aristotle (384–322 B.C.E.) used the word **catharsis,** or emotional release; a performance was designed to engage the audience's feelings and build in intensity
so that the spectator felt "cleansed" or purged of strong emotion by the end of
the play. (Scholars disagree about exactly what the term "catharsis," as applied
to the theatre, meant to the Greeks. We present the most widely accepted interpretation.) Strong and consistent emotional identification with the fictional
events is central to triggering catharsis. European and North American theatre
has often followed this basic premise but with variations.

Exploring Historical and Cultural Perspectives

Brecht versus Wagner

In the early to mid-twentieth century Bertolt Brecht (1898–1956) not only took Aristotle to task for embracing the emotional purpose of drama but also attacked his predecessor, Richard Wagner (1813–1883), a German composer of music drama. Wagner composed many famous operas, such as *Tannhäuser* and *Parsifal,* and was very active in their production. He published theories of drama and music and championed the idea of "total theatre," which sought to unify all the arts. Emotionality and total immersion of the audience in the illusionism of the theatrical event, or "knowing through feeling," were the keys, according to Wagner, to successful theatre and drama. Many other theatre artists embraced this approach, which was consistent with the catharsis theory of Aristotle but went much further.

Brecht, by contrast, was anti-illusionist. He wanted his audiences to remain detached emotionally and to engage intellectually with the dramatic material. Through his plays and published theory he popularized the idea of **epic theatre,** which featured *Verfremdung,* usually translated as "alienation" or "to make strange." Brecht's theatre went to great lengths to call attention to the theatricality of the event: Songs were disconnected from the story of the play, narration frequently interrupted the dialogue, placards and projections delivered lyrics and political messages to the audience, and stage machinery and lighting instruments were placed or hung in full view of the audience. The plays, music, and devices of both Wagner and Brecht are frequently revived today, and they can be seen as

♦ **MOTHER COURAGE,** *by Bertolt Brecht. As can be seen in this photograph, Brecht often used a nearly bare stage to underscore characters' loneliness. Mother Courage, played by Helene Weigel, pulls her wagon against the moving, revolving stage. Note the cabling overhead for a half-curtain pulled periodically through the play, which always revealed partially hidden scenery or projections behind it.*
Photo by KaiDib Films International.

representing polar opposite views of how theatre can function in our world.

Interested? Check out

John Willett, ed. and trans. *Brecht on Theatre.* New York: Hill and Wang, 1964.
Richard Wagner. "Knowing through Feeling." In *Total Theatre,* ed. E. T. Kirby. New York: E. P. Dutton, 1969, pp. 5–8.
Byron Magee. *Wagner and Philosophy.* New York: Penguin, 2001.
John Fuegi. *Bertolt Brecht: Chaos According to Plan.* Cambridge, England: Cambridge University Press, 1987.

In the twentieth century the German playwright and theorist Bertolt Brecht (1898–1956) rejected the cathartic model altogether and insisted that the function of theatre should be to appeal to the intellect of the audience and incite it to social action. In this view, precipitating catharsis is contrary to the very nature of what theatre could and should do. Manipulation of aesthetic distance at appropriate moments could encourage a comparison between fictional events and the real world outside the theatre. Although Brecht sometimes engaged the audience members' emotions, he would interrupt the emotional response and deny its completion. In *The Caucasian Chalk Circle* (c. 1945), for example, two

lovers, Grusha, a servant, and Simon, a soldier, find each other again after a considerable separation due to war. They struggle to communicate with a stream of water separating them. This scene is painful to watch and for the audience is likely to result in considerable emotional involvement. At one point, however, a narrator intrudes to explain what Grusha is thinking but will not say to Simon. The spell is broken. After the interruption the lovers attempt to communicate again, but the narrator intrudes a second time to tell what Simon is thinking but will not utter. Brecht's model has been followed by many artists hoping to encourage social change through theatre.

Japanese Noh theatre embraces an end result of contemplation rather than action or emotional release. The playwright and theorist Zeami (1363–1443) described the ideal image of performance as a flower—a perfect, transitory beauty, an enigmatic and mysterious elegance. The actor should strive to create an unfading flower, despite its temporary nature. The "flower" should also surprise the audience and reveal the unexpected. Above all, the actor should maintain secrets about his art, like a magician or warrior. The slow, carefully choreographed movement, colorful costumes, and simple, open stage of Noh invite the audience to contemplate the story of the play, which is often presented as a memory relived by the central character.

◆ ◆ ◆ ◆ ◆ ◆ ◆ ◆ ◆

The Nature of Acting

At the most basic level every human being who interacts with other human beings is an actor. Every person performs social roles for others, both consciously and unconsciously. On the face of it this is neither a good nor a bad thing but simply a part of the human condition. Psychologists and psychiatrists from Sigmund Freud onward have explored the role-playing of the human animal in order to better understand behavior, to examine internal conflicts, and to treat emotional problems. Major playwrights and other writers of fiction from Aeschylus and Euripides (fifth century B.C.E.) among the ancient Greeks to recent playwrights such as Suzan-Lori Parks (b. 1964) and Tony Kushner (b. 1956) have continually explored the ways in which people pretend to be someone they are not or claim to believe something other than reality for purposes that are helpful or evil, economic or spiritual, comic or tragic. Playwrights often demonstrate that people perform different roles when interacting with different friends, acquaintances, family members, and strangers. People perform differently in private situations than they do in public. Social performance is a basic phenomenon of human behavior and is central to the dramatic content and conflict of the theatrical experience. Is it then surprising that an early Greek word for actor is ***hypokrites,*** from which we glean the more negative words "hypocrisy" and "hypocrite"?

As early as the fourth century B.C.E., Aristotle identified ***mimesis,*** or the artist's process of imitating character and action, as so basic to humanity that it

Exploring Historical and Cultural Perspectives

Hypokrites to Actor

Many cultures have created numerous words for *actor. Hypokrites,* the first Greek word we know for it, actually meant "answerer" and described a performer who answered or responded to the songs and questions of the **chorus** (a group of performers working together vocally and physically). Over time the Greek playwrights added second and third actors to interact with the chorus and the first actor. *Hypokrites* is also related to *Hypokrisis,* meaning the process of acting. In this word we also see the presence of the term "crisis," which plays a large role in both acting and drama.

Some time after the fifth century B.C.E., the Greeks added the word **technitae** for actor. *Technitae* is probably related to the professional status of Greek actors in the fourth century and beyond. The word suggests the technical skill of the actors that was widely celebrated as Greek art and culture spread throughout its many colonies during the Hellenistic period.

The ancient Romans used the word **histrio** for actor, and in this term we see the root of our word "histrionic," by which we usually mean exaggerated human responses. More important, the Romans also gave us the Latin word **actor,** which literally means "doer" but came to be the word of choice for performers in most Western traditions.

◆ **REVELERS AT A MASQUERADE** *wear costumes representing many different periods and styles as they cavort and dance at a ball.*
Hand-tinted lithograph by Pruche, 1837. Collection of the authors.

Makeup as Mask: Kathakali

Some of the most fascinating and complicated stage makeup in the world is fashioned for Kathakali, a form of dance-drama from southern India that is rooted in Hindu mythology. Kathakali originated in the seventeenth century and is traditionally performed in temple courtyards. Actors are all male and are trained from childhood. The actors themselves do not speak but communicate through dance and stylized gesture; their movement is accompanied by singers, drums, gongs, and cymbals. The characters they depict from the ancient *Ramayana* and *Mahabharata* are larger than life—gods and demons come to earth. The actors work acrobatically and in pantomime, often giving the impression that they are possessed by the spirit of the gods.

Costumes in Kathakali are very colorful and elaborate, including enormous headdresses. The makeup is also very colorful, and five conventionalized styles symbolize specific characters and qualities. Actors often apply makeup themselves. *Chutti* (white gill-like extensions) are then applied by a makeup artist while the actor lies on the floor. *Chutti* are built up slowly in layers on the cheeks of the face. A literal mask is not used because the performer must execute very intricate and emotional facial expressions and remarkable eye movements that are said to have developed along with a strict code of gestures from ancient dance, dramatic, and ritual forms. Some actors redden the whites of their eyes with a small seed to accentuate rolling eye movements.

Interested? Check out

"Kathakali," www.cyberkerala.com/kathakali.
M. P. Sankaran Namboodiri. "Kathakali: Dance-Drama of Kerala," www.vvm.com/~pnair/htm/k_kali.htm.
Phillip B. Zarilli. *Kathakali Dance-Drama: Where Gods and Demons Come to Play.* London: Routledge, 2000.

KATHAKALI MAKEUP *is very extravagant. As evidenced in this photograph, we see paper* chutti *on the sides of the face, bright green, red, and gold on the face, an ornate headpiece, long fingernails, and bells on the ankles.*
Photo by and courtesy of Rakesh Solomon.

was necessary to invent theatre. Children love to play roles and often use imitation to learn to speak, to mimic grown-ups, and to understand the world around them. All of us probably engaged in dress-ups early in life, pretending to be adults, playing house, fighting fires, galloping across the great expanses of an American prairie in the theatre of our minds. Once we are grown, some of this activity continues, of course, but often in more controlled, private ways or perhaps during the social freedom of a costume party. Participation in theatrical production gives sanction to this sense of play.

For those who choose to create theatre for an audience, the process of *mimesis* is not merely copying but creating and recreating from the observation and analysis of human models of character and action and from the exploration of self. Here *mimesis* becomes an art form to be studied, practiced, and refined by both playwrights and actors.

In the ancient Roman theatre the *persona* was the mask of the actor. We now more commonly use the word to designate psychologically the social role a person is playing or presenting in life. Both of these meanings are appropriate to the process of the actor assuming a character. The actor dons a mask, whether literal or figurative, and when the preparation is complete, the audience is asked to accept this masked actor as the character designated by the play. The mask might be a literal device placed over or on the face, thus rigidly fixing the character's expression in some emblematic moment. In Japanese Noh theatre the leading actor meditates on his mask for a long time before finally placing it over his face, almost as if trying to become one with the spirit of the mask. The mask could be makeup, applied to age, beautify, or distort the actor's real face. The makeup could be highly stylized like that of Kathakali performers in India who spend hours having layered, colorful makeup applied to help them depict the supernatural figures who move dancelike through the play.

Frequently, however, the mask is figurative. Through language that was conceived not by the actor but by a playwright, through movement unlike the actor's own, by presenting action that is contradictory to the actor's beliefs or normal behavior, the identity and personality of the actor are concealed from the audience while the actor simultaneously reveals a truthful picture of the character.

◆◆◆◆◆◆◆◆◆◆

From Play to Production

While some theatrical performances progress through **improvisation** (the performers make up the words or movements as they go along), most theatre begins with a written text. One writer (or group of writers) creates the **play** or **script**—a written text indicating the words the characters speak and some of the physical action. In doing so, the writer provides the basic action of the play—he or she decides the major events of the play, the basic nature of each character, and the exact words that will be spoken on stage. The play is then brought to life by a team of theatre artists—a director, actors, and designers (the composition of the creative team may change in different situations)—and theatre technicians. This team creates the theatrical **production**—the actual concrete performance of the play with actors, sets, costumes, lighting, and props.

THE PRODUCTION COLLABORATORS

Historically, the work of creating a production has been divided in various ways. Accounts from ancient Greece say that the playwrights staged their own work. In eighteenth-century Europe a leading performer, dubbed an "actor-manager," organized the presentation of a play. Many theatres in the twenty-first century share a basic division of artistic duties. We will refer to the following job titles many times in this book.

Typically (although by no means exclusively), contemporary production begins with a script created by a **playwright,** or author. The financial and business aspects of the production are handled by a **producer.** The producer usually negotiates the rights to a play and hires a **director,** who is in charge of the artistic aspects of production. It is the director's job to guide the transformation of the play to live production. The director interprets the play and heads the artistic team, providing a focus and organization for the creative work. In general, the director sets the tone for the production, approves its overall look and sound, sets the movement of actors, and makes the final decisions when necessary. Often, the director (although sometimes the producer) chooses the actors, sometimes assisted by a **casting director,** and the director always helps the actors to develop and refine their characterizations.

A **scenic designer** creates a visual home for the play on stage. Many people might help to build scenery, but the designer envisions and controls the visual effect. The **costume designer** creates "wearable scenery" for the actors to help define and express character, and a **lighting designer** influences the effect of all visual elements by controlling focus and mood with color, placement, and intensity of light. A **sound designer** creates acoustic and recorded sound. On some occasions, a **makeup designer** may join the production team. A musical adds a **composer** and **lyricist** (who create the music and lyrics), a **music director** (who works with singers and orchestra), and a **choreographer** (who stages dancing). In medium- to large-sized theatres the creative decisions made by this team are executed by a **stage manager** (who ensures that things run smoothly on- and backstage) and management staff, a scene shop crew, a costume shop crew, and a lighting crew.

FRONT-OF-HOUSE PERSONNEL

Theatre operations that deal directly with the audience are called **front-of-house.** The **house manager** is responsible for the safety and comfort of the audience members during their time in the theatre. House managers coordinate ushers, make sure the audience areas of the theatre are clean and safe, resolve any seating problems, and deal with any emergencies. In the case of a fire or other dangerous situation the house manager is in charge of getting the patrons to safety, notifying the authorities, and securing the theatre. The house manager works closely with the stage manager in starting the show and beginning again after intermissions. The **box office manager** works directly with the house manager and is responsible for organizing and overseeing ticket sales, including supervising the staff members who deal directly with the public. Front-of-house personnel act as a liaison between the audience and production and have an influence on the pleasantness of the patrons' experience.

THE REWARDS OF COLLABORATION

Making theatre requires a tremendous amount of work. Although a few individuals make large sums of money in the theatre, most people who are engaged in it professionally make very little, often supporting themselves most of the time through other occupations. A vast number of people participate in theatrical production with no thought of financial reward. What is the attraction for those human beings who step out of the audience to go on- or backstage?

♦ **A JAPANESE THEATRE** *in Tokyo viewed from the stage shows a large Western-style house whose management requires a large front-of-house staff for efficient operation.*
Collection of the authors.

Perhaps most obviously, theatre provides a forum for self-expression. Many possibilities exist for artistic outlet—not only acting and directing but also designing lighting, sound, scenery, costumes, or makeup, as well as drawing, painting, sewing, building, writing, and composing. Individuals with strong organizational and technical skills enjoy putting these to work behind the scenes in theatrical management and technical positions.

The vicarious experience of the audience in the theatre becomes more concrete in the life of the performer; the actor actually inhabits, rather than watches, the character's fictional life. All artists of the theatre, actors and playwrights especially, experience empathy with an intensity that widens their life experience and point of view. Making theatre is a way of trying on different identities—of exploring life from another vantage point, of investigating the human mystery with a unique tool. It provides a safe way of playing out conflict.

One of the most satisfying aspects of working in the theatre is collaboration—first with other artists, technicians, and administrators and finally with the audience. It is important to keep in mind that no one in the theatre creates in a vacuum. Each person contributes a part of the whole, and that part is successful and valid only insofar as it is appropriate to the success of the entire production.

♦♦♦♦♦♦♦♦♦

Space

For a performance to be theatre, it must be presented in a space that accommodates both the performers and the audience at the same time. The space could be

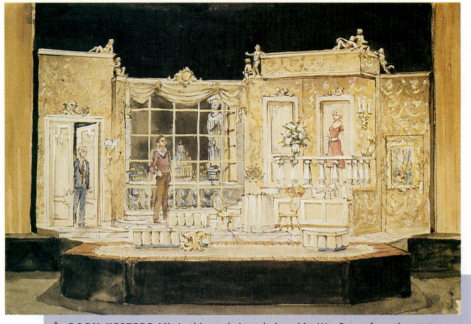

◆ **BORN YESTERDAY.** *In this rendering, designed by Wes Peters for a thrust stage at Brown County Playhouse in Indiana, we see an interior dominated by a façade— a thrust theatre's version of a box set—with two playing levels.*
Courtesy of Wes Peters.

as tiny as a closet with one actor performing for an audience of one, or the space could be as large as a sports stadium with a cast of hundreds, even thousands, performing for an audience of fifty thousand or more. The space could be formally designed by an architect for the express purpose of theatrical performance or could simply be a preexisting space that was never intended by the builder as a theatre. A performance space, however, need not be built at all; an open meadow or hillside might function very well. The audience might be raised above the performers, or the actors might be elevated with the audience looking up. Performers and audience could be in the same horizontal plane. There are few rules other than the one indicated by the first sentence of this paragraph.

The space must be organized with the movement of the actor and the relationship of the actors to the audience in mind. As the Swiss designer Adolphe Appia (1862–1928) reminded other theatre artists, no design for the theatre is complete without the performers. Despite the openness of the spatial possibilities of theatrical performance, several physical arrangements have become traditional in the last 2,500 years. These models have recurred in many cultures and undergone numerous variations, but the essentials of each form are repeated. All three traditional spaces—proscenium, thrust, and arena—are defined to a large degree by the physical relationship of performers and audience.

PROSCENIUM SPACE

If you attend the theatre with regularity, it is likely that you have encountered a **proscenium space** frequently. Invented by the Italians in a temporary form in the sixteenth century and for permanent structures by the seventeenth, the proscenium theatre is most clearly defined by a large open arch—the

proscenium arch—that marks the primary division between audience and performance space. A proscenium space may have an **apron,** an extension of the stage that continues toward the audience from the arch; the apron serves as an important performance space and is usually without scenery. Although some theatres have a large apron that allows freedom of movement, many proscenium spaces have a shallow apron or no apron at all. Most proscenium theatres also have **wings**—spaces offstage left and right for actors, crew, and scenery that are not in the visible performance space. The entire performance space is like a huge box (see Figure 2.2).

Resembling a big picture frame, usually rectangular rather than square, the proscenium arch frequently encloses most or all of the scenery that is traditionally placed upstage of the arch, resulting in a barrier between audience and actors (see Figure 2.3). The frame not only serves to focus the action, but also allows the use of changeable scenery with the ability to mask the offstage activity from the audience. Although there are other theories regarding the proscenium's invention, the frame appears to have been developed for this very reason: to create the effect of watching a picture in motion and in three dimensions. The proscenium's effect is enhanced by the use of a **grand drape** (front curtain) to hide scene changes or to indicate the beginnings and

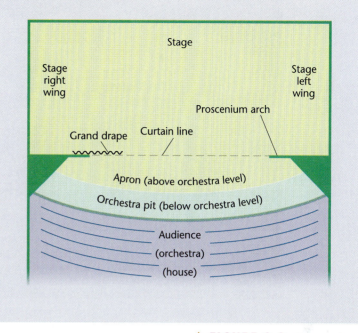

♦ **FIGURE 2.2** *Proscenium Theatre Ground Plan (as Seen from Above)*

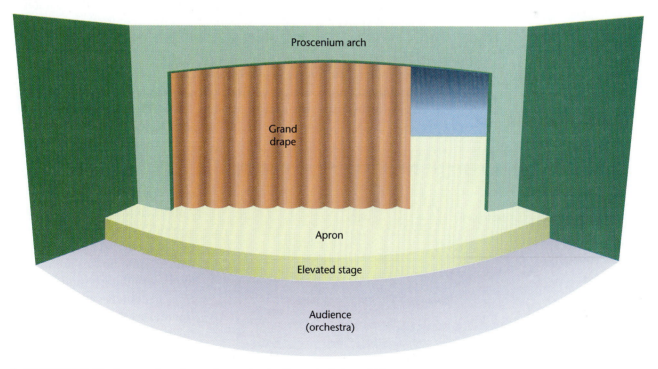

♦ **FIGURE 2.3** *Proscenium Stage from the Audience's Point of View*

conclusions of acts or scenes. The use of the grand drape has diminished, however, since the mid-twentieth century because of growing sophistication in lighting and changes in aesthetic sensibilities. A proscenium theatre can become a box of illusions, and the French called it so in the seventeenth century. Its illusionary possibilities are intensified by the use of artificial light and the clear separation of the performance box from the audience area.

The audience area of any theatrical space is called the **house.** In a proscenium theatre the **orchestra** is the space immediately in front of the stage where seats are on the floor. The theatre might also have an **orchestra pit**—traditionally a sunken area between the apron and the audience—for musicians (see Figure 2.4). Usually, the orchestra floor is gently **raked,** sloping upward from stage or pit to the back of the house. Some houses are divided by aisles running toward the stage to facilitate audience seating. **Continental seating** does not include these aisles except at the extreme left and right; the orchestra seats are unbroken in one long horizontal arc, and rows of seats are placed

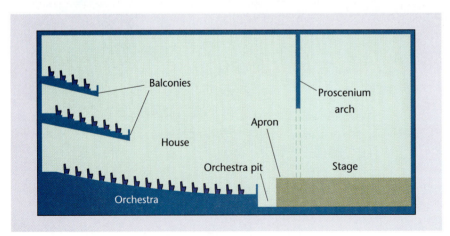

◆ **FIGURE 2.4** *Section View of Proscenium House*

Exploring Historical and Cultural Perspectives

An overwhelming majority of proscenium theatres built before the age of electricity vanished because of fires, rebuilding, or urban renewal. Some were remodeled so extensively that the original structure is unrecognizable. Of the few surviving theatres, the Drottningholm near Stockholm, Sweden, is very important because it is still used for productions, most of which are staged using eighteenth-century scenery and methods except for lighting. (Originally, Drottningholm was lit by candles and oil lamps.) This small court theatre with a deep stage was built for King Gustav III in the 1760s but was closed when the king died some thirty years later. Long boarded up, the theatre was rediscovered in 1921. The most remarkable surprise was the discovery of original scenery and stage machinery that still worked. You can visit this theatre today for a tour or a production of operas, plays, or ballets of long ago. Although still active as a theatre, it also functions as a museum of European theatre in the 1700s with its two-dimensional wing and drop scenery (flat pieces of scenery painted to look three-dimensional) and flying machines of a type rarely seen since the nineteenth century. Ingmar Bergman's film of Mozart's opera *The Magic Flute* (1975; available on VHS and DVD) begins in the Drottningholm Court Theatre. During the first few scenes you can see the eighteenth-century wing and drop scenery at work. A few other court theatres survive in Europe, including a beautiful one at Krumlov Castle in the Czech Republic. Unfortunately, the Krumlov Theatre is no longer used for performances, but it has been preserved with great care. You can visit a wonderful Internet site for Krumlov Castle, including inter-

THE DROTTNINGHOLM COURT THEATRE, *a small surviving eighteenth-century proscenium theatre, still has much of its original scenery as can be seen in this temple set with wing and drop scenery. Notice the balconies on each side of the proscenium opening, the orchestra pit downstage of the apron, and the hood of a prompter's box down center. Throughout the eighteenth and much of the nineteenth centuries, musicians were almost always present in the pit regardless of the type of play being presented. The European continental theatres did not have proscenium doors as the British theatres had.*

Photo by Per Bergström. Courtesy of Sveriges Teatermuseum, Stockholm, Sweden.

active, virtual tours of the spaces at www.ckrumlov.cz/uk/ samek/snadvoni/i_hd.htm.

Interested? Check out

Max Plunger. *The Drottningholm Court Theatre: Its Advent, Fate and Preservation.* Stockholm, Sweden: Byggforlaget, 1993.

Agne Beijer. *Court Theatres of Drottningholm and Gripsholm.* New York: B. Blom, 1972.

The web site for the Drottningholm Court Theatre at www. drottningholmsslottsteater.dtm.es/engelsk/eframes_index.html.

a good distance apart to facilitate audience passage. A proscenium space may include seating in **galleries, balconies,** or **boxes** on levels higher than the orchestra.

Proscenium spaces have been common since the Italian Renaissance, and most European theatres were using them by the late seventeenth century. Nearly every culture with a theatrical tradition adopted the proscenium for at least some of its presentations, including cultures in India, Africa, Japan, and China. It was virtually the only kind of theatre space available in North America until well into the twentieth century. Nearly all the Broadway theatres in New York are proscenium spaces, and most theatres across the United States and Canada as well as in Europe are prosceniums.

THRUST SPACE

The **thrust space** is one of the oldest theatrical arrangements to be formalized as theatre architecture. The classical Greeks, traveling acting companies in the European Middle Ages, classical Chinese performers, some Japanese Noh and early Kabuki companies, *commedia dell'arte* (improvisational comedy) troupes in Italy, Elizabethan actors in England, and many theatre companies in Europe and North America since the mid-twentieth century have all utilized variations on the thrust space.

At its most basic the stage of the thrust is surrounded on three sides by the audience, even though a majority of the audience area is frequently facing the performance space from the "front." Put another way, the performance space extends out into the audience area so that the actors, when facing forward, or downstage, have audience members in front of them and on both sides but not at their backs (see Figure 2.5). The actors then must play to the audience in an arc, since the audience is laid out before the performers like a fan. At the actors' backs might be a simple curtain, painted or constructed scenery, or a screen, but always with entrances and exits for the actors. Some permanent thrust spaces have a **façade**—a generalized standing or hanging structure, often multilevel, that may be neutral or decorated but always resides upstage of the action, creating a background that can suggest nearly any location, inside or out. A generic façade was popular in classical Greece and Rome as well as Elizabethan England and Spain in the Golden Age; in China, Japan, and India; and in more recent times in some thrust theatres in North America. Some thrust spaces allow the performers to leave the stage by aisles through the audience and/or vomitories. **Vomitories** (voms) are entrances to elevated seating for the audience that run underneath the audience and come up to empty out into the seating area. They were invented by the Romans for theatres and amphitheatres (such as the Coliseum in Rome) and are often used today in sports stadiums.

Some thrust stages are portable or mobile to facilitate being moved from place to place by traveling troupes of actors. This kind of stage (often called a **booth stage**) was probably used by ancient Greek and Roman mime performers and was definitely used by actors in the Middle Ages. In the second half of the twentieth century, inspired especially by the theatres that were common in Shakespeare's time, the thrust space became very popular again, and many new professional and academic theatres were built, beginning with the Stratford Festival Theatre in Ontario. Other famous thrust spaces in North America include the Alley Theatre in Houston, the Mark Taper Forum in Los Angeles, the Guthrie Theatre in Minneapolis, and the Vivian

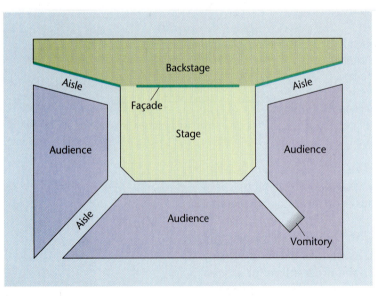

◆ **FIGURE 2.5** *Thrust Theatre Ground Plan*

Stratford Festival Theatre

The first important thrust theatre in North America continues to be a showpiece for productions of classical plays, especially for the works of Shakespeare and his contemporaries (although the Stratford company performs modern plays as well). The stage at Stratford, Ontario, was originally designed by director Tyrone Guthrie (1900–1971) and designer Tanya Moiseiwitsch (b. 1914), who wished to produce a space appropriate for Elizabethan drama and one that reflected many of the known characteristics of the public theatres of Shakespeare's time. The Festival Theatre opened in 1957 with a production of *Hamlet* and was remodeled in 1997. It seats 1,820, but steep, two-level seating areas keep most of the audience close to the stage action and never farther away than sixty-five feet. On stage, part of the upstage façade, which has a central balcony and multiple doors, is removable to give variety and flexibility to the scenic possibilities. A similar but more asymmetrical thrust without the permanent façade, also conceived by Guthrie, resulted in the successful Guthrie Theatre in Minneapolis, Minnesota.

The Stratford Festival in the 1970s added a much smaller and simpler thrust stage, for many years called the Third Stage but renamed the Tom Patterson Theatre in 1991. The space has been modified several times over the years but is maintained for more intimate or experimental productions than the much larger Festival stage. The Patterson seats just under 500 audience members.

♦ **STRATFORD FESTIVAL THEATRE,** *viewed from house center. Note the deep thrust of the stage with the seats surrounding all three sides and the multi-level façade up center.*
Photo by Jeff Speed. Courtesy of the Stratford Festival Archives.

Interested? Check out

The Stratford Festival web site, www.stratfordfestival.ca.
Tyrone Guthrie. *Renown at Stratford: A Record of the Shakespeare Festival in Canada.* Toronto: Clark, Irwin, 1971.
James Forsyth. *Tyrone Guthrie: A Biography.* London: Hamilton, 1976.

Beaumont Theatre in New York. It is now common for actors to train and work in thrust spaces.

ARENA SPACE

The **arena space** is the easiest to describe but one of the most difficult to use well. Quite simply, it is a space in which the audience completely surrounds the performance area. The stage could be square, rectangular, circular, trapezoidal—in fact, any geometric shape (see Figure 2.6). A circular arena space is sometimes called "theatre-in-the-round." Typically, the performers enter and exit the space through aisles or passages that puncture the audience surround, and in most cases the passageways that serve the actors also serve the audience arriving and

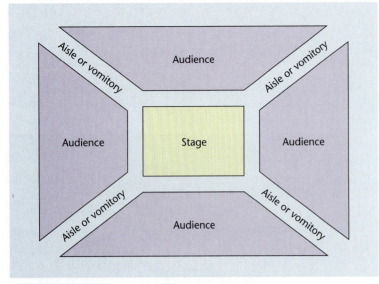

◆ **FIGURE 2.6** *Arena Theatre Ground Plan*

departing. Although arena theatres are usually associated with modern theatre, the spatial form can be found occasionally in ancient theatre such as the medieval rounds of Cornwall. The arena configuration allows more people to be seated close to the action than does proscenium or thrust. Most arena spaces are small and intimate, seating fewer than one hundred, but some rather majestic professional spaces, such as the Fichandler at Arena Stage in Washington, D.C., are quite large. Many college and university theatre programs include an arena space for presentations.

An arena space discourages the use of much scenery that literally depicts a complete locale. Consequently, it is virtually the opposite of a proscenium space in terms of scenic investiture; instead of viewing the action from one side, the audience experiences it from all sides. There can be no scenic façade, no single point of view, and every audience member is facing not only the performance space but other audience members as well. Arena encourages economy in staging—both artistic and financial. Because the audience always has other audience members in view, the arena often enhances aesthetic distance by reminding the audience that it is watching a per-

◆ **ARENA STAGE,** *Washington, D.C., The Fichandler Stage. The performance space is nearly empty except for a few scenic pieces for* Our Town.
Courtesy of Arena Stage.

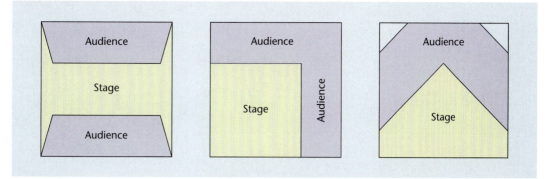

♦ **FIGURE 2.7** *Possible Configurations in a Black Box Theatre Ground Plan*

formance. To make the action clear and open to the audience in arena, actors must move more frequently than they would in other traditional spaces.

THE BLACK BOX

One type of nontraditional theatre space may be quickly becoming a traditional one. The term **black box** at one time described a simple room transformed to a theatre space, usually painted black. In the second half of the twentieth century, however, the black box became so common that some theatre companies, colleges, and universities began constructing them deliberately as smaller, flexible, alternative theatres for plays and performances that were thought to be appropriate for intimate spaces and small audiences. The traditional spatial approaches of thrust, arena, and proscenium tend to be used in a black box. The audience might be placed in an L-shaped configuration or on two opposite sides of the action, with audience members facing one another and stage action taking place in the troughlike middle. Alternatively, the audience members could find themselves in the middle of the space with the performers surrounding them (see Figure 2.7). Because the physical arrangements can be unusual or extreme, some artists call black boxes "lab" theatres, indicating a place where artists are free to experiment with new work or methods.

FOUND THEATRE SPACES

A nontraditional theatre space is often a "found" space but need not be that exclusively. A **found space** is anywhere, indoors or out, that was never intended as a theatrical space when created or designed. A director, designer, and company of actors might discover a space that they find appropriate for a specific play or for the kind of work they wish to pursue. The space could be any

♦ **ROMEO AND JULIET,** *the balcony scene, performed in a found space, an architectural ruin, near Ankara, Turkey. Note the rope ladder for access to the "balcony."*
Photo courtesy Billy Rose Theatre Collection, the New York Public Library for the Performing Arts, Astor, Lennox and Tilden Foundations.

The Performing Garage

A converted garage on Wooster Street in the Soho district of New York City is a good example of a found space that was converted to a theatrical one. Founded in 1967 and directed by Richard Schechner (b. 1934), the Performance Group was inspired by the environmental work of Polish director and theorist Jerzy Growtowski (1933–1999) and the political activism of the Living Theatre, New York's most famous experimental company of the 1960s. Schechner, who wrote the definitive book on environmental theatre, and his company transformed the garage, using scaffolding and platforms to accommodate an audience that was mixed rather freely with the actors in both space and the action for each performance. Perhaps their most memorable production was the ritualistic *Dionysus in 69* (1968), which was based on Euripides' Greek tragedy *The Bacchae.* The audience entered a large space with wooden towers and platforms and could sit on either the floor, platforms, or towers. Actors were at first dispersed throughout the room but then began to congregate in groups. As performers moved through the space, they sometimes touched or spoke directly to the audience members.

After the breakup of the Performance Group about 1980, several members, including Elizabeth LeCompte (b. 1944), Spalding Gray (b. 1941), and Willem Dafoe (b. 1955), reorganized as the Wooster Group, another experimental company that continued to use the Performing Garage. The group now describes its theatre as a flexible black box. The political and nontraditional Wooster Group has used this space in a variety of intriguing ways featuring deconstructions of famous plays. A deconstructed production begins with a well-known play, but as a pretext for a conception that is dramatized commentary on either the play itself or the values inherent in the original play. The Wooster Group created fascinating deconstructions or new conceptions of many well-known plays, such as *The Hairy Ape* (Wooster Group project, 1995) and *The Emperor Jones* by Eugene O'Neill (Wooster Group project, 1993) and Arthur Miller's *The Crucible,* rechristened *L.S.D. (. . . Just the High Points . . .)* (1984). The results are often fascinating and disturbing interpretations of early and mid-twentieth century culture and theatre.

Interested? Check out

Richard Schechner. *Environmental Theatre.* New York: Hawthorn, 1973.
David Savran. *Breaking the Rules: The Wooster Group, 1975–1985.* New York: Theatre Communications Group, 1988.
The web site for the Wooster Group, www.thewoostergroup.org.

room, large or small, in a public building, a house, a church, a factory. The space might be a town square, a field, a football stadium, a street corner, a gymnasium, a rooftop. In the medieval period the town square in Lucerne, Switzerland, was used for religious drama. Performances have frequently been staged at Judson Memorial Church in Washington Square and St. Mark's Church in the Bowery in New York City.

A space might be used as it is found or undergo some kind of modification to make it serve the purpose. In other words, any place can become a theatre. Even traditional theatre spaces sometimes are transformed to serve a different kind of theatrical experience. For example, the stage of a large proscenium theatre might become a more intimate theatrical space by placing the audience on the stage as well as the actors, leaving the traditional house empty and ignored. German director Max Reinhardt staged *The Miracle* in the 1920s many times in cathedrals throughout Europe. In the United States he reversed the process by instructing designer Norman Bel Geddes to redecorate a large theatre throughout to resemble

♦ **AMADEUS,** by Peter Shaffer, performed by the acting ensemble on an open stage with a highly polished floor. Period is indicated by costumes and furniture pieces. Directed by Michael Donald Edwards; scenic design by Michael Ganio; costume design by David Zinn.
Courtesy of Indiana Repertory Theatre.

a cathedral. **Site-specific performance** is a term used for a production that is developed for and closely linked to a particular location. *Another Person Is a Foreign Country* (1991), written by Charles L. Mee and directed by Anne Bogart, was performed among the ruins of the first cancer hospital in the United States.

ENVIRONMENTAL THEATRE

One of the most dynamic uses of nontraditional space is often called **environmental theatre.** Although we can find precedent in older cultures, the twentieth century witnessed an explosion of environmental theatre in the 1960s and early 1970s in Europe and the United States. This approach continues to be used periodically in both professional and academic theatre. The basic principle of environmental theatre is that the audience and actors share the same space. There is little or no separation of acting and observing areas, with the result that the audience members are physically part of the performance. Consequently, the traditional qualities of aesthetic distance undergo severe modification; sometimes audience members feel put on the spot and find it difficult to locate a "comfort zone." Environmental theatre can occur in traditional theatre spaces or found spaces.

Many productions in the twentieth century experimented with placement of the audience even if they were not attempting to create complete environmental theatre. John Dexter's direction of the first production of *Equus* (1973) by Peter Shaffer, for example, placed some of the audience members in a fan shape at the back of the stage (as if witnesses at a trial), even though most of the audience was in the traditional proscenium house. The intended effect was a modified arena, and perhaps it functioned as such for the onstage audience. For the audience in the house, however, it looked as though the onstage audience was being used as living scenery.

More environmental in its approach was the first professional revival in 1974 of Leonard Bernstein's musical *Candide* with a new book by Hugh Wheeler, as directed by Harold Prince. For the Broadway production in a traditional proscenium theatre the orchestra seats were torn out so that ramps and platforms for the actors could meander all around the stools used to seat the audience. These audience members had to look in all directions to be able to see the action. More traditional audience seating, which produced a "safer" if more removed viewpoint, was positioned around the central "environmental" area. The audience members in this traditional area looked down on the dramatic action and were free to observe the intermingling of audience and performers in the orchestra. The production created two very different experiences for the audience members depending on where they were seated: environmental for those in the orchestra and more passive, traditional viewing for those in the surrounding seats.

EXPERIMENTING WITH SPACE

Sometimes playwrights call for radically different approaches to space in their scripts. Maria Irene Fornes often experiments with space in the plays she writes and directs. In *Fefu and Her Friends* (1977) Fornes calls for five different settings in and around the house of the major character, Fefu. Five settings would not be unusual except that the playwright doesn't want five sets changing in the same space; she wants five different spaces to which the audience must move to witness the action. All the audience is together to watch the first scene in Fefu's living room, then the audience is divided into four groups who see four different scenes simultaneously but in a different order. For example, one quarter of the audience visits the study for scene 2, but another quarter goes to the kitchen, another to the lawn, and the fourth to a bedroom. The audience keeps shifting until each group has seen all four scenes in the four spaces, then all return to the living room to view the final scene, reunited. Naturally the production's eight actresses must perform the four middle scenes four times in a row, and all these scenes are approximately the same length. The point of the playwright is not just novelty in moving the audience around but to demonstrate how people behave, talk, and respond differently depending on the kind of space they are occupying at the time. When this play is produced in a traditional theatre, the production team has to choose and convert rooms that are not usually intended for performance—dressing rooms, lobby areas, prop rooms, classrooms, rehearsal studios—to achieve the number of different settings called for by the playwright.

STAGE DIRECTIONS

Most actors, directors, and designers use a standardized set of terms to talk about space and the use of space with a common understanding. These terms were created for proscenium stages and are based on the assumption that the audience is positioned on one side of the performance space or stage. Early proscenium stages were raked—elevated much higher at the back of the stage than closer to the audience (that is, the stage sloped down as an actor moved toward the audience). Consequently, the part of the stage farthest from the

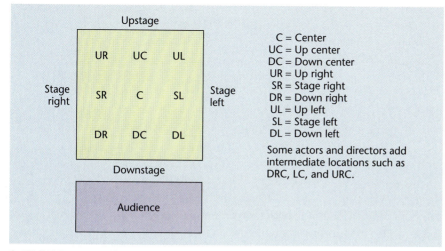

C = Center
UC = Up center
DC = Down center
UR = Up right
SR = Stage right
DR = Down right
UL = Up left
SL = Stage left
DL = Down left

Some actors and directors add intermediate locations such as DRC, LC, and URC.

♦ **FIGURE 2.8** *Stage Areas*

audience became known as **upstage.** The stage area closest to the audience is called **downstage.** Today, if an actor moves upstage of another actor or object on stage, he is moving **above** the chair or actor. If an actress moves downstage of another actor or object on stage, she is moving **below** the table or actor. All **stage left** and **stage right** directions and movements are given in terms of the actors' left and right *as they face the audience;* the space in the middle of the stage is **center.** Various combinations of these terms are used to describe different portions of the stage, such as down center, up right, down left (see Figure 2.8). A movement of any length is usually called a **cross.** Therefore the actress playing a betrayed wife (A) crosses from center to down left below a chair to the table where she picks up a pistol, turns right to face the staggering actor playing her angry, drunken husband (B) upstage right, levels the pistol, and aims it at her adversary (see Figure 2.9). When making notes in a script, most actors, stage managers, and directors use the letter X to indicate a cross, so a cross to down right would read XDR.

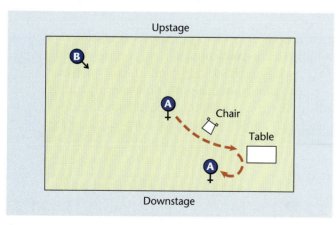

♦ **FIGURE 2.9** *Diagram Showing Actor Movement*

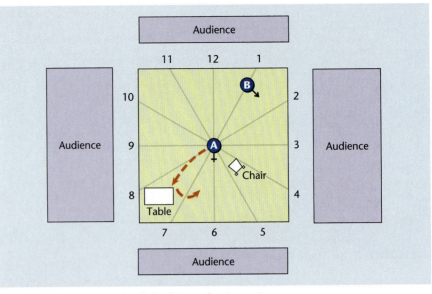

♦ **FIGURE 2.10** *Use of Clock Face for Stage Areas*

Some directors, designers, and actors use standard stage terms in an arena space by simply designating one side as downstage, but many artists have developed other systems, such as dividing the space into a clock face. For example, an actress might now move from center to a position at seven o'clock to confront the villain waiting at one o'clock (see Figure 2.10).

Stage directions, physical descriptions in a play, are frequently about location and movement in space. In the late nineteenth century William Gillette was a successful playwright, actor, and director who created very detailed stage directions that leave little to the imagination in terms of movement, placement, stage business, and sometimes emotionality. The following stage directions from his thriller *Secret Service* (1896) describe the action when the hero Thorne, who is a Union spy pretending to be a Confederate officer during the Civil War, is seized by Confederate soldiers while Thorne is attempting to telegraph an unauthorized message. The spoken dialogue is delivered by General Randolph, who suspects Thorne of treachery:

> *Hold that machine there!* (pointing at telegraph instrument. Sergeant and two men spring quickly across to right; Sergeant rushes against Thorne with arm across his breast forcing him over to right against chair and table on right—chair a little away from table to emphasize with crash as Thorne is flung against it—and holds him there. The two men cross bayonets over instrument and stand motionless. All done quickly, business-like and with as little disturbance as possible. General Randolph strides down center and speaks across to Thorne.) *I'll have you court-martialed for this!*[2]

♦♦♦♦♦♦♦♦♦♦

Theatre and Transformation

Although actors could perform for themselves alone without any intended audience, as an act of theatre the process would be incomplete. To have theatre,

♦ **CLOUD NINE,** by Caryl Churchill. In this production at Towson State University, the character Edward, a small boy played by an actress, swings out over the audience, thereby crossing the proscenium stage beyond the expected limits of traditional stage directions.
Collection of the authors.

collaboration of artists and audience is both an opportunity and a necessity. Because the audience changes with each performance, the nature of its responses and collaboration is different each time. In the process of this interaction in a specific place, transformation occurs on many levels. The space, for a time, is transformed through mutual agreement to a fictional world. The people watching and listening are no longer just individuals but form the collective whole of the audience. The experience of trying on a new identity for even a short time may have a transformative effect on the actor. The engagement of all who come together opens the possibility for change: in thought, attitude, feeling, and perspective.

The mythical story of the origin of the performing arts in Japan embodies both the importance of collaboration and the theatre's transformative power. The ancient gods were squabbling one day. The god of the sun got angry and hid in a cave, depriving the world of light and warmth. A goddess named Uzume impulsively attempted to entice the sun god to come out. In her emotional distress she began to move rhythmically—the creation of dance. Although Uzume's performance was intended for an audience of one, the other gods and goddesses responded approvingly to her efforts. Out of curiosity, and especially intrigued by the reaction of the larger audience, the sun god came out of the cave, only to be enchanted by Uzume's performance. Consequently, the birth of the performing arts arose from emotional distress, found and engaged an audience, and brought light back to a dark world.

QUESTIONS AND ACTIVITIES

1. Identify a play, film, or television show that led you to experience catharsis. Why do you think this experience was so emotionally intense for you? Consider both elements within the production and what you brought to the experience mentally and physically.

2. Identify plays, films, or television shows in which actors address the audience directly. What do you think this device added to the experience?

3. Identify an event other than theatre in your culture that sanctions obvious pretending or role playing. Does this event require costuming or assuming a distinct persona? Why is this event attractive to the people who participate?

4. Discuss effects that different spaces have on television viewing, movie viewing, or sports events. For example, how is watching television in a student lounge different from watching it in your family living room? Are there different types of programs that you would prefer to watch in different spaces? In what kind of theatre space would you prefer to see a comedy? A tragedy? A large-cast musical? A two-character play?

5. Make a list of the various types of spaces where performances took place that members of your class attended (or just heard about). What are some other places on your campus or in your city or town that might be interesting to use for performance? What sort of an atmosphere would each site offer?

6. Learn to give and take stage directions by practicing in a small group. Clear as large a space in a room as possible. Refer to the diagram of stage areas (Figure 2.8) and relate it to the space you have. Take turns moving each other around the space by using the appropriate terms. For example, one person gives the following directions to three other people:

   To Person 1: "Begin at center, cross down right, and stand facing downstage."

   To Person 2: "Enter up left, cross down right to center, and turn left."

   To Person 3: "Enter from up left, cross below person 2, and stand down left facing person 1."

7. Visit an established theatrical space on your campus or in your city or town and take a tour if possible. Identify the type of space. Describe the actor/audience relationship and the feel of the theatre. How does this atmosphere change when it is full of people? Identify the different areas on stage and in the house (wings, apron, orchestra, thrust stage, façade, vomitories, etc.). Stand on stage in various positions and see what the house looks like from the actor's point of view. Practice giving and taking stage directions while on the stage (see Question 6 above).

◆◆◆◆◆◆◆◆◆

KEY TERMS AND CONCEPTS

The Audience Experience
empathy, p. 27
aesthetic distance, p. 28
catharsis, p. 32
epic theatre, p. 33

The Nature of Acting
hypokrites, p. 34
mimesis, p. 34
chorus, p. 35
technitae, p. 35
histrio, p. 35
actor, p. 35

From Play to Production
improvisation, p. 37

play or script, p. 37
production, p. 37
playwright, p. 38
producer, p. 38
director, p. 38
casting director, p. 38
scenic designer, p. 38
costume designer, p. 38
lighting designer, p. 38
sound designer, p. 38
makeup designer, p. 38
composer, p. 38
lyricist, p. 38
musical director, p. 38
choreographer, p. 38
stage manager, p. 38

front-of-house, p. 38
house manager, p. 38
box office manager, p. 38

Theatre Space
proscenium space, p. 40
proscenium arch, p. 41
apron, p. 41
wings, p. 41
grand drape, p. 41
house, p. 42
orchestra, p. 42
orchestra pit, p. 42
raked, p. 42
continental seating, p. 42
galleries, p. 43

◆◆◆◆◆◆◆◆◆

FOR FURTHER EXPLORATION

Daniel Gerould, ed. *Theatre/Theory/Theatre: The Major Critical Texts from Aristotle and Zeami to Soyinka and Havel.* New York: Applause, 2000. For a sampling of ideas about what theatre is and should be.

"Aristotle" in the *Perseus Project Encyclopedia,* www.perseus.tufts.edu.

"Background to Noh-Kyogen," www.iijnet.or.jp/NOH-KYOGEN/english/english.html. For more information about Noh and its related comic form, Kyogen.

John Harrop and Sabin R. Epstein, *Acting with Style,* 3rd ed. Boston: Allyn and Bacon, 2000. For more on acting in the production process.

Richard Leacroft and Helen Leacroft, *Theatre and Playhouse.* London: Methuen, 1984. For more detail on the history of theatre architecture.

W. Oren Parker and R. Craig Wolf, *Scene Design and Stage Lighting.* Fort Worth, Tex.: Harcourt Brace, 1996. For information on the design and technical aspects of production.

MACBETH, Actors Theatre of Louisville.
Photo by Larry Hunt. Courtesy of Actors Theatre of Louisville.

Analyzing Theatre

Thinking and Writing about Live Performance

A udiences in the twenty-first century are used to watching actors perform on film, television, DVD, or videotape. The experience of theatre is different in many ways. An audience member could certainly attend the theatre with no preparation and have a wonderful time, but understanding certain concepts will make the experience fuller and richer. In this chapter we explore how to be an effective collaborator from the house. We discuss ways in which theatre differs from television and film, ways to look and listen to enhance the theatre experience, and how to analyze and evaluate performance, including an exploration of the role of the critic in the theatre and special considerations for writing about theatre.

Theatre, Film, and Television

Periodically, viewers turn on their TV and hear that the program they are about to watch is "Live from Lincoln Center" or "Live from New York . . . it's *Saturday Night!*" These programs are recorded in front of an audience in a theatre or studio, and at home the viewers may be witnessing the events as they occur, although often by tape delay. A portion of the unexpected nature of live performance is recaptured. Of course, viewers realize that the "live" event they are witnessing is very limited because the viewers do not see nearly as much as the on-site audience sees.

ACTIVE PARTICIPATION

Even a "live" broadcast does not require the kind of **active participation** that is necessary in the theatre. In film and TV the cameras and the director who picks the camera shots are highly selective. They make the choices for the viewers. In the theatre you choose what to watch—the actor at the side of the stage playing with his hair, the flickering stage light, or the leading lady delivering a speech at center stage. Theatre practitioners try to direct your attention with movement, actor positioning, and lighting, but ultimately, the choice is yours. Watching live theatre tends to take more concentration than watching film or TV does. Even attending the theatre requires effort; you must be in a certain place at a certain time. You can't pause the performance when you feel like it; on the other hand, your viewing is less likely to be interrupted by events (a telephone call, a doorbell, a conversation in the room).

TV and film images reduce the three-dimensional actor or object to two dimensions (the image is flat). The visual scale of filmed or digital images is also very different from that of live performance. Most TV images are much smaller than live performance; film images can be much larger. Theatre does not allow for a close-up shot (unless the close-up is projected on a two-dimensional screen for the audience, in which case the event is multimedia). Where you are seated in the theatre can make a difference in how you experience performance. If you are far away from the actors, it may take more energy to keep your attention focused on the stage.

Many people feel that the trade-off for more effort expended in watching theatre is an increased intensity of experience. Audience reception of film and television is typically passive (even when the entertainment is enjoyable). In the theatre choosing to participate—taking charge of the viewing experience and listening with special attention—creates a more vivid communication event. Part of this excitement is generated by the possibility for two-way communication. In film and most television there is no shared space for the viewers and performance, so any viewer response goes unseen and unheard by the actors. In the theatre, however, actors are very aware of the presence of the audience, and the actors' performances are in turn affected by the messages they receive: laughs, gasps, silence, even rustling of programs, all communicate to the actors and in turn affect their communication on the stage.

With that two-way communication comes a certain responsibility. The people on stage are human beings; respectful and courteous treatment is important. So much entertainment is brought into our living rooms that it is easy to forget (even in the movie theatre) that talking, ringing cell phones, and beeping pagers disturb other audience members. In the theatre they are even more distracting to the performers on the stage.

THE NATURE OF LIVE PERFORMANCE

There are drawbacks to live performance. Mistakes cannot be edited as in film or television; there is less quality control. A wonderful performance cannot be saved; even a videotape of a theatrical performance represents only a limited record of what happened from one point of view. You can't watch a favorite live performance again and again.

But there is also a special attraction to being "live." Although mistakes can and do occur, part of the theatre's excitement is never knowing exactly what will happen next and perhaps even seeing how performers will deal with the occasional glitch. A very special performance cannot be saved, but that very fact makes the theatre intriguing. Performance is a one-time-only event—one that you have helped to create by your presence—that will never happen in exactly the same way again.

The unique conditions of live performance differentiate it from all other methods of receiving a play. A student's understanding of Henrik Ibsen's *A Doll House* performed in a university theatre must differ from the response from reading a copy of the play *A Doll House* in the library, watching a film of the play starring Claire Bloom and Anthony Hopkins in a movie theatre, or watching a DVD of the play starring Juliet Stevenson and Trevor Eve on a TV screen in a classroom. Even if the translated text of the dialogue were the same, and in performance even if the actors were the same and the director and designers the same, each would be a different *Doll House* because the audience's relationship with the performance or

♦ *A DOLL HOUSE, first Norwegian production in 1880. Notice the box set with ceiling piece and chandelier, the Christmas tree upstage, and multiple entrances, all intended to suggest a real domestic interior in the Christmas season. Nora is seen here rehearsing her tarantella dance, which she deliberately does badly in order to get her husband to help her to avoid reading the letter in his mailbox, which will reveal her forgery.*
Universitetsbiblioteket, Oslo.

reading would differ markedly with each. The scale and feedback opportunities would radically differ, and audiences respond differently to various kinds of spaces. Consequently, the reception must differ as well.

♦♦♦♦♦♦♦♦♦♦

Analyzing Production

When in the theatre, it is important to be as open as possible—to take in or soak up the immediate sensory experience. At some point, however, you will probably want to analyze the event: What just happened? How did it happen? What was its effect on me? With those questions you will begin an analysis of the performance event. Your analysis can be as simple as thinking about the performance in the car going home or talking to friends about the experience over coffee. It can be as structured as an organized paper with clear assertions and strong support.

In the minds of most audience members, reception is followed by understanding, which usually includes "the meaning" of what they are experiencing. It is important to underscore how the meaning of a play or a moment in the play can become something quite different for each audience member. Many theorists of theatre assert that meaning is fluid, based on frame of reference—the previous experiences and cultural context of individual audience members—and the intentions and skills of the actors delivering the dramatic material. Most audience members will assume or assign meaning to what they experience.

There may be many possible meanings for what is communicated from the performance space, but these meanings are authentic for the spectators. The playwright's, actors', or director's intent might not match the interpretation reached by the audience member. This disparity does not signify failure, but the inevitable outcome of any communication or performance system that is addressing or entertaining an audience. The performance (especially including audience response and feedback) has its own unique life each time it occurs.[1]

In analyzing production, it is helpful to make a distinction between observation and interpretation. **Observation** is your recognition of what actually happened on stage: The actress playing Carol sat down heavily in the chair and held her head in her hands. A photograph or videotape could verify your observation. **Interpretation** is your intuitive response, your subjective experience of what the physical action communicated: Carol is depressed, sad, or exhausted. Although you and your neighbor might agree on your observation (though, of course, people may even recall things differently), you could very well have different interpretations of the behavior.

♦♦♦♦♦♦♦♦♦

Thinking about Actor Performances

In the theatre most audience responses and interpretations begin with characters and the actors who play them. Audiences are capable of believing some remarkable and impossible things when these are presented effectively on the stage. They can believe that Peter Pan flies and that Ebenezer Scrooge travels through time, space, and dreams with the ghosts of Christmas Past, Present, and

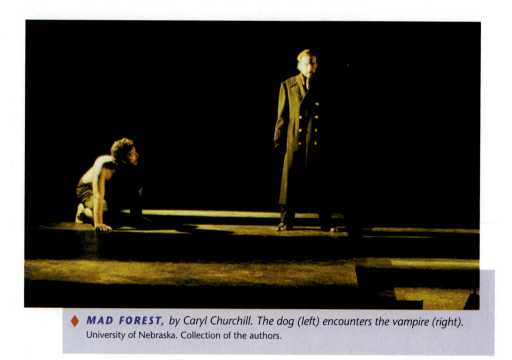

♦ **MAD FOREST,** *by Caryl Churchill. The dog (left) encounters the vampire (right).* University of Nebraska. Collection of the authors.

Future; audiences can believe that ambushed soldiers are being strafed in a Vietnam firefight in *Tracers* (1983), that an invisible orchestra is accompanying the cowboy Curley who opens *Oklahoma!* (1943) singing "Oh, What a Beautiful Morning." As playwright Eugene O'Neill liked to tell his directors when preparing for production, audiences will believe anything if you do it well. This assertion might be overstating the case, but it is clear that excellent execution goes a long way in helping us to accept the impossible. It doesn't matter whether the play is realistic or stylized and whether it is comic, tragic, or melodramatic. The audience can suspend disbelief and accept that character as genuine, at least for the moment of performance.

If we believe an actor's interpretation of a character (even as a cat or dog), then we accept that character as existing truthfully in the theatrical world as dramatized by the production. Caryl Churchill's *Mad Forest* (1990) has a wonderfully imaginative and poignant scene between a talking dog and a vampire (but with no dog suit or vampire cape for the actors). At first the vampire tries to ignore the starving dog, which is frightened of but fascinated by the vampire. Eventually, the dog's loneliness and desperation convince the vampire to make him into one of the undead—a vampire dog. This scene is symbolic of the awful exploitation and power struggles in Romania (where the action takes place), but while the scene is playing, audiences focus on the very personal encounter of these two impossible creatures. The action comes first in creating audience response. Symbolism comes later.

BELIEVABILITY

What enables the audience to accept the authenticity—or **believability**—of a character? The key might lie in beautifully written dialogue, or it could be the actor's delivery of the dialogue. Much of what is identified as character is created first by a playwright, but the actor completes the creative process and provides the key to audience belief or lack thereof. Perhaps the actor creates the illusion that the words are being delivered for the first time; the delivery of a lesser actor might sound memorized. If an actor's vocal delivery cannot be understood because of volume or articulation problems, it hardly matters how well a line is written. A fine performance by an accomplished stage and film actor such as Kevin Kline or Meryl Streep of a weakly drawn character is not much more than an exhibition of the actor's skills. More disheartening to watch are weak performances by unprepared actors of remarkably crafted characters such as Blanche DuBois—a neurotic and sensitive woman on the verge of emotional collapse in *A Streetcar Named Desire*—or Iago, a plotting, intelligent villain trusted by all around him in *Othello*.

In thinking about how and why a production works, it is important to try to separate the character as written from the actor's performance. People often admiringly quote funny or incisive lines delivered by favorite actors in films, TV, or plays. These lines are frequently credited in the imitator's mind to the actor rather than the character. Many people tend to identify the actor so closely with the character played that objectivity is lost. People standing at the water cooler, sitting at a lunch table, or walking across campus might quote Tom Cruise, Bette Davis, Denzel Washington, or Gwyneth Paltrow or even sketchily drawn characters in commercials or animated figures such as Homer Simpson, but viewers are actually quoting writers in most cases. The personality, charisma, or vocal delivery of the actor, however, is likely to be much of what draws the imitator to repeat the dramatic or comic moment out of context.

ACTOR CHOICES

One way to isolate an actor's contribution to character is to think in terms of **actor choices.** These choices may be more apparent if you see an actor perform several different characters. An actor's approach to movement, for example, may be significant. Is the actor setting an appropriate tempo for the character when crossing the stage or gesturing? Is the actor leading with an appropriate part of the body—for example, does movement seem to come first from the head, chest, or pelvis? Just these choices make a remarkable difference in the quality of the movement. Do the actor's movements seem appropriate to the character's age, profession, and social background and to the nature of the dramatic moment? Does the actor's physical bearing seem consistent with the words being spoken? Does the vocal quality seem appropriate for the character?

An emotional life can be identified for nearly every character on the stage. Many characters are frequently given to raucous laughter or perpetual sadness. The jovial Mr. Fezziwig in stage adaptations of Charles Dickens's *A Christmas Carol* never seems to stop chuckling. Anton Chekhov's plays are filled with people who cry at the drop of a hat; Masha in Chekhov's *The Sea Gull* explains that she always wears black because she is mourning for her life. A character's depression (such as that of most of the protagonists in Woody Allen's films and plays) may make audiences laugh, or a character's inappropriate or obnoxious laughter may irritate or anger the audience. Emotionality affects audience belief, but it is also crucial to the dramatic development of a play. Suzan-Lori Parks's plays often have characters who repeatedly exhibit threatening anger. The two brothers who love each other in *Topdog/Underdog* (2001), for example, make scathing remarks to one another.

Although a character's words may define or set the tone for emotionality, nonverbal behavior usually underscores, enhances, or even contradicts the spoken dialogue. Actors and directors make choices for character portrayal and experiment during rehearsal. The audience sees only the ultimate choice. An audience member's response to a character's behavior depends on the circumstances surrounding that behavior and what the audience is able to infer from the actor's facial expressions, body language, and tone of voice. If a character named Sue with difficulty declares her love for a character named Bill and Bill laughs at her, an audience will possibly feel sorry for Sue and angry with Bill. On the other hand, if Sue is constantly belittling and chastening Bill, an audience will possibly be glad that Bill finally gets his revenge. Then again, perhaps the audience suspects that Bill also loves Sue but is very insecure and doesn't believe Sue and so chooses to treat Sue's declaration as a joke out of self-defense. Many questions could be asked of such a scene: What was the nature of Bill's laughter? Did the actors' choices for physical communication match the words and sounds? What were the actors trying to communicate beyond obvious words and gestures?

CHARACTER INTERACTION

Unless the audience is watching a one-person show, it is observing actors collaborating with other actors. Working together as a team, called **ensemble** work in the theatre, is often crucial to the success of a scene. The actors should really seem to be listening to one another and reacting to one another. Dynamic and appropriate character reaction and then, in turn, the creation of new action are

◆ **HAMLET.** *In this production the acting ensemble surrounds Hamlet, played by Bruce McKenzie. Directed by Jon Jory; scenic design by Paul Owen; costume design by Walt Spangler.*
Photo by Richard C. Trigg. Courtesy of Actors Theatre of Louisville.

critical to the dramatic process. The interaction of actors as characters must be both logical and interesting to watch. An unengaged actor might appear to be waiting for his or her next opportunity to speak. Sometimes an audience sees onstage a collection of individual performances that seem virtually independent of one another. When this situation occurs, the audience is not likely to accept the world of the play as authentic.

When the actors are responding to what other actors are offering, however, the audience gets a sense of spontaneity no matter how well rehearsed the action might be. William Gillette, a popular actor at the turn of the twentieth century, was fond of describing "the illusion of the first time."[2] He strove to make the audience accept that his words had never been spoken before, that his actions were invented at that moment in response to what had immediately preceded. Of course, he rehearsed tirelessly, but his secret for success lay in that illusion of spontaneity.

◆◆◆◆◆◆◆◆◆

Thinking about Space and Design

The theatrical space demands a way of looking that is not typical in everyday life. Most of what people see around them is very familiar and repetitious: their home and the routine of work or school or recreation. In a classroom students focus on an instructor or discussion group, a chalkboard or projection screen, or they simply gaze out a window daydreaming of being elsewhere. Several choices

◆ *AGAMEMNON AND HIS DAUGHTERS, 2001 production, adapted from several Greek tragedies by Kenneth Cavander. In the pit Natascia Diaz, as Elektra, undergoes fits of madness while the men, played by Paolo Andino and Ezra Knight, stroll around the perimeter. Much of this production set in an arena stressed the severe anxieties and solitary suffering of the female characters. Directed by Molly Smith; set and lighting design by Pavel Dobrusky; costume design by Lindsay W. Davis.*
Photo by Scott Suchman. Courtesy of Arena Stage.

are made for the students by a professor, and students might or might not co-operate with those choices. But students seldom pay attention to the variety of details around them.

If the students or professor go to a theatre, however, and see a stage set of a classroom, they are likely to notice many details that they could ignore in their own classroom. The audience might scan the stage setting, seeking to authenticate or dispute the choices made by designer and director. Do the details seem true to previous experience? Even if most of the setting seems true to life, is there a detail or set piece that seems out of place or odd? If so, this discrepancy could be deliberate on the part of the production team or the playwright to call the audience's attention to the unusual detail. Suppose, for example, that the set seems exacting except for the fact that it has no doorway, no windows, and no entrance of any kind. The absence might seem like a mistake. Or perhaps the lack of an exit makes the characters appear to be trapped (no way in or out), which can begin to create discomfort in the audience members.

As with choices made by the actor, elements of space and design will be interpreted according to the surrounding action. If the scene escalates emotionally and it slowly becomes evident that the student characters are being terrorized by a cruel and rigid teacher, the set with no means of escape might help to create a sense of paranoia and confinement. It then becomes a symbol of unenlightened education driven by torture and inflexibility. Certain plays, such as *The Lesson* (1951) by Eugène Ionesco, deal with this very theme. In this play a professor is tutoring a single student. As the play progresses, the professor becomes increasingly oppressive, ultimately dehumanizing the student and killing her.

SEEING IN THREE DIMENSIONS

♦ **TANGO**, *by Slawomir Mrożek. In this production we focus on a corpse on the stage floor as two men upstage, one of whom is the murderer, dance to tango music.* Towson State University. Collection of the authors.

Of course, nearly all people see—or think they see—real events in three dimensions. Unlike watching an image on a screen, at a live performance the audience must negotiate three-dimensionality with all of its possibilities for depth and multiple focus. Although most audiences do not consciously think of stage space in terms of its depth, they usually notice if a sense of depth is absent or if the use of depth is especially striking. For example, it is not often in a performance that an audience sees furniture or actors lined up straight across the stage. Such an arrangement would call attention to itself and strike the audience either as amateurish, as the preparation for a chorus line, or as a very formal moment in the action. As a stage director, Ingmar Bergman (b. 1918) often has used depth in significant ways. For example, he has placed actors in nearly the same upstage/downstage plane but very far apart. In live performance this arrangement would create a very different image for an audience member sitting in the center of the house than it would for a spectator sitting far to the right or left. Visually, the impact of different seat locations can be almost like viewing different productions.

When examining the performance in space, it can be instructive to consider **space and design choices.** What are the director and designers attempting to get the audience to see? Where do they want the audience to look and why? What is the spatial relationship of the actors to each other and to the set?

EXAMINING SCENERY

It is no surprise that much of what an audience sees on a stage in performance isn't really what it seems to be. Walls are rarely solid and most often are made of stretched canvas or other lightweight materials so that they can be easily shifted or transported. The audience might see a wall shaking a bit when a door slams on stage. Detail that seems three-dimensional is often painted or enhanced by paint and light. The unseen portions of the scenery are unfinished—only what we see in the playing space matters. The actors in performance often see unfinished scenery, but the audience does not. An audience member knows that the scenery is fake but is prepared to believe in its reality within the world of the play.

There are two basic approaches to creating this world on stage. If the scenery is **representational,** it is crafted realistically to look and function just as the scenic location would in the real world, whether interior or exterior. The audience often wants to believe in that scenery just as it wants to believe in the actors' performances. If the scenery is **presentational,** it is not meant to resemble everyday life; it may be stylized, abstracted, or suggestive scenery. For

♦ **THE CHERRY ORCHARD,** by Anton Chekhov. The original representational production at the Moscow Art Theatre. The famous actor-director Konstantin Stanislavsky, as the character Gaev, addresses the bookcase in this scene. Notice the prompter's box downstage center.
Photo courtesy Billy Rose Theatre Collection, the New York Public Library for the Performing Arts, Astor, Lennox and Tilden Foundations.

presentational scenery authentic appearance is not important, but the scenery should be interesting and functional. When scenery does not perform as intended, belief in the entire fictional world can be destroyed. In 1917 in the play *Peter Ibbetson*, the actor John Barrymore was escorting the actress Constance

♦ **THE GREAT WHITE HOPE,** by Howard Sackler. In this 2000–2001 presentational revival, the crowd for an early twentieth-century boxing match becomes a sea of straw hats suspended above an open trap in the floor. This device creates an image of an anonymous crowd and comments on the period without filling the stage with a host of extras. Actors (left to right) are Richard Henrich, Sarah Marshall, Eric Sutton, Jack Kyrieleison, and David Fendig. Directed by Molly Smith.
Courtesy of Arena Stage.

Collier through a large scenic opera house during a moment of majestic, romantic spectacle. Unexpectedly, the scenery gave way and toppled to the floor in a cloud of dust and debris amid shrieks and curses from the startled actors. Fortunately, the actors were unhurt, but all the expectations for a beautiful illusion were spoiled, to say the least. A planned stage composition was destroyed, and it must have been difficult to recapture the tone of the play after such a disaster.

Most of the time, of course, audiences do not witness such failure, but audience members can still ask themselves, "Does the scenery seem appropriate for the action as it is played? Is the scenery consistent with the style of the play? Is the scenery attempting to suggest a specific historical period? Is the scenery an expression of a completely imaginary location? Is the presentational scenery so highly stylized that it does not suggest any locale but a mood perhaps? Does there seem to be too much or too little scenery for the action of the play? Does the performance seem overwhelmed by the scenery (critics and artists sometimes talk about overdesigned productions or a "trial by scenery"). If the scenery seems appropriate to or effective for the performance, what makes it so? What seems to be the intent of this scenery?"

Imagine watching a production of a tragedy about kings set centuries ago, such as *Richard II* by Shakespeare. The stage floor is painted like a chessboard, and decorations onstage suggest chess pieces and various game imagery. When the actors enter, they are all dressed in either black or white, as if they are game pieces themselves. Such a scheme is more than a little obvious, but the heavy-handed point is likely to make itself evident very quickly, perhaps leading you to think of the entire play in terms of gamesmanship, which is probably what the director and designers wanted you to consider when seeing this play. In most cases scenic messages will be much more subtle.

◆ **THE CHAIRS**, by Eugène Ionesco, presented here at the Guthrie Theatre. Near the end of the performance, the stage is filled with chairs awaiting the much-anticipated arrival of the orator, who turns out to be incapable of communication. The Old Man is played by Christopher McCann; the Old Woman by Barbara Byrne. Directed by Daniel Aukin.
Photo by Michal Daniel.

Exploring Historical and Cultural Perspectives

The Effect of Audience Space on *Angels in America*

Space has a profound effect on an audience member's experience of production. It is not only a question of being able to hear or see better. The relationship of an audience member's position to the performance area can affect the level of emotional involvement with the action. A good illustration of this dynamic is our experience with Tony Kushner's *Angels in America: A Gay Fantasia on National Themes* (1993–94).

Two plays make up *Angels in America: Millennium Approaches* and *Perestroika.* Together they explore the impact of AIDS on the gay community as well as the personal struggles of several gay men with religious backgrounds that are intolerant of their choices, family disapproval, and the underground nature of alternative lifestyles in conflict with modern marriage and the workplace. Real, fictional, and fantasy characters appear in the plays, and they present both representational and presentational scenes in settings ranging from park benches to offices and living rooms, from public restrooms to heaven. An angelic visitation to the bedroom of a dying AIDS victim is contrasted with the fantasy action on an arctic ice floe; a young woman tries to cope with her own drug dependence as well as the discovery that her husband is gay.

When we saw the Broadway production of *Angels in America,* we saw both plays, *Millennium Approaches* and *Perestroika,* on the same day (one at a matinee and the other in the evening). For *Millennium Approaches* we sat on the front row and felt as though we were virtually thrust into the action, which seemed very immediate and vital. In the evening, however, we sat about halfway back in the orchestra and felt somewhat isolated, as if the play's emotional import had difficulty reaching us there. On the other hand, the staging, im-

◆ **ANGELS IN AMERICA,** *by Tony Kushner. Prior Walter, who is dying of AIDS, played here by Bash Halow, is visited by an angel, played by Suzanne Grodner. Directed by Mladen Kiselov; costume design by Suttirat Larlarb.* Photo by Richard C. Trigg. Courtesy of Actors Theatre of Louisville.

ages, and artistic composition of the production were much easier to comprehend with distance. In retrospect we were much more excited about *Millennium Approaches* and more objective about *Perestroika.*

Set properties (usually large additions to the setting such as furniture) also become part of the scenery. Chairs, for example, are frequently recurring set props, and they often blend in with the surroundings. At times, however, they take focus and communicate meaning. We see many, many chairs in the aptly entitled French play *The Chairs* (1952) by Eugène Ionesco. The playwright calls for the actors to steadily fill the space with chairs that remain empty throughout the performance. This presence and absence is part of the point of the play, in which the aging characters anticipate a great moment that never comes. On the other hand, a 1982 modern-dress British production of

♦ **PRIVATE LIVES,** by Noel Coward. In this unusual production a Parisian apartment becomes a distorted box set in which no expected furniture remains except a couch and the surprising intrusion of the Eiffel Tower in the living room. Actors (left to right) are Jefferson Mays, Karenjune Sanchez, Steve Webber, and Ellen Lauren. Directed by Anne Bogart; scenic design by Neil Patel; costume design by James Schuette.
Photo by Richard C. Trigg. Courtesy of Actors Theatre of Louisville.

Bérénice (1670) by Jean Racine placed a single imposing chair on stage and no other furniture. Not only did the chair catch the attention of the audience, it also became a focus of tension because no actor ever sat in it or used it until the play was nearly over. Once the actress playing the title role finally sat in the chair, the action carried dramatic weight because the tension was finally released.

After viewing a performance, you could ask yourself, "Are the set props merely sittable/standable units that are meant to indicate place and provide conversational units for the actors, or do they contribute more? Are the set properties communicating thought or symbolism?"

EXAMINING COSTUMES

It is easy to take costumes for granted and associate the choices strictly with the character being observed, almost as if the character were a real person who pulled these clothes out of the closet that morning. Audiences are sometimes stunned or surprised if the costumes are particularly attractive or detailed or are dismayed if they seem inappropriate to character or to the period in which the play or its production is set. But all costumes are a product of specific choices made by the costume designer and director.

Costumes can be important to locating the play in space and time. Most audience members have an idea of dress in famous periods such as Imperial Rome, Elizabethan England, or "Roaring Twenties" New York, and often recognize the period or location simply by costumes. In many productions, however, the play has been shifted in time or place, or perhaps historical periods are combined or even invented, as often happens in works of fantasy or plays set in the future. In this case audiences are completely free to accept or reject the designer's vision of how things might look in Los Angeles in 2534.

Perhaps the most effective assessment an audience member can make of costumes is appropriateness to character. Questions might be raised about appropriate color and texture, the costume's relationship to the costumes of other characters in the play, or the character's social position, economic status, occupation, age, and gender. Of course, many designers hope that the audience will not leave the show thinking about the costumes or lights or the sound or settings but will simply accept the designs as authentic manifestations of the world of the play as interpreted by the production team.

♦ *CORIOLANUS, by William Shakespeare. This production updates the play to a fascist country in the twentieth century. Here, Coriolanus, played by Andrew Long, is held aloft by other soldiers. Directed by Michael Kahn; scenic design by Walt Spangler; costume design by Jess Goldstein.* Photo by Carol Rosegg. Courtesy of Shakespeare Theatre, Washington, D.C.

♦♦♦♦♦♦♦♦♦

Understanding Style

"Style" is a complex term, and people use it frequently with a variety of meanings and intents. Some people mean it in a superlative sense, such as "she has style and grace," without providing modifiers for the word "style." Such uses of the word "style," however, tell us little about things theatrical. We will use **style** to suggest manner of expression and methods of onstage behavior as they affect composition and performance. It is not the content that dictates style, but the way in which that content is packaged and delivered to the audience. Style is dictated by language—poetry, prose, and dialects. Style is identified by character movement and social manners, by changes and fashions in architecture, clothes, furniture, and decoration (on both low and high economic scales). Style is expressed by music, painting, and dance. In short, style is heavily reliant on the period of history, the economic status of the characters, cultural values, and the geographical region or specific locality of the world that the style reflects or suggests. It is common to talk about a Restoration style (1660–1700 in England) or a Greek classical style, but such labels alone may suggest much or little depending on one's acquaintance with those periods of history.

Style can be a method of "authenticating" a place or time. A production of *The Weavers* by Gerhart Hauptmann could suggest rural Germanic Silesia in 1892 (the place and time of the play as written) through representational setting, costumes, properties, manners, and movement. This approach would require hundreds of peasant costumes (many in rags) because there are hundreds of starving workers exploited by the weaving industry. The audience would see the weavers' hovels because a big part of the play demonstrates their suffering. It would also see some of the rich industrialists and a house of the rich exploiters,

♦ **BIG LOVE,** by Charles L. Mee. Three pilots, played by Ryder Smith, Jeff Jenkins, and Mark Zeisler, move as if in a blue void. Directed by Les Waters; scenic design by Paul Owen; costume design by Marcia Dixcy Jory. Photo by Richard C. Trigg. Courtesy of Actors Theatre of Louisville.

which in turn is wrecked by the workers in revolt. To be representational with this play requires much detail and probably expense. On the other hand, a production team may sometimes impose a style that is quite different from the original on the material to be performed. For example, the hundreds of peasants might be used as a stylized chorus presenting the woes of the downtrodden, or a production could present just a few actors representing a much larger group. They could be costumed accurately but placed on a bare stage to avoid all of the scenic detail but at the same time underscore the austerity of the weavers' situation.

The style of the original play can be altered in production. Many plays from the past that were originally written in poetic form have, in the twentieth century and beyond, been translated into prose. This factor alone radically changes a play's style. When Carlo Goldoni's situation comedy *A Servant of Two Masters* (1743) is produced outside of Italy, the Italian regional dialects are often replaced by local dialects. Working-class dialects of England or New Jersey, for example, are more recognizable to English-speaking audiences. The British play *The White Devil* (1612) by John Webster is a violent tragedy originally set in seventeenth-century Italy. Some modern productions of the play have reset it in 1930s fascist Italy to underscore the political and social corruption running through the play.

Playwrights also indicate stylistic shifts within the play's text. For example, in 1928 Bertolt Brecht rewrote an eighteenth-century British ballad musical, *The Beggar's Opera* by John Gay. In his German-language *Threepenny Opera* Brecht kept the London location but moved the action to the nineteenth century. Composer Kurt Weill threw out all the old music and inserted funky 1920s jazz tunes. Brecht called for the characters to be dressed in one historical style but speak and sing as if in another. Such shifts are by no means unusual in the theatre, and similar incongruities have been used in varying degrees in many different periods. Sometimes a style is actually invented, as we see in work that is meant to suggest the future. *R. U. R.* (1920) by Josef and Karel Čapek, which introduced robots to the stage and the word "robot" to our language, was set futuristically in the 1950s and 1960s. Once we are well past the time of creation of such a style, however, we can usually see that the invented style is heavily indebted to the period in which it was created.

A production team may borrow a performance style from one culture and apply it to the plays of another. A production team in the United States or France, for example, might borrow the performance style of Japanese Kabuki and apply it to Western plays. Over the last several decades the West has seen nearly all the famous Greek and Elizabethan tragedies performed in such a borrowed style. Of course, this has also worked in reverse. Japanese directors, for example, have in turn adapted Western plays to their own classical styles or in some cases have drawn from several sources to come up with invented styles. Chinese, Indian, and other Asian and African theatre companies have also adapted Western plays to one of their own performance styles and

◆ **R. U. R.**, *by Josef and Karel Čapek, Theatre Guild. R. U. R. introduced the word "robot" to languages in this, the first American production of 1922. See how the director and designer at the time envisioned an army of robots in the 1960s. Directed by Phillip Moeller; designed by Lee Simonson.*
Photo courtesy Billy Rose Theatre Collection, the New York Public Library for the Performing Arts, Astor, Lennox and Tilden Foundations.

have adopted Western realistic or stylized methods from the twentieth century, sometimes with great success.

In examining a production, it is helpful not only to recognize the style or styles being used but also to assess how such styles seem to help or hinder the theatrical event. Does the selection of a new style seem to make older material more accessible? Does the strangeness of an old style allow the audience more objectivity in analyzing action that is set in the past? If different styles are used in the same production, does the conflict or contrast make the experience confusing or does it make it more exciting?

◆◆◆◆◆◆◆◆◆◆

Evaluating Production

Audience members tend to evaluate a performance event. It seems natural to affix the terms "good" or "bad" to a production, to recommend the show to others or pan it. Word of mouth is often a powerful tool for getting audiences to see a show, and every performance deserves a fair examination. In deciding what worked and what did not, you can learn a tremendous amount about the theatrical process as well as clarifying your own preferences and values.

CONSIDERING CONTEXT AND ARTISTIC INTENT

To appreciate a show at any one of the myriad theatrical venues available, it is important to consider the **context of performance.** If you attend a professional show such as *The Lion King* (1997) or *Aida* (2000) in a major city such as New York, Boston, Chicago, Atlanta, Montreal, or San Francisco, your major objectives might be to have a social evening out of the house and to experience an enjoyable performance. The purpose of the show in that venue is commercial; producers expect to make money from the performance, or it would not exist. You have paid a considerable amount of money for a ticket, and you come expecting the highest level of professionalism in design, execution, and performance.

Even within the same city, no more than ten blocks away, you could attend a performance by a troupe of young actors aspiring to professional careers but currently making their living at other pursuits during daylight hours. Through sheer commitment, force of will, and inspiration the performers have managed to stage a play in a church basement, a warehouse, or the corner of a coffeehouse. When you choose to attend this theatre, you do so with different expectations. The space will not have the glamour or the comfort of Broadway; you do not expect expensive sets or costumes or glossy performances. You can, however, hope to see inspiration, talent, imagination, ingenuity, and commitment.

Perhaps you need not go even ten blocks. You could exit from the commercial theatre only to encounter street or guerilla theatre. Often geared to political or social agendas and akin to public demonstration, such productions are typically mounted improvisationally with little or no preplanned staging, but some of the speeches, images, props, and placards are formulated in advance and used to confront the audience directly. The issue could be abortion rights, Middle East turmoil, religious oppression, U.S. troops in Iraq—any number of contested issues that are disturbing to the activists. The performers are in your face, making demands, challenging your beliefs or lifestyle. This too is theatre—one in which the cultural context can have a sense of irony, since you are witnessing it just outside a commercial theatre building, with a mostly well-heeled crowd of theatre patrons who had no preparation for the rough theatre they are now encountering. Therefore, you can choose to attend theatre, but sometimes the theatre chooses you.

Beyond the general context of the production, it is helpful to try to articulate the **artistic intent** of a production. Do you believe that the show was meant to entertain you, shock you, comfort you? In establishing the intent of the artists, you can more effectively evaluate how well the production achieved its goals and ask, in the end, whether or not those goals were worth attempting.

TASTE

We will define **taste** as the personal inclination and preferences of the beholder of an aesthetic experience. Taste is inextricably tied to our previous experience with all aspects of culture: leisure activity including sports and the fine and performing arts, television and all types of popular culture, decoration, architecture, reading, fashion, advertising—nearly everything around us that is created by human beings rather than occurring naturally. You might look at a new TV show, music video, painting, film, or play and find yourself alienated; perhaps it lies outside your previous knowledge or experience and you feel unprepared to process the new stimuli. On the other hand, you could be excited, even though you find the new work alien, because through previous experience you have often encountered new or experimental material. The response could be intellectual, emotional, or both.

Some argue in theory that regular exposure to many different kinds of theatrical events is likely to broaden appreciation of an array of styles, methods, and genres of performance. This notion of acquired tastes is not always true, however. No matter how much theatre a person experiences, that person might always prefer a specific genre, style, or period of work. Someone's list of theatrical preferences could begin and end with American musicals—or thrillers, or Greek tragedies, or Shakespearean comedies. After all, most historians and theorists of the theatre have specializations that are likely to be related to their preferences.

"I DON'T KNOW WHY I LIKE IT . . . I JUST DO"

Active examination of personal theatrical experience is likely to heighten not only your understanding of your own tastes but also your ability to express your opinions and formulate meaningful argument. Carefully executed analysis (both written and oral) is likely to improve problem solving, powers of observation,

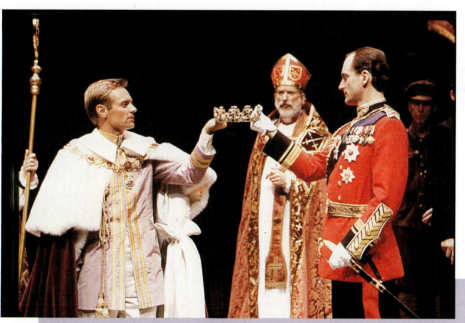

◆ **RICHARD II,** by William Shakespeare, Shakespeare Theatre, Washington, D.C. A traditional image of King Richard II, holding a crown, with Henry Bolingbroke, who will eventually usurp the throne. The sanction of the church is indicated by the archbishop between them. The production was very regal but updated to the early twentieth century. Richard is played by Walter Acton; Bolingbroke is performed by Andrew Long. Directed by Gerald Freedman; costume design by Lawrence Casey. Photo by Carol Rosegg. Courtesy Shakespeare Theatre, Washington, D.C.

recognition of structure and design, understanding of symbolism, and analysis of cultural correspondences. It is important therefore that examination of performance does not include only positive (or negative) comments but reflects the writer's understanding of why a performance was successful or not. It is difficult but instructive to be objective about one's own emotional responses to a production—after the fact, of course.

If you are moved by an actor's portrayal, by a particularly poignant speech, or by a powerful song, try to determine why the moment was so successful. Do particular visual images come to mind? Was the success related to belief in the character? Was the emotional response triggered by the spoken text, by the mimetic action of the actor, by the music underscoring it, by the character isolation created by the lighting? Perhaps this action was very close to the audience or safely removed. What do you remember that could have triggered the emotional response?

"I JUST DON'T LIKE IT"

"I just don't like it" is the too-easy response to a play or performance that confuses, offends, bores, challenges, or mystifies an audience member. A spectator can grow frustrated by an event or simply dismiss it as unimportant. Sometimes audiences give up quickly on an artistic experience, or they might struggle with it for hours or even days. If a production does not appeal to you, it is important to think about why. Were you bored? Offended? Confused? What caused this response? Were the production choices inappropriate? Was the material uninteresting to you?

Different plays and works of art are likely to appeal to you at different ages or levels of experience. Was the production style completely new to you? If a student watches action thrillers full of fast-paced chases, fights, and violent language almost exclusively, the first response to a Japanese Noh performance might well be negative. Noh would probably seem impossibly slow, almost like watching a performance in slow motion. Noh is keyed not just to music, colorful costumes, and demonic possession; it is interpreted through silence and reflection and ghostly memories. Unlike the pace of contemporary life, which is often relentless in the rush to get things done, Noh is in no hurry at all.

◆◆◆◆◆◆◆◆◆◆

The Role of the Critic

A few people make a career out of experiencing and evaluating production and sharing that viewpoint with the public. **Theatre critics** have a difficult job. They work with one foot in the theatrical community and the other in the public arena. They serve as arbiters and entertainers simultaneously. The ideal theatre critic provides a fair yet interesting critique of a very complex event, usually under a deadline. People who write about theatrical productions often have a complicated relationship with the arts community. In the past theatre critics were sometimes closely connected with a particular theatre or performer and used their reviews as a forum to build public support. William Winter, for example, was a good friend of nineteenth-century star actors Edwin Booth and Richard Mansfield and wrote biographies of them along with newspaper criticism. Today we have an expectation of impartiality from our critics; we expect an unbiased evaluation of the shows that they write about. Particularly in the commercial sector, a review in a major newspaper can have a strong influence on the outcome of a production. Broadway producers frequently close a show if opening night reviews are poor, believing that it will be impossible to draw enough of an audience to offset the costs of the production.

THE CRITIC AND THE AUDIENCE

Critics have a responsibility to the readers, listeners, or viewers they serve. Newspapers, radio, television, and Internet sites employ critics to cover entertainment events and pass along information to their audiences. Ever-rising ticket prices make consumers very careful about choosing where to spend their entertainment dollars. Many people use reviews to help them make difficult choices.

The simplest **review** gives information about the show: where, what, when, and how to get tickets. An effective review gives the consumer enough information about the show to make an intelligent decision given personal tastes and priorities. If the review includes **criticism**—in other words, analysis, interpretation, or evaluation of what was done—it is important that the writer support any judgment about the production with description. As a reader you can then decide whether or not you are likely to agree with the writer's viewpoint. Critics are also expected to produce copy that is interesting to read in its own right. This need sometimes conflicts with the desire for even-handed evaluation and leads to an emphasis on humor or a cleverly biting tone. The critic owes the audience a fair and interesting review; whether a production is poorly or beautifully done, it must be honestly described and evaluated.

THE CRITIC AND THE ARTISTS

Some theatre artists who have been hurt by negative reviews understandably look on critics with suspicion or even contempt. It is disheartening to invest the enormous amount of time and energy required by production only to have such efforts spoken of harshly in public. Given the potential damage from a negative review, it is important that critics do their best to provide balanced coverage, praising good work as well as pointing out aspects that were below par. A conscientious critic also cultivates sensitivity to the nature of the production and its aims (professional or amateur, large or small budget).

A fine critic can provide an informed perspective on the artist's work that few audience members can offer, setting a production in a historical context and providing a comparison with contemporary work. The very best writers can pass on a vision for changing theatre, pointing out current needs in the community that the artists may fulfill. Before 1918 many theatre critics in the United States (especially in New York) lamented the state of theatrical entertainment, which many critics called "show-shop," meaning entertainment devoid of meaningful

♦ **MISS JULIE,** a nineteenth-century play by August Strindberg. This production challenges the audience's expectations. Jean, the servant-class character, stands in a trap in formal costume inappropriate for his station in life while Miss Julie wears nineteenth-century garb suggesting a much lower class than her real aristocratic station. Jean is played by Jefferson Mays; Julie is played by Ellen Lauren. Directed by Anne Bogart; costume design by Marcia Dixcy Jory; scenic design Paul Owen. Photo by Richard C. Trigg. Courtesy Actors Theatre of Louisville.

Exploring Collaboration

Effective Performance Reviews

The job of a critic is not just to judge a production. When exciting things are happening on stage, the review helps to spread the word. The critic serves as a link between the theatrical production and its potential audience. The successful review of a production, whether written for publication or as a class assignment, should collaborate with the reader. Besides being clear and accurate, the review should encourage the reader to visualize parts of the performance and understand the writer's point of view. In 1966 critic Walter Kerr wrote an intriguing review of the first production of the musical *Cabaret*. His writing not only provides his opinions and some plot information but also paints a dynamic picture of the performance. He clearly loved the play, the settings, and most of the performances. Despite his assertion that the leading character of Sally Bowles as played by Jill Haworth was miscast, his review still makes the reader desire to see the production. In retrospect his review is an important part of the historical record for this landmark musical. A few excerpts will demonstrate:

◆ *CABARET, the first production. A mirrored surface appeared upstage, which not only reflected the actors but the audience as well. The mirror can be glimpsed in this image in which the emcee performs with the onstage orchestra.*
Photo courtesy Billy Rose Theatre Collection, the New York Public Library for the Performing Arts, Astor, Lennox and Tilden Foundations.

CABARET is a stunning musical with one wild wrong note. I think you'd be wise to go to it first and argue about that startling slip later.

The first thing you see as you enter the Broadhurst [Theatre] is yourself. Designer Boris Aronson, whose scenery is so imaginative that even a gray green fruit store comes up like a warm summer dawn, has sent converging strings of frosted lamps swinging toward a vanishing point at upstage center. Occupying the vanishing point is a great geometric mirror, and in the mirror the gathering audience is reflected. We have come for the floor show, we are all at tables tonight, and anything we learn of life during the evening is going to be learned through the tipsy, tinkling, angular vision of sleek rouged-up clowns, who inhabit a world that rains silver.

This marionette's-eye view of a time and place in our lives that was brassy, wanton, carefree and doomed to crumble is brilliantly conceived. . . . [The production] has elected to wrap its arms around all that was troubling and all that was intolerable with a demonic grin, an insidious slink, and the painted-on charm that keeps revelers up until midnight making false faces at the hangman.

Master of Ceremonies Joel Grey bursts from the darkness like a tracer bullet, singing us a welcome that has something of the old "Blue Angel" in it . . . something of all the patent-leather night-club tunes that ever seduced us into feeling friendly toward sleek entertainers who twirled canes as they worked. Mr. Grey is cheerful, charming, soulless and conspiratorially wicked. In a pink vest, with sunburst eyes gleaming out of a cold-cream face, he is the silencer of bad dreams, the gleeful puppet of pretended joy, sin on a string. . . .

[Despite the miscast Sally,] [t]he style is there . . . driven like glistening nails into the musical numbers, and I think you'll find they make up for what's missing.[3]

Source: Walter Kerr, review of *Cabaret, New York Times,* November 21, 1966, p. 62. Reprinted by permission.

content cranked out for the so-called tired businessman. After the horrors of World War I a few critics began to suspect that surviving the cataclysm of a world war might alter the theatrical landscape, and they were correct. In the late 1910s a handful of intrepid playwrights such as Eugene O'Neill and Susan Glaspell, designers such as Robert Edmond Jones and Lee Simonson, and directors such as Arthur Hopkins and Philip Moeller raised the artistic and intellectual standards of commercial theatre, and many critics rallied around them instantly. O'Neill's first commercially produced full-length play, *Beyond the Horizon* (1920), had a very uninspired production, was poorly cast and cheaply designed (not by any of the artists listed above), and was ineptly rehearsed, yet many critics recognized that it was an important play. This poorly produced but well-written modern tragedy won the Pulitzer Prize for drama that year.

THE CRITIC AND THE HISTORICAL RECORD

Although criticism is often considered nearly as ephemeral as production—it is often produced for immediate consumption and is discarded with the daily newspaper—a piece of criticism essentially becomes part of the historical record. Students of the theatre rely on reviews, for example, to reconstruct productions from the past and learn about preferences in different time periods. The Internet has provided easy accessibility to many newspapers and periodicals that were previously considered obscure. A daily critic must first satisfy the more immediate needs of the contemporary audience and media, but it is important to keep in mind the possible reach of a review and write with as much accuracy and thoughtfulness as possible.

Theatrical reviews are also regularly published in magazines such as *The New Yorker* and *American Theatre*, as well as scholarly journals such as *Theatre Journal*. Unhampered by daily deadlines, critics are able to spend more time evaluating a small number of productions. This kind of criticism is not as timely as daily reviews but is often better able to examine a production with greater consciousness of its importance to the historical record.

A SECOND LOOK AT PRODUCTION

Professional critics sometimes return to a production to see whether their original rave or pan review still seems justified or to see how a production might have grown or diminished. Critics sometimes back off from their original positions or clarify them and declare an even greater admiration or contempt for the production in question. It is clear, however, that these critics, who make their living by reviewing live performance and often have remarkable abilities to analyze incisively after seeing new material just once, still notice many things that they apparently missed the first time.

Seeing a production a second time can be a valuable learning experience for anyone. If you return to a theatre to see a second performance of the same production, the experience must be a different one. The audience members with whom you are in company will differ from the first audience. Some of their responses will vary and will, in turn, affect actors' performances. A full house engages the performers more effectively than a sparse one does, regardless of the

Exploring Collaboration

Follow-Up Reviews

In 1845 Edgar Allen Poe returned to see the play *Fashion* at least nine times and published a follow-up review. This persistence was unusual. For nearly a century, however, it has been common for many newspaper critics to write follow-up reviews. They go to see a second or third performance of a play and publish a second review. In some cases they simply write a revision or extension of the first review after they have had more time to reflect. In most cases the first newspaper review of a new production must be submitted for publication within hours of seeing the show, and the follow-up review allows the critic another chance to share a considered impression with potential audience members.

Alexander Woollcott was a premier critic of the American theatre, writing reviews for a number of newspapers and magazines from 1914 until the 1930s. In 1922 he witnessed the first production of Eugene O'Neill's landmark expressionistic play *The Hairy Ape*. After reviewing the first-night performance he saw subsequent performances, and a little more than a month later he published a second review under his ongoing follow-up title of "Second Thoughts on First Nights." He not only provided more analysis but also took other reviewers to task for misconstruing elements

◆ **THE HAIRY APE**, *original production by the Provincetown Players at Playwrights Theatre in New York in 1922. Louis Wolheim plays the central character, Yank, thrown into a jail cell, isolated from all other humans except for their jeering voices, much like the animal's cage he will find himself in at the end of the play.*

Photo courtesy Billy Rose Theatre Collection, the New York Public Library for the Performing Arts, Astor, Lennox and Tilden Foundations.

capacity of the house. If you are a part of a very responsive audience at your first performance but the second is very quiet, your experience is likely to differ significantly. Such "second sight" can be even more dynamic if you sit in a very different part of the theatre for the second performance.

At a second viewing of a production you are likely to notice many details that you missed the first time. Your focus is likely to shift (as it should), and you are now in a state of expectation because you know what is supposed to happen next. You can be more objective, less emotionally engaged perhaps but probably more intellectually engaged. You can "see" better, you have increased aesthetic distance, and you are better equipped to understand the performance. It is easier the second time to figure out the mechanics of the presentation that might have fooled you the first time through surprise and the power of the unexpected—not unlike a magician's illusion.

of the production. The following excerpts are representative of the whole:

> The Hairy Ape . . . is a brutal, startling, dismaying and singularly vivid play, which will linger in the memory long after most of the stuff this season has produced has faded out of mind. . . .
>
> [The action develops in] short, stabbing scenes so distorted and so fantastic that The Hairy Ape takes on the bad dream accent and aspect of an ugly fable. That is why it seems the most natural of consequences that [Yank, the central character,] should steal into the night-shrouded Zoo at last and acknowledge the gorilla as his brother, that he should open the cage and invite the gorilla to come out and join him in one last bout with an unfriendly world. That is why in the final moment of the play you accept it as inevitable that the gorilla should crunch him to death in two gigantic hairy arms and pitch him dying into the cage. . . .
>
> Both the scene on Blackwell's Island [jail] and the scene in the monkey house are capital examples of inferential stage setting. In the former you see only the one cell and the one crouched prisoner behind its steel bars. But a jabbering chorus of many voices pitch words down out of the surrounding darkness and the very angle of the single cell starts your imagination to constructing a hundred others, fading away into that darkness, row on row, tier on tier. . . .
>
> There have been two especial strictures in the criticism [that] has trailed after The Hairy Ape through the dailies and weeklies. One deplored the sudden fantastic note entering into the composition so late as the fifth scene. [Some critics found the first four scenes realistic and the remaining four scenes expressionistic.] As a matter of fact, a sensitive ear would detect that note in the very first scene, with its regimented motion and its stylicised [we would now say "stylized"] laughter and its abstractions of thought. . . . The notion that those earlier episodes aboard ship are naturalistically wrought is a curious illusion of the playgoer's mind, traceable, probably to the squalor of the language. . . .
>
> The other stricture deals with the oaths [that] flow in a steady cascade from the baffled and unhappy stoker. . . . It ought to be recorded that the speech of The Hairy Ape is rougher talk than the American theatre has heard in our time. As we sit listening to it, it is difficult to believe it was only five years ago that one coarse epithet popping out in the climax of Our Betters seemed so extraordinarily bold and inspired fourteen articles on what the present-day stage was coming to. Evidently it was coming to The Hairy Ape.[4]

Source: Alexander Woollcott, "Second Thoughts on First Nights," *New York Times,* April 16, 1922, Sec. 6, p. 1.

We are not implying that you should always see a performance at least twice to examine it effectively, but we are suggesting that it is helpful to do this from time to time (when practical) to raise your own awareness of your skills and limitations. The more practice you get, the more acute your abilities are likely to become.

♦♦♦♦♦♦♦♦♦♦

Writing about Production

People have probably been writing about theatre as long as they have been going to see theatre. In his comedies Aristophanes wrote about the plays of

Greek tragedians. We're writing about plays and productions in this book. You will probably be asked to write about theatre as a student. Writing about theatre encourages personal exploration. Sometimes one of the great pleasures of experiencing a play is talking about it afterward with friends or colleagues—learning what others saw and what they thought, crystallizing your own reactions, and reaching a greater depth of understanding in trying to communicate with someone else. Writing goes a step beyond talking. It forces you to recognize what you feel and think; it encourages you to verbalize a point of view in a very specific way and requires you to organize your thoughts. Writing about theatre, as about other things, is a way of thinking; it leads the writer to make concrete decisions. Precision of thought is necessary to communicate on paper. When writing, a person must connect in a very personal way with the experience, and in producing a document, the writer is encouraged to support assertions with evidence. Your piece of writing is meant to convey your ideas about the theatrical experience to the reader, and in creating it, you expand the chain of communication that began with a notion in the playwright's mind.

Once you have made arrangements to see a performance, you need to decide whether or not to read the play in advance if it has been published. This choice is a matter of personal preference. Reading the play ahead of time will make you better prepared to analyze the production, but surprise value could be lost. Your choice might be different depending on the play.

When you arrive at the theatre, take note of the theatre space, if it is new to you, and of the audience. What kind of audience are you a part of on this particular evening? Check out the program and be sure to take it home with you. It will give you information that you need about theatre personnel, spelling, and dates. Many theatres provide program notes that are designed to deepen the audience experience. These notes often include chronologies, short biographies, criticism of the play or previous productions, production histories, or related graphics.

When the show begins, turn your full attention to the stage; let yourself become immersed in the world of the play. Don't try to analyze or figure out the play or production yet, and *do not take notes during the show!* We know that this is a common practice, but we firmly believe that it is not a good idea for two reasons: It is very often distracting to the audience members seated around you, and if you are writing, you are not experiencing the performance—you have pulled yourself out of the artistic experience as it is meant to occur.

If you feel panicky that you will not remember enough to write a paper, it is perfectly acceptable to take notes furiously during intermissions, and we highly recommend doing so immediately after the performance. Trust yourself: If you are focusing on the experience, you will retain far more than you ultimately need to analyze the production. It is important to record your impressions as soon as possible after witnessing the performance, however. Take notes quickly (brainstorming); don't worry about sentences or grammar. First briefly describe your own feelings during and after the show, then analyze what made you feel or react in specific ways. Record what you remember: images, lines of dialogue—anything that stood out for you. Write down sensory impressions: colors, sounds, light, and dark. Make lists of adjectives to describe particular parts of the production.

Exploring Historical and Cultural Perspectives

Sometimes confusion arises regarding the spelling and meanings of the word "theatre." The word comes to us from the Greeks, who used the word *theatron* for the portion of the theatrical space in which the audience sat to watch plays. The word literally meant "seeing place." The Greeks, however, had no single word for the entire theatrical space, nor a word for the institution of theatre for which they provided the first important model. Inspired by the Greeks, the Romans built theatres, which in Latin they called *theatrum.* In turn the word became *teatro* in Italian and Spanish, *theatre* in British English, *théâtre* in French, and *theater* in German. In American English both the British and German spellings have become standard, the British spelling often being preferred by theatre artists but the German spelling by most American dictionaries, newspapers, and publishers. Both spellings are correct, and both spellings signify the ongoing institution and practice of the theatre as well as the theatre building.

Unfortunately, some people have the mistaken notion that the building gets one spelling and the practice gets another. The most important thing to remember in writing about the theatre is to be consistent with your spelling, but when writing the name of a theatre building or company, always use the spelling selected by that entity. If you preferred the German spelling, for example, you would have to write "Much theater activity in the United States in the twentieth century was inspired by the productions of the Group Theatre, the Théâtre Libre, and the Deutsches Theater."

Although the theatre is a subjective experience, it is important to be as objective as possible in supporting what you say about production by providing evidence. You will describe the way in which the production elements created (or failed to create) the world of the play. Perhaps you believe that the production did a fine job of creating an eerie, suspenseful mood. Your support might be that the dark atmosphere with patches of isolated light and the music that crept in at the most tension-filled moments helped to create a threatening mood.

Writing about a transitory experience is both challenging and exciting. It requires that you be attentive and present in all senses of the word during the event, that you exercise your skills of observation and interpretation, and that you create symbols (words) that will in some way reproduce your experience for others. Writing about theatre will develop and tune skills that will serve you well far beyond the walls of the theatre or classroom.

♦♦♦♦♦♦♦♦♦♦

When It All Works

Even when we have read the play and/or seen previous productions of the script, we can still be taken emotionally by a production. It is exciting when this happens. We saw a production of *Much Ado about Nothing* by the Royal Shakespeare Company that seemed so complete in its emotional and comic presentation, so precise in its technical skill, so remarkable in its scenic beauty, and so engaging in its acting performances that our immediate response after the applause finally subsided was a wish that it could start all over again, despite the fact that we had been watching in the theatre for some three hours. No matter how sophisticated your analytical skills may become, there is always the possibility of complete immersion—always the chance that you can yield completely to the power of the theatrical event.

◆◆◆◆◆◆◆◆◆
QUESTIONS AND ACTIVITIES

1. Explore the difference between describing (objective) and interpreting (subjective). Choose one scene in a play that you have seen (or a film if a play is not possible). Make a list of terms describing elements of the scene, for example, "red light, screams from offstage." Now add interpretive words for what you saw, for example, "red light—hot, evil, frightening; screams from offstage—startling, bloodcurdling, disturbing."

2. If your class members (or even a small group of them) have seen the same production, choose one scene to discuss. First, have each person make a list of words that convey emotions generated by that scene. Compare your lists. Choose some similar words from different people. Explore what made these people feel that way (elements of performance—actors, set, costumes, lighting, sound)? If there are very different responses, find out why. See whether you can express why people responded differently to the same scene.

3. Discuss productive ways to give criticism (both negative and positive). If you are on the receiving end, what do you think works well? What is counterproductive?

4. Choose a play that has been recently produced by a professional company. Run a search on Lexis/Nexis (or another database that can connect you with newspaper and periodical articles). Use the playwright's last name with an important word from the title as search terms. Choose several reviews, print them, and read them. Did the critics give a clear description of the play and production? On the basis of the reviews, do you think you would like the show? Highlight the main points of the review in one color and the support for that idea in another color. Are the main points well supported? Do you get a strong mental image of what is happening on stage? Do the reviews present different opinions? Is there one review that you believe is stronger than the others? Explain why.

◆◆◆◆◆◆◆◆◆
KEY TERMS AND CONCEPTS

active participation, p. 58
observation, p. 61
interpretation, p. 61
believability, p. 62
actor choices, p. 63
ensemble, p. 63

space and design choices, p. 66
representational, p. 66
presentational, p. 66
set properties, p. 69
style, p. 71
context of performance, p. 74

artistic intent, p. 74
taste, p. 74
theatre critic, p. 76
review, p. 77
criticism, p. 77

♦♦♦♦♦♦♦♦♦
FOR FURTHER EXPLORATION

David Ball. *Backwards and Forwards: A Technical Manual for Reading Plays.* Carbondale: Southern Illinois University Press, 1990.

Robert Benedetti. *The Actor at Work,* 8th ed. Boston: Allyn and Bacon, 2001.

Willmar Sauter. *The Theatrical Event: Dynamics of Peformance and Perception.* Iowa City: University of Iowa Press, 2000.

Richard H. Palmer. *The Critics' Canon: Standards of Theatrical Reviewing in America.* Westport, Conn.: Greenwood, 1988.

Kalina Stefanova-Peteva. *Who Calls the Shots on the New York Stages? The New York Drama Critics.* New York: Routledge, 1993.

ROMEO AND JULIET, Actors Theatre of Louisville.
Karenjune Sanchez as Juliet. Neal Huff as Romeo.
Courtesy of Actors Theatre of Louisville.

CHAPTER 4

Understanding the Play

A Theatrical Blueprint

There must be a plan for most theatrical performances. With few exceptions someone has decided before the audience gathers, even before the actors are selected, basically what will happen on stage. The "play" is a plan or blueprint for the total production. In most cases this means a printed text, which typically contains **dialogue** (words spoken by the characters) as well as **stage directions** (written descriptions of physical or emotional action or physical appearance). The play is to some degree an outline that must be finished by the production team; it is two-dimensional until the artists make it three-dimensional. A wonderfully written play cannot ensure a fine performance but may provide a strong foundation for the successful collaboration of a team of artists.

Theatre, film, and television are very different media, but they share many storytelling techniques. Because most people have seen more film and television than live theatre, we will sometimes use examples from these forms.

In *The Poetics* (fourth century B.C.E.), an early examination of dramatic literature, Aristotle identifies the components of a play. Even though this list is thousands of years old, it is so basic that it is still a useful place to begin. Aristotle identified **six elements of a play:** plot, character, thought, language, music, and spectacle. It is important to understand the definitions of the six elements, since we will use them throughout this book, although you will find somewhat different interpretations as you continue to read about and study the theatre. The six elements are useful as a tool for analyzing and understanding plays and thus furnish a kind of shorthand shared by many people who work in, talk about, and write about the theatre. Each element is defined below and applied to Shakespeare's play *Romeo and Juliet* (1594–95).

◆◆◆◆◆◆◆◆◆◆

Plot

Plot, according to Aristotle, refers to the organization of the action of a play. Playable action is vital to a good play, but plot is not action. Plot is not a story or list of events, but an organizing principle: Plot is what gives a play its unity. Without plot a dramatic performance would seem to be a series of random events with no observable connection. Aristotle believed that plot is the most important element because it organizes all the rest. Another term for plot is **structure.**

CAUSAL STRUCTURE

Plays can be unified in a number of ways. The traditional Western (European and North American) drama is often organized in a linear and causal fashion. **Linear** plot means that the events of the drama progress forward and sequentially in time; **causal** (or "cause-to-effect") plot indicates that one event causes the next: Event A leads to event B, which leads to event C, and so forth. Without A and B, there is no C. Most thrillers and comedies on film and television have a linear and causal structure. Playwrights and critics after Aristotle have looked carefully at the causal plot and established specific terms to describe its function, which we use to examine *Romeo and Juliet.*

The Well-Made Play

European playwrights of the nineteenth century perfected the use of causal structure in a type of drama called **"the well-made play."** The term can be confusing, since, of course, *any* type of play can be written or constructed well. This particular theatrical term (*pièce bien faite* in French) refers to a category of drama in which a meticulous and involved plot takes precedence over all other elements. As perfected by French playwright Eugène Scribe (1791–1861), the well-made play featured an intricate pattern of causality, carefully controlled suspense, and misunderstandings and reversals, leading to an emotionally satisfying climax followed by rapidly falling action. Scribe's plays, such as *A Glass of Water* (1840), tended to be comedies; they were lightly satirical but carried no particular message, and most ended happily. The works of Scribe and his immediate successor, Victorien Sardou (1831–1908), were wildly popular throughout the nineteenth century and were widely produced, translated (often without acknowledging the original authors), and imitated. French playwrights Eugène Labiche (1815–1888) and Georges Feydeau (1862–1921) further developed the comic possibilities of the well-made play and produced fast-moving farces. Other authors used the well-made play structure for melodrama. By the 1870s Henrik Ibsen (1828–1906) had most successfully adapted the familiar structure to address difficult contemporary social issues in plays such as *A Doll House* (1878) and *Ghosts* (1881). Many twentieth-century playwrights rejected traditional causal construction, but writers have continued to use and adapt the well-made play structure for film and television. Whenever you watch a comedy, an action movie, or a thriller, you are probably enjoying a direct descendent of the *pièce bien faite*.

Interested? Check out

Stephen S. Stanton, ed. *Camille and Other Plays*. New York: Hill and Wang, 1957.

John Russell Taylor. *The Rise and Fall of the Well-Made Play*. London: Methuen, 1967.

The action of *Romeo and Juliet* could be described as the attempt of two young lovers to come together in the face of tremendous odds. If the lovers were immediately successful, *Romeo and Juliet* would be a very short play, but all kinds of obstacles present themselves. Romeo and Juliet meet and fall in love; their attempts to be together are thwarted by the enmity of their families, the Capulets (Juliet's) and the Montagues (Romeo's). A desperate attempt to escape together ends in their deaths. The causal relationship of one event to another in the play is complex, and sometimes there are multiple possible causes for any one event, but the existence of causality is always clear. The action continually progresses forward in time in the fictional world, beginning shortly before Romeo and his friends crash the Capulets' party and ending with the suicides of the lovers and the discovery of their bodies in the Capulet tomb. At no time does the audience see action that had occurred previously (although it is often described). We can say, then, that the plot or organization of *Romeo and Juliet* is linear and causal.

At the heart of causal structure is the **conflict** of opposing forces: Two or more characters (generally) want the same thing (money, power, a kingdom, love) or want different things to happen (escape or justice, revolution or consolidation of power). The forces work against each other until, in some way, the outcome is decided. The central conflict in *Romeo and Juliet* is Romeo and

Juliet versus their families and friends. The lovers wish to be together; the old feud between the Capulets and Montagues keeps them apart. Although conflict between characters is the easiest to identify, a complex play will often locate conflict in a number of areas: moral conflict (good versus evil), for example, or conflict between two ideas. Typically, though, the conflict of larger forces is embodied in the characters themselves.

Point of attack refers to the point in the story at which the playwright chooses to start dramatizing the action. Plays are highly selective in terms of the events that are included in performance, and these selections lie at the heart of the play's structure. The story of the play might stretch far into the past, but the playwright selects one moment in that story to begin actually showing (rather than telling about) the progress of events. When *Romeo and Juliet* begins, the feud is already well established, but the lovers have not met; indeed, Romeo begins by professing his adoration for Rosaline. After the lovers meet, the action stretches over a number of days; we witness many events in the struggle of the lovers, including their secret marriage and Romeo's banishment and return to Verona. The play therefore has a relatively early point of attack—the playwright chooses to dramatize most of the important incidents in the story. A play with an early point of attack is often said to be **episodic:** Selected dramatized moments in the story are separated by breaks in the action. The playwright sometimes indicates a passage of time between scenes through dialogue.

In contrast, when a play has a late point of attack, most of the events in the story have already happened, and we see only the last few episodes or only one episode dramatized. If *Romeo and Juliet* had a late point of attack, for example, the last few hours of the lovers' lives would be dramatized in great detail and the early events such as their first meeting would only be described. Marsha Norman's play *'night, Mother* (1983) has a late point of attack. The actual time that elapses for the fictional characters is the same amount of time that the audience is in the theatre—only ninety minutes. The clock is ticking in full view, underscoring the real time of the play. The audience shares the last hour and a half of Jessie's life as she prepares for death.

As a play opens, the playwright usually sets up the dramatic situation for us by using **exposition,** or information that is needed to understand the play. Although exposition may be introduced throughout the play, a great deal of information is typically conveyed in the first few scenes. Character and setting must be established; crucial past events of the story (those occurring before the point of attack) must be described so that the audience can follow the causal connections as the play progresses. Exposition can be conveyed visually; we see two opposing groups of people, for example, in the opening scene of *Romeo and Juliet* and learn immediately of the battle lines drawn between the Capulets and Montagues. Most exposition, however, is conveyed through dialogue. Juliet's father plans to marry her to the wealthy Count Paris. The two men are heard planning the engagement early in the play, so the audience is prepared, late in the play, when the father insists on the wedding, unaware that Juliet is secretly married to Romeo.

However it is presented, the exposition creates a situation in which an uneasy balance of forces exists; nothing major is happening yet, but the audience soon recognizes the potential for conflict. When the Prince breaks up the initial street brawl, he not only gives the history of the feud, but also sets an extreme consequence for another eruption of violence—"If ever you disturb our streets again, / Your lives shall pay the forfeit of the peace," a consequence that later will apply to Romeo.

The **inciting incident** is an event that destroys the uneasy balance and sets off the major conflict of forces. From this point on, the conflict is clearly defined and will build throughout the play. The meeting of Romeo and Juliet is the inciting incident of Shakespeare's play. They fall in love at the Capulet party without knowing each other's identity. When Romeo learns Juliet's name, he characterizes his danger in financial terms: "Is she a Capulet? / O dear account! My life is my foe's debt." When Juliet learns Romeo's identity, she exclaims, "My only love, sprung from my only hate! / Too early seen unknown, and known too late!" The conflict of the lovers versus the ancient grudge is now clearly defined.

Following the inciting incident, small units of action are dramatized that build in emotional intensity; this section of the play is called the **rising action.** The major forces in conflict gather information, lay plans, and pursue their own objectives (or goals). As they encounter obstacles, they must try something

◆ *ROMEO AND JULIET, 1998 production. The Capulets discover their daughter, thinking that she is dead, the morning after Juliet has taken the potion. Left to right, Libby George as the Nurse, Hassan El-Amin as Capulet, Robert Gerard Anderson as Friar Lawrence, Michael Harding as Paris, Angela Iannone as Lady Capulet, Brandy McClendon as Juliet (on the bed).*
Photo by Karl Hugh. Courtesy of the Utah Shakespearean Festival.

new. Audience empathy with the characters becomes stronger; as the stakes get higher for the characters, the audience becomes increasingly involved in the action. Romeo and Juliet meet surreptitiously and declare their love in the famous balcony scene. The stakes are raised as the Friar secretly marries Romeo and Juliet and Romeo kills Juliet's cousin Tybalt in anger over the death of his friend Mercutio. Romeo's subsequent banishment and Juliet's desperate attempt to avoid a forced marriage by drinking a sleeping potion set the stage for the climax.

The **climax** of a play is the emotional high point of the action; the conflict has reached a critical stage, and the outcome is finally decided—often, one side wins and the other loses.[1] All has been leading up to this moment on stage. Playwrights understand that their climactic scene is the most important one of the play. The dual suicide of the lovers is the climax of *Romeo and Juliet.* Hearing of Juliet's supposed death, Romeo returns from exile and kills himself at his lover's side. Juliet awakens too late to prevent his death and kills herself with his dagger. The lovers have chosen death over separation. The outcome of the conflict is decided; in *Romeo and Juliet* neither side wins. The lovers are together for eternity but only in death. The Capulets and Montagues are no longer fighting, but the families have lost a son and daughter; Tybalt, Mercutio, and Paris have been slain as well.

Emotional intensity drops during the **falling action**—the events from the climax to the end of the play. Loose ends are tied up for the audience, and balance is restored, although something clearly is different than at the play's beginning.

♦ **ROMEO AND JULIET,** *the tomb scene, after the deaths of both characters. Note the lovers entwined on the floor as those left behind mourn. In this 1994 production the time of the play is shifted to the 1920s. Directed by Jon Jory; scenic design by Ming Cho Lee; costume design by Marcia Dixcy.*
Photo by Richard C. Trigg. Courtesy Actors Theatre of Louisville.

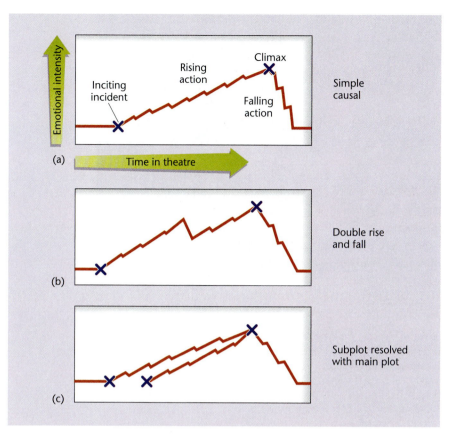

♦ **FIGURE 4.1** *The Emotional Effects of Causal Structure* Graph (a) represents the rise and fall of emotional intensity in the simplest causally constructed plot. Note that the action is not uninterrupted in its rise; each episode or unit of action may have its own rise and fall. Most plays will not fit neatly into the single pyramid structure. Graph (b) represents a play in which the emotional intensity reaches a high point, then falls slightly, only to build again rapidly to its true climax. A play with a subplot (secondary line of action) is represented by graph (c). The development of the subplot begins after the major action has been established and continues independently until both conflicts are resolved in the climax.

Falling action is also sometimes called the play's resolution or dénouement. In the falling action after the death of Romeo and Juliet, the families arrive at the tomb, Friar Lawrence explains the tragic series of events, and the Prince makes his final pronouncement.

In the simplest causal plots, emotional intensity can be graphed as a kind of lopsided pyramid (see Figure 4.1). We can see the emotional intensity established at a relatively low level, begin to rise at the inciting incident, rise slowly, climax, and fall rather quickly. (Once the climax is over, things must be wrapped up speedily, or the audience will lose interest.) Many plays will not fit this graph. Some plays do not rise neatly to the climax but have dips in intensity and secondary climaxes in the rising action.

Other plays may include **subplots,** or secondary lines of action, in which different conflicts are developed. A subplot may be entwined with the major line of action and reach its climax in the same scene, or it may develop independently and climax at another time. In Shakespeare's *A Midsummer Night's Dream* (c. 1595) the main line of action concerns four lovers lost in the woods and the

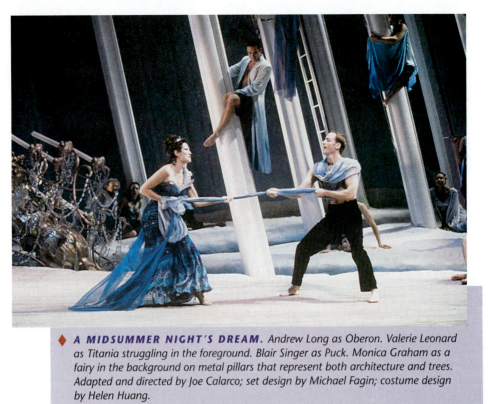

♦ *A MIDSUMMER NIGHT'S DREAM.* *Andrew Long as Oberon. Valerie Leonard as Titania struggling in the foreground. Blair Singer as Puck. Monica Graham as a fairy in the background on metal pillars that represent both architecture and trees. Adapted and directed by Joe Calarco; set design by Michael Fagin; costume design by Helen Huang.*

Photo by Carol Rosegg. Courtesy of The Shakespeare Theatre.

fairies who interfere in the lovers' affairs. A secondary line of action develops around a group of workers who gather in the woods to rehearse a play for the king's wedding. The two strands of action intersect when one of the workers, Bottom, becomes magically involved with the fairies. Both lines of action culminate in the final scene as the workers perform their play at the king's wedding while the lovers watch.

Aristotle identified two more terms that are useful in understanding plot: discovery and reversal. **Discovery** occurs when something important is found, learned, or realized during the action of a play. The discovery might be of an object (the murder weapon is found, for example) or a piece of information (the detective is actually the murderer). The most meaningful discoveries are often those that a character makes about himself or herself or about the nature of the human experience. Powerful discoveries happen in *Romeo and Juliet* when the lovers learn each other's true family identity, when Juliet realizes that she can no longer trust her nurse, and late in the play when Juliet awakens to find her lover's lifeless body beside her.

Reversal occurs when a line of action veers around suddenly to its opposite. The prime suspect in a murder investigation turns up dead, for example, and the detective must look for another solution to the crime. A good example of reversal in *Romeo and Juliet* is Romeo's slaying of Juliet's cousin Tybalt. Until this event the love affair has been clandestine, but there is still some hope that the couple, married in secret, might be able to reconcile their families. Tybalt's murder and Romeo's subsequent flight from Verona lead directly to the play's tragic climax. Aristotle thought that Sophocles' tragedy *Oedipus the King* (c. 430–425 B.C.E.) was perfectly structured because at the play's climax, discovery and

◆ **ROMEO AND JULIET.** *Jane Cowl and Rollo Peters in a 1920s production. In the tomb scene Romeo has already taken the poison and Juliet finds the vial empty. Note the strong side light on the unfortunate couple from stage right.*
Photo courtesy Billy Rose Theatre Collection, the New York Public Library for the Performing Arts, Astor, Lennox and Tilden Foundations.

reversal happen in the same moment: When the tragic hero learns that he is, in fact, the very murderer he has been seeking (discovery), he goes from being the most powerful man in Thebes to an exile, shunned by humankind (reversal).

If you are able to apply the structural terms defined above to a causal play and create a graph reflecting its emotional rise and fall, you have a good start toward understanding how the play works. Sometimes it is difficult to decide how to apply the terms; there might be debate, for example, on which moment is actually the climax of the play, and good arguments could be made for alternative choices. The identification of the climax then becomes a question of interpretation; the choice that you make will have an effect on how you view the play as a whole.

VARIATIONS ON LINEAR, CAUSAL STRUCTURE

Playwrights understand that a familiar structure is comfortable for the audience. Years of watching the dramatization of stories in film and television have developed audience expectations for outcome. Think about how strong your expectations are for what will happen as you watch a play, film, or teleplay (script for television). Writers can play *with* or *against* this expectation. Any challenge to an established pattern can be very powerful on stage. A play that does not include falling action after the climax, for example, can be very disturbing. A **cliff-hanger** stops at the climax; the outcome of the conflict is not shown. Television series sometimes end their seasons with a cliff-hanger episode to encourage

Elmer Rice's *On Trial*

The popular play *On Trial* ran for a year after opening August 19, 1914, in New York. It launched the successful career of Elmer Rice, who is best known for his expressionistic masterpiece *The Adding Machine* (1923). *On Trial* was famous for introducing the novelty of the flashback to the stage. Framed plays, in which the beginning and end are in the "present" and the heart of the play is in the past, had been written and produced a bit earlier. *Romance* (1913) by Edward Sheldon, for example, has a prologue and epilogue set in the 1890s. A grandfather tells a story to his grandson, and this story, set in the 1860s, makes up most of the play. The difference in *On Trial* is that the play makes many journeys into the past and melds them with the present scenes in the courtroom. Witnesses take the stand during a sensational murder trial that turns on adultery and shady business deals. The audience sometimes hears court testimony, but most of the past events are dramatized as if the witnesses are recalling the scenes. The accused, who refuses to take the stand on his own behalf in order to protect the integrity of his wife, is ultimately saved by the testimony (and flashbacks) of his nine-year-old daughter. In 1920 critic Burns Mantle called the flashback "a new technique in play building."[2] Since that time the device has been used frequently in courtroom dramas as well as many other types of plays, films, and television scripts.

Interested? Check out

Anthony Palmieri. *Elmer Rice: A Playwright's Vision of America.* Rutherford, NJ: Fairleigh Dickinson University Press, 1980.
Robert Hogan. *The Independence of Elmer Rice.* Carbondale: Southern Illinois University Press, 1965.

viewers to tune in next season. In 1935 playwright Clifford Odets used the cliffhanger structure to advocate social action. Written during the Great Depression, *Waiting for Lefty* tells the story of cab drivers struggling to unionize against oppressive management. The play ends at the climax as the newly motivated drivers leave the auditorium shouting, "Strike!" In Henrik Ibsen's play *Ghosts* (1881), Oswald, the son of Mrs. Alving, suffers from inherited syphilis. He experiences an attack or seizure that leaves him in a vegetative state. Earlier in the play, in anticipation of this occurrence, Oswald had begged his mother to administer a lethal dose of morphine pills if such a thing ever happened. The play ends with the visual image of Mrs. Alving holding the box of pills, standing by her unfortunate son. The audience does not learn whether or not she will fulfill his wish.

Western playwrights of the early twentieth century introduced the **flashback** variation to linear structure; although most of the play progresses forward in time, occasional scenes actually dramatize events that occurred in the story before the point of attack. Sometimes a play or film begins and ends in the present while the vast majority of the action dramatized is from the past; the "present" scenes serve as a frame for a long flashback. In Tennessee Williams's *The Glass Menagerie* (1945) the narrator, Tom, begins and ends the play by speaking to the audience in the present, but most of the play dramatizes his past life with his mother and sister.

One of the finest uses of the flashback technique is in Arthur Miller's *Death of a Salesman* (1949). By intercutting present and past scenes, the playwright both tells the story of the aging salesman Willy Loman and recreates the confusion in Willy's mind for the audience. In Harold Pinter's *Betrayal* (1978) linear structure is reversed. The first scene in the play is actually the last to happen in the story chronologically; the play begins with the end of an adulterous love affair. As the play continues, each scene is set progressively farther back in time. In the last scene of the play the audience sees the characters' first confession of love and listens to their declaration of mutual affection with the poignant knowledge of all the pain to come. Caryl Churchill's *Top Girls* (1982) begins with a fantasy sequence in

♦ **GHOSTS,** *by Henrik Ibsen. This simplified staging with sparse furniture and eerie atmosphere is a big departure from the literal expectations for this realistic play. Adapted and directed by Scott Wentworth; scenic and costume design by Ann Sheffield; lighting design by Michael Giannitti.*
Courtesy of Indiana Repertory Theatre.

which the main character, Marlene, meets with famous women from the past, then moves to present reality, and finally flashes back to the past; Marlene, her sister, and her niece interact in a scene that occurred before the original point of attack. The last scenes shown in both *Top Girls* and *Betrayal* are actually the earliest in time.

♦ **AFTER THE FALL,** *by Arthur Miller. The first production, Vivien Beaumont Theatre at Lincoln Center. The simplified staging, using a collection of outlined platforms, was appropriate for this memory play that moved about in time and place. The central character (an autobiographical role representing the playwright) was played by Jason Robards. Directed by Elia Kazan; designed by Jo Mielziner.*
Photo courtesy Billy Rose Theatre Collection, the New York Public Library for the Performing Arts, Astor, Lennox and Tilden Foundations.

SITUATIONAL STRUCTURE

Although many plays are organized by causal plot, it is important to remember that other alternatives for unification are possible. Some playwrights choose other types of plots based on idea, image, mood, or character. Japanese Noh dramas, for example, frequently treat a past event, and emphasis is on deepening revelation rather than progressive action. In *Aoi No Uye* (c. fourteenth century and attributed to Zenchiku) a princess, Aoi No Uye, lies very ill and unconscious. She is not played by an actor but is represented by a folded kimono down center. A witch is brought in to help the ailing princess, but the witch conjures up a ghost that turns out to be a manifestation of the intense jealousy of Rokujo, a living enemy who is in love with the princess's husband. Rokujo has tried to hurt the princess in the past, and these attempts are reenacted in the present time of the play by the ghost of her embodied jealousy. Rokujo's spoken words (actually delivered by a chorus) are in the past tense even though Rokujo's body (now transformed into a demon) is threatening the princess with a mallet. Ultimately, a holy man banishes the evil through a kind of exorcism, and peace is restored. So the action is played out in both present and past tense at the same time.

Indian Sanskrit plays do not seek an emotional release or catharsis but create pleasure for the audience through a harmonious balance of moods (**rasa**). The plays imitate a condition, not action as is typical in Western drama. There is no tragedy in *Shakuntala* (c. fifth century) by Kalidasa or in any other Sanskrit plays, which assiduously avoid death on the stage. This play explores the situa-

◆ *WAITING FOR GODOT*, by Samuel Beckett, the first New York production. Estragon, Vladimir, and Pozzo attempt to subdue Lucky, who is out of control. Played by Bert Lahr, E. G. Marshall, Kurt Kasznar, and Alvin Epstein. Directed by Herbert Berghof.
Photo courtesy Billy Rose Theatre Collection, the New York Public Library for the Performing Arts, Astor, Lennox and Tilden Foundations.

tion in which Shakuntala, the heroine and title character, finds herself. Most of the action in the play is created by magic and divine intervention. The heroine and a king fall in love but find themselves separated. The king is placed under a curse that causes him to forget pregnant Shakuntala, and they are never reunited in the earthly world. When Shakuntala is facing complete abandonment, she is saved by a nymph, who spirits her away to a holy mountaintop, the home of the gods. Years later a charioteer of the gods takes the king to the mountain, where, with the curse broken, the lovers are reunited (now with their son) and can return to the king's earthly kingdom. A happy ending (even if it is only cosmic) seems to be the reigning expectation of Sanskrit.

Substitution of condition for traditional action also sometimes finds its way into modern Western drama, as in *Waiting for Godot* (1953) by Samuel Beckett. Here two tramps on a road imitate the process of waiting. Very little of consequence happens in the way of action: They bicker, suffer, complain, and make no effort to make anything important happen. They are waiting for something to come to them. Yet the play is funny, sad, and fascinating in its exploration of the human condition. The same is true of the best surviving Sanskrit plays.

STRUCTURE BY IDEA, CHARACTER, AND IMAGE

Plays can also be unified by idea, character, and image. In *The Blue Room* (1998), David Hare's adaptation of Arthur Schnitzler's *La Ronde* (*The Circle,* c. 1900), the scenes are not causally linked at all, and the action cannot be graphed in the traditional manner. The play dramatizes a string of sexual encounters that cross economic and class boundaries. The first scene is between a Girl and a Cab Driver; the second scene is between the same Cab Driver and a Nanny; the third is between the Nanny and a Student; and so on. In the final scene an Aristocrat has an encounter with the Girl from Scene 1. The play, then, has a circular structure (from which Schnitzler took his title). Unity is provided by idea and character repetition rather than by causation.

Swedish author August Strindberg experimented with providing unity through image. *A Dream Play* (1907) follows the journey of a goddess who visits the earth. The action progresses as dreams progress, not through logical connection but by repetition of character and image. One scene dissolves, and another replaces it; characters appear and disappear, images reappear in new places, and characters reappear in strange guises. Strindberg's stated objective was to create a play organized in a way familiar to the human subconscious rather than the conscious mind. Similarly, the French Surrealists of the 1920s and beyond harnessed aspects of the dream world to make ordinary, everyday events occur in impossible ways, just as they do in our dreams. Jean Cocteau, for example, created *Wedding on the Eiffel Tower* (1921), in which the bizarre is mixed with the prosaic. Even though the action is supposedly taking place on an upper level of the Eiffel Tower in Paris, at one point, without comment or explanation, a girl rides by on a bicycle. Even though there are many actors in the play, all of the lines are delivered by two narrators, who are both dressed as Victrola-style phonograph machines.

One of the most intriguing plays from the Arab world, the Egyptian play *The Tree Climber* (1962) by Tewfik al-Hakim, uses the device of having a very fluid approach to time and place. Time is not chronological, and space changes instantly and without explanation; the action is not causal. The play is a thoughtful murder mystery, but the events and spatial shifts are impossible in the real world. A Western-style inspector attempts to solve the crime but is incapable of entering the spiritual and quirky world of the protagonist, who is also the chief murder suspect. Known only as the Husband, the protagonist communes with the earth, obsessing with his garden. Only the Dervish, a religious figure who is representative of traditional Arab culture, seems to understand the disappearance of the wife and the import of the mysterious events.

Many plays and performances after the nineteenth century (especially experimental works) have attempted to defy, disrupt, or free dramatic structure from its traditional or reigning position. Audience expectations are often undermined (the playwright might deny a dramatic climax, for example). Form may become fluid and not representational of anything recognizable such as a real or logical progression of events. Time may be negated. In Adrienne Kennedy's *Funny House of a Negro* (1964) there is very little story, but the central character, Sarah, an African American, is bombarded by voices and images of the white world (especially Queen Victoria), Africa, Christianity, death, rape, and suicide and confused memories of her own family background. She desires to escape the tortures of a severely conflicted life, but she also desires to free herself from the past and her heritage and become a writer. She is trapped in her mind, which becomes a disturbing "funny house," a nightmare from which she cannot awake.

REPETITION AS STRUCTURE

An event, action, or line of dialogue may be repeated with or without variations and provide a kind of unity for the play. German playwright Heiner Müller's *Hamletmachine* (1978), for example, uses Shakespeare's *Hamlet* (1600–01) as a jumping-off place to comment pessimistically and violently on social and political failure in the modern world, especially Europe. The play repeats distressing images and lines that become a denial of the conceptions audiences are likely to have of Hamlet and Ophelia. Hamlet even claims that he is not Hamlet, and Ophelia violates all of Shakespeare's presentation of her as soft, compliant, gentle, and chaste.

Repetition is even more dynamic and frequent in *America Play* (1994) by Suzan-Lori Parks. The play deconstructs the assassination of Abraham Lincoln and creates a disturbing view of the icons from the American Civil War and racial issues from the point of view of an African American woman at the end of the twentieth century. A revisionist of history, Parks presents the assassination of Abraham Lincoln as if it were a sideshow act. For a fee, people can participate and play the assassin. This action is repeated many times in variations as if burning the images into the brains of the audience. Parks seems to ask, "Where is African American history in a field of sacred white icons?"

POSTSTRUCTURALISM

Dramatic work created after World War II that breaks down traditional causal structure is often identified as **poststructuralism.** Many plays and performances of the last several decades are somewhat like negative photographic images of what were once positive dramatic events. The perception of concrete space becomes negative or impossible space, and events are so negotiable or ambivalent as to be indefinable or so contradictory as to be adrift among definitions. It is sometimes impossible to figure out a logical story, since none is presented. The last three plays mentioned have no story per se but are rich in dramatic event, images, and disturbing problems.

Much of this work is also metatheatrical, that is self-conscious in its presentation of theatre as a theatre. There are many antecedents for **metatheatre,** from the simplest "play within a play," such as that found in Shakespeare's *A Midsummer Night's Dream* (1595–96). The workers (called "rude mechanicals") perform a silly play for the wedding of the monarch (so the audience watches a play about characters watching a play). In the German romantic metatheatrical extravaganza *Puss in Boots* (1797) by Ludwig Tieck, all of the action is set in a theatre. The audience members (some of whom are actors with scripted lines) watch a play break down and never reach completion. At the same time Tieck demonstrates why audiences should reject the old-fashioned neoclassicism of the eighteenth century and replace it with the modern drama of romanticism. In one of many wonderful moments from this hilarious play, the audience rejects the play and the actors they are watching and calls for an encore by the scenery. When the setting is revealed again (without actors), the audience greets it with tumultuous applause.

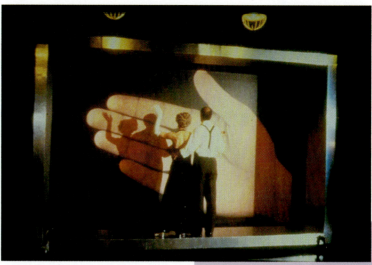

◆ **WAR OF THE WORLDS,** *by Naomi Iizuka. In this post-structural work, actors Ellen Lauren and Stephen Webber appear to be waving to someone unseen; in actuality they are confronting a giant, god-like hand, framed by gleaming metal. Conceived and directed by Anne Bogart; created by the SITI Company; scenic design by Neil Patel; costume design by James Schuette.* Photo by Richard C. Trigg. Courtesy of Actors Theatre of Louisville.

STRUCTURE IN THE TWENTY-FIRST CENTURY

The theatre at the end of the twentieth century was characterized by great diversity, and the structural experiments suggest where dramatic structure is going in the twenty-first century. Playwrights both called on and defied tradition, used and broke rules, pushed boundaries of structure, experimented with emphasizing various dramatic elements, and shattered audience expectations.

Stephen Sondheim has pushed the musical in new directions by introducing unusual subject matter and structural devices; *Assassins* (1990) is circular and linear simultaneously while exploring the motivations of presidential killers. Overseen by a cynical narrator, the play features lyrics that include the creative use and adaptation of some of the actual text spoken by the historical assassins. In Michael Frayn's play *Copenhagen* (1998), time and space are fluid; the action begins after the death of the characters, who reexperience moments from the past in seemingly random order while they struggle to understand one significant but ambiguous encounter.

Playwrights such as Caryl Churchill defied traditional dramatic structure to question contemporary social structure and gender limitations. The first act of Churchill's *Cloud 9* (1979) takes place in British Colonial Africa during the Victorian period. The second act begins in 1979 London, but the stage directions state that twenty-five years have passed for the characters. With her leap in time,

Churchill asks us to compare our attitudes with those of our Victorian ancestors. She lays the groundwork for further exploration of social roles by specifying that some of the characters should be played by an actor of a different gender or race. In the first act, for example, Betty, a traditional Victorian wife, is performed by a man; Edward, a little boy with homosexual leanings, is performed by a woman, and Joshua, the African servant, is performed by a white man.

The experimentation of the late twentieth century has even led us to question the nature of the word "text" itself. Traditionally, we think of the "text" of the play as the words spoken by the actors on stage. There have always been theatrical performances, however, that wholly or in part depend only on the actor's body for expression. In **pantomime** a silent actor creates a scenario without words. Each movement is carefully planned and rehearsed. Many twentieth-century theatre artists have expanded the boundaries of such silent text. Samuel Beckett's play *Act without Words* (1957) uses physical action to express human singularity and frustration. Robert Wilson (b. 1941) and Richard Foreman (b. 1937) have created performances in which image takes precedence over words. The National Theatre of the Deaf pioneered the marriage of aural and visual language on stage; in its work, language and spectacle fold into one category.

Part of the exploration of the twentieth century involved pushing the boundaries of theatre itself. Since the 1950s, for example, many painters, sculptors, and musicians have turned their art into surprising performances through what at first were called **happenings** (events, planned or spontaneous, in which the audience watched or participated in the production of temporary art) and action painting, in which the artist painted while the audience watched. Today these types of productions are more often referred to as **performance art** (usually one-person/first-person shows that purport to make the artist the subject of the performance). Many performance art events of the late twentieth century have centered on the AIDS crisis and gender conflict. In the twenty-first century it is often difficult to say where the art of theatre ends and the arts of music, dance, painting, and sculpture begin.

In analyzing such plays (old or new), it is helpful to think about how the playwright challenges our expectations of traditional structure. What kind of experience does the play create instead, and what might be the purpose behind offering such an experience to the audience? Rejection of traditional dramatic structure often coincides with political or social rebellion and commentary and might represent an artistic response to gender issues, to cultural or artistic conflict, or to political strife. Nontraditional structure sometimes reflects a despairing reaction to horrors and fears generated by the Holocaust, the nuclear arms race and lingering atomic arsenals, waves of worldwide terrorism, racial and ethnic cleansing, and the ever-shrinking global community and ever-expanding and geographically shifting population.

♦ ♦ ♦ ♦ ♦ ♦ ♦ ♦ ♦

Character

Character refers to the fictional persons that are created to perform the action of the play. Character is the element of drama that most people find the easiest to understand, probably because human beings constantly observe and interpret human behavior in everyday life. It seems natural to look beyond surface reality and probe for someone's reasons or motivation, try to understand the true meaning behind a statement, or attempt to reconcile two seemingly incongruous actions. Unlike some other types of literature that utilize imaginative creation of character, a play does not usually have a narrative voice explaining what the character feels or thinks. The audience must watch, listen, and interpret. It is sometimes easy to imagine characters as having a life outside the world of the play, but for the purposes of understanding drama, character exists only within the action and words of the play as supplied by the author.

An accomplished playwright will develop a character only to the extent needed to fulfill its function in the play. We usually learn a great deal about a play's **protagonist** or central character. *Romeo and Juliet* has dual protagonists; both are young, impulsive, and loyal to friends and family. The intensity of their love for each other is fully and magnificently developed in the course of the action, as are the changes in character that this love brings about. We know less about Romeo's friends Mercutio and Benvolio, Juliet's cousin Tybalt, the lovers' parents, Juliet's nurse, or Friar Lawrence, who is instrumental in moving the action. We know as much as we need, however, to understand the play and to have a clear idea of the essence of each character. To spend more time characterizing secondary or minor characters would detract from the unity of the play as a whole. The play is about the struggle of the lovers, not about the problems of their families and friends.

♦ **ROMEO AND JULIET.** *Friar Lawrence marries the lovers secretly. The Friar is played by John Camera, Romeo by Neal Huff, Juliet by Karenjune Sanchez. Scenic design by Ming Cho Lee; costume design by Marcia Dixcy; directed by Jon Jory.*
Photo by Richard C. Trigg. Courtesy of Actors Theatre of Louisville.

CHARACTER CREDIBILITY

Information about character is given in three basic ways: (1) what characters say about themselves, (2) what others say about them, and (3) what the character does. Characters do not always tell the truth. As in life, the audience evaluates the accuracy of character information by considering the circumstances. Tybalt (a Capulet) calls Romeo (a Montague) a "villain." The audience is unlikely to believe Tybalt, given the historical enmity between the families. At the other extreme, when Juliet calls Romeo "the god of my idolotry," we know that her vision is colored by new love. Action, or what the character actually does, is the most important way of defining character. Romeo shows his impulsiveness by scaling his enemy's balcony in the dead of night. Juliet is loyal and determined; these qualities lead her to take the sleeping potion, even though it means that she will be shut up alive in the family burial vault.

LEVELS OF CHARACTERIZATION

One way of understanding how characters are developed in a play is to consider five **levels of characterization:** biological, physical, psychological and emotional, social, and ethical. A minor character may be developed only through the first two levels; a full and complex character will draw on all five.

Biological traits include the species of the character. Usually, of course, plays are written about human beings, but important plays have included fairies, demons, monsters, animals, spirits, gods, and even robots. Typically,

◆ **COMEDY OF ERRORS,** *by William Shakespeare at the Guthrie Theatre (a thrust stage) in Minneapolis. The twin brothers confront each other at the climax of the play. Directed by Dominique Serrand.*
Photo by Michal Daniel.

such nonhuman characters are depicted with human characteristics. Another important biological trait is sex. Whether characters are male or female usually has a profound effect on their behavior in the play and may dictate their social position and range of activity. Similarly, a character's race may influence social position in the dramatic environment. A biological trait that has often been used for comic effect is the creation of twins. In Roman comedy Plautus produced considerable confusion and mayhem when twins are mistaken for one another in *The Brothers Menaechmus* (c. second century B.C.E.), which Shakespeare in turn adapted as *Comedy of Errors* (c. 1592). Shakespeare further complicated the misunderstandings by adding a second pair of twins, who are servants to the leading characters.

Physical traits include stature, weight, hair and eye color, and facial hair. In the theatre, such traits are filled in automatically by the actor playing the role and by changes made with costume and makeup. Sometimes a physical trait is central to a character's personality. Shakespeare's villain Richard III is a hunchback; his revenge is partly motivated by his anger at this physical disfigurement. In Tennessee Williams's play *The Glass Menagerie* (1945), Laura's painful shyness is magnified by her limp. Helen of Troy's stunning beauty brings an entire nation to ruin in Euripides' tragedy *The Trojan Women* (415 B.C.E.), and Rapunzel's magnificent golden hair brings a union with a prince in the Stephen Sondheim and James Lapine musical *Into the Woods* (1987). Sometimes the authenticity of the physical traits are not so obvious. David Henry Hwang created a stunning clash of cultures in *M. Butterfly* (1988). Both his protagonist, Rene Gallimard, a French diplomat in China, and his audience are fooled by an apparently beautiful Chinese actress who turns out to be a young man in drag. Hwang successfully manipulated perceptions of biological and physical traits simultaneously.

Psychological and emotional traits develop the character's basic internal makeup. Richard III is angry, vengeful, clever, and ruthless. Laura is sensitive and withdrawn and lives most happily in her imagination. Juliet's nurse is sympathetic but foolish. Shakespeare's Hamlet is intelligent, thoughtful, and melancholy. As in reality, a character's psychological and emotional life has a great impact on physical action. It provides the motivation for the action of the play. How the character relates to others is important. Is a character an extrovert or an introvert? Gregarious or withdrawn? Joe Pitt, in *Angels in America: Millennium Approaches* (1991) by Tony Kushner, is a frustrated federal legal clerk who is gay but denies it. He is stuck in a bizarre marriage and confused by his religious background, but finally, with great trepidation, he enters the sexual world he has been avoiding. Sir John Falstaff, by contrast, seems secure with his life choices and jokes, drinks, and cavorts his way through three of Shakespeare's plays. A character can be abrasive or helpful to others, as unselfish as Willy Loman's faithful wife Linda, or as self-serving as Harpagon in *The Miser* by Molière (1668), who sees his children's relationships only as means to increase his riches. Cases of maladjustment, however, often end in disaster. *Topdog/Underdog* (2001) by Suzan-Lori Parks has two African American brothers who compete with one another. Booth is an unemployed shoplifter, and his older brother Lincoln (they are named for president and assassin) works as a whiteface Abe Lincoln impersonator at a cheap arcade. For years, however, Lincoln was a street hustler dealing three-card monte. Both brothers have created fantasy lives for themselves with regard to sexual prowess and street skills but continue to suffer (although in denial) about their awful past. They were abandoned and betrayed by their parents when adolescents. The violence and displacement of their wrecked lives finally erupt into fratricide over money as Booth kills Lincoln.

Social traits may include a character's job or profession, socioeconomic status, or religious or political affiliation. It is significant, for example, that Romeo and Juliet are from powerful, upper-class families. Both households have many servants, friends, and relations, many of whom are actively engaged in perpetuating the old feud. It is important to the parents that their children make a "good" marriage; in forcing Juliet to marry Paris, Juliet's father believes that he truly has his daughter's best interests at heart. Hamlet is a prince of Denmark; his social position puts him in the thick of a dangerous power struggle at court. Willy Loman's job is of prime importance in *Death of a Salesman* (1949); Arthur Miller uses Willy's position in society to explore the conflicts inherent in the American dream. Gerhardt Hauptmann's *The Weavers* (1892) features a group protagonist: impoverished characters united by their common working-class status. In Wendy Wasserstein's *The Heidi Chronicles* (1988), the central character is one of the first generation of American women to come of age during the women's movement. She is an art historian, and her perspective on forgotten women of the past has a strong influence on her choices in the play. From a very different sphere in the social fabric comes *Fences* (1985) by August Wilson. The protagonist, Troy Maxson, is a struggling garbage collector in 1957. He has a background of prison and baseball in the Negro League, but he was passed over when integration finally came to major league baseball. While trying to keep his

♦ **M. BUTTERFLY,** by David Henry Hwang. Rene Gallimard, played by John Lithgow, falls in love with a Chinese music drama actress named Song Liling, who is really a cross-dressing male played here by B. D. Wong in this New York production of 1988. Directed by John Dexter; set and costume design by Eiko Ishioka. Photo by Joan Marcus.

♦ *TOPDOG/UNDERDOG, by Suzan-Lori Parks. Lincoln, in the top hat, is played by Jeffrey Wright. His brother, Booth, who will kill him, is played by Don Cheadle. Directed by George C. Wolfe. The Joseph Papp Public Theatre, New York.*
Photo by Michal Daniel.

family afloat, he undermines his son's dreams and betrays his faithful wife with another woman. In the pre–civil rights days he is a victim of racist employment practice; white men are not onstage in the play, but their oppression is felt throughout.

Ethical traits are the moral standards held by a character. Although the audience is frequently given clues to a character's integrity by other means, an ethical or moral choice is often a defining moment for a protagonist, particularly in a tragedy. In Arthur Miller's *The Crucible* (1953), John Proctor, on trial for witchcraft, chooses death rather than incriminate other innocent people. Shakespeare's Macbeth chooses to murder both the king and his closest friend, Banquo, to satisfy his own political ambitions. The results of grasping for power are even more ominous in the Chinese play *The Orphan of Chao* (fourteenth century), attributed to Chi Chün-hsiang. The villain General Tu-an Ku not only kills his political enemy, but also murders every member of his family and extended family—men, women, and children—to ensure that Ku will remain in power. Of course, he misses one infant, who, when grown, learns the truth and exacts revenge from the evil general. All three characters in Michael Frayn's *Copenhagen* (1998) are obsessed with ethical choices posed in the scientific community during the creation of the atomic bomb. Frequently, a character's choice in a time of moral dilemma has a profound effect on the play's action. Jessie has already chosen suicide in *'night, Mother.* Her determination to follow through and her mother's equally determined efforts to stop her furnish the central conflict of the play. A profound but enigmatic ethical choice is made at the conclusion of *Conduct of Life* (1985) by Maria Irene Fornes. The wife of an oppressive and criminal military officer pulls out a pistol and kills him. Then, without explanation, she places the gun in the hands of a twelve-year-old girl who had been repeatedly sexually abused by the officer.

UNDERSTANDING CHARACTER RELATIONSHIPS

Much of our enjoyment in the theatre is derived from watching the interaction of characters. As in life, the audience comes to understand character by observing the impact human beings have on one another and the ways in which characters behave in different situations.

It is helpful to look at the entire network of relationships established in a play. Any past relationship, usually presented through exposition, will be important to understanding present conflict. Romeo's love for his friend Mercutio fires his desire for revenge against Mercutio's murderer, Tybalt. John Proctor's prosecution in *The Crucible* is due in part to the machinations of young Abigail, who hopes to rekindle an adulterous affair. In Lorraine Hansberry's *A Raisin in the Sun* (1959), Mama serves as the matriarch of the Younger family. Her caring and concern for her children and grandchildren are genuine, but in the course

of the play she comes to understand that her well-meaning control has stymied the growth of her son, Walter Lee. Relationships may have a wide impact. The brother/sister relationship between Tom and Laura in *The Glass Menagerie* is full of love, understanding, and compassion; the mother/son relationship between Amanda and Tom is characterized by misunderstanding, impatience, and conflict. The ultimate failure of the mother and son to establish a means of communication (or at least a peaceful coexistence) leads to Tom's abandonment of the family. Tom's relationship with his sister is doomed, not internally but by the dysfunction of the mother/son relationship.

◆◆◆◆◆◆◆◆◆◆

Thought

Thought refers to the ideas in a play and can be generated in a number of different ways. Sometimes a playwright will actually write a speech for a character explicating a particular idea or arguing a point. The famous "To be, or not to be" speech from *Hamlet* (1600–01), for example, is an exquisitely worded argument of the most basic human question: Should I choose life or death? At the end of *Romeo and Juliet* the Prince reminds the bereaved families that their

♦ **HEARTBREAK HOUSE,** *by George Bernard Shaw. The playwright confronts the issues that give rise to World War I in what he calls a* fantasia. *Scenic design by Ming Cho Lee; costume design by Deborah Trout; directed by Jon Jory.*
Photo by Richard C. Trigg. Courtesy of Actors Theatre of Louisville.

own enmity has brought about their sorrow: "Capulet, Montague, / See what a scourge is laid upon your hate, / That heaven finds means to kill your joys with love." The British playwright George Bernard Shaw was a master of working specific ideas into dialogue, often featuring an argument or debate prominently in the action. In *Mrs. Warren's Profession* (1902) a debate occurs between Mrs. Warren and her daughter Vivie. The mother explains the logic of her background as a prostitute and then a madam to pull herself out of the gutter of poverty and servitude. Vivie seems to understand but cannot accept how her mother funded the wonderful education that Vivie has received. With an impossible divide between them, mother and daughter will continue their lives in separate spheres. In stressing intellect over emotion, Bertolt Brecht made many choices as a playwright to support thought. Shen Te, the heroine of Brecht's *Good Person of Setzuan* (c. 1940), finds herself in a dilemma. She is such a thoughtful and selfless woman that she allows everyone to walk all over her. To save herself, she creates a male alter ego, Shui Ta, and performs this role to regain control with demanding, even ruthless, treatment of the people who have been taking advantage of her. In other words, Shen Te must be bad to protect her own goodness.

USE OF IMAGERY TO CREATE THOUGHT

In a complex play, meaning exists on many levels. A concept might be developed through a visual image or expressive language. The youthful, muscular language of *Romeo and Juliet* is made manifest in the actor's climb up the balcony, only to be replaced in the end by the vision of two corpses enveloped by the sounds of mourning. In *Hamlet* thoughtful speeches on mortality are reinforced by verbal images of death and decay ("something is rotten in the state of Denmark"), concrete visual images of skulls and bodies, and the physical action of dueling, poisoning, and stabbing. The characters' dread, guilt, and fear are given physical presence by the appearance of the ghost of Hamlet's father.

In looking for the ideas that are expressed in a play, it is important to take the play as a whole into consideration. Characters have conflicting viewpoints, neither of which might actually communicate what the playwright thinks. Wole Soyinka's *Death and the King's Horseman* (1976) demonstrates the failure of alien cultures to understand one another but, more important, the destruction of sacred parts of native culture by arrogant, uncomprehending British colonial authority. Nigerian Yoruba culture celebrates the beauty of life through a ritual of death, but this is disrupted by both the British and natives, with catastrophic results.

CONTRIBUTION OF PLOT TO THOUGHT

Plot is most instrumental in creating thought. What actually happens in the play—what the playwright chooses to include or exclude, how the playwright chooses to begin and end the play—has a profound effect on ideas that are communicated by the play. *Romeo and Juliet* would be a very different play if the events did not lead to the protagonists' deaths. If the lovers managed to run away and live happily ever after, the play might be seen as a celebration of the power of young love over unreasonable opposition. Instead, the tragedy dramatizes the terrible costs of prejudice and vengeance and the failure of authority figures to provide appropriate counsel and understanding to the young. In *Oedipus the King* the wife/mother of Oedipus commits suicide offstage. Oedipus discovers her body and puts out his own eyes, also unseen by the audience. Because the violence is kept offstage, the audience can focus on how the deeds affect the living rather than on the horror of the physical acts. Unseen action is also critical in *Riders to the Sea* (1904) by John Millington Synge. Here the women of an Irish fishing village repeatedly lose their men to storms at sea. Frequently, they watch helplessly from windows as the play explores not the deaths of the men, but the suffering of the women left behind. The circular structure of *The Blue Room* (and its predecessor, *La Ronde*) raises specific questions about class and sexual behavior as the repeated affairs move through various economic and social groups, bringing all participants to one shared level.

USE OF ALLUSION

Many times thought in plays is communicated by **allusion**—references to previous art, literature, historical event, geography, and culture. When audience members recognize these references, they are likely to find parts of the play opening up in unexpected ways. Allusion is a method of layering and texturing the play, enriching it for those who are prepared for the recognition. In some cases the entire play can function as something of an allusion. *A Tempest* (1969) by West Indian Aimé Césaire, for example, revisits and reconstructs Shakespeare's *The Tempest* to refashion the nature of colonization in the action of the play. Caliban, a literal monster in Shakespeare's play, in Césaire's becomes more clearly a victim of the powerful Prospero, who in turn decides at play's end to remain on the island and continue his struggle with the native Caliban. In the final moments of the play Prospero appears to have sunk into madness. It is much easier now to see the awful consequences of European colonization on native peoples than it was in Shakespeare's time. Or a playwright might turn a play inside out, so to speak. Tom Stoppard took a traditional play—Shakespeare's *Hamlet*—as a point of departure but told the story from the viewpoint of two minor characters. *Rosencrantz and Guildenstern Are Dead* (1967) shows the off-stage action between Shakespeare's scenes. The play can be understood and enjoyed by someone with no knowledge of the older play, but such knowledge offers an extra level of enjoyment as the audience member understands Stoppard's clever use of the original as well as his comments on how our view of the world has changed since the seventeenth century.

◆◆◆◆◆◆◆◆◆◆

Language

Language refers to the playwright's choice of words in a play. Unlike that in a poem, novel, or essay, language written for the stage must be capable of being spoken aloud. It is usually a heightened version of human speech. For many centuries the standard language of the theatre was poetry; a play written in **prose** (language similar to everyday speech) would have been considered inartistic and unworthy of production. The language of plays from the past sometimes seems artificial and strange at first, but an audience can become accustomed to it fairly quickly when it is accompanied by lively staging and clear performances.

Dialogue written in **verse** (poetry) may have a rhyme scheme or just a specific rhythm. In seventeenth-century France, Molière wrote comedies (such as *Tartuffe,* 1664) and Racine wrote tragedies (such as *Phèdre,* 1677) in rhyming couplets. Shakespeare's plays are written largely in **blank verse;** the lines are not rhymed but have a specific, set rhythm. This rhythm is often **iambic pentameter,** which means that there is a stress on each second syllable and five stresses per line. Shakespeare frequently varies this pattern, however. Sometimes the stresses fall in unusual places or extra beats are added; sometimes the ends of lines rhyme; sometimes the characters speak in prose. When plays in verse are translated into another language, it is usually impossible to reproduce the effects of the original poetry. By the eighteenth century in comedy and by the nineteenth century in melodrama and realism, prose had become the theatrical standard. If actual speech were transferred to the stage, however, it would seem boring and repetitive. Even the most authentic-sounding dialogue has been sharpened and shaped by the playwright.

The use of figurative language often enriches dramatic dialogue. When Romeo declares, "Juliet is the Sun," he uses a **metaphor** (equating two unlike objects to suggest a similarity between them) to convey the importance Juliet has assumed in his life. Juliet uses a **simile** (comparing two unlike things using *like* or *as*) to link the depth

◆ **ROMEO AND JULIET** (1998). The initial encounter of Romeo and Juliet with masks at the Capulet banquet. Tom Parker as Romeo and Brandy McClendon as Juliet.
Photo by Karl Hugh. Courtesy of the Utah Shakespearean Festival.

of her love to that of the ocean. **Sensory imagery** brings the physical world of the play alive for the audience and helps to convey the character's experience of environment, as when Romeo describes the dawn: "Look, love, what envious streaks / Do lace the severing clouds in yonder east." Juliet's use of **hyperbole** (overstatement) suggests her impatience when she insists that " 'Tis twenty years" until the next morning.

In most plays dialogue moves back and forth between characters. When one character speaks for an extended period the speech is called a **monologue.** If the character is alone on stage or if the other characters are not supposed to hear the words, such a speech is called a **soliloquy.** A brief remark by a character meant to be heard by the audience but not the other characters is called an **aside.** Asides and soliloquies appear frequently in presentational plays.

CONTRIBUTION TO CHARACTER

Language can communicate a great deal about character and situation. Even knowing the general idea to be conveyed, a playwright must make specific choices about how a character should express that idea. There are many ways to say "no," for example; a character who says, "Negative, sir" is very different from one who says, "Nah, I don't think so." We often infer social class and regional affiliation solely on the basis of how a character speaks. Many of Tennessee Williams's characters are clearly products of the southeastern United States, Neil Simon's of the Northeast. Shaw's play *Pygmalion* (1912) and its musical adaptation, *My Fair Lady* (1956), explore the dynamics of language and social class: Henry Higgins passes off a young Cockney girl as a duchess primarily by altering her dialect.

A playwright's choice of words can also give us important clues about a character's intelligence and emotional state. Is a character's language simple or sophisticated? Straightforward or obtuse? Does the character use many negative or positive words? Words with highly emotional connotations? Once Romeo has seen Juliet, his language reflects the profound impact: "O, she doth teach the torches to burn bright!" He develops his description of Juliet's beauty with a series of strikingly original images of light against dark: "The brightness of her cheek would shame those stars / As daylight doth a lamp." Later, carefully chosen language makes real for the audience Juliet's fear of waking in a tomb "Where bloody Tybalt, yet but green in earth, / Lies fest'ring in his shroud."

Any change in the pattern of language may signal another kind of change: heightened emotion, change of tone, or alteration of circumstance. Even when dialogue is not written in poetry, rhythm still plays an important part in creating mood and establishing a character's state of mind. Consider the following speech from Harold Pinter's *Betrayal*. Jerry is talking to his best friend, Robert. Jerry has been having an affair with Robert's wife, and he has just learned that she has confessed everything to Robert.

> *I don't know why she told you. I don't know how she could tell you. I just don't understand. Listen, I know you've got . . . look, I saw her today . . . we had a drink . . . I haven't seen her for . . . She told me, you know, that you're in trouble, both of you . . . and so on. I know that. I mean I'm sorry.*[3]

Punctuation in the speech indicates a specific rhythm. The character does not speak in smooth, finished sentences, but haltingly, in disconnected phrases.

Exploring Collaboration

W Improvised Text

When the words of a play are not planned ahead of time and written down but are made up on the spot by the actors, we call the creation of the text **improvisation.** Often, some rules or givens are established before the actors begin to make up words and actions, but the important quality of improvisation is that the text is, at least in some measure, based on impulse and is reactive to and dependent on the audience response. Actors must collaborate by anticipating each other's thought and rhythms. Most improvisational work tends to be comic.

Historically, the best-known type of theatre based on improvisation is **commedia dell'arte.** *Commedia* originated in Italy sometime before 1568. We know that some of its characteristics go back at least to the ancient Greek mimes. Some features of the comic plays were fixed; each actor specialized in a role with specific characteristics. Outlines of plots, or scenarios, were available for the actors to use, and standard speeches were memorized and could be inserted when needed. Comic bits, known as *lazzi,* might also be standard. Within each performance, however, *commedia* actors would feel out the crowd, make up dialogue, interact with the audience, and pursue whatever line of business they perceived would be most effective in the given moment.

Commedia dell'arte is the ancestor of today's popular "improv" troupes, such as the famous Second City in Chicago (first home for many *Saturday Night Live* performers), as well as the improvisation-based television show *Whose Line Is It Anyway?*

Improvisational performance requires specific skills: the ability to think quickly, to follow impulse, to cooperate fully with fellow performers. Often, a set structure gives the actors a basic groundwork; the troupe may frequently play a specific "game" based on audience suggestions, for example, but since suggestions will always be different, the performance cannot be planned in advance.

Improvised text does not benefit from the careful shaping and editing of traditional text. We do not expect complex structure, finished dialogue, or profound thoughts. There is great excitement, however, in the spontaneous nature of its performance, and the audience experience includes an appreciation of the quickness of wit, insight, and ability to make connections by the performers who are brave enough to attempt entertaining many people without the security of a written text.

Interested? Check out

Viola Spolin and Paul Sills, eds. *Improvisation for the Theater: A Handbook of Teaching and Directing Techniques,* 3rd ed. Chicago: Northwestern University Press, 1999.

Jeffrey Sweet. *Something Wonderful Right Away: An Oral History of the Second City and the Compass Players.* New York: Limelight Editions, 1987.

The web site for the Second City comedy troupe, www.secondcity.com.

Words are repeated, and pauses occur between thoughts. The rhythm suggests that the character is having difficulty deciding what to say; he is thinking, coming to realizations even as he speaks. On stage, pauses are often just as important as words—sometimes more so. A silent character is often one who is undergoing an intense inner struggle, and this can be reflected in the actor's face and body.

ESTABLISHING MOOD AND ENVIRONMENT

Language can also be used to describe the characters' environment and set the mood of the play. Even the general quality of the world of the play can be established through language. Hamlet compares his home to "an unweeded garden that grows to seed. Things rank and gross in nature / possess it merely." The murder of Hamlet's father has turned the court of Denmark into a place of evil, and the language of the characters reflects that transformation. Conversely, in Oscar Wilde's late Victorian comic universe, language is a tool to be manipulated and enjoyed. *The Importance of Being Earnest* (1895) is full of important words applied to trivial things and vice versa. Gwendolen is "devoted" to bread and butter, but Lady Bracknell tells an orphaned young man, "To lose one parent can be regarded as a misfortune; to lose two looks like carelessness." The misapplication of language reflects the topsy-turvy values of the play's upper-class characters.

The two final elements of a play can only be indicated in a printed text. The production team fleshes out suggestions from the playwright and brings its own creativity to the creation of the two elements that appeal most directly to the audience's senses: music and spectacle.

♦♦♦♦♦♦♦♦♦

Music

Music has been very important in the theatre of most cultures, and in many cases it has been vital. At the time that Aristotle made his analysis, some dialogue and many choral passages in the Greek theatre seem to have been chanted and/or sung, accompanied by instrumental music. In later centuries theatre in the West became highly oriented toward spoken dialogue. This tendency was solidified in the late nineteenth century, when realism was in fashion, since dialogue seemed to be a more accurate depiction of everyday life than song. Music tended to be relegated to specialized forms, such as opera or musical comedy. In contrast, traditional theatrical forms in Asia and Southeast Asia kept music fully integrated into production, with song and musical accompaniment serving important functions in performance.

Music is a powerful tool for encouraging emotional identification; it can increase suspense, excitement, sadness, and happiness. In Western musical theatre, song is frequently used to express heightened emotion, but, following the model of Brecht, song is sometimes used to interrupt the story or emotional development and present ideas about class struggles, corruption in the palaces of power, and the plight of the poor. Shakespeare frequently calls for music in his plays, but the cryptic stage directions tell us little about the type of music that was used. For the Capulet party, Shakespeare includes the instruction "Music plays, and they dance." The music here may be used both to create the atmosphere of a public gathering and to underscore the first meeting of the protagonists. Even in realistic plays, a limited amount of music can serve important functions. In *A Raisin in the Sun,* traditional African music and jazz coming from a phonograph and radio set the mood in the Younger household and help to establish the family's cultural roots. Tennessee Williams's *A Streetcar Named Desire* (1947) has so much offstage music coming from the French Quarter in New Orleans that much of the dramatic action of the play is underscored.

Exploring Historical and Cultural Perspectives

Blast! What Is It?

Sometimes it is difficult to categorize what you have experienced in the theatre. When we witnessed a production entitled *Blast!* (2000), we watched and listened with delight to an odd amalgam of styles and structure. Something like a musical revue (no new music was written for the piece), the presentation was not a play; it had no dialogue or any text to read and very little singing. There was no story to tell, yet the music and the accompanying staging elicited many emotional responses—moments of humor, sadness, and awe. All the musical numbers were connected (the numbers did not stop and start as in a concert). Spectacle mixed freely with music. Although many dancers participated, the musicians, who were usually on their feet, were also cleverly and frequently choreographed while playing. The experience was something of a mix of revue, dance, marching bands, and drum and bugle corps, dominated by brass and percussion with unusual props and lighting effects.

♦ **BLAST!** The brass ensemble also performs as dancers and actors.
Photo by Joan Marcus. Courtesy of James Mason.

The show was created by artistic director James Mason along with George Pinney, James Prime, Jim Moore, and Jonathan Vanderkolff: a creative team. When nominated and selected for a 2001 Tony Award, the production was categorized as "Best Special Theatrical Event." Whatever labels one might wish to assign to *Blast!,* it was clearly theatre and a performance to be enjoyed, talked about, and thought about long after the lights went down on the stage.

It is sometimes useful to expand the definition of "music" beyond traditional song or instrumental underscoring and include the use of other sound. Offstage sound effects can contribute to mood, give important information, or cause action, as when the noise of the approaching watchman hurries Friar Lawrence from the Capulet tomb, leaving Juliet alone to join Romeo in death. The gunshot at the end of *'night, Mother* not only is startling, but also signals the end of Jessie's life. One of the most famous offstage sounds comes at the end of Henrik Ibsen's *A Doll House* (1879) when Nora leaves her husband. We hear only the front door slamming shut.

Spectacle

Spectacle refers to the visual elements called for in a play. It could include scenery, costumes, props, lighting, actor physicality, and movement and can offer a satisfying sensory experience. The intense colors used in Indian Kathakali dance drama and the beautiful, detailed costumes and sets of Japanese Kabuki theatre have appealed strongly to generations of audience members. In addition, visual elements can convey mood, furnish excitement, and convey meaning. Many choices regarding spectacle are left up to the production team, but the play often calls for or implies important visual elements. The opening brawl between the Capulet and Montague factions gets *Romeo and Juliet* off to a rousing start and clearly establishes the feud between the families. The image of Romeo and Juliet touching each other's palms is clearly indicated in the dialogue and has become a familiar symbol of young love. The Capulet party offers opportunity for colorful costumes and dancing—a scene of gaiety—in sharp contrast to the tableau of the lifeless young lovers at the play's end.

Many Western plays open with a description of setting. The playwright defines the world inhabited by the characters as it exists in that playwright's mind. Frequently, this physical description is filled with information about the play's geographic location, about the social and economic position of the characters, about the characters' tastes. Susan Glaspell's one-act play *Trifles* (1916) begins with a description of the deserted farmhouse of a murder victim:

> a gloomy kitchen, and left without having been put in order—unwashed pans under the sink, a loaf of bread outside the breadbox, a dish towel on the table—other signs of incompleted work.[4]

Spectacle, in this case, becomes central to the action of the play, as the female characters, Mrs. Hale and Mrs. Peters, solve the crime by reading the past from small domestic clues—"trifles" overlooked by the male law enforcement officers.

Even when a setting is abstract or minimal, it makes an important contribution to defining the fictional world. Samuel Beckett's *Endgame* (1957) takes place in the aftermath of some kind of unspecified holocaust. The barren reality of the characters is encapsulated in the set. The interior is free of any decoration. The light is described as gray. The windows, too high to be reached without a ladder, suggest an unseen world outside.

In any given play the six elements—plot, character, thought, language, music, and spectacle—work together to create a special world on the stage. The relative significance of the different elements varies considerably from play to play. In *Romeo and Juliet,* for example, plot and character are stronger than thought. In Kathakali dance drama, spectacle and music are of prime importance. The weight of the each element can change according to the time and culture in which the play was written and in which it is performed as well as the preferences of the individual playwright. It is the combination of elements that creates the experience for the audience, but a careful analysis of components can often reveal a great deal about how a play functions in the theatre.

QUESTIONS AND ACTIVITIES

1. Choose a television series that you know well and analyze its structure. How is exposition delivered? Is there more than one line of action in each episode? What kind of climax does it typically use? When do the commercial breaks occur? Try several different types of shows (cop show, sitcom, soap).

2. Read a linear, causally structured play (for example, Susan Glaspell's *Trifles*, Lorraine Hansberry's *A Raisin in the Sun*, or Henrik Ibsen's *A Doll House*). Create a graph that reflects the emotional rise and fall of your play from an audience's point of view. It won't look exactly like the diagrams in this chapter; each play will be somewhat different. Choose specific moments in the play for inciting incident and climax. If your choices differ from those of other students, discuss how the choice of climax affects interpretation of the play.

3. Read a play that is not causally structured (for example, Ntozake Shange's *for colored girls who have considered suicide when the rainbow is enuf*, Tom Stoppard's *The Invention of Love*, or Eugène Ionesco's

The Bald Soprano). How would you describe the plot of this play—in other words, what provides its unity? What holds it together?

4. Discuss the advantages and disadvantages from a writer's point of view of writing for a continuing series versus a single two-hour play or film.

5. Choose a character from a play, film, or television show. List as many character traits as you can think of, putting them in the five levels of characterization. Then discuss *how* these character traits are conveyed.

6. Choose a play or film in which thought is very important. What ideas were conveyed? *How* were these ideas conveyed?

7. Write a critical analysis of a play. Begin by reading and experiencing the play. Think about which of the six elements are most important in this play. Read the play again. Pay particular attention to and take notes on the particular element(s) you have chosen as your focus. (See also the sections "Reading a Play" and "Writing about a Play" in Chapter 5.)

KEY TERMS AND CONCEPTS

dialogue, p. 88
stage directions, p. 88
Aristotle's six elements of a play, p. 88
plot, p. 88
structure, p. 88
linear, p. 88
causal, p. 88
well-made play, p. 89
conflict, p. 89
point of attack, p. 90
episodic, p. 90
exposition, p. 90
inciting incident, p. 91
rising action, p. 91
climax, p. 92
falling action, p. 92
subplot, p. 93
discovery, p. 94

reversal, p. 94
cliff-hanger, p. 95
flashback, p. 96
rasa, p. 98
poststructuralism, p. 100
metatheatre, p. 101
pantomime, p. 102
happenings, p. 102
performance art, p. 102
character, p. 102
protagonist, p. 103
levels of characterization, p. 103
biological traits, p. 103
physical traits, p. 104
psychological and emotional traits, p. 105
social traits, p. 105
ethical traits, p. 106
thought, p. 107

allusion, p. 109
language, p. 110
prose, p. 110
verse, p. 110
blank verse, p. 110
iambic pentameter, p. 110
metaphor, p. 110
simile, p. 110
sensory imagery, p. 111
hyperbole, p. 111
monologue, p. 111
soliloquy, p. 111
aside, p. 111
improvisation, p. 112
commedia dell'arte, p. 112
music, p. 113
spectacle, p. 115

◆◆◆◆◆◆◆◆◆

FOR FURTHER EXPLORATION

J. L. Styan. *The Elements of Drama.* Cambridge, England: Cambridge University Press, 1960.

Ronald Hayman. *How to Read a Play,* 2nd ed. New York: Grove Press, 1999.

MEDEA, by Euripides, Theatre de la Jeune Lune, Minneapolis.
Photo by Michal Daniel.

Interpreting the Play

Understanding Genre, Reading, and Writing

In this chapter we discuss a useful tool for analyzing and comparing plays: dramatic genre. Because a play is meant as a blueprint for production, it needs to be read differently from other literature. To help develop these skills, we discuss effective strategies for reading a printed text as well as writing about plays, which can lead you to new levels of understanding and interpretation.

♦♦♦♦♦♦♦♦♦♦

Dramatic Genre

A culture that creates or sustains theatrical activity often finds a way to classify its plays; putting plays in categories is one way of talking about which ones are similar and discovering how they work. In the ancient Indian Sanskrit drama a play was classified according to the mood, or *rasa,* it evoked. Japanese Noh divides its plays into five categories according to character and subject matter: gods, warriors, women, supernatural beings, and miscellaneous characters. As far back as the Greeks, plays in the Western tradition were classified according to genre. **Genre** relates to the kind of emotional response a play creates in the audience. One genre is not better than another; different types of emotional reactions serve different purposes in the theatre. We will discuss four major genres here: tragedy, comedy, tragicomedy, and melodrama, as well as some of the subgenres that have been used to identify plays at various times. In the twentieth century genres became so combined that many recent plays defy generic identification.

TRAGEDY

While the terms "tragedy" and "tragic" are frequently used in everyday speech to mean "sad" or an event including unexpected death, in the theatre these terms refer very specifically to a particular type of drama. If a play is serious and ends unhappily, it may be a **tragedy.** Traditionally, "serious" and "unhappy" are not the only characteristics of tragedy, however. Aristotle believed that tragedy evoked the emotions of pity and fear in its audience—pity because the audience sympathizes with the protagonist and fear because the audience empathizes with the character who is facing a difficult problem.

Audience members in most periods have expected a certain dignity and importance from tragedy. The nature of this importance—often translated as **magnitude** in Aristotle's definition of tragedy—has been debated for centuries. What makes a play "important"? For the ancient Greeks and for many societies to follow, "importance" was closely related to the social class of the characters. Tragedy was about people of noble birth. Today, many people object to the notion that social class has any relationship to the "importance" of a person's life or story, but it is at least understandable that when something happened to a royal family, the entire kingdom was affected. In *Oedipus the King* (c. 430–425 B.C.E.), Oedipus has been a very successful ruler of Thebes, for example, and his fate is inextricably tied to that of his people. Magnitude might also refer to the importance of the issues treated in the play. The action of tragedy raises serious and difficult questions—the nature of justice for example, or free will versus predestination.

The protagonist in a tragedy frequently faces an **ethical choice,** or choice about a moral issue: Should I kill the king who murdered my father? Should I implicate other people to save my own life? Sometimes a character's ethical choice brings about the character's own downfall. In Sophocles' play *Antigone* (415 B.C.E.) the title character faces a difficult ethical choice. Both of her brothers are dead. The king, her uncle, has ordered that one brother, who fought in a rebellion against the state, should remain unburied. The body must be allowed to rot. Antigone's religion and family loyalty tell her that she must give her brother a proper burial. She follows the dictates of her conscience and buries her brother, disobeying the law of the state. Antigone makes her choice with full knowledge that her uncle has declared any violation punishable by death. The conflicts of personal conscience and obedience to authority, of loyalty to state or religion, of following the dictates of love or honor, have tremendous resonance in the twenty-first century, regardless of when the play was written.

♦ *ROMEO AND JULIET (1899).*
Maude Adams and William Faversham in the balcony scene. This is a traditional nineteenth-century interpretation of this scene from the most famous romantic tragedy of Elizabethan theatre.
By permission of the Folger Shakespeare Library.

The Greeks saw tragedy as a way of explaining why bad things happen; if terrible things happened to a good person for no reason, it would suggest chaos rather than order in the world. Protagonists were often basically good people who made mistakes. Later critics have pointed out that tragedy often depicts a complex moral universe: Things are not just good or bad. As such, tragedy is a true reflection of the world we live in. No one is perfect, and good can be found in "bad" people, just as bad qualities can be found in basically "good" people.

Theorists have wondered about the popularity and longevity of a dramatic form that ends unhappily. What compels human beings to create and seek out this kind of empathic experience? For the ancient Greeks, **catharsis** was one answer—it was healthy to evoke strong emotions and then let them ebb away. Certainly, the ability to experience extreme emotion vicariously is an intriguing part of tragedy. Other commentators have found a teaching value in tragedy; the advice of some tragedies seems to be "Don't make the same mistake." One of the most enduring explanations of tragedy, however, is that the form demonstrates nobility of the human character. Our attention in tragedy is not so much on *what* happens but on *how* it happens and how the people involved deal with adversity. The audience often knows the outcome of tragedy from the beginning. The ancient Greeks knew the legends and myths on which their tragedies were based before they entered the theatre, but the playwrights retold these tales and altered emphasis. Shakespeare tells us in the opening of *Romeo and Juliet* (a romantic tragedy, 1594–95) that the lovers are "star-crossed" or unlucky; we know that their story will not end happily. We are interested in the strength of character that is demonstrated and the kinds of choices the characters make on

their journey. *Romeo and Juliet* was also adapted as a modern urban musical tragedy, *West Side Story,* in 1957.

Although tragedy as a genre is not a focus of most traditional Asian theatre, a number of Japanese Kabuki plays feature situations that are recognized as tragic. *The Scarlet Princess of Edo* (1817), for example, includes complex, violent, and erotic action. Princess Sakura falls into poverty and prostitution and loses her child amid many murders and suicides as well as a visit from a ghost.

In the eighteenth century, as more democratic forms of government began to become a reality, playwrights began to write tragedies about middle-class characters. George Lillo's *The London Merchant* (1731) depicts the death of a shopkeeper at the hands of his apprentice. By the mid-nineteenth century Georg Büchner in Germany was at work on *Woyzeck* (1836), a tragedy with a working-class protagonist. Woyzeck, a poor soldier, is victimized by both the military and a corrupt doctor who uses him as a guinea pig in his scientific experiments. Woyzeck finally snaps and repeatedly stabs Marie, his promiscuous lover, to death.

Tragedy is less common in new work beyond the nineteenth century, but it has occasionally appeared in plays such as Eugene O'Neill's *Desire under the Elms* (1924) and *Mourning Becomes Electra* (1931), two dark explorations of family life that were based on the Greek tragedies of Euripides and Aeschylus. American playwright Maxwell Anderson used historical British figures to depict the clash of political responsibility and personal emotion in *Anne of a Thousand Days* (1948), about Anne Boleyn, and *Mary of Scotland* (1933), about Mary, Queen of Scots. Artists and theorists have speculated about the difficulty of writing modern tragedy, pointing out that a tragic viewpoint is difficult to achieve, since playwrights can no longer assume shared religious or moral be-

liefs in the audience. Some argue that in this age of fragmentation it is difficult to find a person whose fate is of great enough significance to be considered of tragic importance. In 1949 Arthur Miller wrote his essay "Tragedy of the Common Man," advocating a redefinition of "importance" and defending his use of an ordinary protagonist in *Death of a Salesman* (1949). The title of the play is significant; Miller examines the suicide of a salesman, not a king or a queen.

In the last several decades of the twentieth century, some feminist critics found the traditional structure of tragedy (based on stimulating catharsis) to be an inherently male construct, evolving from a male view of reality. Women playwrights, they argued, tended to see human events in less linear terms and often implied the possibility of change and growth in their plays, rather than inevitability.

COMEDY

Of course, if a play is basically humorous, it is probably a **comedy.** Although comedy is a tremendously popular form, the genre of comedy is more difficult to pin down than tragedy. If tragedy creates the emotions of pity and fear, the genre of comedy might be defined through its *lack* of such emotional involvement. If you feel very strongly about something, it is often difficult to laugh. When you find something funny, you are looking at the situation more objectively; sometimes, no matter how bad things get, it is possible to step back and laugh because of the ridiculousness of the situation.

The audience can laugh in comedy because any threat to the characters is much less serious than in tragedy. In comedy there is seldom a sense of impending doom because the stakes in the conflict are lower. Rather than death, a character might be threatened with discovery in an embarrassing situation. Rather than ethical choice, characters typically make expedient choices—not *whether* something should be done, but *how* it should be done: How can I sneak out of this room before my husband finds me here? How can I convince the rich lady to give me the money that I need? How can I meet this attractive woman? How can I steal that delicious pie? Because the stakes are lower, our emotional engagement tends to be less intense than it is with tragedy.

The focus of comedies may differ markedly. Comic action sometimes diverts an audience by taking it out of itself. Mel Brooks and Tom Meehan's musical comedy *The Producers* (2001), about two men who try their hardest to produce a theatrical flop, is pure fun as it depicts many segments of society irreverently. In one of the funniest musical numbers in the show, for example, the dancers are costumed as old ladies and use walkers in their routine. Some comedy uses laughter to render a serious problem less dangerous. The audience is invited to objectify a problem by ridiculing it. In *Volpone* (1606) Ben Jonson treats the subject of greed in a humorous way. The villains at the center of the action, Volpone and Mosca, are so successful that they can be caught by no one but themselves.

◆ **THE CAUCASIAN CHALK CIRCLE,** *by Bertolt Brecht, includes much outrageous comedy in the midst of a serious story. In the second act especially, a completely corrupt imposter is made a judge who actually helps the poor and downtrodden by passing judgments in violation of the laws created by the rich and powerful. Produced at the University of Nebraska.*
Collection of the authors.

Often, the conflict in comedy results from a social norm being violated—an old man wants to marry a young girl, for example, or two characters want to carry on an extramarital affair. Usually, the social norm is reestablished at the end of the play: The appropriate people are paired up, and all is right with the world again. The return to social order is often celebrated festively with a dance or a marriage, and most or all of the characters are reunited in the final scene.

Comedy has a broad appeal, and its development has taken a number of different directions in the last two thousand years. Some critics have found it useful to subdivide the genre into at least five types. Some you will find very familiar; others you might not yet have encountered.

Situation comedy, as the term suggests, emphasizes the humorous qualities of the situation in which the characters find themselves. The type is usually traced back to ancient Roman comedy, which treated the affairs of typical middle-class people. *The Phormio* (161 B.C.E.) by Terence, is a situation comedy about the ridiculous manipulations of a wily servant who helps two young men win the brides they seek. The play was so successful and influential beyond its time that Molière adapted it (but changed the name of the servant hero) as the hit comedy *The Tricks of Scapin* (1671). Playwrights from many periods have adapted the major servant character under various names—Phormio, Scapin, or Scapino—and continue to use the role as a wonderful vehicle for a comic actor. Shakespeare based *Comedy of Errors* (1592–93), the crazy exploits of two sets of twins, on the Roman comedy *The Brothers Menaechmus* (c. second century B.C.E.).

Neil Simon has been very successful in writing situation comedies for the American stage. *Barefoot in the Park* (1963) follows the adventures of a newly married couple living in a fifth-floor walk-up in New York City. Although Simon's more recent plays have usually maintained a basic situation comedy format, they often contain serious and contemplative moments, creating a bittersweet tone. The TV "sitcom" is the most prevalent example of the situation comedy in current society. *Frasier* is a good example of a family-based situation comedy. The nuclear family was replaced by the bar regulars in *Cheers,* by a workplace "family" in *Just Shoot Me,* and by the extended family of peers in *Friends.*

Farce is a type of situation comedy that emphasizes broad physical action. In this case the term "broad" means large or exaggerated action. The performers of commedia dell'arte (an improvisational form from Italy) specialized in this type of comedy. Use of the term **slapstick** to designate broad comic action originated with *commedia* actors and their use of a long, flat paddle with a flap that literally made a loud slapping sound when used for comic beatings. The *commedia* legacy can be traced through the Marx Brothers, the Three Stooges, and into animated cartoons. Coincidence and mistaken identity occur frequently in farce, and the characters are put in situations that require specific physical action. Japanese Kyōgen plays serve as comic interludes for the more somber Noh drama. *Tied to a Pole* (c. 1350), also adapted for the Kabuki theatre, revolves around two servants. To prevent them from stealing his liquor, their master binds one servant's hands together and lashes another servant to a pole. Despite this incapacitation, the servants try to drink their master's wine and ultimately succeed. The physical comedy that results is communicated clearly to the audience members, whether or not they share a language with the performers. The French

♦ **COMMEDIA DELL'ARTE**
comic character Arlecchino dressed in traditional diamond-pattern costume (a formal development of a patched costume), wearing his half mask and chin-piece, and armed with his slapstick.
Illustration by Maurice Sand. Archives Charmet/Bridgeman Art Library.

◆ **TIED TO A POLE.** *In this Japanese Kabuki farce the two servants are chided and threatened by their master before he leaves the house. The master has bound his two servants because he doesn't trust them while he is gone, yet they acrobatically manage to raid his supply of wine without using their hands. Kabuki world tour.* Photo by Japan Society.

medieval farce *Pierre Pathelin* (c. 1470) dramatizes a lawyer tricking a merchant, then a supposedly stupid peasant in turn tricking the lawyer. *Pierre Pathelin* was popular in France for centuries. In fact farce is frequently associated with France. Molière wrote many farces in the seventeenth century, such as *The Flying Doctor* (c.1650). At the end of the nineteenth century Georges Feydeau created some of the most enduring farces; in *Hotel Paradiso* (1894), as in many farces that have followed, there are many doors on stage because characters are constantly running in and out, just missing each other, just barely escaping discovery. Feydeau's characters typically pursue clandestine affairs and are forced to hide under beds, in closets, and in trunks, afraid that they will be caught in a compromising position. British playwright Alan Ayckbourn capitalized on this sexually suggestive situation by entitling one of his comedies *Bedroom Farce* in 1977.

Farce provides the opportunity for highly physical actors to display their technique. *A Funny Thing Happened on the Way to the Forum* (1962), a musical farce cobbled together from bits and pieces of Roman comedy by Stephen Sondheim, Burt Shevelove, and Larry Gelbart, has utilized the talents of comic actors Zero Mostel (in 1962), Phil Silvers (in 1972), and Nathan Lane (in 1996). *Noises Off* (1982) by Michael Frayn follows the antics of an out-of-control theatrical company. The play ends with a fast-paced scene in which the characters onstage perform a play, and everything that can go wrong does. Some favorite "classic" TV shows are farces; *I Love Lucy,* for example, was created around Lucille Ball's talent for physical comedy.

Comedy of character is driven by the eccentricities of its major figure. Molière also specialized in this subtype, often playing the major roles himself. The action of *The Imaginary Invalid* (1673) revolves around a hypochondriac;

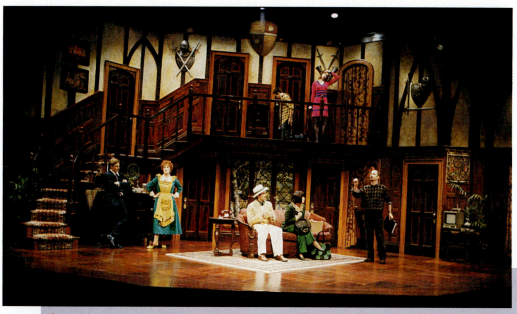

◆ **NOISES OFF,** by Michael Frayn. The Act I setting for this farce depicts the interior setting for the production of a play. The audience watches the characters rehearsing a play. Notice the plentiful doors on different levels, which encourage farcical chases, hiding, and near discoveries. Directed by Risa Brainin; scenic design by Nayna Ramey; costume design by Devon Painter. Courtesy of Indiana Repertory Theatre.

Harpagon in *The Miser* (1668) is blinded by his own greed. A musical example of comedy of character is *Hello, Dolly!* (1963), based on Thornton Wilder's *The Matchmaker* (1954). Dolly Levi is a colorful and persistent character who drives the action of the play. Based on a comic strip from the 1930s, the musical comedy *Annie* (1977), by Charles Strouse, Martin Charnin, and Thomas Meehan, is unified by its focus on a precocious orphan girl searching for her parents. Beth Henley's *Crimes of the Heart* (1979) features three eccentric sisters who are reunited during a time of family crisis.

Comedy of idea is focused on thought rather than character or situation. The plays of the Greek author Aristophanes are comedies of ideas. During the years of a real war between Athens and Sparta, Aristophanes staged *Lysistrata* (411 B.C.E.), in which women take over the fortress of the city and refuse sex to all their mates until the men decide to stop fighting. George Bernard Shaw is the master of comedy of idea in English. *Arms and the Man* (1894) debunks the concept of heroism, and *Man and Superman* (1905) predicts the next wave of human evolution: new emancipated, independent, and modern men and women who will replace the obsolete, frail human beings of Shaw's time. George C. Wolfe's *The Colored Museum* (1986) uses the musical revue form (songs and short scenes tied together by a theme) to satirize stereotypes from black history, ranging from an experience in a slave ship to a lampoon of *A Raisin in the Sun.*

Comedy of manners, as the term suggests, explores the behavior of a particular segment of society. Characters frequently find that their own desires are at odds with social expectations. Historically, comedy of manners has focused most often on upper-class society to both celebrate and poke fun at its pretensions. The English Restoration period (1660–1700) is known as the golden age for comedy of manners and produced plays in which the idle rich entertain

♦ **NOISES OFF,** by Michael Frayn. The backstage scene represents the reverse of the on-stage scene, frequently achieved by using a revolving stage. We still have the multitude of doors as seen from the other side. "Offstage" becomes "onstage." Directed by Risa Brainin; scenic design by Nayna Ramey; costume design by Devon Painter.
Courtesy of Indiana Repertory Theatre.

themselves with sexual intrigue and clever dialogue. In William Wycherley's *The Country Wife* (1675) the major character, Horner, circulates the rumor that he is incapable of having sex in order to gain access to other men's wives. Oscar Wilde's frequently revived *The Importance of Being Earnest* (1895) is a fine example of comedy of manners from the Victorian period; in it two young ladies vow that they can only love and marry someone named Ernest. The play seems to make fun of the new movement of realism, including some of Wilde's own plays, such as *Lady Windermere's Fan* (1892). George Bernard Shaw's *Pygmalion* (1912), a comedy of manners that was later adapted by Lerner and Loewe as the musical *My Fair Lady* (1956), explores the relationship between social class and speech.

In 1845 Anna Cora Mowatt created a comedy of manners with American characters; *Fashion* makes fun of the newly rich who mimic the fashions of Paris. In the end truthfulness and integrity triumph over social pretension and hypocrisy. American playwright Philip Barry developed a distinctive style of comedy of manners in the 1920s and 1930s with plays such as *The Philadelphia Story* (1939), which features a vivacious young heroine (originally played by Katharine Hepburn) who has rejected but is later reunited with her true love. Stephen Sondheim and Hugh Wheeler's musical *A Little Night Music* (1973) follows this tradition by exploring the erratic behavior of upper-class society with both a satirical and sympathetic eye.

Romantic comedy follows the attempts of lovers to get together. It shares this basic structure with many situation comedies, but romantic comedies more often produce a feeling of well-being and sympathy at the end, rather than

♦ **THE COUNTRY WIFE,** *a comedy of manners by William Wycherley. Mr. Horner,
played by Leigh Lawson, romps on the floor with Lady Fidget (Elizabeth Meadows
Rouse), Dainty Fidget (Helen Hedman), and Mrs. Squeamish (Robin Moseley). The
2000 production directed by Keith Baxter; set design by Simon Higlett; costume design
by Robert Perdziola.*
Photo by Carol Rosegg. Courtesy the Shakespeare Theatre, Washington, D.C.

strong laughs. Shakespeare's *Much Ado about Nothing* (1598–99) is a good
example, as avowed enemies Beatrice and Benedick end up confessing their
love for each other as the result of a trick orchestrated by their friends. The
perennially popular musical *The Fantasticks* (1960, which finally closed in 2002
after an almost forty-two-year initial run), by Tom Jones and Harvey Schmidt, is
a romantic comedy in which the lovers weather misfortune and hard experience
before ultimately satisfying their fathers' hopes of union. Tom Hanks and Meg
Ryan teamed up as performers in two highly successful romantic comedies on
film: *Sleepless in Seattle* (1993) and *You've Got Mail* (1998).

Most comedies combine elements of several different subtypes. Farcical
action is an important part of *Much Ado about Nothing* and *The Fantasticks*,
even though the main thrust of action in these plays is romantic. In categorizing
a play, it is important to think about what drives the major action: the situation,
a character's eccentricities, an idea, social behavior, romance, or perhaps a different element.

Tragedy and comedy treat the two poles of human experience, and their
symbols, the tragic and comic masks, have come to denote the theatrical experience in its entirety. Although most societies have recognized the importance of encompassing both the tragic and comic in theatre, they have differed
in their viewpoint of what the relationship between the two genres should
be. In the ancient Greek theatre and the classic Noh theatre, tragic and comic
action were kept separate and were seldom combined in the same drama. The
serious plays were also separated from the comic plays by being performed on
different performance days in Greece or in different parts of the program
in Japan. The Elizabethans did not mind combining genres and indeed used

humorous scenes as **comic relief**—action created to ease emotional tension or contrast with a major event—at strategic points within a serious play. In *Macbeth* (1605–06) Shakespeare brings on the comic character of a drunken Porter just as the title character and his wife have killed King Duncan (an excruciatingly tense scene). The Porter makes sexual jokes that have nothing to do with the tragic action, and he never appears again. In spite of occasional comic moments in serious plays or serious moments in comic plays, a play is categorized by its overall emotional effect. Few people would call *Macbeth* a comedy on the basis of the Porter scene.

TRAGICOMEDY

When the tragic and comic tendencies seem equally mixed, the play might be called a **tragicomedy.** During the Italian Renaissance, tragicomedy came to mean a middle form that incorporated serious action, everyday (rather than noble) characters, and a happy ending. The Elizabethans created plays with serious action but happy endings, such as Shakespeare's *A Winter's Tale* (1610–11), which ends with a repentant husband discovering that the wife he thought was dead is actually alive. This middle or third form had many manifestations in the eighteenth and nineteenth centuries. In France Denis Diderot theorized the need for a serious play without a tragic conclusion and called the form *drame*. His own versions of this type were dull, but he inspired many others to experiment with the idea. In the early nineteenth century, German romantic playwright von Kleist insisted on calling any of his serious plays, such as *The Prince of Homburg* (1811), simply *spiel*, or "play," and many who followed him have

◆ **THE THREE SISTERS,** by Anton Chekhov, produced in New York in the 1940s with Katharine Cornell and Ruth Gordon. At the end of the play the sisters have failed to get what they want and have lost people close to them. Throughout the play's action they have been unable or unwilling to act on their strongest desires, and they end with little but their love for one another. This play is of mixed tone and is often labeled a tragicomedy. Photo courtesy Billy Rose Theatre Collection, the New York Public Library for the Performing Arts, Astor, Lennox and Tilden Foundations.

done the same. In the twentieth century many playwrights called their mixed tone efforts "plays," and since the 1950s television has grown fond of identifying serious teleplays as simply "drama."

In the late nineteenth and early twentieth centuries, Russian playwright Anton Chekhov perfected the drama of mixed tone: Comic and tragic points of view are presented almost simultaneously. A typical Chekhovian stage direction is "laughing through tears." In *Uncle Vanya* (1899) a well-meaning, middle-aged man comes to realize that he has spent his entire life supporting a priggish and pretentious fraud. Mid-twentieth-century playwrights took such tragicomedy in different directions. Tennessee Williams wrote with mixed tone but tended to emphasize the serious in plays such as *A Streetcar Named Desire* (1947). Samuel Beckett explored the dark side of the human condition using traditional comic turns in *Waiting for Godot* (1953). In *A Raisin in the Sun* (1959), Lorraine Hansberry depicted both the strength and the tensions within a family as they pursue different and sometimes conflicting routes to escape poverty. Many contemporary artists find tragicomedy an appealing form, since it seems to reflect the ambiguity in modern life.

MELODRAMA

If the action of a play is serious but ends happily and if the focus is more on *what* happens rather than *how*, the play might be classified as a **melodrama.** Although melodrama shares the combination of seriousness and happiness with tragicomedy, certain characteristics set it apart; because of its enormous popularity, melodrama is often thought of as a separate genre. In everyday speech, we often use the term "melodramatic" in a belittling way to mean "over-emotional." In theatrical terminology, however, "melodrama" refers to a specific genre of play with recognizable characteristics. Melodrama tends to rely on fast-paced action and suspense, and the audience's main concern is whether or not something will happen rather than how the characters will react: Will the cops arrive in time? Will the beautiful woman kill her lover? Sometimes the action may be highly emotional rather than physical, as in the television sub-genre of soap operas, or "soaps." Will John divorce Mary? Will Harry discover his son's true identity? Discovery and reversal play large roles in the action of melodrama: The murder weapon is discovered, the old friend is revealed to be a traitor (discovery), the villain lifts a key from the jailer and escapes (reversal).

The climax of a melodrama is usually a scene in which spectacle plays a major role. Exploding mines, fiery steamships, heroines teetering on cliffs, and car chases have all been used to raise dramatic tension to the breaking point. Westerns have shoot-outs with pistols, science fiction adventures have shoot-outs with lasers. In some subgenres of melodrama the climax is less dependent on spectacle, but the emphasis is still on suspense. Murder mysteries, such as the many dramatizations of the Sherlock Holmes stories, rely on revelation of the killer (discovery) for the climax.

Traditionally, the conflict in melodrama is between the forces of goodness and evil. A hero or heroine is usually pitted against a villain, and the play ends with **poetic justice:** Good is rewarded; evil is punished. Melodrama shares with tragedy the emotion of fear but also stimulates hate. The clarity of moral definition in melodrama is quite different from that in tragedy.

♦ *WAITING FOR GODOT,* subtitled "a tragicomedy" by its playwright Samuel Beckett. The four principal characters have many clown-like qualities, and often create comic action, but much of the action and the characters' ongoing predicament are sad. Here we see the character of Lucky played by Alvin Epstein.

Photo courtesy Billy Rose Theatre Collection, the New York Public Library for the Performing Arts, Astor, Lennox and Tilden Foundations.

THE BELLS. *In Henry Irving's famous production of this melodrama in the nineteenth century, he used a scrim and gas lighting to create a vision scene. The character is standing in a realistic box set, but the upstage wall of the apparent room is a scrim concealing a scene behind it until the lighting is added upstage and dimmed downstage. Traditionally, melodrama has utilized sensation and intense situations.*
By permission of the Folger Shakespeare Library.

Melodrama may or may not deal with serious issues. It has been a favorite way of advocating social and political causes. *Uncle Tom's Cabin* (1852) was trumpeted as an important contribution to the abolition of slavery, and the temperance movement used melodramas such as *The Drunkard* (1844) and *Ten Nights in a Bar-Room* (1858) to depict the dangers of drunkenness and the possibility of redemption. The clear-cut definition of good and bad makes melodrama a useful tool for encouraging and discouraging various types of behavior while holding out the possibility of reward.

Twentieth-century melodramas include murder mysteries such as Agatha Christie's *The Mousetrap* (1952) and thrillers such as Frederick Knott's *Wait until Dark* (1966), in which a blind woman is terrorized in her home by two men. Television and film quickly adapted melodrama. Most story-based television series that are not sitcoms are melodramas of one type or another. The spectacular action of melodrama is especially well suited to special effects films. One of the best-known and finest examples of twentieth-century melodrama is George Lucas's *Star Wars Episode IV: A New Hope* (1977), the first of the *Star Wars* films to be released. It pits the (good) rebels against the (evil) empire. Darth Vader is a perfect villain (evil through and through). Luke, Leia, Han, and Obi-Wan team up as a collective hero. Luke destroys the Death Star in the spectacular climax, and the final scene shows the heroes receiving medals and applause. In subsequent *Star Wars* films, Lucas kept the basic form but began playing against audience expectations in selected scenes: Darth Vader is revealed to be Luke and Leia's father and later redeems himself to some extent by saving Luke from the emperor. The enormous popularity of the *Star Wars* films (as well as the steady stream of those featuring superheroes) is a testament to the satisfaction that audiences derive from melodrama that is done well.

DEPARTURES FROM TRADITIONAL GENRE

Many plays, particularly from the twentieth century on, do not seem to fit neatly into a traditional genre. It is not necessary to declare unequivocally that a play belongs in one genre or another. In trying to decide, however, you will often discover some important qualities. Playwrights sometimes work against our traditional expectations. As we watch a melodrama, we anticipate a happy ending; the destruction of a good character (such as the death of the hero Qui-Gon Jinn in *Star Wars Episode I: The Phantom Menace,* 1999) makes a tremendous impact. A play that seems like a comedy at the beginning and then becomes serious is often very disturbing. A taboo subject treated in a comic tone makes us uneasy; such a play can make us question our own value system. Joe Orton's play *What the Butler Saw* (1969) makes farce out of the taboo subject matter (at the time the play was written) of homosexuality and incest. *Copenhagen* (1998) by Michael Frayn does not correspond to any of the traditional Western genres but is structured much like a traditional Noh play: The dead reflect on the past, trying to find meaning. Some playwrights find the whole notion of genre irrelevant and take advantage of the freedom to craft plays without the restrictions of a label. Others use or adapt genre to serve their own purposes. Many plays do not fit neatly into the generic box, but identifying *why* they do not is often enlightening.

Reading a Play

When you read a play, you are not seeing the finished product as imagined by the playwright; it will not be complete until it is staged as a production and living actors are speaking the lines and moving through space. Reading is not the ideal way to experience a play. However, if you limit your knowledge to only those scripts that you can see produced, you will never experience many beautiful, funny, and inspiring plays. If you choose to become a theatre practitioner, you will read and interpret many plays in order to create production.

It is therefore important for everyone who has an interest in theatre to develop the skill of imagining the play in three dimensions while reading. When you experience an actual production, the directors, designers, actors, and technicians have already done much of the work for you. When you read a play, you take on all of these roles in your own imagination.

VISUALIZING THE ACTION

As you begin to read a play, try to create a mental picture of each of the characters and the space that they inhabit. Sometimes a writer will give you very complete descriptions; sometimes a writer will provide almost nothing. David Mamet, for example, sets parts of *Glengarry Glen Ross* (1983) in a Chinese restaurant. There is no description. You can imagine the space as spare and monochrome or filled with color. The intensity with which you "see" the action of the play will have a strong effect on your emotional reaction to it.

It is important to understand the action of the play as immediate, even when reading. If we think of the play as something that has already occurred, it loses much of its power. Imagine that it is happening now, just as it would occur with action in real time in a theatre. Watching the drama unfolding before you, even within your own mind, is the most fruitful way to experience a dramatic text.

To get the broad sweep of action and most immediate emotional impact, it is best to read a play for the first time in one sitting without stopping. Once you have a sense of

♦ *ROMEO AND JULIET,* the banquet scene, an important moment early in the play. In the first encounter of the two lovers, they not only make their first overtures of attraction but also dance as part of the play's spectacle. Directed by Jon Jory; scenic design by Ming Cho Lee; costume design by Marcia Dixcy. Photo by Richard C. Trigg. Courtesy of Actors Theatre of Louisville.

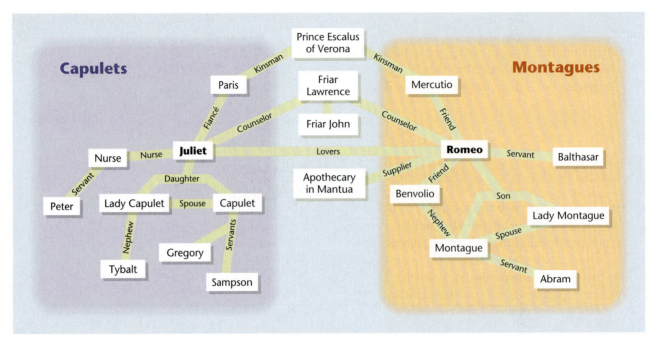

FIGURE 5.1 *Character Relationships in* **Romeo and Juliet**

the play as a whole, you can begin to analyze the play to increase your understanding of how it works. The most important thing to grasp as you read a play is the basic action: What is happening? It is usually not difficult to answer this question for a fairly simple play with five or fewer characters; it is more of a challenge in a play with several lines of action and many characters. Making a diagram in which character relationships are represented spatially can help you to keep things straight. We have included a diagram for *Romeo and Juliet* that illustrates graphically how the characters are related to each other (see Figure 5.1). When you look at the diagram, Shakespeare's symmetrical use of character becomes apparent: Each side (Capulet and Montague) is represented by one young lover, a servant attached to that person (Nurse, Balthasar), two parents, one nephew of a parent, and a kinsman of the Prince. In other plays, Shakespeare organized the character relationships differently to facilitate a different kind of action.

Most of the text of a play is dialogue; the playwright's primary means of communication is through the words of the characters. When reading a play, however, it is important not to overlook stage directions, which can give important information. A character's physical movement, posture, or gesture may be significant. A particular visual image as described by the playwright may be essential for a complete understanding of the text. Indeed, the climax of a play may occur in a moment of action, unsupported by dialogue. Much of the hysterical comedy in the last act of *Noises Off* is furnished by event: Props appear, disappear, and fall apart, and three different "burglars" break onto the stage set in a matter of minutes. At times dialogue and stage directions may contradict one another. At the end of both acts of Samuel Beckett's *Waiting for Godot,* the two tramps agree to leave, but in the final (and very significant) stage direction the reader is told that the characters do not move. It is important to visualize

"Exit, Pursued by a Bear": Those Problematic Stage Directions

Exploring Historical and Cultural Perspectives

In Shakespeare's *The Winter's Tale,* Antigonus lays a baby on the seacoast of Bohemia, only to be chased offstage (and apparently devoured) by a bear. The cryptic stage direction "Exit, pursued by a bear" tells us little about how the playwright imagined the bear or how his company made such a completely unexpected device (the animal appears out of nowhere) work on stage.[1]

Such problematic stage directions can drive directors crazy. Unimportant ones may be cut, but some (like the bear) set up important situations later in the play. Each production team must do its best to come up with an imagina-tive solution. The history of *The Winter's Tale* is littered with different approaches to "Exit, pursued by a bear," including realistic bear costumes, stylized bears, and shadow bears shown on stage.

Less of a problem, but still a challenge, are terse stage directions such as "They fight." Each director (often aided by a fight choreographer) who takes on the challenge of *Hamlet* must carefully stage an exciting, convincing fight to meet the demands of the play's climax. As you read such a script, it is important to remember all that might be implied by the simple direction "They fight."

the action as you hear the dialogue so that you are aware of the discrepancy. Research into human communication indicates that when verbal signals (words) and nonverbal signals (such as posture, gestures, facial expressions, tone of voice) seem to contradict each other, people tend to believe the nonver-bal. In the theatre as well, an audience tends to interpret visual cues as "truth"; a reliance only on dialogue as you read may lead to confusion about the play's action.

It is also important to be aware of action suggested in the dialogue. Some playwrights, either through artistic choice or because of expectations during the period in which they wrote, have kept the use of stage directions to a mini-mum. Elizabethan plays, for example, usually contain few and sometimes cryp-tic stage directions. In such cases it is important for the reader to look for implied stage directions—actions suggested by the dialogue. The "kiss" of the lovers' palms in *Romeo and Juliet* is suggested not in a stage direction but in a verbal exchange. Two sets of twins separated at birth encounter each other for the first time at the end of Shakespeare's *Comedy of Errors.* Their initial shock as each character encounters "himself" is a wonderful visual moment that is only implied by the dialogue.

UNDERSTANDING CULTURAL AND HISTORICAL DIFFERENCES

Because a play is always the product of a particular time and place, certain assumptions were made when the play was written—assumptions about how the play would be produced, who would or would not be reading or seeing

Exploring Collaboration

East and West: *Death of a Salesman* in China

In 1983 playwright Arthur Miller watched the Chinese premiere of *Death of a Salesman* at the Beijing People's Theatre in a production with Chinese actors whom Miller had directed himself. It was an extraordinary cultural and theatrical event. China's arts community was just recovering from the communist government's Cultural Revolution, which had subjected many artists to imprisonment, death, and degradation as well as cutting off any contact with the West. Playwright Cao (or Tsao) Yŭ and director and actor Ying Ruocheng, who had previously visited the United States, had conceived the idea of the Chinese production to bring a classic of Western dramatic literature to a Chinese audience.

Understandably, Miller was at first afraid of disaster. How would such a quintessentially American play communicate to an audience from such a different culture and political system? How could he direct actors when he did not share their language or culture? Intrigued by the prospect, however, Miller agreed. Ying played the role of Willy Loman, the salesman caught in his own mistakes in pursuit of the American dream. An enormous task faced the entire production team: Miller had to learn about and try to communicate with the Chinese; the Chinese had to fit as artists into a foreign universe. The actors had not been trained in the subtle, realistic acting style that the play called for. In the end the production was a resounding success. Miller recorded his last thoughts on leaving China:

At some point in our milling around for our last farewells, for what reason I have no idea, I felt a kind of despair; maybe it was a fear that when all was said and done I could not know what I suppose I had come here to find out—what my play really sounded like to the Chinese, and what in their heart of hearts these actors had made of it. In a word, the old opacity of "China" was once again descending over my vision. I know the audiences laugh in just about the same places as we do in the West, and I have seen many of them weeping for Willy, so maybe my questions don't matter. It is possible that I ought to heed my own advice, given when Chinese would ask in what place the play was happening, since they were not permitted to make up like Westerners: namely, that it all happens in some country of the mind where people with Chinese faces and straight black hair speak and behave as though they were in another civilization. So I will try to console myself with our having met and together created a kind of house, and a family, and a struggle to live, on the plain of imagination where indeed it is possible to share everything we have come to be.[2]

Interested? Check out

Arthur Miller. *Salesman in Beijing.* New York: Viking, 1983, a published account of Miller's remarkable cross-cultural experience, based on a diary he kept during the rehearsal process of *Death of a Salesman* in China.

---

the play, how certain characteristics and ideas would be viewed by the potential audience. Shakespeare's plays change location often and rapidly because he took for granted the use of a flexible, bare stage with minimal set pieces that could be easily changed. His plays were not meant for publication; the only people reading them would be members of his company who were actively involved in the staging and with whom Shakespeare had continuous contact. There was no need for many stage directions; the action would evolve during rehearsal.

The term **convention** refers to an agreement between the production personnel and the audience. A widely used convention in the twenty-first century is the dimming of the house lights, which tells the audience that the performance is about to begin. In seventeenth-century France the house and stage remained fully lit by candles throughout the performance. The audience was called to attention by a theatre employee pounding on the floor with a large staff three times. The fact that characters speak in poetry in some plays is accepted as a convention, as are characters bursting into song (with orchestral accompaniment) in a musical. Different kinds of theatre have different conventions attached to them. In classical Chinese music drama a table becomes a mountain when used as such, and in Noh drama a fan can symbolize many things. Sometimes a playwright or director will establish a convention to work only within a particular play or production. Perhaps there are no doors in the set, but the actors perform as if there were. The audience figures out that the doors exist, even without seeing them.

Conventions are often so much a part of our experience that we don't even think about them. What does it mean to you when on television you see a close-up of an actor's face and his lips are not moving but you hear him speaking? You probably assume that you are hearing his thoughts. You learned this convention at some point in your viewing experience; it seems second nature now.

Conventions change from culture to culture and are developed, modified, and abandoned through time. A Western audience member watching Japanese Kabuki theatre for the first time might be startled to see an actor strike and hold a pose and exaggerated facial expression with his eyes crossed. This pose is a *mie* and is accompanied by a burst of wooden percussion in performance. It is a heightened expression of emotion and exhibits the skill of the actor. Audience members who are familiar with the convention look forward to a *mie* with anticipation and call out to the actor in the midst of performance, encouraging him to sustain the *mie*.

When reading a play, you may be confused at moments because you are unfamiliar with a convention. If you are reading for emotional response and to get a basic sweep of the action, you might want to mark such passages to investigate later. Conventions are sometimes explained in editorial notes, you can ask someone familiar with the period or culture, or you can do some research about theatre of the time period.

Playwrights are often unaware of many cultural assumptions they make while writing a play, since these are so deeply imbedded in the particular culture. The Greeks did not explain the significance of their gods; the Elizabethans did not explain the symbolism of herbs and flowers; the Neoclassicists did not explain contemporary medical procedure; the Japanese did not explain the use of fans. Yet all these made their way into plays that we still read and perform today. Sometimes the audience perception of the play's basic action changes through time. Henrik Ibsen's plays were highly controversial in the late nineteenth century. He could assume that his audience would be shocked by the idea of divorce; Nora's decision to leave her "doll house" was radical, frightening, and, to some, immoral.

Whether you are reading for enjoyment or as preparation for staging a production, a lack of familiarity with the playwright's culture can sometimes cause confusion or even lead to misinterpretation. It often takes extra effort to come to a clear understanding of a play from the past or from a different contemporary culture. The most important tool in interpreting plays from the past or plays from a different culture is an open mind—a realization that physical environment, customs, and values change over time and from place to place. In

♦ **TWELFTH NIGHT,** *by
Shakespeare, a nineteenth-
century production. Mrs. Scott
Siddons plays Viola, a female
character who masquerades as
a male during most of the play.
This is a good example of female-
to-male cross-dressing in which
the femininity of the actress
is soundly preserved.*
By permission of the Folger Shakespeare Library.

seeking a full understanding of any play, we need to consider its place and time of origin. Any background that we can discover in the time we have available will be helpful.

RESEARCH

Often, the easiest way to acquire such background is through introductions and notes provided by editors that share the knowledge of experts in language, literature, and history, often reinforced by significant research. If you embark on your own search, you might look for information on the playwright, the society, and, specifically, the theatre of the time and place. When you learn that Molière himself played the role of Arnolphe and that he, like the character, was enamored with a much younger woman, it gives his play *The School for Wives* (1662) a new dimension. When you know that Shakespeare's female roles were played by young male apprentices, it gives an added level of humor to plays such as *Twelfth Night* (1600–01) and *As You Like It* (1599–1600), in which female characters (who were actually male actors in female costume) disguise themselves as men. When you understand that married women could not own property and had no rights to their children, it makes Nora's decision in *A Doll House* (1879) to leave her family even more frightening and poignant. Without an awareness of the repressive power of the state, it is not possible to understand the fear and paranoia depicted in plays set in Eastern Europe before or during the disintegration of the Soviet Union, such as Caryl Churchill's *Mad Forest* (1990).

An appreciation for the background of a play and the theatrical conventions that were current at the time of its composition will make reading more pleasurable and allow a more informed interpretation. Our reaction will never be exactly like that of the first audience who saw the play, and we might choose not to stick strictly to the conventions of the past, even in our imaginations. To be freed as much as possible from our own (often unconscious) assumptions, however, gives us greater freedom of choice and therefore a wider imaginative scope.

♦ ♦ ♦ ♦ ♦ ♦ ♦ ♦ ♦

Writing about a Play

As part of your study of theatre, you might be asked to write a critical paper that analyzes a play in order to come to a deeper understanding. A work of criticism (as we are using the term) does not necessarily judge the quality of the play (although it may), and it is not just a summary of the action. In a critical paper you are sharing your ideas about how the play works with your reader.

If you find it difficult to begin this kind of project, try the following procedure. After you have finished an initial reading of the play, take notes. Record quickly (not worrying about how it sounds) how the reading made you feel, what it made you think about, what struck you particularly in the play. When you have

Juliet Was a Guy in Drag? Changing Theatrical Conventions

Exploring Historical and Cultural Perspectives

How important are the theatrical conventions with which a play was first produced?

Audiences in the Elizabethan period were used to males performing female roles. Seeing a woman perform in one of Shakespeare's plays would have been shocking to them; such public display by a female was considered inappropriate and dangerous. The tragic heroines of ancient Greece were also performed by men. Juliet, Cleopatra, Beatrice, Ophelia, Cassandra, Hecuba, Clytemnestra—all the great female characters from Elizabethan England and ancient Greece—were first created by male performers.

From the historian's perspective it is fascinating to speculate about how cross-gender casting might have influenced a play's meaning, even though we can never recreate for ourselves the mind-set of the original audience. Because we are used to performers playing characters of the same sex, our response to the convention would be quite different, and use of the original convention might change or distort the meaning of the play. From time to time modern directors have returned to cross-gender casting for classical plays, with both interesting and ludicrous results.

There have also been experiments in reconstructing original stage conditions, settings, and costumes: a replica of the Globe Theatre (as it was understood at any given time) for Shakespeare and his contemporaries, wing and drop scenery for Restoration comedies, the use of masks for Greek tragedy. Learning about historical performance conditions can help us to understand the way a play was meant to work, but each new production must be reconceived for the present audience. Practitioners today do not feel an obligation to reproduce a period's performance conditions. However, research often provides a starting point for design and helps theatre artists to conceive an environment that supports the needs of the text.

Interested? Check out

The National Theatre of Great Britain's production of the *Oresteia* by Aeschylus (including three plays, *Agamemnon, Choephori (The Libation Bearers),* and *Eumenides (The Furies),* English version by Tony Harrison, directed by Peter Hall, 1983 (available on VHS and DVD). The production successfully adapted a number of conventions from Greek tragedy (masks, male actors for female roles, extensive use of the chorus) for a modern audience.

---

cleared your mind onto paper, take a break if possible, and when you come back, look over your notes for correspondences. Which things seem to belong together? What ideas or images seem related or keep recurring? You might want to rewrite and organize your notes.

With these ideas in your mind, read the play again. Look for words and visual images suggested by either dialogue or stage directions that helped to create your feelings or thoughts about the play. How did the playwright create these impressions? What, specifically, made you react in the way you did?

You will need to narrow your discussion of the play, depending on the scope of paper you plan to write. A thorough analysis of all aspects of a play (as a director would do in preparation) would produce quite a long document. If you are writing critical essays for class, it is more likely that you will focus your discussion on one aspect of the play that interests you.

You might examine the play on the basis of structure, character, thought, language, or spectacle or a specific part of one element, such as the use of animal imagery in Shakespeare's *Othello.* You might focus on how one aspect of the play is developed through several different elements (e.g., how the images of death and decay are worked out in the language and spectacle in *Hamlet*). You might do a comparative paper on two plays (e.g., the use of the past in *The Homecoming* and *Fefu and Her Friends*). There are many avenues to reaching a better understanding of a script. Your method of analysis should be chosen to suit the play you are dealing with.

It is often necessary to go beyond your own responses and limited frame of reference to find more information about a play and inform yourself about other people's interpretations. A **critical research paper** must include the ideas of others as well as your own conclusions. The purpose of the research is to aid your understanding of the script. You are presenting your analysis of the play, but the paper should be an informed interpretation, drawing on previously published works. If you are dealing with a well-established play or author, you will need to be selective and deal with the most important sources. For recent or more obscure work you will probably be reading articles in newspapers and periodicals. The ideas of other people that you mention must be clearly documented (with footnotes, endnotes, or parenthetical documentation) so that it is clear which ideas in the paper are your own.

Reading and thinking about plays can be fun and enlightening. When you read actively and imaginatively, a play jumps to life. Comparing that play to others by thinking in terms of genre can lead you to notice interesting things you might have missed before. As a reader of plays, you collaborate with a playwright from the past (whether the play was written two thousand years ago or two months ago) to create present meaning.

◆◆◆◆◆◆◆◆◆

QUESTIONS AND ACTIVITIES

1. Make a list of the four major genres. Think of the plays and films you have seen recently. How would you categorize them according to genre? Explain why you made each choice. Do the same for your favorite films and plays from any period.

2. Make a list of the subtypes of comedy. Take the comedies from your list in Question 1. Decide how you would categorize each play or film and explain why you made the choice.

3. Make a list of current actors whom you have seen recently in a film or play. Do any of these actors tend to specialize in a genre? What qualities make them appropriate for this type of play or film? Which actors seem equally effective in multiple genres?

4. There is a long tradition in theatre and then film of burlesque—making fun of popular genres and subgenres by imitation. Some examples in the theatre are Ludwig Tieck's *Puss in Boots*, Richard Brinsley Sheridan's *The Critic*, and Charles Bush's *Psycho Beach Party* (a play about a type of film). Some examples in film are Mel Brooks's *Space Balls, Blazing Saddles,* and *Young Frankenstein.* Choose one play or film to read or watch. What did the burlesque point out that is true (although usually exaggerated) about the original genre or subtype?

5. Choose a contemporary play and analyze it according to genre. What characteristics does the play share with the traditional genres? If you had to categorize the play, what would you call it? If you feel you could not place the play in a genre, explain why.

6. Identify conventions at work in different types of entertainment events: theatre, film, TV, sports events, rock concerts. What happens if the convention is broken?

KEY TERMS AND CONCEPTS

♦♦♦♦♦♦♦♦♦

FOR FURTHER EXPLORATION

David Ball. *Backwards and Forwards: A Technical Manual for Reading Plays.* Carbondale: Southern Illinois University Press, 1990.

David Scanlan. *Reading Drama.* Mountain View, Calif.: Mayfield, 1988.

James Thomas. *Script Analysis for Actors, Directors, and Designers.* Boston: Focal Press, 1992.

LES MISÉRABLES.
Photo by Joan Marcus.

Producing the Play

Connecting Theatre and Audience

After a play has been analyzed, the visual elements designed and built, and the actors rehearsed, the theatrical production still needs an audience to reach completion. In this chapter we describe the major types of theatre currently available in North America, since these are the forms to which most of our readers have access. We then discuss the work of the producer—the person most responsible for getting the show and the audience together—and the economics of the theatre in the United States, which has a profound effect on the type of theatre available and accessible to the viewing public.

♦♦♦♦♦♦♦♦♦♦

Theatrical Choice in North America

Depending on where you are in North America, you might have many professional shows to choose from on a given night or you might get a chance to see theatre only several times a year when plays are performed at a school. Metropolitan areas tend to have a wide variety of theatre available, but there is usually some kind of theatre in small towns. Although similar categories exist in other areas of the world, the precise nature of theatre produced depends on the traditions of the region as well as performers and funds available. If there is truly no theatre available in your area, you can always make your own!

PROFESSIONAL THEATRE

Professional theatre is created by individuals who make a living (or at least attempt to do so) in the theatre. The professional venue can be commercial or nonprofit, and many theatre artists and technicians work in both. All Broadway and Off-Broadway theatres, touring shows, and major resident theatres are professional. The economic interests of artists and technicians are protected by various unions and guilds that negotiate with the producing organizations.

Commercial theatre is that which is meant to earn a profit for investors. Typically, a commercial company is put together for a specific production. A producer or producing organization finds a show that seems to have great potential for drawing an audience. Financial backing is usually sought beyond the resources of the producers. The hope is that money taken in at the box office and funds from foreign, film, and television rights as well as theme merchandise will at least allow the investors to break even. A long-running hit means that those who are willing to take a chance on the play receive financial reward. Global box-office receipts for the musical *Les Misérables* exceeded $1.8 billion. Sometimes, however, even a failure at the box office can bring financial reward in the form of a tax write-off.

Given the enormous financial risk, producers often look for shows that have been highly successful at an earlier time or in other countries. In the 1980s the blockbuster musicals *Cats, Les Misérables,* and *Phantom of the Opera* were imported from British to American stages. In 1996 *Rent* moved from a successful Off-Broadway production to Broadway.

◆ **CABARET** *has been another commercially successful musical. Here we see "Willkommen," the welcoming song with the emcee and girls of the cabaret. Directed by Sam Mendes; scenic design by Robert Brill; costume design by William Ivey Long.*
Photo by Joan Marcus.

Although commercial theatres can be found in all major metropolitan areas, New York City has a particularly large concentration. The term "Broadway" refers both to a particular area of New York (the theatre district bordered by 41st to 53rd Streets and Sixth to Ninth Avenues) and to the size of the house (some Broadway theatres seat as many as 1,900 patrons). The designation "Off-Broadway" dates from 1955 and refers to theatres with fewer than 500 seats in Manhattan that are not located in the Broadway district.

A successful Broadway show runs as long as it is making money. Companies are also put together for national (and sometimes international) tours. These companies travel across the country taking costumes, scenery, lighting—everything necessary except a space—along with them. Variations of whole-production touring have been occurring in North America since the 1850s, when so-called combination companies took advantage of the new network of railroads. Entire productions with complicated scenery and properties were transported easily and quickly throughout the United States and Canada. Like the old combination companies, modern tours are booked into various theatres, called touring houses, for limited runs and then move on to the next city, thus expanding the audience for any show. Tours of Broadway shows sold more than 15 million tickets in the 1997–98 season—over half of the Broadway industry's total ticket sales.[1] The League of American Theatres and Producers, made up of theatre owners and operators, producers, presenters, and general managers, is the national trade association for the commercial theatre industry. The organization provides support for its members and aims to further the interests of Broadway theatre across North America.[2]

♦ **OUR TOWN,** *by Thornton Wilder in 1938, the first Broadway production in a commercial professional theatre. The famous graveyard scene displays Wilder's simplicity in the midst of a nearly empty theatre. The use of open umbrellas can prove very powerful on stage, and many directors have exploited this device over the last century. Directed by Jed Harris.*
Photo courtesy Billy Rose Theatre Collection, the New York Public Library for the Performing Arts, Astor, Lennox and Tilden Foundations.

Nonprofit theatres may be professional but are not commercial. They share the characteristic that no individual or organization realizes a profit from the investment in production; any money that is taken in at the box office or earned from other sources is funneled back into the arts organization to support other shows and programs. Many theatres are incorporated and approved by the Internal Revenue Service as nonprofit organizations, and donations are therefore tax deductible. Like public radio and television stations, nonprofit theatres rely on annual fund drives, fund-raising events, and numerous grants to survive.

Resident theatres are professional, nonprofit organizations that maintain a constant presence in a community and produce an entire season of plays. These theatres are sometimes called **regional theatres;** the oldest ones were founded in order to establish professional theatre in areas of the country other than New York City, but resident theatres now include professional, nonprofit companies in the New York area as well. Shows are produced with the understanding that they will run for a designated period of time, then will close to make way for the next selection. Typically, resident theatres hire both local artists and those from around the country. Their aim is to produce a balanced season of plays, and they hope to fill as many seats as possible with subscribers (patrons who buy tickets for an entire season of plays rather than individual shows). When the national economy is down, however, season ticket sales often decline while individual sales rise. Resident theatres often maintain a multitheatre complex and run several seasons of shows simultaneously. Arena Stage in Washington, D.C., for example, offers shows in the 827-seat Fichandler Stage, the 514-seat Kreeger Theater, and a flexible, intimate performance space known as the Old Vat Room. Resident theatres offer outreach programs to further integrate the theatre with

♦ **OUR TOWN**, *by Thornton Wilder, as produced at La Jolla Playhouse, a professional resident theatre in 2001, more than sixty years after the original. In stark contrast to the original production, the stage manager confronts Emily in the graveyard scene. Here, the role of the Stage Manager is played by Lizan, an African American woman, rather than the traditional white man. Emily is played by Emily Bergl. Directed by Michael Greif.*
Photo by Russell Caldwell.

the local community, including classes, performances for local schools, play development series, after-show discussions, and tours.

The League of Resident Theatres (LORT) provides support for its members, particularly in communicating with the federal government and by serving as a collective bargaining agent with the various employee unions.[3] The LORT membership includes such theatres as the Shakespeare Theatre (Washington, D.C.), the Guthrie Theatre (Minneapolis), the Alliance Theatre Company (Atlanta), and the Mark Taper Forum (Los Angeles). The analogous organization for English-speaking theatre in Canada is the Professional Association of Canadian Theatres (PACT).[4] Theatre Communications Group (TCG) serves nonprofit theatres in the United States by publishing books, providing employment services, awarding grants, and conducting research on finances and practices.[5]

AMATEUR THEATRE

The designation **amateur theatre** is used when the practitioners do not rely on theatrical activity for their livelihood. Amateur theatres exist for many reasons and come in all shapes and sizes. Such productions may range from highly polished and imaginative work to efforts in which the emphasis is on recreation and camaraderie rather than a finished product. Typically, amateur theatres are nonprofit organizations that combine box-office receipts with grants and other fund-raising to continue serving their clientele. Although all or most of the labor is volunteer, the expense of maintaining or renting a space, building sets and costumes, and providing the technical aspects of production is considerable.

Exploring Collaboration

New Audience Initiatives: The Cleveland Play House

Among those who work in and support the theatre, there is great concern over the "graying" of the American audience. As younger generations grow up with computer games, video games, videos, and DVDs at their fingertips, the average live theatre audience member seems to get older and older. Many professional resident theatres are working to turn this tendency around by incorporating new audience initiatives into their programs and by collaborating with schools and social service organizations.

The Cleveland Play House (a resident theatre) has an impressive array of educational activities. In its statement of commitment to education the Play House cites a study from UCLA that showed that arts education had a positive effect on academic achievement. Besides a variety of classes and workshops for teens and adults as well as children, the Cleveland Play House offers the Children's Theatre, performing on Saturday and Sunday afternoons. Elementary schools are offered a three-play season at the Play House, and special morning matinees of the adult mainstage productions are attended by middle and senior high school students. In addition, the Literature Alive! series presents a play based on great narrative writing or a curriculum subject to middle and senior high schools. The Play House offers student talk-back sessions with performers, backstage tours, and study guides, as well as inviting teachers to preview any production free of charge.

As part of its Urban Initiatives, the Cleveland Play House collaborates with the Cleveland Municipal School District/Project ACT to offer the Reading Company literacy program. Homeless families from shelters visit the Cleveland Play House to see a children's book dramatized by students from the Cleveland School of the Arts. With the help of the local schools and other organizations, the Cleveland Play House offers the Early Learning Initiative to preschools and the Reading Family, a series of classes and a workshop to develop better parenting and improve reading skills.

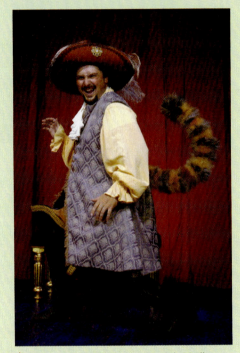

♦ **PUSS IN BOOTS**, by Eric Schmiedl, Cleveland Play House. The cat (Boots) is played by James Mango. This production is part of the outreach program of the Cleveland Play House, doing plays for children and youth.
Courtesy of Cleveland Play House.

Interested? Check out

The Cleveland Play House web site, www.clevelandplayhouse.com.

Educational theatre may be extracurricular or integrated into classroom structure. On the primary- and secondary-school levels, dramatic activity is used to develop student skills and widen interests. The Educational Theatre Association (ETA) serves as an advocate for theatre education as well as rewarding excellence in student work.[6] Theatre programs in colleges and universities add to these goals the possibility of professional training for students as well as the opportunity to offer a wide range of viewing possibilities to the local community. At many schools students may pursue a Bachelor of Arts degree with a major in theatre; some schools offer a Bachelor of Fine Arts with additional credit hours devoted to professional training. Graduate work in performance, playwriting, design, or technical theatre leads to the Master of Fine Arts degree and, in some schools, a Doctor of Fine Arts. Resident theatres often collaborate with colleges and universities to provide internships for students completing professional training programs. Students who are interested in the history, theory, criticism, and literature of the theatre may study for the Master of Arts and Doctor of Philosophy degrees. The Association for Theatre in Higher Education (ATHE) promotes excellence in theatre education and actively supports scholarship through teaching, research, and practice.[7]

Community theatre is created by residents of a particular area who come together to create theatre without being part of a larger institution. Such theatres tend to focus on the quality of experience for the practitioners, and audience members tend to be family and friends. Plays are often chosen with local appeal and satisfactory roles for available performers in mind and tend to be fairly traditional. Comedies and musicals, for example, are perennial favorites. Community theatres may specialize in producing for a special audience (children, for example) or involve a particular type of community member in performance (seniors, veterans, women). The American Association of Community Theatre (AACT) exists to help such theatres across the country provide challenging artistic opportunities and contribute to their communities.[8]

◆ *JESUS CHRIST SUPERSTAR,* Lincoln Community Playhouse, Lincoln, Nebraska. *Directed by Robin McKercher; set design by Brenda Sabatka; costume design by Cate Wieck; lighting design by Renee Tuchscher.* Courtesy of Robin McKercher.

◆ **THE TIME OF YOUR LIFE,** *by William Saroyan, revived by the Steppenwolf Theatre in Chicago in 2002. This theatre company is famous for ensemble acting as is suggested by this group shot at the bar. Most of the action of this large-cast play requires carefully crafted and sensitive interaction of many actors at once. Most of the characters are lost, lonely souls. Directed by Tina Landau.*
Photo by Michael Brosilow.

HYBRID THEATRES

Many theatres do not fit neatly into either the "professional" or "amateur" category; for our purposes we will use the term **hybrid theatres.** Small resident theatres may hold a contract with Actors' Equity (the union in the United States for actors and stage managers) that allows the hiring of both union and nonunion performers. Summer stock theatres may hire well-trained students and experienced community members for seasonal work. Students who have recently graduated often form their own nonunion companies, holding down "day jobs" to support themselves while investing energy and time in rehearsal and performance at night. The designation "semiprofessional" is sometimes used for companies that aspire to professional status but currently are not well established enough to maintain the payroll of a professional theatre. The dedication of these artists may produce exciting shows even though the performers are not technically "professional." For example, the young actors who formed Chicago's Steppenwolf Theatre Company in 1974 and began performing plays in a church basement were committed to developing a strong ensemble while taking artistic risks.[9] The exciting productions of Steppenwolf launched the stage and film careers of Terry Kinney (b. 1954), John Malkovich (b. 1953), and Gary Sinise (b. 1955). The company is now professional and boasts a subscription base of over 25,000.

The term "Off-off-Broadway" was coined in the 1960s in New York to identify performances that occurred outside the traditional theatre spaces of Broadway and Off-Broadway. Such work was typically experimental and often occurred in alternative spaces—coffeehouses, church basements, warehouses, and private homes. As part of the 1960s counterculture, Off-off-Broadway rejected the "establishment" theatre and sought to cross both social and artistic boundaries. Today, the term "Off-off-Broadway" is used to refer to professional or semi-professional performances that are not Equity. Performance runs tend to be limited and may occur only a few days a week. Production quality varies widely, but this type of small theatre can offer innovative, unusual artistic experiences. Although the term "Off-off-Broadway" originated in New York, this kind of theatre may exist anywhere. Such theatres in Chicago are known as "off-Loop" and in Los Angeles as "Equity waiver."

Omaha, Nebraska, was the home of an unusual variation. As veterans of Off-off-Broadway from the 1960s, Megan Terry and Jo Ann Schmidman brought a nontraditional approach to the Omaha Magic Theatre. Omaha Magic was known for nontraditional performance techniques and for developing and producing new works that addressed current social and political issues, from women's experiences in prison (*Babes in the Big House*, 1979) to adult literacy (*Headlights*, 1989) to self-censorship (*Body Leaks*, 1990).

◆◆◆◆◆◆◆◆◆◆
The Role of the Producer

The person who is most responsible for getting an audience and show together is the **producer**—the person in charge of all financial aspects of production. In nonprofit theatres the job title is often **managing director.** Whatever the title, the producer must collaborate with theatre artists as well as the general public. The job requires finely developed organizational and persuasive skills as well as a thorough understanding of finance. Producing responsibilities may be taken on by one person, or they may be shared by a group.

PRODUCING IN COMMERCIAL THEATRE

An independent commercial production such as a Broadway or Off-Broadway show typically begins with a producer. This position has a long history, but the current commercial producer is often based on a nineteenth-century model. In the late nineteenth century producer-directors such as Augustin Daly and David Belasco created powerful organizations dedicated to careful, detailed single productions of plays that were intended to turn a profit. By 1898 a collection of businessmen who were not artists organized the Theatrical Syndicate to control haphazard professional touring and did so very effectively. The Syndicate, however, also created a monopoly with theatre ownership and control of actors and playwrights, who were not as yet organized as a union or guild. The monopoly was broken in 1915 but was replaced by a rival organization, the Shubert Brothers, which created its own monopoly. Through government action and internal reform, the monopolies are long gone, but the role of the producer as a nonartistic agent of oversight and fiscal responsibility is still very much in place. A Shubert Organization still produces plays and operates theatres, but it is one of many, including the very successful Nederlander Producing Company.

A commercial producer finds a play. Sometimes a playwright or director working on a script actively seeks out a producer. If the producer believes in the

ARTISTS of the THEATRE

HAROLD PRINCE

The most famous producers in theatre history have also worked as artists, usually as directors. As both producer and director, **HAROLD PRINCE** (b. 1928) has had a powerful influence on American theatre, particularly the musical. He began coproducing shows at an early age for the legendary director George Abbott, including the very popular *The Pajama Game* (1954) and *Damn Yankees* (1955). In 1957 he coproduced *West Side Story,* a musical reworking of the Romeo and Juliet tale. The show was directed and choreographed by Jerome Robbins, was later turned into a film, and has become a favorite musical to revive in both professional and amateur venues.

In the 1960s Prince produced some of the decade's most successful musicals, including *A Funny Thing Happened on the Way to the Forum* (1962), which was inspired by ancient Roman comedy, and *Fiddler on the Roof* (1964), the story of a Jewish ghetto in Russia. He began directing in the 1960s as well and in 1966 both produced and directed *Cabaret,* which follows the loosely woven story of the romance between a nightclub singer and a writer in 1930s Germany. The basic story, however, is intercut with scenes set in the nightclub or cabaret, during which the performers dance and sing, not to advance the story but to depict the decadence of German society and creeping influence of Nazism. Prince's production was surprising not only for the ultimate seriousness of its subject matter but also for the highly presentational (not realistic) style of the cabaret sequences. The set (designed by Boris Aronson) featured a mirror that reflected and distorted a view of the audience, encouraging a link to be drawn between the degeneracy of 1930s Germany and contemporary America.

In the 1970s Prince teamed up with composer and lyricist Stephen Sondheim to break new ground in musical theatre. In 1970 Prince produced and directed *Company,* which was widely acknowledged as the best example to date of a concept musical—one that was organized more by theme than story. *Company* evolved from related playlets about marriage. Boris Aronson designed a chromium and glass set, complete with working elevators. Both the look of the show and the blend of music and dialogue to investigate human psychology and relationships were startling at the time.

Company was followed by *Follies* (with Stephen Sondheim, 1971) produced by Prince and codirected with Michael Bennett (who later went on to direct *A Chorus Line,* 1975). Inspired by a picture of actress Gloria Swanson standing in the remains of a demol- ished theatre, *Follies* depicts the reunion of two aging showgirls, their husbands, and a theatrical impresario in a theatre about to be demolished. The past is explored through song and dialogue and represented visually by ghostly apparitions of the female characters' younger selves. Prince's production was a visual feast, featuring a massive set and extravagant costumes. It was a financial failure, losing $665,000, perhaps suggesting poor decisions on the part of Prince as a producer. Prince, Bennett, and many who saw it, however, considered *Follies* an artistic triumph. The production has become legendary among musical theatre buffs.

Prince directed and recovered his reputation as a producer with *A Little Night Music* (1973), an elegant, bittersweet comedy about sexual role-playing, based on the film *Smiles of a Summer Night* (1955) by Ingmar Bergman. His next collaboration with Sondheim again broke new ground. *Pacific Overtures* (1976) told the story of the opening of Japan to the West, focusing on the subsequent erosion of Asian tradition. The cast was all-Asian (a rarity in the United States at that time). Prince incorporated traditional Japanese Kabuki theatre techniques in staging. The production again was a financial failure but, like *Follies,* is now believed to have been

play and thinks it likely to make a profit, he or she may secure production rights to the play. Money must then be raised to cover the cost of staging the production. Many backers may be brought on board, each contributing a significant amount, to fund the preproduction work. Backers must be convinced that the show is likely to run long enough to earn back the initial outlay. The producer must find both rehearsal and performance space. Some modern producing organizations own their own theatres, but many rent available commercial spaces. The producer hires (and can fire) all personnel connected with the show but normally collaborates with the director in engaging leading actors and designers. Negotiations must take place with different unions for each aspect of pro-

ahead of its time and is considered an artistic milestone.

Prince directed but did not produce the Sondheim show *Sweeney Todd: The Demon Barber of Fleet Street* in 1979. The piece is a musical thriller featuring extremely complex music by Sondheim. The story was taken from another unusual source: an adaptation of a nineteenth century British melodrama about a barber who kills his patrons and sends the bodies to a woman who bakes them into pies.

Another important Prince contribution from the 1970s (without Sondheim) was the revival of *Candide* (1974). The musical had failed in the 1950s; believing that the show would be more successful if it were truer to the original novel (by the eighteenth-century writer Voltaire), Prince contacted the artists of the 1950s version and received their permission to remake the musical. Prince directed the revised version at the small Chelsea Theater Center in Brooklyn. The Chelsea then produced the play on Broadway in conjunction with Prince. Broadway traditionalists were again shocked by the renovation of the Broadway Theatre to accommodate environmental staging (intermingling audience and actors without a clear separation of space), but the energetic production won a following.

In his autobiography, *Contradictions: Notes on Twenty-Six Years in the Theatre* (1974), Prince tells of the excruciating process of moving *Candide* from the small, nonprofit theatre seating 180 to the larger Broadway house. Because of environmental staging, the theatre could seat only 900 (a small number for Broadway). Prince and others on behalf of the show petitioned the Musicians Local 802, the union for stage musicians, three times, asking to be allowed to employ only thirteen musicians—the number used at the Chelsea. According to union regulations, twenty-five was the minimum number for Broadway shows. The request was denied, but the production could not afford to reorchestrate the show. In the end, twenty-five musicians were on the payroll; eighteen performed, and the other seven sat in the basement. The *Candide* story (as well as many others throughout the book) illustrates the enormous frustrations often encountered by producers in the theatre.

Prince went on to direct (but did not produce) two blockbuster musicals from the British composer Andrew Lloyd Webber: *Evita,* which opened on Broadway in 1979, and *Phantom of the Opera,* which opened on Broadway in 1988 and was still running in 2003, having logged over 6,000 performances. In 1993 Prince directed *Kiss of the Spider Woman,* and in 1994 he opened a stunning revival of *Show Boat* on Broadway. Prince has continued directing (with some producing) and opened *Bounce,* a new collaboration with Stephen Sondheim and John Weidman, in 2003 at the Goodman Theatre in Chicago.

At last count Prince had been awarded twenty Tony awards for Broadway productions. His collaborations with other gifted artists have changed the face of the American musical numerous times, and his career is a fascinating study of the tensions of artistic versus financial decisions in the theatre. Although Prince began in commercial theatre, he now (like most theatre artists) tends to develop new works at resident theatres before subjecting his shows to the high-stakes world of Broadway.

Interested? Check out

Carol Ilson. *Harold Prince: A Director's Journey.* New York: Limelight Editions, 2000.
See the Internet Broadway Database, http://ibdb.com (maintained by the League of American Theatres and Producers), for a complete list of credits for the shows mentioned above.

duction. The producer must weigh the cost of talent needed to produce a fine show against the need to keep the production costs as low as possible.

The producer hires the show's director. Although most artistic control rests with the director, the producer controls the purse strings and therefore maintains a certain amount of artistic power. The producer is answerable to the backers and so must try to keep the production within budget as well as meeting payroll and keeping adequate financial records. Ultimately responsible for creating an audience for the show, the producer oversees marketing and publicity. In commercial theatre the producer typically works with a public relations firm. Marketing and publicity include designing and distributing posters and

♦ *HEDDA GABLER, by Henrik Ibsen. Kate Burton, as Hedda, holds her father's pistol. Notice the contrast with warm lighting in the library upstage and cold lighting in the room in which Hedda handles the pistol. Directed by Nicholas Martin; scenic design by Alexander Dodge; lighting design by Kevin Adams. Huntington Theatre Company, Boston.*
Photo by Charlie Erickson.

billboards, writing and distributing news releases and direct mail campaigns, producing TV and radio commercials, and serving as a liaison with the media.

Tony Awards (Broadway) and Obie Awards (Off-Broadway) for an entire show are presented to the producers, since they are the ones who get the ball rolling in the commercial arena. In their book *The Producers: How We Did It* (2001), Mel Brooks and Tom Meehan include an entertaining account of getting producers and artists together to launch their remarkably successful musical.

PRODUCING IN NONPROFIT THEATRE

In nonprofit theatre the managing director usually works closely with the **artistic director,** who is responsible for the theatre's artistic mission. This team must focus on the continuity of the organization rather than a specific show. Casting and design choices must take the entire season into consideration, and although all shows will have a particular budget assigned, the entire season must stay within a larger budget as well. Along with taking care of publicity and marketing, an audience development staff may also coordinate special outreach programs to bring in new audience members and to help current patrons stay involved in the life of the theatre. Tickets are often sold at reduced rates to large groups, special backstage tours are arranged, guest speakers are provided for group functions, and special promotions may be offered for specific shows or days of the week.

Periodically, productions from resident or summer theatres move into commercial houses. The successful revival of the 1963 play *One Flew over the Cuckoo's Nest,* with Gary Sinise and directed by Terry Kinney, began at the Steppenwolf Theatre Company in Chicago in 2000 and moved to Broadway in 2001. Nonprofit theatres sometimes collaborate on a production, continuing development at each presentation and sometimes moving the play to a commercial venue. In this way the production is given a wider audience, and the theatres share the cost of development as well as increased national visibility and potentially any profits from the commercial run. *Hedda Gabler* (2001), with Kate Burton and directed by Nicholas Martin, began at Williamstown Theatre Festival in Massachusetts. When a production moves, the originating theatre may become one of the commercial producers mounting the venture. In the case of *Hedda Gabler* the production began at Williamstown but was also developed at the Bay Street Theatre in Sag Harbor, New York, and the Huntington Theatre Company in Boston before opening on Broadway. All theatres were listed as producers. The artistic director at Huntington became the Broadway director of record.

PRODUCING IN AMATEUR THEATRE

In amateur theatre the producing duties are often shared by a number of people. In a large educational theatre department or community theatre, producing may be primarily the responsibility of an administrator (the department chairperson, for example, or an executive director). In those theatres the producer's major concern is for the overall health of the organization. In smaller theatres the duties are assumed by a number of people, many of whom may be volunteers. Working on publicity, fund-raising, or public relations committees is a way for people with strong organizational and communication skills to support the theatre.

♦♦♦♦♦♦♦♦♦♦
The Economics of Theatre

The live nature of theatre creates one of its biggest challenges: financing. A film can be copied thousands of times and distributed to movie theatres, video stores, and private homes; it begins earning its money once the creative work is complete. A theatrical performance, however, must be recreated every night for a particular audience. The show needs its actors, technicians, and other staff until it closes. Unlike film, the product cannot be resold; it is intangible and cannot be held in the hand but constantly must be created anew. Consequently, the immediacy of the theatrical experience sometimes comes at a high price.

PRODUCTION COSTS

In amateur theatre the initial outlay for a production includes a royalty fee paid to the playwright, the cost of materials for sets and costumes, the cost of technical equipment that must be purchased or rented, advertising costs, as well as the salaries of professional staff hired to lead and guide the volunteers. In addition, a professional production must pay all company members: directors, designers, technicians, actors, ticket sellers, and others, most of whom are unionized. Any organization that has its own space must pay for upkeep and repairs as well as all utilities. A show with no home base will need to pay the owner of the performance space for its use.

Not surprisingly, professional theatre is expensive, especially in first-run houses in cities such as New York and Chicago, where property values and taxes are exorbitant. The owner of a theatre must pay taxes and upkeep on the building whether or not the theatre is empty or the current show is successful at the box office. In rented spaces this expense is passed on to the show's producers and ultimately to the audience.

Since the early twentieth century, production costs have escalated much faster than the rate of inflation. In the 1920s most first-run professional productions of Broadway plays could be staged for about $10,000 to $20,000, but many were done for much less. A typical outlay for a non-musical with three or more sets was about $14,000. *The Straw,* a failure by Eugene O'Neill in 1921, closed after twenty performances, but the producer George Tyler lost only $9,000 on the venture.[10] In the early twenty-first century, however, even a simple, single-set show with two or three actors can cost from $800,000 to $1 million to get to opening night on Broadway (the most expensive of the professional venues). Emanuel Azenberg, lead producer for the 1999 revival of *The Iceman Cometh,* estimated that it would cost approximately $5 million to present this relatively large-cast but single-set show on Broadway for thirteen weeks, including an estimated $1.5 million to open the show and $3.25 million to keep it running.[11] Musicals are even more expensive to produce, because of typically large casts, multiple sets, hundreds of costumes, more extravagant lighting, and payment for extra personnel: music director, composer, lyricist, choreographer. The musical *The Full Monty* (2000) reportedly cost $7 million to stage, and *Aida* (2000) cost at least $15 million. Theatres in smaller cities with lower overheads still struggle with climbing production costs. Seventy-seven nonprofit theatres that participated in a Theatre Communications Group survey reported that total expenses grew by 35.6 percent from 1997 to 2001, while earned income only increased by 18.4 percent.[12]

A hit show, particularly a musical (which tends to tour more extensively than a spoken word play), can be extremely lucrative. By 1997, when *Cats* set the record for the longest-running Broadway show, it had been seen by an estimated eight million people on Broadway and fifty million worldwide and had sold 390,000 T-shirts, 130,000 sweatshirts, and 1.14 million souvenir books.[13] When it closed on Broadway in September 2000, it had played 7,485 performances over eighteen years. When *Les Misérables* closed on Broadway in 2003, it had played 6,612 performances over sixteen years and had been seen by nine million people. Worldwide, the show has been seen by over fifty million people and has been produced in thirty-four countries in twenty different languages.[14]

Unfortunately, most theatrical productions do not earn a profit. A more likely scenario is for a show to close before it has time to recoup the producers' original investment. Perhaps the most infamous Broadway flop is the musical *Carrie,* based on the novel by Stephen King, which closed after only five performances in 1988 and lost $8 million.

EFFECT ON TYPES OF PLAYS PRODUCED

Because of prohibitive production costs, many commercial producers are hesitant to invest money in a show that might close quickly, so they opt for what they believe will prove to be a major box-office draw. The result has been a narrowing of material on Broadway and other commercial venues to mostly safe plays that are likely to appeal to a mass audience. Large-cast, spoken word plays are very difficult to get produced, since the chances are great that the show will not earn a profit and might not even break even. Producers sometimes sign on recognizable film and television actors (who also may have extensive stage experience) in an attempt to ensure full houses, but this practice often limits the show's run. The 1999 revival of *The Iceman Cometh,* for example, counteracted the financial liability of a large cast by featuring Kevin Spacey in the leading role. The run was limited to thirteen weeks because of Spacey's film commitments. In the 1920s it was not uncommon for an amateur production to catch the attention of critics and find itself in a Broadway house within the year. The Provincetown Players, for example, staged the first productions of the modern classics *The Emperor Jones* (1920) and *The Hairy Ape* (1922) by Eugene O'Neill in a converted stable in Greenwich Village, seating only about two hundred people, yet both productions moved into Broadway houses less than two months after opening. Such a move is inconceivable in today's high-stakes entertainment world.

In effect, commercial theatre tends to consist of musicals (which, if successful, produce a high return on investment), comedies, and the occasional

♦ **THE HAIRY APE,** by Eugene O'Neill, in a multimedia production by the Wooster Group in 1995. Actors, left to right, are Roy Faudree (on monitor), Willem Dafoe, and Scott Renderer.
Photo by Paula Court.

unusual serious play (usually with one set and a small cast) that has proven successful in other venues. *Proof* (2000), for example, a four-character show with one set, opened on Broadway and played successfully after performances at the Manhattan Theatre Club. *Frankie and Johnny in the Claire de Lune,* a show with one set and a cast of two, also had a successful run at the Manhattan Theatre Club in 1987 and was revived on Broadway in 2002. For the most part, production of pre–twentieth century dramatic literature presents too high a risk in the commercial world and is carried on by resident theatres and educational theatres. Artistic experimentation happens in resident and educational theatres as well as Off-off-Broadway and some nontraditional companies scattered across North America but is increasingly difficult to fund. Nonprofit theatres find that programming traditional crowd-pleasers is important if they are to bring in the funds to keep the theatre functioning. In difficult economic times the number of such shows that are necessary to pay the expenses often crowds out more difficult, but often exciting, work.

THEATRE FUNDING

A dependence on box office receipts severely limits the options available for an audience. Many important, thought-provoking plays have been artistic but not commercial successes. In many European countries theatres are subsidized by the government as cultural institutions of equal importance with art galleries, museums, and libraries. Government funding for the arts has been more difficult to sustain in the United States. Founded in 1965, the **National Endowment for the Arts (NEA),** an independent agency of the federal

Exploring Historical and Cultural Perspectives

The Federal Theatre Project

During the height of the Great Depression the federal government created the Works Progress Administration, which in turn developed many thousands of jobs in a variety of sectors using federal funds. One of these sectors was the **Federal Theatre Project (FTP),** a nationwide effort representing the first time that the U.S. government directly subsidized theatre (an idea that was controversial then and continues to be as Congress regularly challenges decisions of the National Endowment for the Arts).

Between 1935 and 1939 thousands of theatre artists were taken off the relief rolls in some forty states and put to work creating new plays, unusual productions of classic plays, children's theatre, Yiddish and African American companies—all with inexpensive ticket prices. Some of these productions were dynamic experiments such as Orson Welles's production of *Doctor Faustus* (1937) and the all-black production of Gilbert and Sullivan entitled *The Swing Mikado* (1939). Some were tough examinations of widespread poverty, such as *One-Third of a Nation* (1938), and at times they were critical of government policies, such as *Triple-A Plowed Under* (1936). In a remarkable national project, an antifascist play by Sinclair Lewis entitled *It Can't Happen Here* (1936) was produced simultaneously by at least twenty-one companies in as many cities from coast to coast.

In 1937, reacting to rumors that some new plays were highly critical of the government, federal authorities, often in distress over content in previous FTP productions, announced an immediate halt to all new productions for two months. The now famous musical *The Cradle Will Rock* (1937) was just about to open. Finding their theatre padlocked, the actors rebelled against federal authorities by staging the play anyway without an orchestra or settings or any technical support in an empty theatre. The only accompaniment was the composer Marc Blitzstein at a piano. From this rebellion emerged the experimental Mercury Theatre, headed by Orson Welles and John Houseman. This event is memorialized in the 1999 Tim Robbins film, *Cradle Will Rock*. Although FTP continued to operate beyond *Cradle,* the House Un-American Activities Committee began hearings on FTP in 1938, and by June 1939, Congress had pulled the plug on the Federal Theatre Project, calling it left-wing and a haven for communists.

Interested? Check out

John O'Connor and Lorraine Brown. *Free, Adult, and Uncensored: The Living History of the Federal Theatre Project.* Washington, D.C.: New Republic, 1978.

Hallie Flanagan. *Arena.* New York: Limelight, 1969.

government, "serves the public good by nurturing human creativity, supporting community spirit, and fostering appreciation of the excellence and diversity of our nation's artistic accomplishments."[15] As the largest single funder of nonprofit arts organizations in the United States, the NEA supports arts education and preservation as well as the development of new projects. Although the NEA's budget is quite small in comparison to other government expenditures—almost $105 million in 2001, costing each American less than 37 cents per year—the Endowment has been frequently attacked for its grants to artists whose work is objectionable to some segments of the taxpaying public. Since the 1950s nonprofit theatres have increasingly sought corporate sponsorship to help with escalating production costs. This financial contribution might take the form of underwriting a season of plays, a specific production, or even an actor's performance. Not surprisingly, corporate gifts evaporate quickly in a slow economy.

Two Audience Studies

Two studies provide valuable information on audience demographics for two particular segments of the theatre audience in North America. The League of American Theatres and Producers conducted a study of the audience for touring Broadway shows in the United States and Canada during the 1999–2000 season. The study found that the audience for touring Broadway shows was 68 percent female. The average age was forty-eight; 67 percent of audience members under age twenty-five had graduated from college, and 28 percent had earned a graduate degree. The average annual household income was $81,800. The finding that the audience for touring Broadway was largely female, educated, and affluent suggests that continued outreach programs are critical if theatre is to reach a more diverse audience. On a brighter note, the same study indicated that the number of theatregoers under age eighteen grew from 1.3 percent in 1990–1991 to 4.5 percent in 1999–2000.

A second study, authorized by the Theatre Development Fund and League of American Theatres and Producers, was conducted on the audiences of Broadway and Off-Broadway (in New York City) for the 1997–1998 season and indicated a more ethnically diverse younger audience. From 4.9 percent of the total audience in 1966, theatregoers under twenty years of age made up 13.9 percent during the 1997 season. In the eighteen- to twenty-four-year-old range, Asian, Hispanic, and African American individuals made up 20 percent of the Broadway audience and 25.4 percent of the Off-Broadway audience. The report clearly showed that early exposure to the theatre with school classes and families was important to the development of young audiences.

Interested? Check out

League of American Theatres and Producers. "The Audience for Touring Broadway: A Demographic Study 2000." www.livebroadway.com/audiencetour-2000/audience.html.
Theatre Development Fund. "1998 New York Theatre Audience Study." www.tdf.org/information/pressreleases/wachtelrelease.htm.

EFFECT ON THE AUDIENCE

Rapidly rising production costs have driven ticket prices up. In 1920 the highest-priced Broadway ticket for spoken word productions was $2.00. Musicals usually charged no more than $2.50 per ticket. By the end of the economic boom of the 1920s the top price was still usually under $4.00. By contrast, a ticket to a Broadway show in 2002 might range from a low of $20–40 (for weekdays and less desirable seats) to a high of $75–100 (for weekends and better seats). Even non-profit theatres find themselves passing unsubsidized costs on to the consumer. A theatregoer in 2002 might expect to pay anywhere from a low of $15–32 to a high of $44–60 to see a show at a major resident theatre. When you read this, ticket costs may be even higher.

A regrettable byproduct of high ticket prices is a narrowing of the potential audience to those individuals with disposable income. An awareness of the prohibitive nature of ticket prices has led to a number of steps, even in commercial venues, to make tickets affordable to a wider audience. The Theatre Development Fund (TDF), a nonprofit organization dedicated to supporting new productions and broadening the audience for the performing arts, offers discount

programs to increase the number of potential theatre-goers in New York City. Its popular "TKTS" booth in Times Square, for example, sells Broadway and Off-Broadway day-of-show admissions at 25–50 percent reductions. TDF also sponsors a voucher program for more experimental productions in out-of-the-way spaces to encourage adventurous theatregoing.[16] The producers of *Rent* (a 1996 show about young, poor artists in New York City) reserved the first row of seats for students at reduced prices, both during its Broadway run and on tour. Many nonprofit theatres offer discounted tickets to students and senior adults. "Student rush" lets young people into the theatre close to opening time at a reduced price, and many nonprofit theatres allow volunteer ushers to see shows free of charge.

Still, the cost of professional theatre (whether commercial or nonprofit) makes it unavailable to many people. How can live theatre be made more accessible to a wider audience? The question is difficult, but answering it will be vital to the theatre's future.

THEATRE AND THE COMMUNITY

Besides the more intangible contributions that theatre can make to a community, studies have shown that a lively arts scene is healthy for a city's economy. Theatre audience members tend to patronize restaurants and bars, parking facilities, and public transportation. By 1997 *Cats* had contributed an estimated $3.12 billion to New York City's economy.[17] According to a study released in 2002, the nonprofit arts

Exploring Collaboration

The New 42nd Street

Perhaps the most dynamic example of the role of theatre in urban renaissance is the collaboration of government, artists, and corporate America to renovate the Times Square area of New York City. **The New 42nd Street,** Inc. is a nonprofit development corporation created by New York City and State to revive theatres and the area around them as new construction appeared. In the decrepit neighborhood of Times Square, filled with X-rated movie theatres and seedy retail shops, New 42nd Street renovated the old Theatre Republic built in 1900 by Oscar Hammerstein (father of the lyricist Oscar Hammerstein II). After having much of the original decoration restored and state-of-the-art technical facilities installed, the theatre opened in 1995 as the New Victory, a theatre dedicated to children and families. The unprecedented success of the New Victory served as the catalyst for continued renovation. Disney chairman Michael Eisner negotiated a deal including low-interest loans from the city and state to cover 75 percent of the restoration of the New Amsterdam Theatre, which became the home of *The Lion King* in 1997. The old Lyric and Apollo theatres were turned into the Ford Center for the Performing Arts, and the Selwyn became the American Airlines Theater for the Roundabout Theater Company.

Besides finding new uses for old theatres and creating approximately 5,000 new seats for live theatre, the New 42nd Street opened a ten-story, 84,000-square-foot facility featuring fourteen badly needed rehearsal studios for the performing arts community as well as office space for non-profit cultural organizations, and a 200-seat theatre. Critics of the development project have lamented the homogenization (or "Disneyfication") of the area and the increasing role of big business in the arts. Supporters point out that the crime rate in Times Square has dropped even faster than that in surrounding areas and that the success of the theatres generated interest from hotel and retail companies. Governor George E. Pataki celebrated the revival of Times Square as a premier tourist destination.[19] Cora Cahan, President of the New 42nd Street, noted that in this case the arts led the way: Renovation of the New Victory helped to stimulate and guide development of the entire block.[20]

Interested? Check out

Robin Pogrebin. "From Naughty to Bawdy to Stars Reborn; Once Seedy Theaters, Now Restored Lead the Development of 42nd Street," *New York Times,* December 11, 2000, www.42ndstreetbroadway.com/press_nytimes_12_11_00.htm.

Bruce Handy. "Miracle on 42nd Street," *Time* 149, no. 14 (April 7, 1997), www.time.com/time/archive/preview/from_search/0,10987,1101970407=137500,00.html.

Mary C. Henderson. *The New Amsterdam: The Biography of a Broadway Theatre.* New York: Hyperion, 1997.

---

industry in the United States (including all the arts, not theatre exclusively) "generates $134 billion in economic activity every year, including $24.4 billion in federal, state, and local tax revenues." Furthermore, 4.85 million full-time equivalent jobs are created.[18] Performance events serve as major tourist attractions and can even be a part of urban renovation designed to bring people back to the city after working hours.

The relationship between any society and its theatre is complex and ever changing. A frequently repeated argument for arts funding is that societies of the past speak to us today mainly through the works of art that they left behind. Theatre leaves only clues—but important ones: play scripts; reviews; theatre buildings (whole or in ruins); personal accounts in letters, diaries, and periodicals; stories handed down by word of mouth; paintings; and, more recently, photographs and videos. The reconstruction of theatre from the past gives us a fascinating perspective on the culture that produced it. Theatre in the present serves its community in many ways. No matter what the venue, no matter what the ticket price, it can serve as a vibrant means of human communication.

The interrelationship of the theatre and its society is sometimes most poignantly illustrated during difficult times. In the wake of the attacks on September 11, 2001, potential audience members sought comfort in their own homes. Broadway theatres reported losing between $3 million and $5 million a week. Five productions closed.[21] Big musicals that survived reported losing approximately $250,000 a week. To weather the storm, parties that typically engage in competitive bargaining pulled together: Unions agreed to 25 percent pay cuts, theatre owners gave breaks on leases, and rental companies reduced equipment fees.[22] In January and February of 2002 (a short four months later), a troupe of Broadway actors toured eight U.S. cities in a musical revue called *NY Loves America*. The show was produced by the League of American Theatres and Producers as a "thank you" from New York City to the nation following the outpouring of support after September 11. The tour was made possible by a combination of corporate and nonprofit contributors. The audience was admitted free of charge.[23]

◆ **A NINETEENTH-CENTURY FRENCH AUDIENCE** *at intermission, busy with conversation, taking refreshments, looking to see who else is here. The audience shifts from a mostly unified entity engaged with the play to a community more socially interactive before uniting once more to witness the production. Notice the man at left pouring something from his cup on the head of another audience member, the child climbing a pillar, other children climbing from one area of seating to another. At least two audience members appear to have copies of the play or music being used in the production.*
Hand-tinted lithograph by Pruche, 1837. Collection of the authors.

◆◆◆◆◆◆◆◆◆
QUESTIONS AND ACTIVITIES

1. Investigate the types of theatre that are available in your area. Check out your local newspaper, run an Internet search, or ask at a public library. Make a list of theatres categorized by type. Collect or print out season brochures giving the lists of plays and dates. Which shows would you most like to attend? Which ones are within your price range? Which theatres use volunteer ushers? Which theatres have student discounts or student rush? If your questions can't be answered by a web site, call the theatre box office.

2. How much are you willing to pay to see a live theatre performance? A rock concert? A sports event? Does it make a difference whether the people you are watching are amateurs or professionals? Why or why not?

3. Assume that you or a small group from your class is going to produce a play on your own with students from the college or university acting classes. Select a play that you have read. Make a list of all the specific things that need to be done on your end. The artistic side is being taken care of by another group. What will you need to do?

4. Go a step further in your imaginary production. Choose one of the jobs and do whatever is necessary—for example, create a budget, decide on a space, and so on. Do any research necessary to complete the task. Report back to your group or class.

◆◆◆◆◆◆◆◆◆
KEY TERMS AND CONCEPTS

professional theatre, p. 144
commercial theatre, p. 144
nonprofit theatres, p. 146
resident theatres, p. 146
regional theatres, p. 146
amateur theatre, p. 147

educational theatre, p. 148
community theatre, p. 149
hybrid theatres, p. 150
producer, p. 151
managing director, p. 151
artistic director, p. 154

National Endowment for the Arts (NEA), p. 157
Federal Theatre Project (FTP), p. 158
The New 42nd Street, p. 161

◆◆◆◆◆◆◆◆◆
FOR FURTHER EXPLORATION

www.nytheatre.com includes a listing of New York City shows, ticket prices, theatre descriptions and directions (including accessibility), and brief descriptions of plays.

Jill Charles, ed. *Regional Theater Directory, 2001–2002.* Dorset, Vermont: Dorset Theatre and Colony House, 2001; and Joseph Wesley Ziegler. *Regional Theatre: The Revolutionary Stage.* New York: Da Capo, 1977. For a list and overview of contemporary American resident (also called regional) theatres and for a history of resident theatres.

Stanley Green. *Broadway Musicals, Show by Show,* 5th edition. Milwaukee: Leonard, 1996; and Andrew Lamb. *150 Years of Popular Musical Theatre.* New Haven, Conn.: Yale University Press, 2000. For a history of American and British musicals.

Jack Poggi. *Theater in America: The Impact of Economic Forces.* Ithaca, N.Y.: Cornell University Press, 1967.

Stephen Langley. *Theatre Management and Producing in America: Commercial, Stock, Resident, College, Community, and Presenting Organizations.* New York: Drama Publishers, 1990.

Photo Gallery

Theatre of Diversity

Theatre is often a meeting place for past and present—a meeting place for different cultures. Theatre of diversity suggests many theatres, many cultures, and cross-cultural efforts. The term suggests diversity in subject matter, in *style, in relationship to the past, as well as diversity of race, gender, and sexual orientation. The photographs presented here are only a sample, but they demonstrate in visual terms the vast offerings of the theatre of our time.*

REINTERPRETATION THROUGH RACE AND GEOGRAPHICAL LOCATION

The Oedipus Plays, in translation by Nicholas Rudall, is a trilogy of the Greek Theban plays of Sophocles (*Oedipus the King, Oedipus at Colonus,* and *Antigone*). Inspired by the dance and music of Zimbabwe, director Michael Kahn cast all African American actors in this 2001 production. The artistic collaborators created an African tribal environment and community spirit through an array of visual and aural splendor. The production bombarded the senses with percussive music and athletic choreography and had special significance in a community where African Americans make up a majority of the population. Here we see the dancing chorus awaiting the return of Oedipus, who will enter through the large central doors upstage (a traditional scenic arrangement for Greek tragedy decorated as if African). Scenic design by Charles McClennahan; costume design by Toni-Leslie James; choreography by Marlies Yearby.

Photo by Carol Rosegg. Courtesy of the Shakespeare Theatre, Washington, D.C.

AFRICAN LEGACY
FROM FILM TO THEATRE

It is uncommon for a film to be converted to theatre. In 1997 Julie Taymor and her collaborators adapted an animated Disney feature to the stage but with remarkable shifts created through puppetry and masks. A significant feature of this adaptation was the African influence that extended well beyond that of the film. Nearly all of the African animals, and even some of the vegetation, were played by black actors. The result was diversity in casting, design, and performance style. In this photo the masks are used as puppetlike extensions of the actors. John Vickery as the villain Scar faces off with the heroic Mustafa, played by Sam Wright. We can still see the actors' faces as the movable masks get within inches of one another, yet the actors' heads are some three feet apart. Direction and costume design by Julie Taymor, masks and puppets designed by Taymor and Michael Curry.
Photo by Joan Marcus.

CLASSICAL LEGACY IN INDIA

Indian Sanskrit plays and epics are still widely read outside India, and some of these plays and epics are performed and adapted in the West, just as director Peter Brook staged *The Mahabharata* in 1985. Indian Kathakali, however, has become the most popular window for the West on Indian culture and the classical stories of that diverse country. Of the classical theatre forms still performed in India, Kathakali is the most familiar in the West. Audiences are fascinated by the display of colorful, exotic, buoyant costumes; the masklike makeup that is unique in the theatrical world; the dancelike movement; and the emblematic gestures. Details are in the costumes and makeup of the performers, not in scenery, since all is performed on an open stage. The principal performers are typically boys steeped in demanding physical training that is in some ways more akin to Western training of gymnasts than actors. The Kathakali actors perform barefoot with bells on their ankles. The musical accompaniment is percussive, and sometimes the performances last through the night while lit by torches. In this photo the bright green facial makeup is framed by white built-up *chutti* carefully added to the face in layers.
Photo by and courtesy of Rakesh Solomon.

KABUKI WOMEN PLAYED BY MEN

The classical Kabuki theatre of Japan fascinates audiences in both Eastern and Western cultures. Kabuki is exotic even in Japan because most of its plays and performance styles are centuries old. Of all the Asian theatrical forms and styles, Kabuki is the most accessible to North American audiences because Kabuki tours internationally and shares a number of characteristics with traditional Western forms while providing elements that are alien to the West. Kabuki includes melodrama, comedy, and tragedy, violent physical action, and both presentational and representational performance. The *onnagata* (male actor who performs female characters) seems completely transformed into the image of a woman in costume, makeup, and movement. Yet he speaks with an obvious falsetto voice that alters our reception of the female character. Although some of the characters and action are extravagant and supernatural stylizations, some of the action is literal in its presentation. The Kabuki style has inspired playwrights, designers, and directors in the West to borrow or adapt many of its methods and images. In this photo the *onnagata* actor Utaemon portrays a heroine in distress. Bondage is a recurring image in many Kabuki plays. The distress at the same time is made beautiful by the shower of cherry blossoms raining down on the character.
Photo by Chiaki Yoshida.

ASIAN-INSPIRED PUPPETRY

Japan has also inspired the West with its unusual puppet theatre, Bunraku, wherein the puppet master becomes one with the puppet and creates the characterization beyond the physical image of the doll. If the puppeteer is particularly skilled as an actor, the audience might find itself responding to both puppet and master. The theatrical company Mabou Mines has long been an extraordinary center of theatrical experiment. In this 2002 production of *Peter and Wendy,* adapted by Liza Lorwin from the Peter Pan story, the principal performer, Karen Kandel, does all the character voices and works at the center of the action with the puppets in the midst of a sword fight. Note the other puppeteers fully engaged with the action of the puppets. Directed by Lee Breuer.
Photo by Ken Howard. Courtesy of La Jolla Playhouse.

ASIAN INFLUENCE MEETS SHAKESPEARE ON HIGH-TECH GROUND

This production of *Macbeth* drew on Asian imagery in masks and costumes but placed the action in a nearly cybernetic world of projections. All roles in the play were taken by three actors, who quickly shifted characters and masks. Minor characters in this *Macbeth* were sometimes presented by projections of performers who "took the stage" alongside the principals. This graphic, often disturbing production was a visual marvel of confrontation and something of a postmodern take on the Elizabethan tragedy. This photo demonstrates vibrant color, one of many lighting projections as scenery upstage of the actors, and dynamic gestures necessary to match the theatricality of the masks and costumes, which appear almost sculptural at times. The actors are Will Bond and Kim Martin-Cotten. Directed by Marc Masterson.

Photo by Larry Hunt. Courtesy of Actors Theatre of Louisville.

POPULAR ENTERTAINMENT ADAPTED FROM THE ANCIENTS

One of the best ways to understand diversity in the theatre is to examine the biggest hits of popular culture, which capture the attention of regular theatre-goers. *A Funny Thing Happened on the Way to the Forum* by Stephen Sondheim, Burt Shevelove, and Larry Gelbart, was very popular when it first appeared in 1962 and has been revived many times in Broadway and other commercial theatres, resident theatres, colleges, universities, community theatres, and high schools.

Yet the raw material for this musical dates to Roman comedy of the second and third centuries B.C.E., especially for character, comic structure, and farcical situations. Pictured here is the 1996 Broadway revival directed by Jerry Zaks and starring Nathan Lane as Pseudolus, appearing with his fellow servants played by Brad Aspel, Cory English, and Ray Roderick. The bright colors of the costumes designed by Tony Walton are typical of traditionally produced musical comedy that is meant to be pure entertainment. Few overt messages are sent by such plays, yet we have a fuller understanding of the popular culture of any period that has left us texts or images of popular entertainment. This production underwent an interesting diversity shift when Lane left the production for other work and was replaced by an African American actress, Whoopi Goldberg.

Photo by Joan Marcus.

CONCEPT MUSICALS

Another popular musical, *Cabaret* (1966) by Joe Masteroff, John Kander, and Fred Ebb, was first produced and directed by Hal Prince just four years after the first *Forum.* This concept musical, which is only partially organized around a book, made different demands on the audience by taking a dark look at pre–World War II Germany and the rise of Nazism in the midst of a chaotic and hedonistic cabaret environment. Traditionally written dialogue and musical scenes taking place in domestic environments alternated with cabaret numbers that commented on the 1929 carefree lifestyle punctuated by anti-Semitism. Like *Forum,* this musical is

also revived frequently in many different venues. The Broadway revival of 1997 directed by Sam Mendes went even further than most of its predecessors in depicting decadence. In the production's final moments the artistic team created a haunting Holocaust-like image. Depicted here is Natasha Richardson as Sally Bowles in Mendes's Roundabout Theatre Company production with members of the chorus singing directly to the audience (many of whom were sitting at cabaret tables).
Photo by Joan Marcus.

GENDER ISSUES FROM THE NINETEENTH CENTURY

August Strindberg's *Miss Julie* (1888) is a famous examination of the war of the sexes and class differences placed in a time and location that was far from friendly to the rights of women. Frequently revived and reinterpreted by placing the action in periods later than the original, this disturbing play raises many issues that have hardly been settled in our own era. Pictured here is a 1997 postmodern production directed by Anne Bogart. The costumes that were used throughout alternated between nineteenth-century and twentieth-century designs, sometimes combin-

ing the two to underscore the blending of ideology and gender issues since Strindberg's time. Strindberg had written the play for a realistic box set, but director and designers opted for an open setting that allowed freedom of movement. The bright red floor became a field of battle and stressed the contested nature of gender issues. The affair between the two principals, servant-class Jean and aristocratic Julie (here played by Jefferson Mays and Ellen Lauren) also alternates between animal attraction and disgust. Jean's fiancée Christine (played by Kelly Maurer) is asleep in the trap while Jean and Julie carry on their verbal dance of sexual suggestion. Scenic design by Paul Owen and costume designs by Marcia Dixcy Jory.
Photo by Richard C. Trigg. Courtesy of Actors Theatre of Louisville.

GENDER AND GAY ISSUES IN THE ERA OF AIDS

Angels in America: Millennium Approaches stunned the theatrical world when it first appeared in 1991 in San Francisco. Produced internationally, this play has had many interpretations, but it nonetheless challenges political and public opposition to gay rights and the horrible toll taken on the population by the pandemic of AIDS. There are many other plays dealing with these issues. *Angels,* however, through its sensitive subject matter, clever dialogue, droll presentation, and splendid theatricality became the popular hit representing gay rights and AIDS. In this photo from a 1998 production, we see an invasion of the twentieth century by figures from the thirteenth and seventeenth centuries. Prior 1 and Prior 2 (played by Jon Brent Curry and William McNulty) are ghosts of ancestors of Prior Walter (played by Bash Halow). The ghosts died of the plague in Europe just as the current Prior is dying of the plague of AIDS. One ghost emerges through the bed (as in the dreams and imagination of Prior Walter), resulting in a comic history lesson as mistakes in the past are connected to the crisis of the present. This production was directed by Mladen Kiselov; costumes were designed by Suttirat Larlarb.

Photo by Richard C. Trigg. Courtesy of Actors Theatre of Louisville.

GENDER-BENDING COMMENTARY

Cross-dressing is an ancient theatrical tradition dating at least from the Greeks. In recent times cross-dressing has often been used to comment on gender issues—especially conflict over sexual preferences and the socially created issues of power and desire in relationships, family, and politics. The idea of sexual politics is evident in many plays and productions, beginning in the 1970s. *Cloud 9* (1979) by Caryl Churchill opens in the nineteenth century, as we see in this photograph. A sexual affair is struck up between Harry Bagley, a British explorer, and Betty, the wife of Harry's friend. The irony is that Betty is played by a man, so a heterosexual relationship is represented on stage as homoerotic. Because Betty is modeled on a man's image of woman, she is played by a man. In the second half of the play, however, set in the twentieth century, Betty is played by a woman but is still full of nineteenth-century doubts and confusion. Produced at Towson State University.

Photo from collection of the authors.

CHANGING ROLES OF WOMEN IN THE WORKPLACE AND HOME

Another play by Caryl Churchill, *Top Girls* (1982), explores the changing roles of women in the workplace and in the home. The character in this photograph is Pope Joan, a semi-mythical figure from the distant past. Pope Joan was a woman masquerading as a man who headed the Catholic Church before her sex was discovered, resulting in her murder by an enraged mob. In this production at the University of Nebraska, Pope Joan was played by an African American actress. Such nontraditional casting is intriguing for an audience because it contradicts expectations and further complicates the power and gender issues raised by the play.

Photo from collection of the authors.

HISPANIC CULTURE CROSS-EXAMINING ITSELF

Many poignant Hispanic plays have emerged in North America since the mid-twentieth century. José Rivera has been widely produced, especially in resident theatres across North America. His *Marisol* depicts a Puerto Rican woman attempting to suppress her ethnic identity and blend in the commercial world of New York. In *Adoration of the Old Woman*, pictured here, Rivera explores statehood or independence for Puerto Rico, but domestically, in the confrontations of a hundred-year-old matriarch and her seventeen-year-old great granddaughter. Their problems are complicated by the ghost of a woman who long ago slept with the matriarch's husband and now haunts the old woman's bed. Played by Ivonne Coll, the old woman confronts her past and attempts to bridge a generational barrier. This image is from a 2002 production directed by Jo Bonney. The young actresses are Marisol Padilla Sanchez as the ghost and Tamara Mello as the great-granddaughter.

Photo by J. T. McMillan. Courtesy of La Jolla Playhouse.

RACE AND GENDER AMONG
STOCKS AND BONDS

Serious Money (1987) by Caryl Churchill joins a host of other plays that explore the corporate world and commercialism. This theme has fascinated playwrights since the end of the nineteenth century, and dramatic treatments of gender issues in big business date from the 1910s. Churchill complicates the theme, however, by introducing racial tension along with gender issues. Although frantically paced (imitating the business world of London) and cynically postmodern, the play is also surprisingly written in verse that suggests connections with the past. The pictured production is from 2002 in San Francisco, directed by Jonathan Moscone. The actors David Ryan Smith (left) and Billy Corman (right) play a cocoa deal maker from Ghana and a British corporate raider, each out to exploit the other.

Photo by Ken Friedman. Courtesy of American Conservatory Theater.

GENERATIONAL AND FAMILY CONFLICT

Buried Child (1978) by Sam Shepard incorporates one of the playwright's recurring themes of disturbing generational and family conflict, often violent and bizarre. Shepard typically creates unsophisticated characters who are close to the land. This play juxtaposes young city people with dark, incommunicative, midwestern farm dwellers who harbor awful secrets. Conflicts of cultures and language result in soul-searching by the young protagonist, who yields to violence and experiences humiliation. This powerful "homecoming" play is a fascinating study in American values gone horribly wrong and the unwillingness or inability of people to cope with horrors of the past. Actors John Seitz and Marco Barricelli depict father and son in a mysterious and disturbing relationship. Directed by Les Waters.

Photo by Kevin Berne. Courtesy of American Conservatory Theater.

Collaboration in History

"Life moves and changes and the theatre moves and changes with it. By looking at the theatre of the past, we may come to see our own theatre more clearly. The theatre of every age has something to teach us, if we are sensitive enough and humble enough to learn from it."[1]

ROBERT EDMOND JONES

When we look at the ways in which different cultures have created and defined theatre, we see how people thought about life and sometimes the afterlife, what they valued, what they feared, and how they made sense out of the events around them. Studying theatre of the past is a fascinating activity. What we are struck by, however, is the way in which the past does not remain the past. Theatre artists of each "present" look backward to the creations of their near and distant predecessors. They revive, adapt, reinterpret, reconceive, and deconstruct. Some of the most innovative approaches to theatre were born when artists reacted against the status quo; in other words, the "new" defined itself in opposition to what was already in place, and artists made a conscious attempt to push established art into the "past." Sometimes reacting to the status quo meant resurrecting a much older viewpoint or device. We also see interconnections between different cultures, often distant from one another in geographical location as

well as time. Theatre artists have always been creative borrowers. Artists do not necessarily steal the ideas of others (although that has occurred more than a few times). Theatre artists often discover or rediscover inspiration and solutions both far away and close to home. They adopt, change, and revitalize the borrowed elements. Shakespeare, who was not subject to copyright laws, and the German playwright Bertolt Brecht, for example, were great borrowers, but they also reveled in originality and novelty. The theatre artists' roots run deep and far in the history of theatre.

In this section we hope to convey the sense of a dynamic process. Because of our belief that the past is still a vital element in the life of the present, we have chosen to present information about previous theatrical events throughout this book. We realize, however, that you need some sense of historical continuity and chronology. We hope to provide an overview for you in these three chapters and the accompanying timeline, "Key Theatrical

THEATRE OF DELPHI in Greece.
Photo by and courtesy of Louis J. Spear.

Events." Selecting what to include in an overview of 2,500 years of activity is, of course, extremely difficult. In some ways the choice is highly subjective; other theatre historians could give you their own versions, which would no doubt differ from ours. And of course, what we see as important is in-formed by the time at which we write. Ten years ago, portions of this section would have been written differently. We hope that you will take the following chapters as a basis on which to build your own knowledge of the theatre, adding to it as you continue to read and experience productions.

ROMAN MOSAIC of theatrical masks.
Museo Capitolini, Rome. Scala/Art Resource.

Foundations

Classical Theatrical Forms

Classical Greece

Classical Rome

Classical India

Medieval Europe

Classical China

Classical Japan

No one knows how the theatre really began, but at least since the fourth century B.C.E. many theories have been offered to explain its appearance and rise to prominence. Religious ritual appears to be a likely major source, but theatre was almost certainly preceded historically by music, dance, storytelling, oral history, and ancestor veneration, all of which contributed dynamically to the models theatre took in its earliest forms. It can be argued that the first performers in history were shamans—priests in ancient Asia, Africa, the Middle East, North America, and parts of Europe—who communed with their gods and ancestors to heal disease and affect natural events through ritual and dance. Surviving hieroglyphics in Egypt indicate that religious theatre existed there as early as 2500 B.C.E. and continued to be performed at Abydos in honor of the god Osiris for many centuries. What we know about these theatrical events is sketchy at best (short descriptions of what a priest performed). The Greeks in Athens created the earliest theatre that has left us the texts of plays and theatre architecture. The efforts of the Greeks, although grounded in religious ritual, are generally accepted as the oldest surviving dramatic studies of humanity as part of an ongoing public institution.

Classical Greece

In 534 B.C.E. the city of Athens added contests for tragedy to its annual city festival honoring Dionysus, the god of wine, fertility, and ecstatic celebration. Subsequently, all theatre presentations in Athens for over a century were produced only in honor of this god. Like the famous Olympic games, theatre for many years was a contest, at first among playwrights for the best set of tragedies, but later for best comedy and best actor, among other competitions.

Nearly all of the Greek plays that have come down to us were first produced in the fifth century B.C.E. We have thirty-one tragedies by three playwrights (plus one anonymous tragedy) and eleven comedies by one playwright. Although we are happy to have these remarkable plays, it is sad that probably a thousand or more plays have vanished from such a dynamic period of theatre activity. If current estimates of Greek output are roughly accurate, we have no more than 3 percent of the Greek plays produced between 534 and 404 B.C.E.

Theatre was occasional, and one could not earn a living as a playwright or actor; all practitioners technically were amateurs, although they were highly skilled. Contributing talent or money to the theatre of the festival was an important civic responsibility. Later Greek theatre professionalized when touring actors organized into guilds (The *Technitae* or Craftsmen of Dionysus) by the late fourth century B.C.E. Only one full play, a domestic comedy by Menander (c. 342–291 B.C.E.), has survived from that era, which is called Hellenistic (named for the spread of Greek culture beyond Greece).

At the beginning of the process in 534 B.C.E. the actor and playwright were the same person. The early tragic playwrights, such as Thespis (sixth century B.C.E.), performed their own plays, which featured one actor and a **chorus** (a group of singer/dancers who interacted with and responded to the actor). Later

Exploring Historical and Cultural Perspectives

Rediscovering Menander

After several thousand years, scholars are grateful that any texts from the ancient world survive. What we know about ancient Greek theatre depends on what people at the time and in subsequent periods valued, recorded, and saved—either purposely or by accident. Most of the Greek plays that still exist are available because people through the centuries thought they were worthy of study or production, copied them by hand (before the invention of the printing press), and taught them in schools.

The twentieth-century rediscovery of the work of the Hellenistic comic playwright Menander is an exciting story of archaeological and detective work. Menander lived from about 342 to about 291 B.C.E. There are records of his having written over one hundred plays, eight of which won first prize in contests. Menander's work was highly thought of in the ancient world; his reputation grew in stature in the centuries after his death. His plays were known until late antiquity, but during the Middle Ages, any surviving texts were lost. At the beginning of the twentieth century only a few papyrus fragments of Menander's plays were available to read and study. Papyrus (from which our word "paper" is derived) is a plant material that was used to write on in ancient Egypt. Other bits and pieces of Menander's work were saved because they were quoted by later critics, grammarians, and other authors. Otherwise, Hellenistic comedy was known only by what people had said about it and by some Roman comedies that were known to use Hellenistic comedy as a source.

In 1905 an excavation in Egypt turned up part of a papyrus book, or *codex,* dating from the fifth century C.E. These fragments, called the *Cairo Codex,* were published in 1907. Large parts of three plays by Menander were now available, as well as smaller pieces of two other plays. Half a century later, the *Bodmer Codex* (named for the European collector who bought it) was discovered in Egypt. This papyrus, dating from the third century C.E., contained one nearly complete play, *The Dyskolos* (often translated as *The Grouch* or *Old Cantankerous*), which had first been performed in 316 B.C.E. Published in 1959, this comedy about a grumpy old father who gets along with no one revolutionized the study of Hellenistic comedy. The *Bodmer Codex* also contained parts of *The Girl from Samos* and *The Shield,* which were published in 1969. The dry climate of Egypt is credited with allowing the papyri to survive for such a long time.

Other fragments of Menander have turned up in surprising places: in the outer wrappings or cases of mummies. A material called cartonnage, made from papyrus or linen and plaster and then painted, was often used to decorate or enclose mummies. The Egyptians made cartonnage with recycled pieces of papyrus (to use new papyrus would have been extremely expensive). Painstaking stripping of mummy cartonnage has resurrected a number of valuable papyri. Pieces of another Menander play, *The Sikyonian,* were found in Egypt in 1906 in part of the cartonnage of a mummy case. Almost sixty years later, large pieces of the missing sections of *The Sikyonian*—from the *same document*—were found in two mummy cases in a Paris museum. These fragments were published in 1965. Together, these discoveries produced about 500 lines of the play. Scholars are still hopeful that some day the missing 300 lines of *The Sikyonian* might be rediscovered.

Even once a papyrus fragment has been found and identified, it is often damaged and difficult to reconstruct. Its publication and translation are painstaking processes calling on years of expertise and research. For a description of the process involved in translating one small piece of Menander's *The Girl from Samos,* see the paper by W. G. Arnott, "On Editing and Translating Menander," which includes a picture of the papyrus fragment, available at www.open.ac.uk/Arts/CC99/Arnott.htm.

Interested? Check out

Menander. *Plays and Fragments.* Translated and Introduced by Norma Miller. New York: Penguin Books, 1987.

Stanley Ireland. *Menander: Dyskolos, Sami and Other Plays: A Companion to the Penguin Translation of the Plays of Menander by Norma Miller.* London: Bristol Classics Press, 1992.

For more on papyri, see the Duke Papyrus Archive at http://scriptorium.lib.duke.edu/papyrus/, especially "From the World of the Papyri" (http://scriptorium.lib.duke.edu/papyrus/texts/world.html) and "Writing in Egypt under Greek and Roman Rule" (http://scriptorium.lib.duke.edu/papyrus/texts/rule.html), which includes a picture of a papyrus fragment of a play by Euripides.

a second and then a third actor were added, but all of the surviving tragedies were written for three actors who performed multiple roles with a chorus whose size is usually estimated at twelve to fifteen. The chorus, however, might have begun with fifty performers, since that was the size of the traditional **dithyramb** (a choric presentation sung and danced in homage to Dionysus). The dithyramb is older than tragedy and is claimed to be a source for it. All actors and chorus members were strictly male (even though many characters and choruses represented females), and they performed in a large, typically circular performance space called an **orchestra** (dancing place). The chorus entered and exited through the **parados.** At some point a retiring space called a **skene** (our source for the words "scene" and "scenery") was added upstage of the orchestra, and the audience of many thousands watched the action from a large **theatron** (seeing place) on a hillside to which seats were eventually added (see Figure 7.1). All parts of the theatre, though temporary at first for each Dionysian festival, were set in stone permanently by the fourth century B.C.E. Although a few theatres held only a few thousand spectators, most of the surviving theatres are so large that they remind many people of stadiums. The extant architecture creates a dilemma for modern historians, since nearly all of the surviving plays are from the fifth century B.C.E. but extant Greek theatres are from the fourth century B.C.E. or later. Therefore, because the theatres and plays were created in different eras, the theatrical spaces that still exist may not be good indications of the staging that was originally used for the plays.

The action of tragedies, comedies, and other theatrical forms was performed with music and dance, singing, chant, and speech. All actors and chorus members wore full masks covering the entire head, and actors surely performed with dynamic movement and large gestures to reach such large audiences. The vocal and physical skills needed by the actors would have been impressive indeed.

At the Dionysian festival Greek tragedies were performed by three actors in three groups of three plays by three competing playwrights. After all the performances a group of judges, chosen from the ten tribes of Athens, selected the set of plays they found the best. Sometimes a playwright told one story through all three plays (a **trilogy** that can be read as one three-part play today), but other playwrights presented three different stories in their three tragedies. All Greek tragedies that we now possess except one are based on myths that were ancient even when the plays premiered. The famous stories were familiar to many in the audience, but it is clear that playwrights retold them in a variety of ways. The story of Electra, a princess who conspired with her brother to murder her mother and the mother's lover, survives in tragedies by Aeschylus (c. 525–456 B.C.E.), Sophocles (c. 496–406 B.C.E.), and Euripides (c. 480–406 B.C.E.), and each tragedy has a very different focus and point of view. These three playwrights won numerous Dionysian contests and some of their plays continue

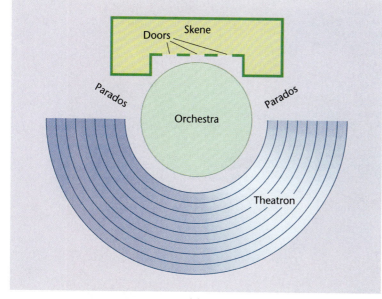

(a)

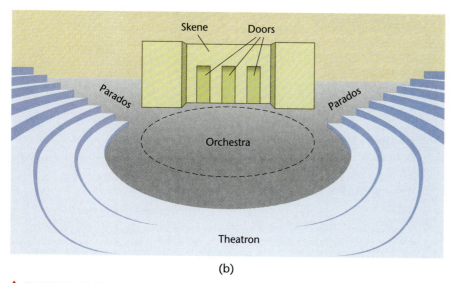

(b)

♦ **FIGURE 7.1** *(a) Greece: Classical Theatre Ground Plan*
(b) Greece: Audience View

to inspire us in modern **revivals** (any productions of a play occurring after the original production).

The only surviving trilogy of plays, *The Oresteia* (458 B.C.E.) by Aeschylus, is still performed, translated, and adapted and has proven to be one of the most enduring dramatic presentations in theatre history. The three plays that make up *The Oresteia* (one of which dramatizes the story of Electra) explore personal vengeance and the creation of a standard for criminal justice. Aeschylus also wrote the only Greek tragedy we have that was based on events in the playwright's own time rather than mythology: *The Persians* (472 B.C.E.) examines with sympathy enemies of Greece whom the playwright had fought a few years earlier.

♦ **GREEK HELLENISTIC THEATRE** at Epidaurus. Note the vast scale, the circular orchestra, the remains of the foundation of the skene upstage of the orchestra, and the always-present natural environment beyond. This theatre is still used for performances of classical Greek plays.
Bildarchiv Steffens/Bridgeman Art Library.

Some of the plays of Sophocles, especially *Oedipus the King* (c. 430–425 B.C.E.) and *Antigone* (c. 441 B.C.E.), both explorations of guilt and crimes against divine law, are often studied as perfect examples of Greek tragedy and are frequently revived and anthologized for courses in dramatic literature. Although written and first performed at different points in the career of Sophocles, *Oedipus the King, Oedipus at Colonus* (406 B.C.E.), and *Antigone* in our own time are sometimes performed together as if they are a trilogy. All three plays deal with the family of Oedipus.

Euripides left us many poignant depictions of suffering and domestic conflict, perhaps most notably in *Medea* (431 B.C.E.), a tragedy of revenge in which the title character kills her children in order to punish her adulterous husband, and *The Trojan Women* (415 B.C.E.), an examination of the victims of war and the horror of its aftermath. Euripides also wrote *The Bacchae* (produced after the playwright's death), the only tragedy still surviving in which the god Dionysus appears as a character. *The Bacchae* continues to fascinate audiences with its conflict of mortals and the god surrounded by a chorus of women possessed by Dionysus. In 2002 Euripides' play *Hypsipyle* was performed in outdoor Greek theatres for the first time since the fifth century B.C.E. This play was lost until major fragments were discovered in 1906. Most of the reconstructed text for production was conjectural, but audiences for the first time in some 2,400 years heard more than 400 lines of Euripides' dramatic verse. The styles and intent of these three poetic playwrights differed markedly, yet the extant tragedies are united in presenting a searing, mournful, magnificent display of agony, endurance, grandeur, fall from greatness, and a remarkable human spirit, which rises in the face of despair.

◆ **MEDEA,** *by Euripides. In this production note the central door, open space, and architectural façade, which are traditional in interpretations of Greek tragedy and are based on our understanding of Greek space and plays. Medea (on the ground) is played by Barbara Berlovitz; her nurse, by Sarah Agnew; King Ageus by Charles Schuminski. Directed by Steven Epp; scenic and lighting design by Dominique Sarrand; costume design by Sonya Berlovitz.*
Photo by Michal Daniel. Theatre de la Jeune Lune, Minneapolis.

The Greeks also left us comedy. The satirical, ridiculous extravaganzas of Artistophanes are infused with fantasy and bawdy jokes. His attacks on contemporary people whom he found corrupt, governmental practices he found misguided, or artistic endeavors he found inferior abound in his lyrical plays full of choric songs and impossible events. Often a political and social reactionary in his plays, Aristophanes staged *The Clouds* (423 B.C.E.) as an attack on the philosopher Socrates. He placed an actor wearing a Socrates mask high in the air in a basket (head in the clouds) hanging from a crane and surrounded him with a bizarre chorus of singing and dancing clouds. In *The Frogs* (405 B.C.E.) Aristophanes dramatizes a mock competition between the real but deceased playwrights Euripides and Aeschylus in the underworld. Aristophanes favors the more conservative Aeschylus, who could save Athens from its woes, it is said, if only he could return from the grave. This fantasy becomes the first important document of dramatic criticism. It is unfortunate that we have no comedies from any other playwrights who preceded or competed against Aristophanes, but his eleven plays still leave a vivid picture of Athenian social, political, and cultural life.

Despite the importance of the plays and the significance of Greek theatre in the Western theatrical tradition, we really know very little about Greek classical theatre production, since the playwrights left no stage directions and most of the surviving information is sketchy. We are intrigued, for example, that some "pass the hat" street performers called **mimes** seemed to include women in their companies (Plato records an example), but the institutional theatre never allowed women to perform. Unfortunately, we know little about Greek mimes.

♦ **RUINS OF A ROMAN THEATRE** at Sabbratha, Libya. Note the high façade upstage with three doorways, the long, low stage (pulpitum) approximately five feet in height with a doorway at each end, and the half orchestra downstage of the pulpitum. For purposes of scale the actor standing on this stage would be only a little taller than the height of the stage. The doorways are huge.
Bridgeman Art Library.

Nonetheless, the plays and ideas that are evident in Greek theatre are replete with exciting possibilities. Greek plays continued to be written and performed in Greek-controlled territory long after the fall of Athens in 404 B.C.E. It was well after the Athenian decline that the Hellenistic philosopher Aristotle wrote his influential *Poetics* (c. 335–323 B.C.E.), which stands as the first important examination of the tragic form. When combined with the remarkable philosophy, art, and architecture of the Greeks, the legacy of their theatre inspires many play revivals, new plays, dramatic theory, uses of masks, theatre architecture, and contemporary scenic design.

♦♦♦♦♦♦♦♦♦

Classical Rome

The Republic of Rome conquered all Greek territory by 146 B.C.E., but nearly a hundred years earlier Romans had begun performing plays based on and inspired by the tragedies and comedies of Greece. Like their forebears, the Romans performed plays at religious festivals but differed by dedicating the productions to any of their gods as long as the festivals honored one god at a time. Legend credits Livius Andronicus (third century B.C.E.) with the first plays and acting performances, but no plays survive until the comedies of Plautus (c. 254–184 B.C.E.) and Terence (c. 195/185–159 B.C.E.). Roman comic playwrights adapted Greek comedies, like those of Menander, but eliminated the chorus (a major depar-

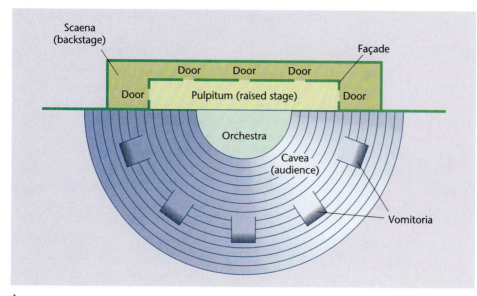

♦ **FIGURE 7.2** *Rome: Theatre Ground Plan*

ture). Although heavily influenced by Greek theatre, the Roman theatricals should not be seen as strictly derivative. The Romans made many stylistic and content changes, and when we are able to compare fragments of the work, it is clear that the Romans provided numerous original touches, which reflected their own values and culture.

Roman theatre spaces and production techniques also built on the Greeks, but the results were very different. Instead of using hillsides, the Romans erected freestanding theatres that surrounded the audience and performers while remaining open to the sky for light. These were the first theatres to focus the audience's attention strictly on the stage without distractions from the surrounding environment. Roman architects exploited the arch to extend their structures high into the air. Because some of these imposing theatres have survived remarkably intact throughout Europe and North Africa, we can reconstruct the Roman structures more authoritatively than we can the Greek ones (see Figure 7.2). Romans introduced many devices that continue in modern usage such as stage **traps** (openings in the stage floor for ascents and descents) and **vomitories** (stadium-like entrances for the audience) as well as a front curtain. Roman Latin also contributed many words permanently to our theatre vocabulary such as *actor, auditorium,* and *histrionics.*

Like the Greeks, the Roman actors were males who performed in masks in large open spaces backed by a stone **façade** (architectural background) punctuated by a series of doors. A half-orchestra still remained in the space, but it was no longer used by the actors. The orchestra became a place for special audience seating or sometimes water shows. The Romans added walls to the orchestra so that they could flood it with water when the occasion arose. A few names of actors have survived, and one of them, Roscius (c. 131–62 B.C.E.), became synonymous in the popular mind with great acting. Until the twentieth century,

♦ **ROMAN ACTOR** *perhaps contemplating his tragic mask held by a servant or assistant. From a fresco of the first century* B.C.E.
From House of the Tragic Poet Index/Bridgeman Art Library.

when the term faded from common usage, a talented actor was often referred to as a "Roscius."

The comedies of Plautus and Terence are rollicking farcical situation comedies focused on domestic trivialities, pratfalls, misunderstandings, and mistaken identities. These plays (which were really musical comedies, although the music vanished long ago) influenced many playwrights beyond their time, especially in the European Renaissance. Plautus created the definitive mistaken identity play in *The Brothers Menaechmus* (c. 205–184 B.C.E.), wherein twin brothers are reunited after much confusion. The model of the masterful trickster is enshrined in *The Phormio* (161 B.C.E.) by Terence. A wily servant tricks two stodgy fathers into accepting their sons' romantic choices. Roman sitcoms and their form have continued into the present adapted as musicals (*The Boys from Syracuse*, 1938; *A Funny Thing Happened on the Way to the Forum*, 1962), movies (the Marx Brothers, Mel Brooks), and television shows. The antics of Roman comedy are still very familiar to audiences of nearly all ages and cultures, and they seem much more modern than do the surviving Greek comedies.

Roman tragedies, although rarely revived anymore, also influenced later periods. The tragedies of Seneca (c. 4 B.C.E.–65 C.E.) have Greek sources but are extensively reconceived adaptations of *Oedipus, Medea,* and others. In Seneca's interpretations the violence escalates. Seneca was fascinated by revenge as a motivation, and only he (at least in surviving plays) maintained something of a chorus. Supernatural figures also stalk the plays of Seneca, whose tragedies and dramatic devices were in turn reworked by Shakespeare and his contemporaries. Many aspects of Elizabethan tragedy are often identified as Senecan. Like Aristotle in Greece, Horace (65–8 B.C.E.) provided a critical document—his ***Poetic Art***—that influenced the Italian Renaissance as much as Seneca and perhaps more than Aristotle.

Attempts to generalize Roman theatre are problematic, since all surviving comedy was written and produced in the Roman Republic (509–27 B.C.E.), while all extant tragedies date from the early Roman Empire (27 B.C.E.–476 C.E.). Yet both forms were performed in both eras, and Roman theatre lasted for some eight hundred years. Like the Greeks, the Romans had mime troupes (which definitely included women). The mimes, along with musical pantomime performers in the late years of the empire, became more popular than the regular theatre. Some mime troupes even included sex acts and scatological parodies of early Christian ritual. It is not surprising that with the conversion of Rome to Christianity as a state religion and the fall of the Roman Empire, the institution of the theatre crumbled and disappeared in Europe for a considerable time.

◆◆◆◆◆◆◆◆◆◆

Classical India

About the time of Seneca, perhaps earlier, **Sanskrit plays** appeared in Hindu culture and suggested directions that later Asian theatre would take. A detailed document by Bharata, ***The Natyasastra*** (sometimes translated as "Doctrine of Dramatic Art"), which appears to predate the most important surviving Sanskrit plays, outlines the principles of performance, staging, and dramatic form as practiced in India and applied to Sanskrit plays. Theatrical origins are associated with the priest caste and the form is closely tied to religion, but lower-

♦ **KUTIYATTUM PERFORMANCE SPACE.** *Note the columns and open playing space, which are assumed to be typical of Sanskrit performance spaces long ago.* Photo by and courtesy of Rakesh Solomon.

caste actors soon joined in. Performance was very presentational and included colorful costumes, music, dance, and a complicated emblematic system of hand gestures. The type of theatre space varied, but it was decorative and symbolic rather than scenic. The actors performed on a mostly open stage. Unlike the Greek and Roman theatre, women often participated as actors in Sanskrit plays and performed prominent roles.

Most of the stories of Sanskrit drama are based on epic Indian literature such as the *Mahabharata* and the *Ramayana,* which featured heroic adventures of gods and mortals. The dramas are structurally organized around *rasas* (moods or sentiments), rather than action and event as we see in typical Western plays. All the plays end happily after a nearly free-form journey through time and space. Of the surviving plays, most are dated to the fourth and fifth centuries. Most famous among these are *Shakuntala,* the travails of an abandoned young mother, by Kalidasa and *The Little Clay Cart,* the narrow escape of a virtuous courtesan from a jealous villain, attributed to King Sudraka. By the 1200s and hastened by an Islamic invasion of India, the creation of Sanskrit plays ceased, but Sanskrit contributed important drama that is still regularly studied and occasionally performed in both India and the West. Like Roman comedy, Sanskrit now exists primarily on paper, but early Indian performance styles cast a long shadow, which can still be glimpsed, often breathtakingly, in two related forms: Kutiyattum and Kathakali.

Before the decline of Sanskrit plays, another religious theatrical form based on ancient epics appeared in India called **Kutiyattum,** which was performed in temples and can still be seen by modern audiences. It appears to combine elements of the *Natyasastra* (including using actresses) with folk traditions. The visual and aural manifestations of Kutiyattum bear correspondences to early Indian practice, using music, open space, and colorful costumes but without

the philosophical texts of its Sanskrit predecessor. By 1700 or so, another remarkable dance-drama, **Kathakali,** appeared and is now often identified as the dominant classical theatre of India. This all-male epic theatre features some of the most incredible makeup and costumes found in any theatrical experience, and its complex system of gestures bears resemblance to the performance descriptions in the *Natyasastra.* Although little text exists in Kathakali, singers provide a narrative. The actor-dancers sometimes enact violent scenes, which were supposedly absent from the Sanskrit plays. Unlike the legacies of Greece and Rome that survive as a small collection of plays and influences, one can still see performances in India that reflect ongoing connections with ancient practices.

◆◆◆◆◆◆◆◆◆

Medieval Europe

While Sanskrit plays were flourishing in India, the Roman Empire was crumbling. Well before its fall, the empire had converted to Christianity, which ultimately dominated both religion and government in Europe after 500 C.E. New church leaders such as Tertullian in c. 200 C.E. stringently attacked theatre, acting, spectacle, and any kind of secular, imaginative literature such as plays. Although there is evidence to support ongoing itinerant theatrical activity during the so-called Dark Ages (500–900), there is no evidence of any formal, legal theatre in Europe until the tenth century. Ironically, accepted theatre practice was reborn in the church itself. Hrotsvitha, a tenth-century German canoness (associated with a nunnery), wrote apparently in seclusion, creating remarkable adaptations of Terence's Roman comedies with a Christian concept. Hrotsvitha's plays might not have been performed in her lifetime, but celebrations of famous stories from the Judeo-Christian Bible proliferated throughout Europe. **Tropes** were presented as early as around 925. In these exchanges of dialogue in musical form, the singers or chanters represented characters from the Bible, such as the three Marys at the tomb of Jesus in a trope called *Quem Quaeritis* ("Whom Do You Seek?"). For centuries these and other types of **liturgical drama** (plays included as part of the worship service) were performed in Latin by the clergy in many monasteries and cathedrals. The clerics also established an approach to staging that used an open space (*platea*) in front of an emblematic background (**mansion**). This system remained the chief model for nearly all medieval staging practices both inside the church and in the community (see Figure 7.3).

Although liturgical plays continued to be performed, after around 1200 many extravagant religious **cycles,** or collections of plays, were performed outdoors and were not confined to cathedrals and monasteries. Cycles were performed in the vernacular (the local language) rather than Latin and appeared throughout Europe. The plays in these cycles, often called **mystery plays,** were based on biblical stories and ranged from the creation of the world to the last judgment. These collections of mysteries, such as the Wakefield Cycle in England and the Valenciennes cycle in France, remained the cornerstone of medieval theatre because they were so popular, plentiful, and remarkably theatrical.[2]

Like the theatre of Greece and Rome, the cycles were performed as part of religious festivals, most frequently in association with the holidays Corpus Christi, Easter, and Christmas. Famous mysteries depicted Cain killing his brother Abel, Noah and the great flood, and the trial, crucifixion, and resurrection of Jesus. The most famous and one of the finest of the mysteries is *The Second Shepherds' Play* from the Wakefield Cycle. This mixed-tone play ends with a solemn presentation of the nativity of the Christ child, but most of the play is given over to comic action about shepherds trying to outwit a sheep thief. The action is full of ironic parallels between a fake birth (using a lamb) and the birth of the "lamb of God."

Some communities also presented **miracle** or **saint's plays** such as *Mary Magdalene* (c. 1500) that recounted the real or apocryphal lives of saints. The

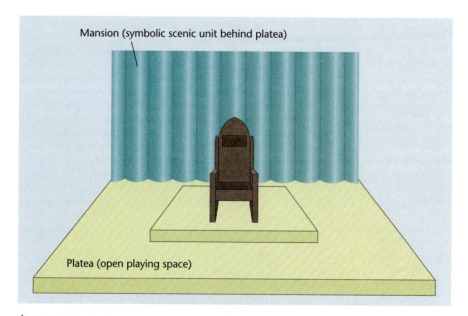

♦ **FIGURE 7.3** *Medieval Mansion/Platea*

Exploring Collaboration

The Community, the Church, and the Feast of Corpus Christi

In 1311 Pope Clement V instituted a new holy day (holiday). Corpus Christi ("body of Christ") was meant to be a day of thanks and celebration for the sacrifice and redemptive power of Christ, symbolized by the Eucharist (Communion). The Roman Catholic Church had recognized the power of theatrical performance as a means of spreading its doctrine. By the end of the fourteenth century, cycles of plays were an integral part of the midsummer Feast of Corpus Christi. Although it began as a single day, the holiday grew over the centuries to three or four days in some places and a week, two weeks, or almost a month in others. Not surprisingly, the most elaborate productions occurred in population centers—market towns with a fairly large number of residents and ample resources. These towns developed complex cycle plays to honor and celebrate the holiday. The massive undertaking required the collaboration of many different parties.

Guilds became well established in the medieval population centers as a means for people in the same field to support each other and further their professional interests. Merchant guilds became prominent in the civic arena as growing towns replaced the old feudal way of life. Craft guilds provided a way for artisans and craftsmen (such as weavers, painters, and bakers) to set standards, train new workers (using an apprentice system), and regulate competition. The craft guilds came to play a vital role in the Corpus Christi festivities as individual guilds took responsibility for staging specific plays. In some instances the type of guild was matched to an appropriate story. The York Cycle, for example, included nearly fifty plays. The shipbuilders produced the play about the building of the ark; the fishers and mariners produced the story of Noah and the flood; the bakers produced the Last Supper. In a rather macabre pairing, the butchers produced the mortification of Christ and his burial. The goldsmiths took charge of the coming of the three kings (magi) bearing gifts, perhaps displaying their handiwork on stage. Some guilds were established for the express purpose of funding and organizing plays.

Plays for the cycles were written for and became the property of specific towns. There was work to be done in preparation for the festival, including construction of scenic units and props, making or borrowing costumes, finding and rehearsing actors and musicians, erecting viewing or performance platforms, and selling tickets. Crowd control had to be organized, and housing had to be provided for the flood of audience members from nearby villages and farms. Successful and impressive production became a source of pride and a status symbol for both the individual guilds and the town as a whole. Guild members who did not abide by the rules that were set for appropriate conduct were fined.

The production of plays for Corpus Christi served many functions. The clergy saw an opportunity for bringing the stories of the Bible vividly to life in the language of the people when church services and the Bible were in Latin and the public was largely illiterate. Community leaders saw an opportunity to build prestige; merchants benefited from the influx of potential customers; craftsmen were able to perform a community service and raise awareness of their professional organization simultaneously. The creative activity was no doubt a welcome change from the rigors of medieval life for performers, technicians, and audience members.

Interested? Check out

Glynne Wickham. *The Medieval Theatre.* Cambridge, England: Cambridge University Press, 1974.

Visit http://arts-sciences.cua.edu/engl/toronto/york98.htm to read about a revival in 1998 of the entire York Cycle at the University of Toronto, the first production of *all* the surviving plays since the final performance in York in 1569. Instead of medieval craft guilds, the various plays were sponsored by companies of actors from Canada, the United States, and the United Kingdom. The site includes a photograph from each play, as well as a link to a searchable online text of *The York Cycle Plays.*

cycles drew on the community for actors and sometimes had a version of a director (called **play master**); the scenic support was often spectacular and full of wondrous events depicting transformations and miracles. The cycles and miracle plays grew in number and complexity (lasting from one to twenty-five

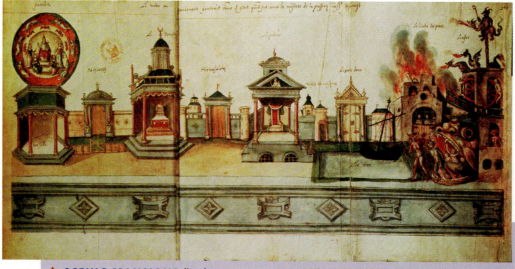

♦ **SCENIC MANSIONS** *lined up on an open stage (platea) at Valenciennes in France c. 1547 for a cycle of biblical plays. The mansion, representing Heaven, is on the far left, and Hellmouth is on the far right emitting flames, smoke, and demons. In between are locations associated with the life of Jesus: Nazareth, a temple, the gates of Jerusalem, the palace of King Herod, and the Sea of Galilee.*
Painted by Hubert Cailleau. Bibliotheque Nationale/Bridgeman Art Library.

days) until conflict over the Protestant Reformation led the Catholic Church to reconsider some of its practices; Protestant countries banned the cycles and all religious plays as corrupt in the 1500s. Despite the official bans, some cycles continued for a while, but only Spain continued to perform them until the eighteenth century.

Most playwrights and actors of medieval Europe remain anonymous to us, but we know much about staging practices because of many detailed accounts and **promptbooks** (books containing scripts, detailed stage directions, and production practices). The promptbook from the Lucerne (Switzerland) cycle also includes drawings of the setting laid out in the town square. Such staging usually had the mansions of heaven and hell as the boundaries. All other mansions and dramatic action took place between these poles of biblical redemption and damnation. Some productions used **processional staging:** moving wagons or **pageants** (think of floats in a parade) traveled through the streets carrying actors and scenery to perform in various locations.

One of the most famous religious dramatic forms of medieval Europe was the **morality play,** which depicted humanity's struggle with good and evil. Structured as a journey, most morality plays followed a generic character through his lifetime. *The Castle of Perseverance* (c. 1425), for example, follows the central character, Mankind (representing all humanity), from cradle to grave. The most famous morality play, however, *Everyman* (c. 1500), dramatizes only the final hours of a man facing his death. All morality plays were peopled with symbolic allegorical characters such as Good Deeds, Pride, and Gluttony, giving human characteristics to abstract ideas.

Secular plays (nonreligious dramas) began to be written and performed again by the 1200s. Some of these farces are still performed. *Johan, Johan* (1533), for example, which was written by John Heywood in England, follows

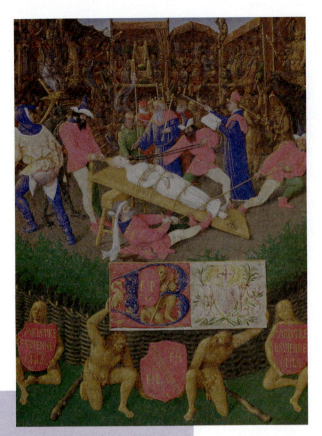

a credulous husband as he gets revenge on his wife who betrays him with a lustful priest. Some intriguing secular musical plays, such as Adam de la Halle's *Robin and Marion* (c. 1283, from France), have a mixed tone. Often presented between courses at a banquet, such plays were called **interludes.** Through narration and direct audience address, the characters in medieval drama frequently move between the fictional world of the play and theatrical reality. A famous interlude, *Fulgens and Lucrece* (1497), by Henry Medwall, features two narrators (named "A" and "B"), who at one point stop narrating and join the action of the play's story because one of them is attracted to the heroine. The interlude and the morality play, both of which were often performed by professional acting companies, are the most important indications of a European return to institutional theatre outside religious drama. Aspects of the interlude are often evident in Shakespeare's plays written for professional companies. Unlike the classical European forms that preceded and followed medieval practice, medieval Europe produced no tragedy. Mixed tone in medieval mystery cycles, moralities, and interludes, however, appears to have influenced Renaissance theatre in England and Spain.

Classical China

Although some kind of theatrical activity in China seems to have been brewing as early as the eighth century A.D., there is no evidence of professional theatre before the tenth century, after which differing forms of plays and theatrical styles developed in both northern and southern China. By the thirteenth century, as mystery cycles were flourishing in Europe, the first great Chinese plays appeared, identified as Yüan plays, since they were written during the Yüan Dynasty (1280–1368). Many of these plays fascinated the public and continue to be read and adapted in both Asian and Western culture. Most of the surviving plays remain anonymous or are credited to playwrights about whom we know little or nothing. *The Orphan of Chao*, an episodic adventure keyed to family revenge, made its way to the French stage in adaptation by the mid-eighteenth century. The wonderfully lyrical *Romance of the Western Chamber* by Wang Shifu is as long as a novel but still charms through its host of songs and the lightly erotic tale of two secret lovers. *The Circle of Chalk* (about a battle for custody of a child) by Li Xiandou is one of the most famous in the West through its adaptation by Bertolt Brecht as *The Caucasian Chalk Circle* (1944).

The Chinese culture apparently produced no tragedy for the stage, but most of the plays feature a mixed tone like Sanskrit and might end either happily or sadly but with a sense of **poetic justice:** Virtue is rewarded; evil is punished. Instrumental music of strings, flute, and percussion was important, and many of the plays included solo singing. Unfortunately, as with Greece and Rome, the original music has not survived. Plays from the north were tradition-

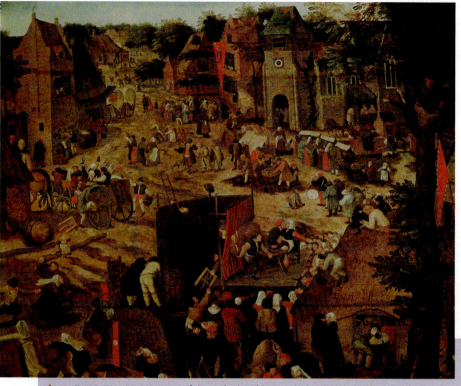

◆ **A BOOTH STAGE** *at a fair as depicted in a painting by Pieter the Younger Breughel. Note the wooden plank stage elevated to head height of the standing audience and the red curtain separating the performers from backstage, where a stool is being passed to or from the stage. The onstage action seems to be a comedy. Such stages were easily transported and assembled by traveling troupes of actors in the Middle Ages and the Renaissance. Versions of the booth stage seem to date from classical Greece.*
Musees Royaux d'Art et d'Histoire, Brussels, Belgium/Bridgeman Art Library.

ally organized into four parts or acts and an additional scene called a *wedge*, but southern plays (often more comic), were written in many acts—up to fifty in some cases.

What is perhaps most striking about classical Chinese theatre, however, is the approach to performance, which was highly stylized with movement, dance, chant, and music. Different Chinese regions developed individual styles. In the early 1800s Chinese artists combined many of them to form what is now known as **Chinese music drama** or **Beijing Opera.** The earliest known stages were nearly bare thrusts except for a carpet, a table, and two chairs; this configuration remains traditional for music drama. A performance could be indoors or out, but the stage was sometimes roofed. The traditional space had only two doorways upstage: one for entrances, the other for exits. The musicians and stage attendants remained onstage with the actors throughout (see Figure 7.4).

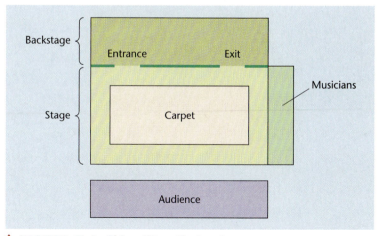

◆ **FIGURE 7.4** *China: Yüan Playing Space*

◆ **CHINESE ACTORS** *engaged in a stylized combat in music drama, c. 1843. Notice the musician sitting on the floor and the canopy over the performance space held up by pillars. The audience is seen in the background; therefore, the view of the artist is upstage of the action. In the nineteenth century evening performances of Chinese plays were often lit by gaslight.*
From "China in a Series of Views" by George Newenham Wright. Illustration by Thomas Allom. The Stapleton Collection/Bridgeman Art Library.

Music drama still tells epic and domestic stories, but the literary qualities of the earlier work are substantially diminished and replaced with remarkable acrobatics and various kinds of spectacle created by the actors themselves or through their ornate and colorful costumes and masklike makeup. Although both men and women performed in the early years of Chinese theatre, by the eighteenth century women were banished from the stage; they were not restored until 1912. Before banishment actresses often cross-dressed as males and sometimes led the acting troupes. Once women were removed, however, male cross-dressing featuring falsetto voice was established as a convention when music drama was being defined. Women have now returned to many of the female roles. Through contemporary performance we can still see many traditions inherited from a sophisticated professional theatre that flourished in China at a time when Europe saw little but religious dramas performed by amateurs.

◆◆◆◆◆◆◆◆◆

Classical Japan

Toward the end of the Yüan Dynasty in China, the first great classical theatre of Japan, **Noh** theatre, developed in the court of the shogun in the feudal samurai system of the late fourteenth century. Noh has always maintained music and dance as part of the dramatic presentation. Two early master actor-playwrights created and perfected the Noh theatre. Kan'ami (1333–1384) is credited with defining Noh's essential form, and his work is represented well by *Sotoba Komachi,* a play in which an aging woman is possessed by the spirit of her dead lover. *Sotoba Komachi* and nearly all the Noh plays are products of reflection as practiced in Zen Buddhism. Typically, the play is in the past tense, recalling painful events of long ago. Kan'ami's son Zeami (1363–1444) is considered the most important figure of Noh, not only because he wrote hundreds of plays, many of which are still performed, but because he wrote theory

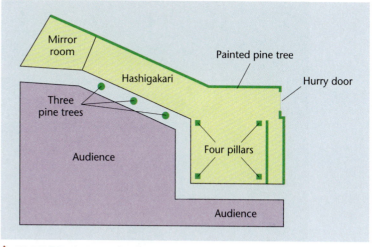

♦ **FIGURE 7.5** *Noh Theatre*

of performance and composition. His **Kadensho** presents the central image of Noh, *yugen,* which means the creation of temporary beauty—likening the Noh performance to a flower: elegant, lovely, transitory.

Noh theatre traditionally presents a varied program of plays, reflecting different moods and styles. A favorite play is *Hagaromo* (attributed to Zeami), which depicts a goddess who removes her magical robe to bathe in a stream, only to have the robe taken by a fisherman. She must enchant him with a dance to get him to return the robe. This climactic dance is an expected event in Noh structure. All is performed on a templelike, open, semithrust stage with a highly polished floor. The audience is seated on two sides (downstage and stage right). On the upstage wall is a large painted pine tree, and the main square of the stage, outlined by four pillars supporting a roof, is connected to backstage by a railed bridge (*hashigakari;* see Figure 7.5). The leading character (*shite*) is masked, but most other characters are not. The actors perform in front of onstage musicians playing flute and percussion, and a chorus, which often speaks for the *shite.* Actors are traditionally male (even though most *shite* roles are female) and assisted on stage by neutrally costumed stage attendants whom the audience pretends are not visible. The gestures of actors are highly stylized and often accentuated by remarkable uses of fans. Noh continues to be performed, and new audience members are struck by the colorful costumes, enigmatic masks, and slow, stately, ritualistic approach to performance.

The most popular classical Japanese form is **Kabuki,** which began in 1603 through the dancing performances of the priestess Okuni. Although Kabuki was begun by a woman and the form was dominated by female performers for over twenty-five years, the government banned women from Kabuki in 1629. It has been traditionally performed by men ever since, with female roles, or **onnagata,** performed by men who specialize in this form of cross-dressing. Kabuki features original plays as well as many adapted from Noh and puppet theatre (**Bunraku**), which includes some of the most famous plays of Japan. The most celebrated playwright, Chikamatsu (1683–1725), wrote for both Kabuki and Bunraku and has been widely translated. One of his most famous plays, which explores social and domestic problems, is *Love Suicides at Sonezaki* (1703), in which two lovers kill themselves because they are unable to realize the marriage they dream of. For the most part, however, the playwrights are not considered nearly

◆ **THE KABUKI PLAY** *MASAKADO*, *performed here by Utaemon and Koshiro, who has his sword drawn as she kneels on the floor. The setting upstage will fall apart later in the play when an earthquake strikes.*
Photo by Lennox and Katherine Tierney, KaiDib Films International.

as important as the actors in Kabuki. It is first and foremost an actors' theatre; the best actors are given names associated with great actors of the past who performed the same roles. Danjuro XII, for example, performed for many years as Ebizo X before he was "promoted" in 1985 to Danjuro, the most famous acting name in Kabuki.

As in Noh, music, dance, and colorful costumes are significant in Kabuki. It was originally performed on stages adapted from Noh, but ultimately Kabuki took a very different direction. Kabuki actors do not wear masks, but the makeup is often intricate and masklike. Typically, Kabuki performance is spectacular, using a revolving stage (the first in the world, created in 1758), huge elevator traps, and special effects that delight audiences with a mixture of realism and stylization. In *Masakado* (*The Demon Princess,* 1836), for example, the princess creates a magical dance that causes an earthquake, and the play ends with all the scenery collapsing. Kabuki is a great borrower and added the proscenium arch after encountering it in the late nineteenth century. The most dynamic element of the performance space, however, is the **hanamichi,** a stage-level ramp that passes directly from the stage apron down right center to the back of the house. This narrow path, which places the actor in the midst of the audience, is used for many important entrances and exits (see Figure 7.6).

Many Kabuki plays feature betrayed romance, eroticism, and military themes. In *Kumagai's Camp* (1751) a samurai warrior must confront the severed head of his own son and pretend that it is the head of his enemy. Any display of

Kabuki Cross-Dressing: The *Onnagata*

EXPLORING HISTORICAL and CULTURAL PERSPECTIVES

Although the Japanese classical theatre form called Kabuki was created by women, it was taken over by men in 1629 according to government decree. *Onnagata* is the Kabuki term for the actor who is a female impersonator. The male performer attempts to create as complete and literal a transformation as possible through makeup, costume, movement, and gesture. In speech, however, the actor uses a falsetto voice that ultimately stylizes the presentation. The *onnagata* performance is marked by grace, charm, and elegance, and the *onnagata* is often a dancer as well. Many famous Kabuki actors have specialized as *onnagata*. In the eighteenth and nineteenth centuries some *onnagata* actors actually took up the role and lifestyle of women in daily life. This seems extreme but indicates how seriously they took their work—they wished to live it.

In our own time two actors especially, Nakamura Utaemon VI (1917–2001) and Bando Tamasaburo V (b. 1950), have been particularly popular and effective and have shared their performances through worldwide tours. Watching these two actors perform at the same time in the 1980s was an extraordinary experience because their styles were so different. Utaemon was much older than Tamasaburo. His dance and gestural work were subtler, and he seemed very vulnerable, although he often suppressed emotionality except for extreme moments of tension. Tamasaburo, by contrast, seemed more direct. His physical work was more dynamic and at times flashier. Both actors, however, despite the falsetto voice, were very convincing as women. When watching them, one thought of "she," not "he."

◆ **UTAEMON** *as the* onnagata *Princess Takiyasha in* Masakado. *He is seen here in a dance reflecting both graceful presence and demonic possession. Note the spider web motif on his costume, which is important imagery for his character.*
Kabuki, grand tour of the United States. Courtesy of the Japan Society.

◆ **TAMASABURO** *as the* onnagata *Princess Taema with Ebizo as Narukami (a priest) in* The Thunder God.
Kabuki grand tour of the United States. Courtesy of the Japan Society.

Tamasaburo continues as a star not only in Kabuki but also in film and dance. He has played Shakespeare's Lady Macbeth, for example, and has choreographed and danced to classical music by Bach as it was played live by the sensational cellist Yo-Yo Ma.

Interested? Check out

http://metropolis.japantoday.com/biginjapanarchive299/275/biginjapaninc.htm for an article on Bando Tamasaburo V.
The Art of Kabuki. Princeton, NJ: Films for the Humanities, 1992 (videotape) to watch pieces of Kabuki in performance.
Earl Ernst. *Kabuki Theatre.* Honolulu: University Press of Hawaii, 1974.
"Kabuki for Everyone," at www.fix.co.jp/kabuki/kabuki.html. The *onnagata* Ichimura Manjiro actively participates in this web site.

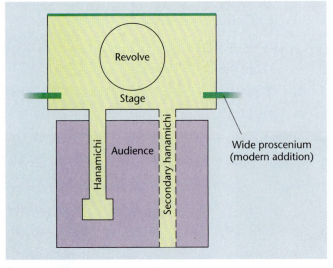

♦ **FIGURE 7.6** *Kabuki Theatre*

emotion would be seen as betrayal by Kumagai's shogun. The actor's remarkable skill with *mie* (a showy pose and facial expression suggesting sustained emotion) must reveal his grief to the audience while concealing it from his lord. Kabuki tends to be the classical form most accessible to Western audiences who are first encountering theatre in Japan.

Most of these Western and Asian classical and seminal forms continue to be performed and adapted in theatrical production, deconstructed or revised by experimenters, and studied by scholars and students of the theatre. Much of what we continue to pursue in the theatre and its scholarship has either built on this work or rebelled against it; the plays and styles and approaches to production developed so long ago by the Greeks, Romans, Indians, Medieval Europeans, Chinese, and Japanese make up our artistic legacy—inspiration to those who followed and the foundation for the theatre's ongoing journey with audiences of the twenty-first century.

♦♦♦♦♦♦♦♦♦

QUESTIONS AND ACTIVITIES

1. Theatre was an important part of religious and civic celebrations in ancient Greek and medieval communities, involving the entire town, even the region, in the event. Do we have an equivalent today?

2. Noh is the product of a time and place very different from ours. The first time an audience member sees Noh theatre, it is often necessary to adjust his or her approach to time: Noh proceeds at a slow, ritualistic, and meditative pace. Do your perceptions change as you participate in different types of activities or experience different forms of entertainment? Do you

prepare yourself in different ways, mentally and/or physically? Do you think people who grew up playing computer and video games perceive the world in a different way from those who did not?

3. How do you think the different theatre spaces of Greece and Rome would affect an audience's viewing experience? Both were open air, but the Greek theatres were built into a hillside (the audience was often facing a magnificent landscape), and the Roman theatres were freestanding.

♦♦♦♦♦♦♦♦♦

KEY TERMS AND CONCEPTS

◆◆◆◆◆◆◆◆◆
FOR FURTHER EXPLORATION

See the list of sources at the end of Chapter 9 on pages
    246–247.

Macbeth.

Mrs Siddons as Lady Macbeth.

Drury Lane 1792.

SARAH SIDDONS AS LADY MACBETH in 1792.
By permission of the Folger Shakespeare Library.

CHAPTER 8

Reinterpretations

Europe Rediscovers the Western Classics

The Italian Renaissance

Elizabethan England

The Spanish Golden Age

Seventeenth-Century France

Restoration England

Eighteenth-Century Europe and the Americas

F ollowing a few precedents in nondramatic literature, by the sixteenth century European artists and scholars were seriously revisiting classical thought in playwriting and theatrical practice. Europeans at this time had little or no awareness of the Asian theatrical forms; serious melding of East and West in theatre would not occur until the late nineteenth century. For some two hundred years or more, however, Europeans rejected medieval thought and practice and attempted to create a new classicism inspired by what they could learn about the Greeks and Romans. After remarkable experiments in Italy, England, Spain, and France, the European theatre settled into a nearly uniform approach to theatrical practice and dramaturgy (we will note the important variations). This uniformity, in plays at least, is usually called **neoclassicism:** a systematic approach to playwriting based on interpretations of classical Greek and Roman models of plays and theory.

♦ ♦ ♦ ♦ ♦ ♦ ♦ ♦ ♦

The Italian Renaissance

Between the Japanese eras of Zeami and Chikamatsu, Italy launched its Renaissance of art and literature. This rebirth of classically inspired creativity produced few plays of lasting importance, but Italy's contributions to the theatre between about 1500 and 1700 were enduring achievements. Of course, Italian art looked back to the humanistic art, literature, and philosophy of the Greeks and Romans. This ferment led directly to the Italian inventions of perspective painting of scenery and easily changeable scenery for the stage. Italians also invented the **proscenium** (picture frame) theatre, and because Italian theatre moved indoors,

theatres standardized artificial illumination using candles and oil lamps. The Italians created opera as an attempt to understand and reconceive Greek tragedy, developed neoclassical principles for the writing of plays, and launched the vibrant, improvisational *commedia dell'arte.*

Italianate scenery was developed in part through inspiration from developments in perspective drawing and painting but also out of a keen desire to provide scenery for specific types of plays (tragedies, comedies, and pastoral tragicomedies) as well as spectacular scenic effects for court entertainments and opera. Perspective scenery for plays appeared as early as 1508, and standardized approaches to such scenery were popularized in the designs and writings of Sebastiano Serlio in 1545. Although Serlio and others experimented with a variety of methods for transfer-

♦ **GENERIC SIXTEENTH-CENTURY DESIGN** *for tragedy during the Italian Renaissance. Designed by Sebastiano Serlio. Note the single central vanishing point and that all scenery is drawn and painted to appear much farther away from the audience than it actually is. This became the standard visual approach to theatrical scenery in Western countries as they adopted the proscenium theatre and changeable scenery.* From Serlio's *Architettura, Book 2,* 1569 edition. Courtesy Fine Arts Library, Indiana University.

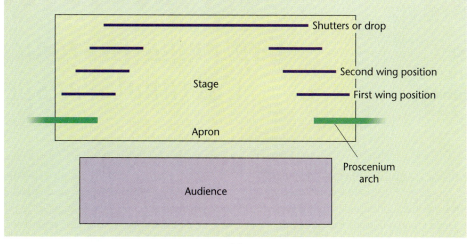

(a)

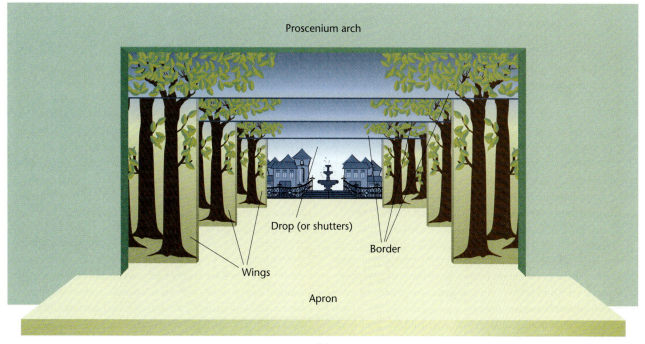

(b)

♦ **FIGURE 8.1** *(a) Italian Renaissance Changeable Scenery (Wing, Drop, and Border) Ground Plan (b) Wing, Drop, and Border Audience View*

ring perspective to the stage, the standard became two-dimensional, changeable **wings** or **flats** that could be pulled quickly on- and offstage in grooves on the floor and at the top of the tall wings. This system, fully implemented by Giovan Aleotti by 1606, eventually became the standard for all of Europe and North America. Consequently, there was great international demand for Italian designers such as Giacomo Torelli, who in the 1640s developed the chariot and pole system (winch, line, and tackle machinery that could change all the scenery simultaneously), (see Figure 8.1).

Italianate scenery was at first presented on platforms in halls without any kind of framing. After experiments with temporary prosceniums, new theatres

Exploring Historical and Cultural Perspectives

Renaissance Court Entertainment

From the early Renaissance in Italy and for centuries thereafter throughout Europe, most royal courts supported, subsidized, or commanded acting troupes, dancers, and musicians and sometimes enjoyed plays and special court productions created specifically to honor or please the royalty. Such entertainment was provided whether the court was led by kings and queens, dukes, and other nobility associated with the Holy Roman Empire; great national powers such as France and England; or economic power centers such as Venice and Florence. Many professional actors, playwrights, designers, and composers were associated with such court theatre and often supplemented their income or worked exclusively for the courts of power throughout the European continent. In many cases members of court also participated, including women, even if women were forbidden to perform on the professional stage.

From the 1400s to the 1600s in Italy such court entertainments were often called *intermezzi* and were spectacular pageants full of symbolism and allegory frequently performed between other entertainments or during the intervals between acts of a play or opera. Many of the Italian scenic experiments resulting in changeable and flying scenery were developed for intermezzi. Costumes for intermezzi were also flamboyant and sometimes bizarre, since the characters portrayed were often cosmic, classical gods and goddesses, or mythological characters. *The Judgment of Paris* (1608), drawn from Greek mythology dealing with the beautiful Helen and jealous goddesses, is typical of Italian applications of myth to Renaissance courts. The designers could afford to be more extravagant and adventurous than in the professional theatre, since their efforts were subsidized by the court.

England's version of court entertainment in the sixteenth and seventeenth centuries was the **masque,** a poetic extravaganza with dancing, often celebrating the monarch (particularly King James I or Charles I) or a royal visitor to the court.

The successful satirical playwright Ben Jonson wrote many masques (a number of which survive) and often produced them in conjunction with designer Inigo Jones. For their first effort together, *The Masque of Blackness* (1605) with an African theme, Queen Anne, wife of James I, appeared in the performance in blackface makeup along with her ladies-in-waiting. It is clear that the visual displays, which often included flying machinery, were just as important to the court as the text that was spoken or sung, if not more so, and this led to turf feuds between Jones and Jonson. The masque designs of Jones were also influential in the Restoration shift from an Elizabethan theatrical façade to changeable scenery for the proscenium arch. Jones's surviving designs demonstrate that he was very aware of the developments in Italy.

Some of the most sumptuous court entertainments were created for Louis XIII and especially Louis XIV in France, where they were often called court ballet. Louis XIV was fond of performing in such shows himself, being flown onto the stage outfitted as the sun, for example, in honor of his nickname "the Sun King." Court entertainment could be performed indoors or out and was sometimes created on lakes and other small bodies of water like the water shows and *naumachia* (miniature sea battles) begun by the ancient Romans. The excesses and visual feasting of such seventeenth-century court productions in France are recreated stunningly in the film *Vatel* (2000), directed by Roland Joffé and starring Gerard Depardieu as a masterful creator of court entertainment.

Interested? Check out

Roy C. Strong. *Splendor at Court: Renaissance Spectacle and the Theater of Power.* Boston: Houghton Mifflin, 1973.

A. M. Nagler. *A Source Book in Theatrical History.* New York: Dover, 1952.

Barnard Hewitt. *The Renaissance Stage: Documents of Serlio, Sabbattini and Furttenbach.* Coral Gables, Fla.: University of Miami Press, 1958.

dedicated to court entertainments, opera, and theatre began to appear with permanent frames separating the audience from the scenery. The oldest proscenium theatre surviving to the twentieth century (reconstructed after being destroyed in World War II) is the Teatro Farnese in Parma, which was designed by Aleotti in 1618. By the late 1600s nearly every European theatre had a proscenium, and this kind of theatre architecture is still the most common throughout most of the world.

Italian neoclassicism began to develop early in the 1500s. By the late 1600s it was standard practice throughout the Western world and remained so until the early nineteenth century. Although playwrights from other countries wrote more significant plays using neoclassicism, the system was developed by Italian playwrights and theorists. Neoclassicism, which had accumulated all of its principles and rules by 1570 in a treatise by Lodovico Castelvetro, was an attempt to justify secular literature (including plays) and to get official and church sanction for the creation of nonreligious plays. The new method was inspired by the classical writings and plays of Greece and Rome as well as the authoritative treatises on drama written by Aristotle in Greece and Horace in Rome.

Once established, neoclassicism no longer needed to justify its existence, but the standards became rather inflexible rules against which the romantics finally rebelled in the late 1700s. Three basic tenets were central to neoclassicism: reality, morality, and universality. Reality did not mean realism but what the Italians called **verisimilitude,** which established that theatrical events as written and staged should be reality-based (events that could really occur in life). Some aspects of verisimilitude were drawn from the classics, some were not, and what often seemed a tendency in Greek and Roman plays became rules for the neoclassicists. The **three unities,** for example, can be found in some of the classics but were by no means rules in Greece. These were the unity of time (the action of the play should take place in twenty-four hours or less), unity of place (action should occur in one location), and unity of action (no subplots unless fully integrated with the central conflict). One of the most entertaining Italian comedies, Niccolo Machiavelli's *The Mandragola* (c. 1520), for example, takes place on a street in front of several houses in Florence. The events of the play span one day and night. All of the action is geared to an intrepid young man's successful seduction of a young wife and his trickery at the expense of her credulous old husband. The unities were meant to enhance believability of the action and scenic presentation while unifying the artistic integrity of the play. The pursuit of reality also led to avoiding onstage violence and supernatural events (no one would believe or accept them, it was thought).

Neoclassicism also demanded that plays should teach a moral lesson, at first to help justify secular subjects and receive the sanction of church and political authorities. Sometimes the moral lesson was clearly stated at the conclusion of the play, or it was clearly implied throughout. Typically, the conclusion states the importance of not foiling true love, the rewards of remaining virtuous, or the idea that peace and human understanding only come after significant suffering. The early *Mandragola* did not follow this rule, but most Italian plays did. The neoclassicists also strove for an idealism and universality in morality and characterization, which led to much stereotyping of character. Known as **decorum,** this universality of character led playwrights to draw characters according to current notions of appropriate behavior, values, and language in terms of age, sex, social class, occupation, and economic condition.

Another unifying device was standardizing dramatic form by insisting that all plays be written in five acts, mostly based on the idea that appeared in Horace and the five-act division of Roman plays as received in the Renaissance. Even though the Italians reached a consensus with tragedy and comedy, they also experimented with tragicomedy and popularized it, especially through pastoral (rural and idyllic) mixed-tone plays such as *The Faithful Shepherd* (1590) by

Giambattista Guarini. This play, dominated by romance and the failed efforts of villainy, along with Guarini's published theories, had a huge influence on tragicomedy in Spain and England.

When not working with fully scripted plays, the Italians ventured far from the restrictions of neoclassicism. Professional Italian ***commedia dell'arte*** (improvisational comedy) also became an international phenomenon whose import outlasted neoclassicism, but *commedia*'s origins are less certain. It appears that by the mid-1500s popular professional *commedia* companies were performing throughout Italy, and some had moved to other countries such as France by 1548. Because of similarities in character types, scenarios, and style, some historians surmise that *commedia* had its origins in the Greek and Roman mimes. However these actors might have developed their art, they found a huge following for their improvisational methods, acrobatic clowning, farcical plots, and attractive lovers. Many characters wore masks; for example, the servant clowns (***zanni***) such as Arlecchino and Brighella carried out foolishness and intrigues against ridiculous older masters such as Pantalone (a miser) and Capitano (a braggart soldier). But many unmasked characters were central to the action. Actresses played unmasked types such as the leading lady (***prima donna***) and young lover (***innamorata***), supposedly to reveal the beauty of the actresses. Of course, young male lovers (***innamorato***) were also unmasked for similar reasons. Actors followed a scenario or plot outline. Although the story of each scenario was fixed, the actors improvised much of the dialogue and action with each new performance.

Commedia dell'arte predated and worked outside the conventions of neoclassicism until the mid-1700s, when neoclassical playwrights in Italy and France convinced many *commedia* actors to start performing fully scripted plays, eliminate masks, and soften the broad humor. This neoclassicized *commedia* spelled the end for *commedia* as a continuing improvisational and farcical acting style. Because *commedia*'s characters, costumes, and the idea of improvisational style still fascinate us, many theatrical companies frequently revive plays based on *commedia*. Ironically, many plays that brought traditional *commedia* to an end are revived and performed in what is intended as a *commedia* style. In fact a multitude of contemporary "commedia" acting troupes have attempted to reconstitute the style and methods, and they frequently perform throughout Europe and North America.

◆◆◆◆◆◆◆◆◆

Elizabethan England

Beyond doubt the period of theatre history that tends to fascinate most contemporary Western theatregoers is that of William Shakespeare, who is usually lionized as the preeminent playwright of the English language, if not the world. Whether his importance is exaggerated or not, he is clearly the most famous playwright of Western civilization. What other playwrights can claim so many theatre festivals dedicated to them? Who does not know about *Hamlet* even if

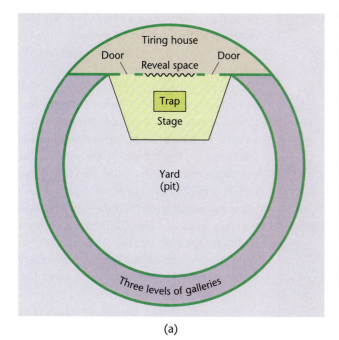

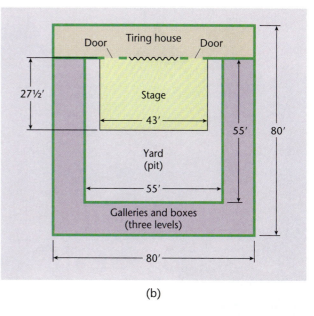

(a)

(b)

◆ **FIGURE 8.2** *(a) Elizabethan Public Theatre Ground Plan (b) Fortune Theatre Ground Plan (Based on Seventeenth-Century Builder's Contract)*

he or she has never read the play? Although most people today view the Eliza-bethan period of theatre through Shakespeare's work, Shakespeare's fellow Elizabethans would not have done so.

During the reign of Queen Elizabeth I, professional theatre in London forged a union between acting companies and a host of writ-ers (mostly university-educated). The all-male companies (women's roles were played by boys or young men) often attracted noble pa-trons, but the box-office receipts were vitally important to the success of the players. This period of greatness in English theatre is identified as 1587 to 1642, a short era that coincided with British exploration, conquest, and nationalistic fervor.

The English at first showed little interest in Italian neoclassicism or changeable scenery, although they would adopt both in 1660. In-stead, the actors performed in three-story, polygonal **public theatres** that were open to the sky. All action transpired on a thrust stage fronting a façade with probably two doors and sometimes a cur-tained discovery space between them. The façade also had a second level for such things as the balcony scene in *Romeo and Juliet* (c. 1594). The audience stood in the pit or yard surrounding three sides of the elevated stage or sat in galleries or boxes extending three stories into the air (see Figure 8.2). The most famous of these struc-tures was the Globe Theatre created by Shakespeare's company, the Lord Chamberlain's Men, who were led by actor-manager Richard Burbage. These companies also used indoor "private" theatres, but the standard of performance seems to have been established in the public theatres. The companies doubled many roles and performed with a **rolling repertory** (a system of daily changes of plays) with

**◆ THE ADAMS
SHAKESPEAREAN
THEATRE** *since 1977 has
served as the main stage for the
Utah Shakespearean Festival. It
was loosely based on what was
known about Elizabethan public
theatres.*

Photo by Karl Hugh. Courtesy of Utah
Shakespearean Festival.

more than thirty plays a year. A popular play reappeared throughout the season.

Also inspired by classical models, especially the Roman tragedies of Seneca, English playwrights returned to tragedy as well as comedy, tragicomic romances, and historical chronicles. Most of these plays were written in **blank verse** (unrhymed **iambic pentameter**), but the playwrights also made extensive use of prose and rhymed verse, which were often mixed with the blank verse as "home base." Elizabethan drama is typically marked as beginning with Thomas Kyd's *The Spanish Tragedy* (1587), a study in vengeance, madness, and grotesque onstage violence, which long stood as a model of tragedy of revenge.

Although many important plays and playwrights are identified with the Elizabethan theatre, several playwrights are of paramount importance and enjoy frequent revivals. Christopher Marlowe was the first to master blank verse, and he created significant models of heroic, antiheroic, and historical tragedy. His *Doctor Faustus* (c. 1588) was the first important play on the recurring subject of selling one's soul to the devil; *Edward II* (c. 1592) was the first important **chronicle** (a dramatic adaptation of historical events dealing with kings and frequent struggles for the crown) of a deposed English king; *Tamburlaine* (c. 1587) was apparently the first play whose popularity inspired a sequel, *Tamburlaine II* (c. 1588). We have been suffering with sequels ever since. Most of Marlowe's tragic heroes were first performed by Edward Alleyn, the leading actor of the Admiral's Men (Richard Burbage's chief competition). About the time Marlowe was murdered at the age of twenty-nine, Shakespeare's playwriting career was catching fire.

Unlike Marlowe, Shakespeare was an actor and was not educated at a university. He fully understood the company for which he was writing and must have performed some of his roles himself. Most of Shakespeare's tragic heroes were first performed by Burbage. Also unlike Marlowe, who specialized in tragedy, Shakespeare created masterpieces in nearly every major dramatic form of the era. From situation comedies such as *Comedy of Errors* (c. 1593) to romantic comedy such as *Much Ado about Nothing* (c. 1598) to fantastic comedy of the supernatural such as *A Midsummer Night's Dream* (c. 1595), Shakespeare created lasting renderings of romance, foibles, and mistakes in both the seen and unseen world. His tragicomic romances such as *The Winter's Tale* (c. 1610) and *The Tempest* (c. 1612) are laced with supernatural wonders and include a dark mood that tempers the comic structure. His chronicle plays have been so effective that many people confuse his renderings in *Richard III* (c. 1593) and *Henry V* (c. 1599) with genuine history. He is most frequently noted for his tragedies, however, especially the rise-and-fall action of *Macbeth* (c. 1606), the study of

Exploring Historical and Cultural Perspectives

In 1587 the Rose Theatre was the first theatre built across the Thames River from London (the Bankside) by manager Philip Henslowe and actor Edward Alleyn, the chief competition for Burbage and Shakespeare's company. Some of Shakespeare's early plays, such as *Henry VI*, and famous plays by Marlowe, such as *Doctor Faustus,* and Kyd's *The Spanish Tragedy* were performed at the Rose. The site of the Rose is close to that of the later Globe Theatre. Both theatres, however, were destroyed during the Commonwealth (1642–1660), when theatre was outlawed and many documents relating to the theatres were destroyed. For centuries scholars tried to piece together the nature of the Elizabethan public theatres with the remaining evidence: building contracts for the Fortune and Hope Theatres and a collection of images of interiors and exteriors that are woefully incomplete and out of scale and raise as many questions as they answer.

Little was known about the construction of the Rose until more than 60 percent of the foundations were uncovered during a new construction excavation in 1989. This discovery provided important evidence to support or negate speculation about the structure and size of the Elizabethan public theatres. Although not all Elizabethan theatres can be extrapolated from the architectural remains of the Rose, its excavation certainly lifted part of the veil shrouding Elizabethan theatre construction. The Rose foundation demonstrates that this theatre was polygonal in shape (some thirteen or fourteen sides), had a thrust stage about fifteen feet deep, later extended to sixteen, which was trapezoidal in shape surrounded on three sides by a yard and elevated galleries for the audience. The interior was nearly fifty feet wide, and the exterior was about ninety feet. Eventually, a new building was placed over the site (as was originally planned), but it was built to protect the remains of the Rose.

A bit later in 1989 a smaller part of the foundation of Shakespeare's famous Globe Theatre was also excavated. (Most of the site is covered by an early nineteenth-century building, which is protected as a historical monument.) On the basis of these remains the Globe was estimated to be also polygonal but larger, about one hundred feet wide, with perhaps twenty sides. The new Globe Theatre in London (intended to be modeled on what is known about the original Globe and used for performances of Elizabethan plays) was already designed and partially constructed at that time, but some changes were made after the 1989 discoveries. Today you can visit the site of the Rose, which is still being prepared for permanent preservation, as well as the fully functional new Globe nearby, which gives regular performances. The film *Shakespeare in Love* (1998) includes a set representing the Rose Theatre, based on an interpretation of the remaining evidence.

Interested? Check out

Andrew Gurr. *The Shakespearean Stage 1574–1642,* 3rd edition. Cambridge, England: Cambridge University Press, 1992.

Christine Eccles. *The Rose Theatre.* New York: Routledge, 1990.

www.rdg.ac.uk/rose, maintained by University of Reading, includes information on the history, excavation, and ongoing preservation efforts for the Rose Theatre, as well as numerous illustrations.

The Shakespeare Globe Centre (USA) web site, www.sgc.umd.edu, maintained by the University of Maryland.

---

jealousy in *Othello* (c. 1604), the forestalled revenge in *Hamlet* (c. 1600), and the domestic tragedy played out in public in *King Lear* (c. 1605).

The one popular type of play that Shakespeare did not master became the specialty of Ben Jonson, another actor-playwright, who created some of the most biting satire of his time and sometimes got in trouble with the authorities for his barbed tongue. His *Volpone* (1606) creates a comic villain surrounded by fools and a manipulator so masterful that he cannot be overthrown except by himself. He must ridiculously overreach to be overwhelmed by the **wheel of fortune** (the

notion that fortunes change if we wait long enough). In fact, most of humanity in Jonson's plays, such as *The Alchemist* (1610) and *Every Man in His Humour* (1598), is shown as foolish, stupid, and easily duped. Recalling the Greek Aristophanes, Jonson was an acidic commentator on his times.

After the death of Queen Elizabeth in 1603 and the ascension of James I, many playwrights created plays filled with terror and a host of malcontents. Similar to today's horror movies, *The Duchess of Malfi* (1613) by John Webster and *The Revenger's Tragedy* (c. 1606) by Cyril Tourneur created a pessimistic tone with sensational scenes of torture, poisoning, strangulation, sword fights, and runaway vengeance. All was enacted in the midst of remarkable, hard-edged poetry, however. Toward the end of this era, John Ford created *'Tis Pity She's a Whore* (c. 1630), which combines beautiful lyrical poetry with scenes of crime, incest, and suicide. Perhaps its most poignant image, a brother interrupting a banquet with the heart of his sister impaled on his dagger, is a telling image for the tragedy of this age. Officially, this remarkable period ended with the closing of the theatres in 1642 at the outbreak of a horrendous political and religious civil war. For eighteen years of Puritan control there was no monarch, theatres were dismantled, acting companies were outlawed, and aside from a few underground performances, public theatre in England was dead.

◆◆◆◆◆◆◆◆◆◆

The Spanish Golden Age

Developing simultaneously with but independent of the Elizabethan theatre, Spain's professional theatre entered what is called a Golden Age that lasted from c. 1580 to 1680. Professional actors had been working for some time before 1580, however, in both religious (*autos sacramentales*) and secular plays (*comedias*) with companies made up of both men and women. The actors performed in temporary spaces, often courtyards, until professional public theatres were built in Madrid, Seville, and elsewhere beginning in 1579. The public theatre, called a *corral*, resembled the Elizabethan public theatre in many ways: a raised, roofed stage backed by a façade with doors and a discovery space; a second balcony level; three levels of galleries and boxes for the audience; and a pit (*patio*) for standees open to the sky. The stage was not a thrust, however, and limited seating was provided in the *patio* close to the downstage edge. As indicated in surviving plays, the performance space also seems to have included some kind of onstage access to the second performance level. The most distinct difference from the Elizabethan theatre, however, was a segregated seating area for unmarried or unaccompanied women, called the *cazuela*, at the back of the house facing the stage (see Figure 8.3). The existence of the cazuela was itself ironic, since actresses were performing on the stage. The history of theatre is littered with contradictions.

Like the Elizabethans, the Spanish practiced an episodic, almost free-form style in writing and staging their plays and showed no interest in neoclassicism until a much later date. Although many playwrights created popular *comedias*, which tended to be mixed in emotional tone and tragicomic in form, the work of two playwrights was especially important during the Golden Age and continues to be regularly revived, translated, and studied. Lope de Vega was one of the most wildly popular playwrights in theatre history. He wrote hundreds of plays, and his fan following could easily be compared to more recent pop phenomena such as the intense popularity of the Beatles, *Star Wars,* and the Harry Potter books. When he died in 1635, one theatre staged an apotheosis in which an actor playing Lope ascended into heaven like a saint. Most of his plays explore the very complex Spanish code of honor and feature love affairs, intrigues, awful villains, and restoration of honor after many tribulations experienced by the hero and heroine. *The King, the Greatest Alcalde* (c. 1620), for example, ends with the King of Spain stepping in and forcing a villain of noble birth to marry the peasant woman he violated, then executing the villain and giving his wealth to the woman as a dowry so that she can marry the man she really loves. Lope's most intriguing play might be *Fuente Ovejuna* (c. 1614), which features a **collective hero** (all the inhabitants of a village) who rise up against their evil overlord and kill him after he rapes and tortures an innocent village woman. No one among the brave and steadfast villagers will name a killer, even when tortured severely by the authorities. Their only answer, even on the rack, is the name of their village, Fuente Ovejuna.

Overlapping Lope's career was that of another prolific and remarkable *comedia* and *auto* playwright, Calderon de la Barca, who also explored the love and honor themes and was equally fascinated by philosophical questions. *The Constant Prince* (c. 1635) is a disturbing examination of self-sacrifice in which a prince captured in war refuses to allow himself to be ransomed. Calderon's most famous play, *Life Is a Dream* (c. 1636), explores illusion versus reality through the struggles of a prince who from birth has been kept imprisoned and ignorant of any social activity until he is grown. When released into the world as a prince once more, he believes that he is in a dream and, not surprisingly, often reacts with comic misunderstanding and deadly savagery. After the death of Calderon in 1681 the professional theatre continued, but no more great playwrights emerged for centuries; stage censorship after 1680 in Spain became quite severe. After the Golden Age, Spain (like England after its civil war) adopted neoclassicism.

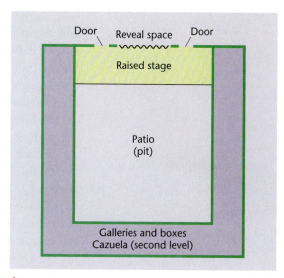

♦ **FIGURE 8.3** *Corral (Public Theatre) Ground Plan*

♦♦♦♦♦♦♦♦♦♦

Seventeenth-Century France

While England and Spain were exploding with vibrant theatrical activity at the end of the 1500s, France was still struggling to find an artistic identity. Through the guidance and patronage of Cardinal Richelieu, the prime minister under Louis XIII, however, theatre and drama found prominent voices in the 1620s and well beyond. Avoiding the style of their enemy England, French theorists, artists, and playwrights found themselves attracted to the neoclassical model of drama and the Italianate models in theatre and scenic design. They endeavored to "out-Italian" the Italians, and in playwriting at least they were quite successful in their quest, so much so that many artists and scholars by the mid-eighteenth century began to identify neoclassicism with the French instead of the Italians.

The French were also attracted to *commedia dell'arte,* whose methods were especially influential on the development of French comedy after a *commedia* troupe took up residence in Paris in 1548. In the same year, Europe's first new theatre since the Roman Empire was built in Paris. The new Hôtel de Bourgogne eventually became the first home of French professional theatre companies. By 1641 Paris got its first proscenium theatre, the Palais Cardinal, built in the palace of Cardinal Richelieu. After his death it became known as the Palais Royal and was ultimately the theatre of Molière, the premier actor and comic playwright of the era. Other theatres also quickly added proscenium arches, which became the European standard.

Neoclassicism did not triumph in France without a bit of a fight, however. Pierre Corneille was the first of three great playwrights of seventeenth-century France. He tested the waters of neoclassicism in 1636 by writing and producing *The Cid,* a fascinating tragicomic tale inspired by Spanish history and drama. Although written in neoclassical form, the play features events that should really transpire over years, but Corneille forced the action into a single day. The play was popular, but Richelieu and many literary figures challenged the appropriateness of the play. The newly formed French Academy ruled that the play should have conformed more closely to the rules and spirit of neoclassicism. Corneille never wavered from neoclassical form again, but this early "irregular" play is his most admired and studied in our own time.

Jean Racine remains the most revered writer of tragedy in all of French theatre. He reworked famous plays and stories from Greek and Roman originals and in several cases produced the most profound versions. His tragic verse was written in rhyming couplets, making translation into English a monumental task. At the center of his plays is always a psychological struggle in which the protagonist (usually a woman) is given an impossible choice—a lose/lose situation. She is torn between her desire and her duty, and desire always wins. This triumph over duty is the heart of the tragedy. Racine's most enduring play in this vein is *Phèdre* (1677), a reworking of earlier tragedies by Euripides and Seneca in which a queen falls in love with her stepson and descends to despair.

In our own time it is the comedies of Molière from this period that are most frequently revived and studied. Unlike Corneille and Racine, Molière was also an actor and the manager of his theatre company, the most successful in Paris. Molière wrote farces and comedies of manners (depicting and satirizing upper-class society), but many of his plays feature eccentric central characters who are given to excess such as miserliness and hypochondria. The most popular of these are *The Misanthrope* (1666), which examines a man who hates humanity yet falls in love, and *Tartuffe* (1669), a satirical study in religious hypocrisy. Molière often took the leading male roles himself; late in his career, his talented young actress wife, Armande Béjart, often took the female leads.

The success of both Molière and his company was so great that when he died suddenly in 1673, the Parisian theatrical world was thrown into a tizzy (such as that sparked by our contemporary corporate raiding and scandals in the business world). The crown interceded and forced three professional theatres

♦ **THE PALAIS CARDINAL,** *the first proscenium theatre built in France (1641). Here, Cardinal Richelieu, who commissioned the new space, attends a performance with his king, Louis XIII. The cardinal died soon after opening his theatre and willed the space to the king. Thus the theatre was renamed the Palais Royal, under which name Louis XIV made the theatre available to Molière, who presented his most famous plays there. This space was intended for court theatre, so it is small compared to professional proscenium theatres built in the eighteenth century.*
Musee des Arts Decoratifs, Paris (Lalance).

to combine. The new company was called the Comédie Française, and for many years it exercised a monopoly on drama in Paris. Although the monopoly is long gone, the Comédie Française continues still and considers itself the "House of Molière."

♦♦♦♦♦♦♦♦♦

Restoration England

When the monarchy was restored in England in 1660, the theatre was also revived after an eighteen-year absence. For the new actors, playwrights, and managers, the influence of France was more prominent than the memory of Elizabethan theatre practice. Many royalists loyal to the king had lived in exile in France along with the new king, Charles II. They became close to the French court and very conversant with professional theatre, which then featured actresses, Italianate scenery, and the neoclassical plays of Corneille and Molière. Once back in England, Charles II granted patents (official licenses) to new theatre managers to open professional theatres. Most theatre buildings had been demolished by the Puritans, and performance spaces had to be adapted from existing buildings such as indoor tennis courts. Once new theatres could be built, they featured proscenium arches and changeable scenery. Unlike other European theatres, however, the English spaces

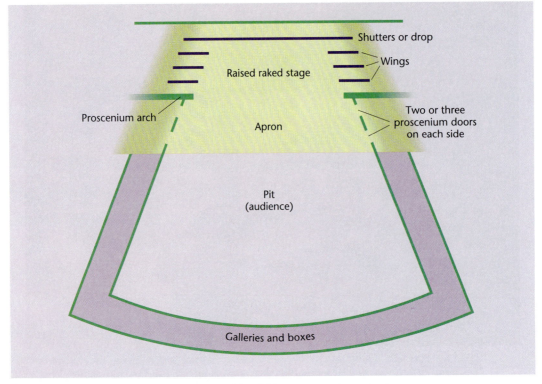

♦ **FIGURE 8.4** *Restoration Theatre Ground Plan*

included functional doors just downstage of the proscenium arch that the actors used for most entrances and exits (see Figure 8.4). This device (perhaps inspired by the memory of Elizabethan theatres) remained in place in Britain and British colonies or former colonies, such as Canada, Jamaica, and the United States, until the first decades of the nineteenth century (see Figure 8.5). Some proscenium theatres in our own time include variations on these proscenium doors.

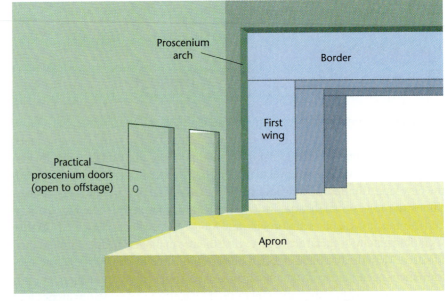

♦ **FIGURE 8.5** *Restoration Proscenium Doors, Audience View*

◆ **THE COUNTRY WIFE,** *by William Wycherley. Actresses in late seventeenth-century England often dressed as young male characters. In this 2000 revival we see the famous scene where Margery Pinchwife (played by Tessa Auberjonois) is in disguise as a boy so that her overprotective husband will allow her to move freely in society. Other men, such as Horner (played by Leigh Lawson), are not fooled. Horner kisses Margery while pretending to believe that the woman is really a boy. The audience enjoys the joke on Margery's silly husband at the same time that sexual tension mounts. Directed by Keith Baxter; costumes designed by Robert Perdziola.*
Photo by Carol Rosegg. Courtesy of The Shakespeare Theatre, Washington, D.C.

Also in 1660 the professional theatres introduced actresses to the English-speaking stage. This novelty soon became the standard, and the second generation of actresses included very talented performers such as Anne Bracegirdle and Elizabeth Barry, who inspired playwrights to create roles specifically for them. The new actresses were the first women to play Shakespeare's famous female roles such as Juliet, Ophelia, and Desdemona, all of which had originally been played by boys or young men. A great male actor, Thomas Betterton, also appeared in the Restoration and created a tradition for performing Shakespeare's leading men that influenced a long line of classical actors stretching to our own time with the likes of John Gielgud, Alec Guinness, and Ian McKellen. Betterton also specialized in comedy of manners.

The comedy of manners reached a kind of perfection in the Restoration as upper-class characters were caught in a comic struggle between their own personal desires (often sexual) and prevailing social codes of behavior. In these plays, the most clever and intelligent people who could manage to control their emotions were always victorious over those who revealed their emotions too easily. Masterpieces of these comedies abound. *The Country Wife* (1675) by William Wycherley depicts a naïve young woman caught up in sophisticated liaisons; *The Way of the World* (1700) by William Congreve includes a famous wooing scene in which a couple desperately in love pretends indifference as they work out what might be the first prenuptial agreement in dramatic literature.

The Restoration period is also noteworthy for the earliest known plays written by professional women playwrights. Aphra Behn's intrigue comedies have found new audiences in our own time, especially her delightful romp *The Rover* (1677), the original production of which featured Elizabeth Barry and Thomas Betterton. This play of chases and disguises was so successful that it led to a sequel. While securing a popular audience, Behn was adept at comically attacking the sexual double standard and the position of women in society.

Although British playwrights had embraced neoclassicism by 1660, they did so with a few variations that persisted until the romantic rebellion at the end of the eighteenth century. For the British, unity of place was defined not as a single location, as the French and Italians defined it, but as any set of locations that could be reached within a twenty-four-hour period. Consequently, the British had many changes of scene in the traditional genres, unlike the French and Italians. The British also maintained violence on the stage, with numerous sword fights, which their audiences seemed to admire but the French strictly avoided. Otherwise, the British stage was very neoclassical for about one hundred and fifty years. The Restoration period, however, lasted a mere forty years. After 1700 the new plays in England and its colonies moved toward sentimentality, eliminated obvious sexual scenes in comedies, and more stringently followed the principle of teaching moral lessons.

◆◆◆◆◆◆◆◆◆◆

Eighteenth-Century Europe and the Americas

When looking back on eighteenth-century Western theatre now, we are often struck by a remarkable similarity from country to country in terms of dramatic style, acting methods, theatre architecture, and scenic design. Of course, the subject matter and language of plays often differ dynamically, but nearly all plays follow the principles of neoclassicism. The plays of the eighteenth century that tend to be revived in our own period are comedies of manners, some of which enjoy popularity, especially in resident professional and university theatres. The tragic plays of the eighteenth century, although popular in their own time, rarely inspire us today.

From England Oliver Goldsmith's *She Stoops to Conquer* (1773) and Richard Brinsley Sheridan's *The School for Scandal* (1777) have held the English-speaking stage since their creation. They continue to entertain audience members who still recognize incisive social criticism, duplicity of character, the dangers of gossip, and misguided attempts of elders to force their intentions on grown children. *The School for Scandal* inspired the most intriguing neoclassical play created in the new United States, *The Contrast* (1787) by Royall Tyler, a comic comparison of European and American society and values. In France René LeSage wrote one of the most biting satires of social and economic cheating in any period: *Turcaret* (1709); the title character is a corrupt tax collector. It was Pierre Marivaux and Beaumarchais, however, who made the most lasting

◆ **DAVID GARRICK** *(left) and* **JOHN PHILIP KEMBLE** *(right) in costume as Macbeth. In 1768, Garrick, by dressing in contemporary clothing—in this case a British military uniform—took an approach to Macbeth that was typical of his period. There was little or no attempt by actors and managers of the time to capture the period or location of the original play. Theatre practitioners did not attempt to unify the production visually. Actors chose or commissioned their own costumes based on their tastes and what they could afford. In 1794, Kemble, a popular actor-manager, attempted to make Macbeth look a bit Scottish by adding a kilt and fur hat to otherwise typical eighteenth-century English attire, including the rosettes on his shoes.*
By permission of the Folger Shakespeare Library.

impact on later periods with Marivaux's comedies such as *The False Confessions* (1737), which center on characters surprised by their own love for another. Beaumarchais' *The Marriage of Figaro* (1784) introduced a remarkable level of democratization by making his central characters servants who are meant to receive the lion's share of empathy from the audience. Beaumarchais also got in trouble with the authorities by attacking nobility of birth as an indication of superiority.

Italy produced entertaining comedies through the efforts of Carlo Goldoni, whose reforms brought *commedia dell'arte* to an essential end by fully scripting plays for the Italian actors, beginning with the farce *The Servant of Two Masters* (1743/1753). Goldoni eliminated *commedia* masks and also created wonderful roles for women, especially in *The Mistress of the Inn* (1753). The heroine Mirandolina outwits all the men in the play and takes complete control of her life.

Female willfulness is also prominent in the English comedies of Susanna Centlivre, whose *The Wonder: A Woman Keeps a Secret* (1714) examined the themes of confinement and freedom as well as the concept of honor and held the stage for more than a hundred years. Shortly after the work of Centlivre,

Exploring Collaboration

The Hallam Company in the American Colonies: A Family Affair

Although amateur theatre was practiced in the thirteen original American colonies from 1665, there was no attempt to create professional theatre until 1749, when a group of performers led by Walter Murray and Thomas Kean, with no apparent previous professional experience or training, declared themselves a professional company and performed in New York, Philadelphia, Williamsburg, and elsewhere. This semiprofessional troupe lasted until 1752, when a bona fide professional company arrived from a small theatre that had recently closed in England. The actors hoped to free themselves from the Licensing Act (1737), which technically made their company illegal in England because of a monopoly held by two major theatres in London. They hoped to establish themselves in the New World. This London Company of Comedians was led by actor-manager Lewis Hallam and backed by his brother, William, who remained in England. The actors were on a **sharing system,** which means they split any profits after the day's expenses on the basis of how many shares each had invested in the speculative venture or had been granted by the manager depending on his or her duties and importance to the company.

The troupe was a family affair. Lewis played supporting roles. His wife (we know her as only Mrs. Lewis Hallam) played female leads in tragedy, and their children also performed and were trained in acting. There were other adults,

some related to the Hallams, some not. Their oldest son, Lewis Hallam, Jr., within six years would graduate to the leading male tragic roles, resulting in odd casting such as playing Romeo to his mother's Juliet. By sometime in the 1760s Lewis was playing opposite his cousin Nancy Hallam in the younger tragic roles. His mother maintained the mature tragic leads until the American Revolution. The company first performed in Williamsburg, Virginia, and went on to towns in the circuit first played by the Murray and Kean company. Touring throughout the colonies was a necessity because no one town was large enough to support a permanent theatre company. When the first census was taken in 1790, the largest city in the new United States, Philadelphia, consisted of only 42,000 people. The actors often struggled to get local permission to play, since many colonists, especially the clergy, Puritans, and Quakers, had prejudices against the theatre and often passed laws prohibiting it. Philadelphia was especially problematic, but the Hallams managed to get permission in the difficult areas by offering performances and giving all the proceeds to local charities. New England, with its Puritan leadership, was off-limits until the 1760s, and no serious inroads were made in that area until after the Revolution.

In 1755 the company left the American colonies and traveled to Jamaica, where a professional company already resided led by John Moody and David Douglass. While there,

John Gay created a sensation in England by devising a satirical ballad opera (a musical with a comic story set to already existing popular music of the time but with new lyrics) about a highwayman and his gang entitled *The Beggar's Opera* (1728). It was not strictly an opera because it included much spoken dialogue. The play was so popular that it had more than one thousand performances in England alone in the eighteenth century. The ballad opera is one of several models that led eventually to the modern musical comedy.

It is very difficult to reconstruct acting methods for eighteenth-century theatre, but several things are clear. Actors performed in front of, not inside, the changeable Italianate scenery. Many theatres had a generous apron downstage of the proscenium arch, and it was on this open apron that most of the per-

Lewis Hallam died. In 1758 the company reorganized and re-turned to the American colonies; Mrs. Hallam remarried and became Mrs. David Douglass, her new husband becoming the new company manager. Actors in the altered organization came from both original companies. Lewis Hallam, Jr., was now an adult and a reasonably accomplished actor. Under the leadership of Douglass the company tried braver things. They ventured into New England with some success in 1761 and advertised that they were not playing "evil" plays, but moral dialogues and public presentations in the art of rhetoric and public speaking. Few people were fooled by this ruse, but Douglass continued in the Northeast by pre-tending not to be a theatre company. Under the Douglass leadership the troupe performed as far south as Charleston, South Carolina, and north to Rhode Island. Probably sensing the unrest in the colonies over British practices that culmi-nated in the Revolution, the company renamed itself the American Company in 1763 even though all the actors were British. About this time Lewis Hallam, Jr., also joined the man-agement of the company. Except for sojourns in Jamaica, he would remain an actor and theatre manager on the Ameri-can stage until his retirement in 1806.

Douglass and his company built the first permanent structures intended from the beginning as theatres, first the Southwark in Philadelphia (1766), then the John Street The-atre in New York (1767). These were the two most important American theatres until the end of the eighteenth century, when a new wave of improved theatre building got under-way. The American Company continued to perform until shortly after the Continental Congress forbade the perfor-mances of plays and other kinds of public entertainment in 1774 as a response to the growing conflicts with England. The all-British-born troupe retired to Jamaica during the Rev-olution. The actors returned after the Revolution as the "Old American Company" but without Mrs. Hallam-Douglass or David Douglass. The troupe eventually made New York their base of operations, but now there was a new Mrs. Hallam on the American stage: Eliza Tuke, the wife of Lewis, Jr. By the time he retired, Lewis Hallam, Jr., was the only link to the original 1752 company and provided valuable information to William Dunlap, a playwright, theatre manager, and the first person to write a history of the American theatre, in 1832.

Interested? Check out

Hugh F. Rankin. *The Theater in Colonial America.* Chapel Hill: Uni-versity of North Carolina Press, 1965.

Don Wilmeth and Christopher Bigsby. *The Cambridge History of American Theatre,* Vol. 1. Cambridge, England: Cambridge University Press, 1998.

William Dunlap. *History of the American Theatre.* New York: Burt Franklin, 1963. (Originally published in 1823.)

formance took place. Theatres were becoming quite large, with the result that actors needed to have great vocal facility; the gestures were probably quite ex-pansive. Actors often attempted to make very direct contact with the audience rather than interact directly with other actors (at least as the norm). This style of performance is often described as **rhetorical**—a "stand-up" actor or actress, whose big voice and grand gestures were intended to capture the attention and admiration of a fully lit and social audience. Many names and descriptions of ac-tors and actresses have come down to us, but one is especially prominent. David Garrick of London is often singled out as the actor of the age. He was said to have had a "natural" style, but we should not read this as "realistic" in our sense of the word. He was subtler than his contemporaries, and he engaged in dynamic mimetic movement on the stage; Garrick was considered a genius of gesture and facial expression. He became internationally famous, which was most unusual for any actor before the nineteenth century.

Professional acting companies first came to North America from England in the eighteenth century. Professional theatre here is usually dated from 1745 in Jamaica and 1752 in Virginia, when first one and later several acting companies toured the colonies. Amateur theatre in English, however, appeared occasionally in North America from 1665 onward from South Carolina to New York. New England prohibited theatre for many years under its Puritan leadership. Amateur theatre appeared in French in Canada in the seventeenth century and in Spanish in the Southwest even earlier. Spanish religious plays were performed by conquistadors and Jesuits in many parts of the New World, including Central and South America. Mexico had active theatre based on the Spanish *auto* and *comedia* models from the 1500s and had practicing local playwrights, some of whom date to the late 1500s. In later years Spanish Golden Age plays would also find important homes in the Americas in Mexico and throughout much of South America. Of course Native American ritual and story-telling reenactments and theatrical activity throughout the Americas predate all of the European-inspired theatre.

As Europe and its colonies reveled in discoveries of the New World and rediscovered the glories of the Western classical past, they hurried to shuck off the sensibilities of the medieval world and express an enlightened attitude. In their Renaissance and post-Renaissance plays, whether it was through neoclassical idealism or comparatively free-form, mixed-tone dramas devised by the Spanish and Elizabethans, European theatre artists were simultaneously looking back at the Western classics and forward to a new world of exploration, discovery, and nationalistic zeal. The postmedieval world was more conscious of its national identity than any Western society since perhaps the Greeks of the fifth century B.C.E. As Elizabethan, Spanish Golden Age, and seventeenth-century French plays became themselves new classics, and as neoclassicism eventually played itself out in the eighteenth century, however, many artists were primed for radical change—and it came quickly.

◆◆◆◆◆◆◆◆◆◆

QUESTIONS AND ACTIVITIES

1. The rules of neoclassicism were developed to produce a specific kind of play, similar to the rules for writing a particular kind of poetry (a sonnet, for example, always has fourteen lines). Choose some other forms of entertainment or art and list the rules. Some of these may be stated; others may be understood.

2. Imagine having seen plays performed only in a thrust configuration. How do you think the viewing experience would change if you attended a performance in which the actors stayed behind a proscenium arch and you viewed the action through a picture frame?

3. In Elizabethan England, women could attend and sit anywhere they could afford in the public theatre but could not perform on stage. In Spain during the Golden Age, women could perform on stage, but unmarried female audience members were restricted to seating in the *cazuela*. Discuss why these restrictions might have existed. What differing concerns might have led to the different types of restrictions?

♦♦♦♦♦♦♦♦♦

KEY TERMS AND CONCEPTS

neoclassicism, p. 200
proscenium, p. 200
wing, p. 201
flat, p. 201
intermezzi, p. 202
masque, p. 202
verisimilitude, p. 203
three unities, p. 203
decorum, p. 203

commedia dell'arte, p. 204
zanni, p. 204
prima donna, p. 204
innamorata, p. 204
innamorato, p. 204
public theatre, p. 205
rolling repertory, p. 205
blank verse, p. 206
iambic pentameter, p. 206

chronicle, p. 207
wheel of fortune, p. 207
auto sacramentale, p. 208
comedia, p. 208
corral, p. 208
cazuela, p. 208
collective hero, p. 209
sharing system, p. 216
rhetorical, p. 217

♦♦♦♦♦♦♦♦♦

FOR FURTHER EXPLORATION

See the list of sources at the end of Chapter 9 on pages
    246–247.

THE ADDING MACHINE, by Elmer Rice.
Courtesy of Actors Theatre of Louisville.

CHAPTER 9

Revolutions

Romanticism to Postmodern Experiment

Once artists grew weary of neoclassicism, they found the form so entrenched that a revolution was necessary to dislodge it. **Romanticism,** a rejection of nearly every aspect of neoclassicism and a celebration of the natural world, was hardly itself a generation old when it came under serious challenge. In retrospect the romantic rebellion seems to have opened a Pandora's box; as each movement wins acceptance, another is formed to rebel against it. Unlike neoclassicism, aspects of the romantic movement as well as many other major movements to follow continue to wield their influence on the theatrical professions that we currently practice and enjoy.

◆◆◆◆◆◆◆◆◆◆

Romanticism

The artistic and social movement of romanticism, which is so strongly associated with the nineteenth century, actually began in the eighteenth. It became the dominant style in both acting and playwriting in the first half of the nineteenth century. The first strains of theatrical romanticism can be found in Germany among young, rebellious theorists and playwrights who were sick of the limitations—the strict form and moral teachings—of neoclassicism. The rebels sought to overturn this monolith of art and culture. Preromantic playwrights who called themselves *Sturm und Drang* ("storm and stress") deliberately broke all the rules of neoclassicism. The *Sturm und Drangers* shocked their audiences with plays full of violence and forbidden topics such as teen pregnancy, rape, self-mutilation, and infanticide. One of the most successful and disturbing of these plays, *The Tutor* (1774) by Jacob Lenz, presents a young tutor who seduces his even younger student and later, filled with guilt, castrates himself. Heinrich Wagner's *The Childmurderess* (1776) begins with the rape of a girl by a soldier. The girl runs away, discovers she is pregnant, has the child, goes mad, and kills the baby.

These dramatic iconoclasts were soon followed by the romantics, led by theorist August von Schlegel, who wanted more than rebellion. The romantics wished to replace neoclassical structure with organic structure: Form should be dictated by subject matter, not classical precedent, they argued. The romantics were fascinated with the wild forces of nature, with the unexplainable, the gothic and mystical, and looked for correspondences between their beliefs and those of the Elizabethans, the Spanish Golden Age, and even the medieval world. Romantics championed democratic principles and dramatized emotion triumphing over reason. They found beauty in disorder and pleasure in expressions of characters divided against themselves. Their chief model from the past was Shakespeare, and the play of choice was *Hamlet*. Through the efforts of the romantics, Shakespeare (dead for more than 180 years) first became an international phenomenon and rose to the top of most evaluations of dramatic literature. The Germans, led by Schlegel, soon translated Shakespeare into their own language, and many other countries followed during the nineteenth century.

Romantic playwrights in Germany created both funny and disturbing works. Ludwig Tieck's fairy tale extravaganza *Puss in Boots* (c. 1797) is a comic

♦ **HAMLET** *continues to fascinate and challenge modern audiences and artists, just as it did the romantics in the nineteenth century. Here we see the duel between Hamlet and Laertes. Left to right, the actors are Diane Venora, Mahish Linklater, Robin Weigert, Francis Jue, and Liev Schreiber as Hamlet. The Public Theatre (New York).*
Photo by Michal Daniel.

metatheatrical play (a self-referencing play that presents the theatre as a theatre) in which the audience takes a major role as the characters argue romantic versus neoclassical principles before the play self-destructs. A haunting, disturbing vision permeates Heinrich von Kleist's plays such as *Pentheselia* (c. 1808) in which an amazon warrior on the battlefield eats out the heart of the man she loves. Later she suggests that there is little difference in biting and kissing; we often do one, she claims, when we mean the other. Although not fully romantic, Georg Büchner's *Woyzeck* (c. 1836) provided one of the earliest examples of a working-class antihero. Woyzeck loses his mind and kills the woman he loves because he not only is betrayed by her but also is the victim of an irresponsible scientific experiment. Büchner didn't find an audience in his own time, but his plays have been regularly revived since the early twentieth century and had a powerful influence on modern theatre.

Two German playwrights, Johann von Goethe and Friedrich Schiller, who began their theatrical work with the *Sturm und Drang* movement, are associated with the romantic movement, although Goethe denied connections. What Goethe and Schiller accomplished with their playwriting and production work at the court theatre of Weimar is labeled Weimar classicism. They combined ancient classics and stories with romantic sensibilities and created remarkable interpretations of familiar work. Goethe's *Iphigenia in Tauris* (1787), a reworking of a Euripides play, focuses on inner turmoil and the need to listen to one's heart. In his most famous play, *Faust* (1808), the old story of selling one's soul to the

The Audience Has Its Say: Theatre Riots and Demonstrations

Exploring Historical and Cultural Perspectives

As long as the house remained fully lit during theatrical performances (from the beginnings until the late nineteenth century), there was always the likelihood of active, even vociferous audience response and interaction during performances of plays. Historical evidence suggests that beginning with professional theatre in the seventeenth century and continuing through the eighteenth and nineteenth centuries, audience behavior included talking back to the actors, sword and stick fights, and open demonstration and riots over actors, ticket prices, responses to a new play, and political issues. Descriptions of such theatre audience behavior sound more like contemporary disturbances and riots occurring throughout the world at popular sports events such as soccer, football, and basketball than like modern theatre audiences.

In 1809, when the popular actor-manager John Philip Kemble managed the Covent Garden Theatre in London, he created a firestorm of protest. Following a destructive fire, he rebuilt Covent Garden and made significant changes that favored wealthy patrons but angered theatre-goers of the lower economic classes. To cater to the richer folk, for example, Kemble changed open galleries in the third tier to private boxes (which were more expensive than gallery or pit seating); the only remaining public gallery was so high above the stage that audience members could see little of the stage action. Kemble added insult to injury by raising the prices of admission to the pit by half a shilling (apparently to pay for his new construction and improvements). The price increase seems slight to us now, but many audience members took offense at the loss of good seats and higher prices and decided to attack Kemble's decision. The resultant audience response is called the Old Price (O.P.) Riots.

When the theatre reopened, a large percentage of the first-night audience arrived with signs and placards demonstrating their displeasure with Kemble's unfair and greedy practices. Their jeers and catcalls were so loud during the performance that no one could hear any words delivered from the stage. Kemble attempted to ride out the storm, but he never had a chance. Soldiers were called in to control the crowd, but their efforts were unsuccessful. The audience not only demonstrated that first night, but essentially rioted (apparently without loss of life) and prevented any real performance for more than sixty consecutive nights. Kemble finally succumbed to the inevitable, offered a public apology, and restored the old prices.

Sometimes audience demonstrations were planned in advance. In France champions of the romantic movement held pep rallies and open demonstrations attacking the neoclassicists—for example, with the opening of Victor Hugo's *Hernani* in 1830. Sometimes, however, demonstrations were spontaneous. Audiences frequently talked back to the actors or, in the Restoration period, even tried to compete with actors. On a number of occasions when a famous actor entered the stage obviously drunk, audience members would tell him to go home. The theatre did not close for the night, however; management would offer the audience a different play (most theatres operated a rolling repertory of plays with many possible productions in the repertory at any one time). In some cases the management had to negotiate with the audience to determine what play they wished to see. Sometimes, however, the results of theatrical disturbances were deadly, as occurred in New York with the Astor Place Riot of 1849. The number of casualties varies depending on the account one reads, but it appears that at least thirty-one people died in this conflict created by reactionary American attacks over feuding actors and what the violent demonstrators perceived as British and aristocratic elitism at odds with "American values."

devil for pleasure or power is altered to a search for perfection. Schiller, also a historian, dramatically revisited European history such as the tragic political demise of the title character in *Maria Stuart* (1800).

France resisted the romantic movement for a time, remaining neoclassical under Napoleon and beyond while the rest of Europe succumbed to the in-

HAST A SURGEON, SHYLOCK—
TO STOP HIS WOUNDS LEST
HE BLEED TO DEATH ?

CONGRESS

PUBLIC OPINION

20% TAX ON THEATRES

THEATRE INCOME $3

U S TREASURY

♦ **"EXACTING A POUND OF FLESH THAT LIES VERY NEAR THE HEART"** *This political cartoon depicts theatre business threatened by the U.S. Congress, with Congress portrayed as Shylock in Shakespeare's* The Merchant of Venice, *demanding his pound of flesh. The public intervenes on the theatre's behalf, just as Portia comes between Shylock and Antonio in the play. Published in the* New York Tribune, *January 19, 1919.*

Many audience demonstrations had happier endings for those involved. One in particular involved popular audiences siding with theatres against attempts by the U.S. Congress to raise ticket prices to increase revenue for the federal government. In January 1919, shortly after the conclusion of World War I, the government was searching for ways to pay for the enormous debt incurred by the war effort. Among the many taxes proposed by Congress was a 20 percent federal tax on professional theatre ticket prices (a 10 percent increase since the wartime theatre tax) to raise an estimated eighty million dollars. Both theatre managers and audiences hit the roof, resulting in almost instantaneous public demonstrations both inside and outside the theatres, a flood of letters and telegrams to Congress, and petitions that gathered almost nine million signatures from well over two thousand cities in eight days. This unusual collaboration of actors, managers, audiences, and newspapers from different regions of the country orchestrated a forceful but peaceful revolt against government action. Overwhelmed by the public outcry over threats to theatrical entertainment, Congress backed down, and the tax increase was dropped. At the time a typical Broadway theatre ticket in the orchestra ranged from $2.00 to $2.50. The tax increase, if passed, would have raised the price range to $2.20 to $2.75.

Interested? Check out

George Rowell. *The Victorian Theatre, 1792–1914,* 2nd edition. Cambridge, England: Cambridge University Press, 1978.
Richard Moody. *The Astor Place Riot.* Bloomington: Indiana University Press, 1958.
Ronald H. Wainscott. *The Emergence of the Modern American Theater, 1914–1929.* New Haven, Conn.: Yale University Press, 1997.

toxication of romanticism. It arrived amid great consternation in Paris when performances of Victor Hugo's *Hernani* in 1830 resulted in vociferous argument and near-rioting in the audience, since the play deliberately violated every principle of neoclassicism. Hugo's romantic theory, which adds the idea of the grotesque to the romantic vision, is more significant than his plays. The character

♦ **EDWIN BOOTH** *as Hamlet, c. 1870. Booth is often remembered as the premier American actor of Shakespearean leading roles in the nineteenth century. He was very successful as an international touring star and had the misfortune to be the brother of presidential assassin and actor John Wilkes Booth. This studio shot is typical of nineteenth-century photos of actors. Although Booth is wearing his real costume, the photo was made in a studio rather than on the set of his stage production.* By permission of the Folger Shakespeare Library.

Quasimodo from Hugo's novel *Notre Dame of Paris* can stand as an image of the entire romantic movement: a beautiful spirit trapped in a grotesque body. Hugo's fellow romantic Alfred de Musset created haunting romantic conflicts in plays such as *No Trifling with Love* (1834), which mixed the comic and trivial with deadly events as an on-again-off-again couple plays games with the emotions of people they don't care about.

Romanticism was very popular in the United States and found curious expression in many plays. *Metamora* (1829), a tragedy by John Augustus Stone, for example, featured Native American characters sympathetically at the center of the action. In the romantic language of the day any aboriginal race was portrayed as the "noble savage," a race destined, it was thought, to be removed or destroyed by the encroachment of "civilized" white settlers in ever-increasing numbers. Although a few evil Indians appeared in plays of the 1830s, it was not until after midcentury that Native Americans began to be routinely characterized as alcoholics and vicious villains in plays. Unfortunately, this stereotype persisted for at least a century.

Although few romantic plays in England left a lasting impression, the romantic actors of that nation created a new standard of performance marked by emotional overflow, athleticism, sudden outbursts, and mixed tone. Sarah Siddons (1755–1831), who was often painted in portraits as the personification of the tragic muse, was enormously popular for her instantaneous reversals of mood and her long-suffering portrayals, which set a standard for the century. Siddons, along with Edmund Kean (1787–1833), created a romantic style in both classical and contemporary plays. Kean erupted on the stage with such clamorous force that reports describe emotionally overwrought audience members screaming and fainting—responses not unlike those of modern audiences at the performance of an enormously popular rock star.

Beginning in the early nineteenth century, each country that boasted a popular professional theatre developed a number of touring stars—actors and actresses who usually toured alone and performed with local companies throughout Europe and North America. Actors such as the American Edwin Booth (1833–1893), one of the biggest stars of the entire century, toured internationally with both melodrama and Shakespearean tragedy. It was soon evident that the test of any male actor of the era was the role of Hamlet, although other tragic figures such as Othello, Macbeth, Lear, and Richard III were considered mandatory roles for most stars. This notion was so prevalent that even some famous actresses—Sarah Bernhardt (1844–1923) from France, for example, and Charlotte Cushman (1816–1876) from the United States—took on Hamlet. Although Cushman created the era's definitive Lady Macbeth, she also frequently played male roles, including a very successful Romeo played to her sister Susan's Juliet. The test role of the nineteenth century for actresses, however, turned out to be "Camille," the protagonist (actually named Marguerite Gautier) in Alexandre Dumas *fils' The Lady of the Camelias* (1852), a romantic tale of a courtesan (a high-priced prostitute) with a heart of gold who succumbs to tuberculosis and lost love.

Staging and design in the romantic era introduced the **box set,** a scenic device that imitated the interior of a room with walls, furniture, and visual detail. This kind of scenery was very important to actors, moving their performances away from the apron and within the walls of the set. After a time actors were no longer playing just in front of the scenery. They were inside the box. We do not know who invented the box set, but it was popularized by actress-manager Madame Vestris (1797–1856) in England and North American tours beginning about 1830. Also associated with Vestris was the work of James Robinson Planché (1796–1880) who introduced **antiquarianism** (the creation of historically accurate costumes and scenery) to the stage in the 1820s. This idea of dressing characters and recreating locations as they would appear at the time indicated by the play was at first a novelty. For centuries actors had traditionally costumed themselves in clothes that were contemporary with their own time regardless of the age or time setting of the plays. Antiquarianism became a new model for design; historical accuracy obviously continues to be important to many directors, actors, and designers of our own day.

The romantic era also ushered in the first known professional African American theatre, the African Company (1821) in New York. Unfortunately, this troupe, which performed both Shakespearean and original plays, was harassed and chased out of town by white bigots. A young African American who might have been a member of that company, Ira Aldridge (1807–1867), soon left the United States and became a highly successful touring star in Shakespearean roles and romantic drama throughout Europe. The "African Roscius" never returned to the United States, and no African Americans, only white actors in blackface makeup, performed in the professional American theatre for a very long time.

CHARLOTTE AND SUSAN CUSHMAN
AS
ROMEO AND JULIET.

Nineteenth-Century Melodrama

The dramatic form that dominated the nineteenth century and continues to dominate in television and film is **melodrama.** This form became the most popular application of romanticism and, later, early types of realism. Many variations of the formula for melodrama were created in the nineteenth century, and most of them continue to be reworked in our own time: disaster epics on land and sea (from volcanic eruptions to tenement fires to shipwrecks), crime and detective thrillers, supernatural horror stories, American West

Nineteenth-Century Women Theatre Managers in Britain and the United States

Exploring Historical and Cultural Perspectives

When Lucy Elizabeth Bartolozzi Vestris took control of London's Olympic Theatre in 1831, she publicized herself as the first woman manager. Technically, this was not true, since one German and several British women had managed companies, but Vestris was certainly the best known and most significant up to that time. The theatregoing public knew her as an actress and singer who specialized in **breeches roles** (male characters performed by women in costumes more revealing than the voluminous skirts of the nineteenth century). Sexual attractiveness was an important part of Vestris's appeal. Assuming the duties of a manager meant accepting many responsibilities that were normally considered masculine: hiring and firing, planning, and financial and artistic decision making. Vestris turned the small Olympic into a fashionable theatre and built a reputation for careful staging of productions using realistic props and scenery (the box set, for example). After leaving the Olympic in 1839, she teamed up with her husband, Charles

♦ **MADAME VESTRIS,** *a popular actress-manager in London, in a cross-dressing role, as Orpheus in* Olympic Devils, *1831, Olympic Theatre.* Photo by permission of the Harvard Theatre Collection, the Houghton Library, Harvard University.

Mathews, to manage the larger Covent Garden (1839–1842) and Lyceum (1847–1856) Theatres, producing several important revivals of Shakespeare and elaborate holiday entertainments. The middle-class audience had nearly deserted the theatre, but Vestris's attention to tasteful subject matter and audience comfort (meant to lure the middle-class patrons back) was widely noted and praised.

More women turned to management as the century progressed. Marie Wilton (1839–1921), also a popular

shootouts, tales of adventure in exotic locales, everyday domestic conflicts featuring love and divorce, reprieve from alcoholism, and an endless parade of villainous big businessmen, lawyers, and outlaws. Although all Western theatre centers (and a few in the East such as Japanese Kabuki) wrote and staged melodrama, those in England and the United States were exceptionally adept and prolific with the form. Planché in England popularized the monster with *The Vampire* (1820); Augustin Daly in the United States introduced the victim tied to the railroad tracks in 1867 with *Under the Gaslight.* Some people are surprised to learn that it was a man tied to the tracks; he was rescued by a woman. A successful actor and one of the best writers of melodrama, Dion Boucicault became an international phenomenon with his spectacular tales of Irish, British, and American struggles and hardships such as *The Poor of New York* in 1857. Five years earlier, George Aiken, followed by many others, had adapted Harriet Beecher Stowe's abolitionist novel *Uncle Tom's Cabin* to melodrama,

breeches role performer, entered management at the age of twenty-five. She turned a dirty theatre known as "the dust hole" into the elegant Prince of Wales's Theatre in 1865. Like Vestris, Wilton was complimented for bringing a domestic atmosphere to a public space, thus making theatregoing more acceptable to the Victorian middle class. She later married her leading man, Squire Bancroft (1841–1926), and the two managed The Prince of Wales's Theatre together until 1879, then the Haymarket Theatre from 1880 to 1885. In producing the plays of T. W. Robertson, they helped to further realism and ensemble performing in Great Britain and raised the status of actors with increased salaries. Sara Lane (1823–1899) managed the Britannia Theatre in Hoxton with her husband Sam until 1871. After his death, she ran it alone for over a quarter of a century until her own death. The working-class audience of the Britannia loved her, and she played the breeches role in the Christmas play until she was in her seventies.

Laura Keene (c. 1820–1873) had worked for Madame Vestris before coming to the United States as an actress to support her mother and two daughters. She specialized in ingénue (young woman) roles in eighteenth-century comedies of manners and Shakespeare's romantic comedies. Keene added management to her career, running theatres in Baltimore and San Francisco before forming a resident company in New York City in 1855 and moving into Laura Keene's New Theatre in 1856. Her strong company specialized in lavishly produced comedies that fit Keene's performance style. She gave up the New York theatre in 1863 and became one of the first managers to tour a combination company (one in which an entire cast traveled with all scenery and equipment). In 1865 Keene had the misfortune to be managing and performing the comedy *Our American Cousin* when actor John Wilkes Booth (brother of the famous actor Edwin Booth) assassinated Abraham Lincoln at Ford's Theatre in Washington, D.C. She was arrested, along with her company, but was released, and the company continued its tour.

Although these women must have faced enormous challenges in a very male-dominated world, they were often successful and carved out specific identities for their companies, frequently at the forefront of innovative stage practice.

Interested? Check out

Jane Kathleen Curry. *Nineteenth-Century American Women Theatre Managers.* Westport, Conn.: Greenwood Press, 1994.

William W. Appleton. *Madame Vestris and the London Stage.* New York: Columbia University Press, 1974.

George Rowell, *The Victorian Theatre, 1792–1914,* 2nd edition. Cambridge, England: Cambridge University Press, 1978.

and this play was performed in the United States more than any other in its time. The lists of popular melodramas are legion, but they are marked by similarities that are easily recognized regardless of language or spectacle or period or local references.

A very important change occurred during the reign of stage melodrama. In the 1820s, along with many other spectacular devices, gaslight was introduced to the stage; it quickly replaced candles and oil lamps even though it was volatile and dangerous. Gaslight produced greater intensity of light and could easily be dimmed up and down. Nighttime scenes could for the first time be dark and shadowy, blackouts were possible, and colored light using silks and glass could be projected in dynamic ways. It was also possible to put the audience in the dark, thus altering its behavior and making it quieter and more focused on the stage. Lowering of the house lights did not occur until late in the century, however.

♦ **EDWIN BOOTH** *as Hamlet being restrained by his friends in the ghost scene at Booth's Theatre (c. 1870). Note the literal castle scenery combining two- and three-dimensional forms and extensive painting. There is little doubt that the gas lights would have been lowered on stage for this scene and perhaps a ghostly limelight follow spot used to illuminate the ghost (unless Mr. Booth insisted that the limelight be used for himself). The ghost appears as a literal manifestation, which was typical in the period. Later, some twentieth-century productions would use only the voice of the ghost, so that we must imagine how the ghost appears.*
By permission of the Folger Shakespeare Library.

Spectacle became very literal and was aided by remarkable inventions applied to the stage: conveyer belts that transported gliding ghosts and racing horses and wagons, hydraulic and electric lifts that created bridges and levels high in the air, three-dimensional scenery that replaced some of the flat painted scenery, traps in walls that enabled sudden entrances of vampires, collapsible scenery for earthquakes and fires. Many devices that we now associate with realism or special effects for film (from James Bond to Harry Potter, from *Mission: Impossible* to *Lord of the Rings*) were first developed for the spectacle of stage melodrama. The pod race in *Star Wars, Episode I,* for example, is an updating of *Ben Hur*'s Roman chariot race, but such chariot races were first done on stage, not on film.

Even parodies of melodrama did not seem to dampen the power of the form in the period. The team of W.S. Gilbert and Arthur Sullivan satirized melodrama in wildly successful melodramatic/comic operettas such as *H.M.S. Pinafore* (1878) and *The Pirates of Penzance* (1879). Although many musical forms appeared on the stage in the nineteenth century, the plays and music of Gilbert and Sullivan provide hints for the modern musical, which in the twentieth century frequently adopted devices and techniques from the operetta form. It was also in the first production of Gilbert and Sullivan's *Patience* that electric light was introduced to the theatre in 1881.

Nineteenth-Century Realism and Naturalism

Realism was a rebellion against romanticism and melodrama, but at the same time a realization of what romanticism and melodrama had approached visually—a very detailed evocation of scenery and costume along lines of historical and contemporary accuracy. Whereas French melodramatic playwrights in the 1850s such as Alexandre Dumas *fils* were attempting to move the subject matter of plays in a more realistic direction, the first fully realistic plays are usually credited to Norwegian Henrik Ibsen. His influential *A Doll House* (1879) centers on a wife leaving her husband and children, and *Ghosts* (1881) broached the forbidden topic of sexually transmitted disease. Ibsen and the other realists were inspired by a scientific revolution that increasingly looked at the human being not as the center of the universe, but as another subject for scientific study. One of these scientists, Charles Darwin, in his *On the Origin of Species by Means of Natural Selection* (1859), created a firestorm with his version of evolutionary theory. For Darwin and other thinkers such as Herbert Spencer, the first sociologist to apply evolutionary theory to social development in the 1850s, the importance of heredity and environment was deemed critical to all animal life. Playwrights such as Ibsen began to use heredity and environment in their plays as strong determinants of human character and behavior. It was not just biological evolution that fascinated artists, but cultural and social evolution as well.

The importance of environment to character behavior extended to creating settings that were not just authentic in every detail, but also connected to the characters who worked or lived in them. Many of the physical trappings of realism had been developed earlier by the romantics through such things as antiquarianism and the box set, but the new realists labored to connect space to character and event both in production and in the written play texts. The realists insisted on creating conversational dialogue that avoided the poetic and included repetition, inane remarks, pauses, and imperfect responses to imitate the way people really speak and interact in everyday life. The subject matter of realism often disturbed audiences and critics the most: frank discussions of prostitution, adultery, and divorce; depictions of the travails of everyday life; treatment of monumental social problems in marriage, rights for women, and the plight of the working class. With realism the theatre became a forum for current, volatile social issues that could polarize the audience.

Unlike the romantics, Ibsen did not try to change everything at once in his plays but utilized easily recognized structure that remained popular throughout the romantic era (melodrama and the **well-made play**). At

◆ *GHOSTS, by Henrik Ibsen, in an early production in Norway. In this opening scene from the play, note the box set and how the stage is crowded with furniture. This crowding is deliberate and typical of many domestic interiors in the late nineteenth century. It is rare to see such crowding today unless the director and designer are making some kind of statement about hindered interaction of the characters. For actors to use this space, they must make circuitous paths through the furniture. Long direct crosses to one another are nearly impossible.*
Bergens Teatermuseum.

the conclusion of his plays, however, he did not provide an easy solution or a happy ending, thus throwing his audiences into a tailspin. When Nora walked out on her husband and children at the end of *A Doll House,* it was more than many audiences could stand; some even demonstrated and waited for Nora to return. Early realists, whose plays are still regularly revived, quickly followed Ibsen's techniques and challenged their audiences to face their own social and personal demons. August Strindberg in Sweden provided *Miss Julie* (1888), a study in both class and gender struggles in which a socially mismatched couple (servant and mistress) play sexual games that end in disaster and apparent suicide for the young woman; George Bernard Shaw in England wrote *Mrs. Warren's Profession* (produced 1902), in which a former prostitute (now a madam) must explain her early life choices to her incredulous daughter—in effect defending logically her decision to become a prostitute in order to haul herself out of poverty. In the United States the title character of James Herne's play *Margaret Fleming* (1890) discovers that her husband has had an affair with and impregnated a poor woman whom he abandoned. Margaret shocked audiences by rejecting her husband and taking the orphaned baby of the wronged woman as her own. She even prepared to nurse the baby on stage—an act that for some audiences was the most shocking of all.

Unlike Ibsen, Shaw, and Herne, some playwrights wanted to throw out traditional structure as well. In 1880 Émile Zola in France called for **naturalism,** in which playwrights should create a "slice of life," following the actual pace of everyday life—in short, imitating novels of the period. Many playwrights, in fact, began to think of themselves as novelists of the stage. Such an approach was very difficult to take without boring an audience, but several playwrights came very close to the ideal. They avoided central characters and created a collective hero or focused the action on a group. For example, the Russian play *The Cherry Orchard* (1904) by Anton Chekhov follows the demise of a wealthy family when its members fail to recognize the social and economic changes going on around them. They end by losing the things that seem to mean the most to them, but they do nothing to prevent the loss. Similarly, *The Lower Depths* (1902) by Maxim Gorky, also a Russian, centers on a group, but this time a collection of down-and-out people at the bottom of the social hierarchy who live in squalor and slowly seem to fade away while no one notices. These and other plays, such as the German Gerhart Hauptmann's *The Weavers* (1892), dealing with starvation and labor problems, created a large array of eccentric characters requiring detailed psychological exploration and ensemble acting.

In the nineteenth and early twentieth centuries most productions of realistic and naturalistic plays were presented in independent theatres, which for a number of years operated outside the sphere of commercial theatre and government censorship. The first of these was the Théâtre Libre, founded by André Antoine in Paris in 1887. Antoine's work, and that of Konstantin Stanislavsky at the Moscow Art Theatre beginning in 1898, created a climate for a radical change in acting style as well as a love among many young and developing actors for the new realism and naturalism. The new acting model was not the romantic touring star, but the actor who worked in an ensemble and created character through close observation of real life, careful examination of character history and motivation, and psychological evaluation. This shift is the apparent beginning of actors psychoanalyzing characters as if they were real people. Urged to do so by directors from Antoine onward, actors pretended that the audience was not present during the performance, creating an imaginary **fourth wall** at the

◆ **THE CHERRY ORCHARD,** by Anton Chekhov. This 1977 production is not updated in costumes or properties, but all of the walls are missing, and the action takes place in an open white space as if the cherry orchard and the house of the estate occupy a single space. Some of the trees of the soon-to-be sold and destroyed orchard are always present. Directed by Andrei Serban and designed by Santo Loquasto for the New York Shakespeare Festival at Lincoln Center.
Photo courtesy Billy Rose Theatre Collection, the New York Public Library for the Performing Arts, Astor, Lennox and Tilden Foundations.

proscenium curtain line. The change must have been startling. Much of what we associate with contemporary directing was created as a response to the need for careful control of the realistic presentation.

◆◆◆◆◆◆◆◆◆◆

The Avant-Garde from the Late Nineteenth Century to the 1960s

Two important terms that have been associated with theatre since the late nineteenth century sometimes lead to confusion, since they are used in various ways. *Modernism* and the *avant-garde* are closely identified with the century that recently ended. **Modernism** in theatre is often used to designate the shift beginning with realism; throughout the twentieth century scholars noted that modern theatre and drama began with Ibsen. Many late twentieth-century scholars associated modernism with the type of theatre that rebelled against realism and naturalism. In this book we will use the term "modernism" to refer to both realistic and much nonrealistic theatre from the late nineteenth century to the present day.

Avant-garde is also a complicated term and often is used synonymously with the term "experiment." Originally a French military term meaning *vanguard* (the front line of troops who are the first to engage the enemy), it was appropriated by artists to signify those who venture into new, unknown territory in the arts. By definition art that is avant-garde cannot remain so for very long. The work either fails or succeeds. If it fails, it usually disappears from practice as well as historical memory; if the art succeeds, it generally joins accepted practice and therefore is no longer at the vanguard. Technically Ibsen was avant-garde for a few years, but his work then became a commercial standard.

The term "avant-garde," however, is usually a label for experimental work that rebelled against realism and naturalism. Beginning in the 1890s, nonrealistic and antirealistic theatre and drama appeared regularly in many different artistic movements and experiments, which continued almost nonstop through the 1960s. Sometimes the avant-garde shocked or surprised; it experimented with subject matter, dramatic form, and staging techniques. Experimenters challenged values and the moral order or often attempted to posit a new way of viewing the world. They were fascinated with dreams, the unconscious, psychoanalysis, alternative realities, the supernatural, and irrationality.

Symbolism in the 1890s and early twentieth century was the first major challenge to realism. Its leading playwright, Belgian Maurice Maeterlinck, created plays such as *The Blue Bird* (1908), a symbolic pursuit of elusive happiness. The legacy of symbolism is still very much alive in theatre for children, Disney films, and many romantic musicals such as *The Fantasticks* (1960), which presents a simple story of love found, lost, and found again with emblematic characters and imaginary scenery on a nearly empty stage. The Irish symbolist William Butler Yeats (1865–1939) discovered traditional Asian theatrical forms such as Japanese Noh and started incorporating similar methods into his stage work, using masks, open stages, folk music, and dance. Many in the avant-garde were fascinated with the possibilities of the relatively bare stage of some Asian theatre. This East/West fascination was a two-way street, with Asian practitioners appropriating Western melodrama, realism, and the proscenium stage. Touring companies from both hemispheres visited foreign theatres. Many classical Asian plays were first translated into English and other European languages in the first half of the twentieth century and became the subject of serious study and inspired periodic theatrical performances.

Also intrigued by Asian forms, August Strindberg in Sweden created not only realism, but also bizarre dramas such as *A Dream Play* (1907), which abandons causality as an organizing principle and substitutes dream or music as a model for form. Time and space shift suddenly in defiance of logic or causality, just as in our dreams. New directors such as Lugné-Poë (1869–1940) in France attempted to create an abstract stage focusing on color or substituting drapes for traditional scenery. Lugné-Poë directed plays by Maeterlinck, as well as one of the most famous outrageous plays of the avant-garde, *Ubu Roi* (King Ubu) by Alfred Jarry, a play that in 1896 seemed designed to offend everyone with its stupid antihero, scatological jokes, and runaway violence. The first word of the play (one that is subsequently repeated persistently) is "merdre," a fabricated word resembling the French word for "shit," which caused the first audience to erupt in a mixture of outrage and delight. Some historians see the notorious production of this play as the event that truly launched the avant-garde on its path to grotesque and sometimes shocking experiment.

Designers too joined the rebellion, and the majestic but simple designs of Adolphe Appia (1862–1928) and Gordon Craig (1872–1966) swept the theatrical world with their images of platforms, stairs, open spaces, and great, even impossible heights. A guiding principle was simplicity, avoiding detail and reducing a location to its most significant elements. In the United States this was called the **new stagecraft,** and it quickly made its way into commercial theatres; sometimes such scenery was used even for plays that were written to be realistic.

Experimental directors and designers took on Shakespeare and other classics anew and sought to return to a simple stage where the space could suggest any location without filling the space with detailed, realistic scenery. As Shakespeare had been the test for actors in the nineteenth century, his plays became the measure of directors in the twentieth. Harley Granville-Barker in England (in 1914) eliminated the traditional forest scenery of *A Midsummer Night's Dream* and replaced it with open platforms and diaphanous drapery. Many new directors were especially successful at combining classical plays with new, open stages. The Japanese revolving stage found its way to Europe in the early twentieth century and helped to revolutionize stagecraft. Even the Kabuki *hanamichi* was used in Max Reinhardt's German production of *Sumurun* (1910), a tale of Arabian intrigues, which toured throughout Europe and the United States. The permanent architectural façade returned in the French work of Jacques Copeau (1879–1949), who sought to focus all of the audience's attention on the performer and the text, not on the scenery. The new directors were eclectic in their tastes and practice.

Early in the twentieth century, many Asian countries, especially Japan, would in turn borrow from the West and develop movements following European realism and then departures from realism. It was not long until Japanese playwrights and directors began to develop their own approaches to theatrical experiment. Theatres following a Western tradition, *shingeki,* and original experimental groups, *Shougekijo-engeki,* continue to proliferate in Japan and work alongside mainstream commercial productions and the classical forms of Noh, Kabuki, and Bunraku puppetry. As early as the late nineteenth century Kabuki adopted the Western proscenium to frame its classical productions.

German and American **expressionism** in the 1910s and 1920s dramatized the dehumanization or destruction of humanity at the hands of industry and war. Written long before Hiroshima, Georg Kaiser's *Gas II* (1920) presents an apocalyptic view of an entire culture wiped out by a superweapon. A principal effect of antirealistic theatre and drama was to dramatize and make concrete (objectify) an internal or figurative thought, idea, feeling, or imaginative event. Consequently, the antirealist might objectify a subjective experience. In expressionism what was seen on the stage, including the scenery, suggested the anxiety and mental breakdown of the central character. Eugene O'Neill's *The Hairy Ape* (1922) was first produced by the Provincetown Players, who were dedicated to American experiment. In the play, Yank, an animal-like ship's stoker, searches

◆ **THE GORDON CRAIG DESIGN FOR *HAMLET*.**
Note the high drapes that dominate the image and almost dwarf the actor who must play Hamlet. The low multi-level platforms are typical of both Craig and Appia and lend the space a sense of architecture and permanence. A brilliant touch is the image of the moon, which seems to be peeking out between the drapes.
On the Art of the Theatre by Edward Gordon Craig.

◆ **MAX REINHARDT'S PRODUCTION OF** *OEDIPUS THE KING*, *which he produced all over Europe, making variations in each city. All, however, featured carefully choreographed and populous crowd scenes such as this one in which the suppliants appeal to Oedipus early in the play to do something to relieve their suffering from the plague.*
Max Reinhardt Archive/SUNY–Binghamton.

in vain for a place where he belongs. In *Machinal* (1928) by Sophie Treadwell, a young woman oppressed by the workplace and her mother—in fact all adults in her life—finally cracks and murders her husband. The play ends with her execution in the electric chair. French **surrealism,** such as Jean Cocteau's *Orpheus* (1926), reconceived Greek mythology in an attempt to combine the dream world so completely with the real world that one could hardly distinguish the two.

Two avant-garde innovators, whose important work was created between the two world wars, had a profound impact on the rest of the century. Bertolt Brecht in Germany popularized epic theatre through theory and his Marxist plays such as *Mother Courage and Her Children* (c. 1939), an episodic journey in which the title character loses her children to the ravages of war and her own preoccupation with capitalist practice. **Epic Theatre** is anti-illusionist theatre featuring emotional detachment, narration, songs, and obvious theatricality; it has been adopted and adapted by countless directors and playwrights. In France Antonin Artaud was not very successful as an actor and director, but his theory of **Theatre of Cruelty** from the 1930s (included in the collection of his work, *The Theatre and Its Double*) is still considered required reading by many avant-garde artists of the theatre. Artaud's theory is focused on personal rather than social change and advocates working on emotions by assaulting the audience's senses. He stressed process over product and visual imagery over text. Many avant-garde artists since the 1950s have created work inspired by *both* Brecht and Artaud.

♦ **THE ADDING MACHINE,** by Elmer Rice. In this revival of the American expressionist play, a party of people known only as numbers are entertained by Mr. and Mrs. Zero. This play and production are typical of expressionism in its anonymity of character and in repetition. Directed by Anne Bogart; scenic design by Neil Patel; costume design by James Schuette; lighting design by Mimi Jordan Sherin. Photo by Richard C. Trigg. Courtesy of Actors Theatre of Louisville.

World War II left artists disturbed by its horrors, especially the Holocaust and the atomic bomb. Artists of the avant-garde created a body of work dominated by plays centered on characters who are strangers to each other, trapped in a violent, meaningless world seemingly without design or purpose. Such plays are often dubbed **Theatre of the Absurd.** The bleak, existential, repetitious world of Samuel Beckett in *Waiting for Godot* (1953), a study of tramps on a road awaiting something or someone that never arrives, continues to haunt theatres around the world. Much of the almost random action of Act I is repeated with small variations in Act II. The manic absurdities of Eugène Ionesco, beginning with *The Bald Soprano* (1950), demonstrate the impossibility of meaningful communication among human beings. Although not strictly of the absurd style, the menacing plays of Harold Pinter, such as *The Homecoming* (1965), lack exposition and many events seem random and disconnected. His characters are often savage to one another in language if not in deed. The audience often feels that it has been dropped into an ambiguous but clearly dangerous conflict.

The 1960s also saw many disturbing experimental plays by African Americans: *Funnyhouse of a Negro* (1964) by Adrienne Kennedy is dominated by images and snatches of dialogue demonstrating a young black woman in conflict with her own feelings and all of her cultural and family baggage. *Dutchman* (1964) by Imamu Baraka presents a white woman randomly selecting and killing young black men on a train after ritualistically taking them through a psychosexual diatribe of insecurities and desires. These and many other African American plays continue to challenge and fascinate audiences and readers.

Exploring Collaboration

Founding an Alternative Theatre: The Provincetown Players

At the outbreak of World War I, George Cram (Jig) Cook and his wife Susan Glaspell were writers from the Midwest who had moved to Greenwich Village in New York. They were also part of a colony of artists of all sorts—writers, painters, sculptors—who gathered in the summer in Provincetown, Massachusetts, to be near the sea, share ideas with other artists, and work on their craft.

It was apparently Cook's idea to create a summer theatre in Provincetown in 1915, a theatre based exclusively on new plays and very anticommercial in its approach. Nearly everyone Cook met became a candidate for dramatic author, as he seemed to invite any new acquaintance to join his revolution to create an important body of dramatic work for the American theatre. Cook wrote plays himself, of course, and emerged as the artistic director of what became known as the Provincetown Players, but his talent was not as an artist—he was a mover and shaker, an inspiration to others. Cook insisted that the playwright would be in charge of producing his or her own work, that the playwright's intent would always be followed precisely. The playwrights frequently directed their own plays and they had the last word, an unusual power for a playwright to have in the modern era. The very first play the Provincetown Players produced was *Suppressed Desires* (1915), a one-act play written jointly by Cook and Glaspell.

Susan Glaspell was the true artist of the two, and she wrote some of the most important one-act plays of the period, such as *Trifles* (1916), as well as a number of full-length plays such as *The Verge* (1921), the first produced American play to have significant expressionistic elements. The Provincetown Players first produced the plays of other dynamic members, such as *Aria Da Capo* (1919), the first American antiwar play after World War I, by the poet Edna St. Vincent Millay. The couple of Cook and Glaspell was the founding heart of this theatre, however, and when they were joined by the as yet unknown Eugene O'Neill in the summer of 1916, the Provincetown Players quickly took off as an influential force in the American professional theatre. By the fall of 1916 they had a tiny theatrical home in Greenwich Village that they fittingly called the Play-wright's Theatre. Even though they were amateurs, they regularly produced bills of one-acts and sometimes full-length plays that attracted the attention of major newspaper critics.

Despite Cook's leadership, the Provincetown Players was a group effort. All of the members collaborated in all aspects of theatrical production: playwriting, acting, directing, scene painting, taking tickets. Even O'Neill, who was painfully shy, acted a few times. The results of production sometimes looked amateurish, in part because the group seemed willing to produce nearly any new play that the members wrote—good, bad, or indifferent. Yet the spirit of their artistic community was strong, and their commitment to experiment was enduring, even when the experiment sometimes proved silly.

The world of the Provincetown Players changed when it produced O'Neill's *The Emperor Jones* in 1920. Within a month the play was on its way to a Broadway theatre, and it ultimately became an international phenomenon. Recognition of their work proved to be a mixed blessing for members of the Provincetown Players. Becoming professionals was ultimately devastating to the vision and efforts of Cook and Glaspell because they and their community of artists, many of whom worked only occasionally with the group, began to struggle with their artistic mission. By late 1922 this welcoming home of dramatic experiment dedicated to the vision of the playwright was at an end. In 1924 it was swallowed by the professional company Experimental Theatre, Inc., which was led in part by O'Neill but no longer with Cook, Glaspell, or the other visionaries who began their collaboration in a living room and an old fishing shack on a wharf in Provincetown.

Interested? Check out

Robert Karoly Sarlos. *Jig Cook and the Provincetown Players: Theatre in Ferment*. Amherst: University of Massachusetts Press, 1982.

Susan Glaspell. *The Road to the Temple*. New York: Frederick A. Stokes, 1927.

Helen Deutsch and Stella Hanau. *The Provincetown Players: A Story of the Theatre*. New York: Farrar & Rinehart, 1931.

During the era of the Vietnam War the avant-garde in Europe and the United States was preoccupied with communal performance groups, environmental staging, and angry political messages. Jerzy Grotowski's Polish Laboratory Theatre became an international phenomenon with environmental productions such as *Akropolis* (1962), a stylized examination of survival and death in concentration camps. Grotowski led an ensemble of actors with a near-religious dedication to their projects. The Living Theatre in the 1950s and early 1960s was an **off-off-Broadway** collective experiment led by Judith Malina and Julian Beck, but by the mid-1960s this company functioned as a group of radical expatriate Americans, wandering Europe with incendiary political productions such as *Paradise Now* (1968), which insisted on instant revolution. Some of the most fascinating group productions were created by the Open Theatre under the leadership of Joseph Chaikin (b. 1935). The Open Theatre production of *The Serpent* (1968) by Jean-Claude van Itallie combined the Garden of Eden, Cain's murder of his brother Abel, and the assassination of John Kennedy, all done with doubling of characters by actors and no reliance on scenery.

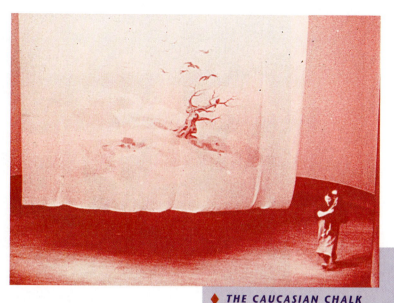

◆ **THE CAUCASIAN CHALK CIRCLE,** *written and directed by Bertolt Brecht and designed by Karl von Appen. The heroine, Grusha, flees the war, saving the child of another. Her journey is depicted by walking in one direction while the revolve moves in the other. Notice the open, empty stage, except for the partially lowered billowing drop above her.*
KaiDib Films International.

◆ **THE HOMECOMING,** *by Harold Pinter. The plays of Pinter are also sometimes grouped with Theatre of the Absurd. The violent and dysfunctional house of men, the decaying living space, and the menacing action is comically ominous as we wonder what dark and unknown activity transpires beyond the staircase. Throughout the performance of the play, mysterious occurrences upstairs suggested by the dialogue make the staircase itself become threatening. Directed by Howard Jensen.*
Indiana University.

♦ **THE AMEN CORNER,** *by James Baldwin. This was an important part of the explosion of new plays written and produced by African American artists in the 1950s and 1960s. This 2001 revival was produced by the Huntington Theatre Company, Boston. Directed by Chuck Smith.*
Photo by Charlie Erickson.

♦♦♦♦♦♦♦♦♦

Twentieth-Century Popular Theatre

In the twentieth century many theatre artists found themselves both among the avant-garde and in the mainstream commercial theatre. Eugene O'Neill in the United States produced many experimental dramas between 1916 and 1934, but some of his plays, such as *The Emperor Jones,* were commercial hits as early as 1920. This was the first professional production (outside variety entertainment) to present a black actor with white actors on a Broadway stage. Inspired by Strindberg, O'Neill created both realism and nonrealism, but most of his late famous plays, such as *The Iceman Cometh* (1946) and *Long Day's Journey into Night* (1956), are strictly realistic.

The realistic trend has continued unchecked since Ibsen. We continue to create box sets and train actors in a realistic style; domestic family conflicts abound on the stage as well as in film and television. The realistic acting style, identified with Stanislavsky, made its way to other countries in the early twentieth century and received one of its most influential incarnations in the work of the Group Theatre in New York in the 1930s. This ensemble found its strongest expression in the Depression-era plays of Clifford Odets such as *Awake and Sing!* (1935), which depicts a hard-edged Jewish mother struggling to make ends meet and trying with little success to hold her family together. The Group Theatre disbanded in 1941, and from the ashes of the defunct company director Elia Kazan and others created the Actors Studio in 1947. The Actors Studio was formed as a workshop for professional actors (many of whom, such as Geraldine Page and Marlon Brando, became household names). Other members of the Group Theatre such as Stella Adler and Sanford Meisner became acting teachers whose methods continue at the center of many acting programs.

Realism has persisted in the plays of many famous and frequently revived playwrights. Arthur Miller in *Death of a Salesman* (1949) gave us the exemplar of twentieth-century tragedy. Some of the most unforgettable American characters fill the plays of Tennessee Williams such as *A Streetcar Named Desire* (1947). Director Elia Kazan and designer Jo Mielziner gave the first productions of both *Salesman* and *Streetcar* visual nonrealistic touches but maintained realism in characterization and action. This kind of modified realism (without all the traditional details of realism) has been common since the midtwentieth century. You can see this approach in which realism dominates in the works of many playwrights: In *Who's Afraid of Virginia Woolf?* (1962), Edward Albee dramatizes in one night a catastrophic emotional breakdown in a dysfunctional marriage. In *True West* (1980), Sam Shepard presents the struggle of two brothers whose disparate lifestyles erupt in violence and role reversal. In *'night, Mother* (1983), Marsha Norman follows the final self-destructive path of a woman who no longer finds any meaning in her life. In *Glengarry Glen Ross* (1983), David Mamet demonstrates the business world out of control but presents it as a model for the American way of life. In *The Heidi Chronicles* (1988), Wendy Wasserstein episodically but realistically tracks the life of an art historian who is searching for meaning in her life beyond her successful occupation.

The first nonmusical Broadway production written and directed by African Americans was *A Raisin in the Sun* (1959), a poignant and traditionally structured play by Lorraine Hansberry. The first production was directed by Lloyd Richards, who in the 1980s began directing the century's most popular and effective African American plays such as August Wilson's *Ma Rainey's Black Bottom* (1984), a conflict of race and power in the popular music world of the 1920s. Nearly all of Wilson's plays are realistic, and some, such as *The Piano Lesson* (1990), have an occasional touch of the supernatural and spiritual. Some productions of *Jitney* (1979/2000), have included a nonrealistic moment by adding a kind of apotheosis of the major character Becker after he dies in an accident offstage.

The African continent has become a major theatrical player in the late twentieth century, offering many new plays since the 1960s. Two playwrights especially have become international phenomena: Athol Fugard through realistic plays such as *Master Harold . . . and the Boys* (1982), a study in the issues of apartheid, and Nigeria's Nobel laureate Wole Soyinka with *Madmen and Specialists* (1971), which attacks political repression in Nigeria by depicting a bizarre power struggle during wartime. Soyinka incorporates ritual and ceremony in his plays, drawing on the ancient practices of shamans and tribal religion and performance from his African region. He even adapted a Greek tragedy, *The Bacchae of Euripides* (1973), as African ritual.

◆ *A STREETCAR NAMED DESIRE,* by Tennessee Williams. This 1992 revival was directed by Gregory Mosher in New York. Alec Baldwin plays Stanley and Jessica Lange plays Blanche. Photo by Brigitte Lacombe. Photo courtesy Billy Rose Theatre Collection, the New York Public Library for the Performing Arts, Astor, Lennox and Tilden Foundations.

◆ *JITNEY*, by August Wilson. The central character, Becker (played by Charles Weldon), a man who runs a jitney taxi service, confronts his son, Booster (played by Charles Parnell) recently released from prison for murder. Directed by Timothy Douglas; scenic design by Paul Owen; costume design by Randall E. Klein. Courtesy of Actors Theatre of Louisville.

Without doubt the most popular theatre (in both economic and crowd-pleasing terms) of the twentieth century has been the modern musical, dominated at first by the United States but now generated in many parts of the world. England's Andrew Lloyd Webber gave us *Phantom of the Opera* (1986), Elton John and Tim Rice created *Aida* (2000), and *Les Misérables* (1985) by Alain Boublil and Claude-Michel Schönberg originated in France. Musicals are sometimes categorized as a separate genre, but the musical is a play and can be of any genre (comedy, tragedy, melodrama), and most theatre before realism incorporated significant music, singing, and dance. The **book musical** (a play that tells a story and has spoken text as well as songs) was inspired by nineteenth-century operettas and has been dominant since the tragicomic, racially mixed *Show Boat* (1927) by Jerome Kern and Oscar Hammerstein II. The book musical peaked in sentimentality with the enormously popular efforts of Hammerstein and Richard Rodgers, beginning with *Oklahoma!* (1943). It then adapted tragic form with Bernstein's *West Side Story* (1957); incorporated rock music with Jerome Ragni, James Rado, and Galt McDermott's *Hair* (1967); experimented with development of the musical form in Michael Bennett's *A Chorus Line* (1975), which is dominated by dance because of the subject matter; reached some of its most sophisticated musical and structural efforts with Stephen Sondheim in such plays as *Sunday in the Park with George* (1984); and tackled contemporary social and sexual issues in *Rent* (1996) by Jonathan Larson. Many of these accomplishments are hilariously parodied in *Urinetown* by Greg Kotis and Mark Hollman (2001).

The Recent Avant-Garde and Postmodern Experiment

Experimental work in the last several decades of the twentieth century has often been categorized as **postmodern,** which can be interpreted as work that is no longer "modern" in the sense that Tennessee Williams and Bertolt Brecht were modern. The postmodern is not of the modern but comments on, satirizes, or reinterprets the modern. The postmodern artist is sometimes identified as artist and critic simultaneously. Some critics see it as an artistic style, hence post-modern*ism.* Others claim that it is a mind-set, a point of view that looks back on the previous century of artistic work with cynicism or futility—and some-times despair. In visual terms it is dominated by simultaneous action and electronic or cybernetic technology; structurally, it features repetition and de-construction of masterpieces of the past.

The last several decades have witnessed considerable blurring of the avant-garde and commercial theatre, so much so that some critics argue that the avant-garde died in the 1960s and refer to experiment from 1890 to 1970 or so as the "historical avant-garde." We will continue to use the term "avant-garde" for noncommercial experiment but verify that experiment since about 1970 has been very different from that which occurred before.

In subject matter many experimental plays have focused on gay and lesbian lifestyles and conflicts, a host of gender issues headed by feminism, and the isolation of the individual in a self-centered world. Theatrical companies dedi-cated solely or primarily to gay and lesbian issues have been appearing since the 1970s. The company Split Britches, for example, deconstructs famous plays such as *A Streetcar Named Desire*; in *Belle Reprieve* (1991), Stanley Kowalski is re-placed by a lesbian and Blanche DuBois by a man in a dress. Gay material has been mainstreamed, of course, most notably with *Angels in America* (1991/1993) by Tony Kushner. *Angels in America* and many other plays since *The Normal Heart* (1985) by Larry Kramer have focused on the horrors and social fallout of the AIDS pandemic.

Feminist issues have been a dynamic part of experimental work since the 1970s, when many women's acting companies and female playwrights prolif-erated in North America, Britain, and Germany. Audiences have been chal-lenged by Caryl Churchill's comic and disturbing *Top Girls* (1982), a scathing examination of gender issues in the business world. Maria Irene Fornes dissects gender power struggles in Latin America in *The Conduct of Life* (1985). Ntozake Shange calls her play *for colored girls who have considered suicide when the rainbow is enuf* (1976) a choreopoem; the poetic speech is delivered by a cho-rus of young women. These playwrights and others have introduced new and exciting types of dramatic structure. Because so many artists have been preoc-cupied with gender issues in the last few decades, we have seen an explosion of cross-dressing on the stage—a whole new wave of gender-bending tied to sexual politics.

Many postmodern directors have deconstructed classics of the stage with startling revelations, imbuing old plays from Greek tragedy to Gilbert and Sullivan

♦ **ANGELS IN AMERICA**, by Tony Kushner. In a scene reminiscent of Romeo and Juliet's kissing palms, two characters—Hanna and Joe Pitt, played by Adale O'Brien and Jon Brent Curry—struggle with their relationship troubled by oppositional sexual preferences and overshadowed by the AIDS crisis. Directed by Mladen Kiselov. Photo by Richard C. Trigg. Courtesy of Actors Theatre of Louisville.

comic operettas with contemporary political contexts. **Deconstruction** in theatrical production means a radically reinterpreted famous play in which the original play may still be recognized. The new production, however, uses the written play as only a pretext and frequently comments on or negates the apparent intent of the original play. Peter Sellars (b. 1957), for example, directs postmodern interpretations of musicals, operas, and classical plays, often using collections of video screens, onstage cameras, and contemporary locations. In Germany Peter Stein (b. 1937) produces radical stage environments and unusual audience relationships for classics ranging from *The Oresteia* of Aeschylus to Ibsen's *Peer Gynt*. Sometimes the classics are so modified by the directors that they seem to become entirely new plays, as occurred with Ariane Mnouchkine's French production of *Les Atrides* (1990–1992), a Kathakali-like reconception of *The Oresteia*.

Wholly new work dominated by visual images, dynamic music and dance, or closely choreographed movement has become the hallmark for many **conceptual directors** such as Martha Clarke, who conceived *Vienna Lusthaus* (1986) with text by Charles Mee, Jr., and created a culture at the crossroads primarily through visuals. Robert Wilson is also a master of visual images and has combined minimalist and postmodern music (by Philip Glass and David Byrne) with remarkable designs and movement in vast projects such as *the CIVIL warS* (1983). One of the most intriguing postmodern artists is Tadashi Suzuki (b. 1939) from Japan. Suzuki combines different periods, cultures, and styles with international casts of actors trained in the martial arts for his experiments such as *Clytemnestra*, a reworking of Greek tragedy.

Prominent among postmodern trends at the end of the twentieth century
was solitary work of performance artists, utilizing media and direct audience
address. Karen Finley's one-person, semiautobiographical shows are con-
frontational and controversial, using nudity and strong political and social messages as in *We Keep Our Victims Ready* (1989). Spalding Gray gives his audience
the convincing impression that his monologues such as *Monster in a Box* (1991)
are entirely autobiographical and embarrassingly revealing of his psychological
problems. Although Anna Deavere Smith often has performed alone (she also
appears as a traditional actor in TV productions), she impersonates many different characters based on real people she has interviewed. Her *Fires in the Mirror* (1992), like much of her work, focuses on racial conflict in the United States.

Early in a new century it is difficult to know whether the patterns and models of the late twentieth century will persist for long or soon be replaced by new
forms and styles. The play *The Guys* (2001) by Anne Nelson is a poignant two-
character play that is simply written without any obvious theatricality. She focuses on the humanity of the dialogue and suffering characters to create an
exploration of people trying to cope with the aftermath of the horrors of September 11. Early in the play one character, when referring to the morning of that
day, says, "That moment marked the end of the Post-Modern Era."[1] Only time
will verify or negate this statement. Although change is inevitable, it is equally
certain that plays and performance of the past will continue to inspire new art
and be themselves reworked and adapted to meet the demands and desires of
future audiences. Some of you who are reading this book will be an important
part of this change.

QUESTIONS AND ACTIVITIES

1. Class distinctions were considered important to a number of plays and events described in this chapter. Discuss the perceived relationship of social class to the current theatre and other forms of entertainment.

2. Theatres were the focus of artistic, social, and political conflict in the eighteenth and nineteenth centuries. What do you think could provoke a demonstration (or even a riot) in a theatre today? Consider plays, production elements, and management practice.

3. Selective realism has become a popular style: An actual location is suggested by realistic scenic pieces and props, but the audience is left to fill in the rest through imagination. The choice of what to include on stage becomes very important. Think about several different rooms or spaces that you know well. If you had to choose one item to suggest the space, what would it be? A second item? A third? Try this exercise with different kinds of spaces: a specific classroom, bedroom, living room, spot on campus, place in a city, specific store, and so on.

4. As a cultural institution, theatre is always a combination of using preestablished practices and reacting against them. Think of other areas of cultural change. How has your generation kept or changed what you inherited from the last? Discuss fashion, manners, vocabulary, and morality. How is film or television different now from what it was ten years ago? Twenty? Thirty? (Sometimes it is easier to notice differences. The similarities seem to be givens. Try to think of different ways in which things *could* have developed in order to see the similarities.)

KEY TERMS AND CONCEPTS

romanticism, p. 222
Sturm und Drang, p. 222
metatheatre, p. 223
box set, p. 227
antiquarianism, p. 227
melodrama, p. 227
breeches role, p. 228
realism, p. 231
well-made play, p. 231

naturalism, p. 232
fourth wall, p. 232
modernism, p. 233
avant-garde, p. 234
symbolism, p. 234
new stagecraft, p. 235
hanamichi, p. 235
expressionism, p. 235
surrealism, p. 236

Epic Theatre, p. 236
Theatre of Cruelty, p. 236
Theatre of the Absurd, p. 237
off-off Broadway, p. 239
book musical, p. 242
postmodern, p. 243
deconstruction, p. 244
conceptual directors, p. 244

FOR FURTHER EXPLORATION

Oscar Brockett and Franklin Hildy. *History of the Theatre*, 9th edition. Boston: Allyn and Bacon, 2002.

Edwin Wilson and Alvin Goldfarb. *Living Theater: A History*, 3rd edition. Boston: McGraw Hill, 2000.

Victor Turner. *From Ritual to Theatre: The Human Seriousness of Play*. New York: Performing Arts Journal Publications, 1982.

T. B. L. Webster. *Greek Theatre Production*. London: Methuen, 1970.

Richard Beacham. *The Roman Theatre and Its Audience*. Cambridge, Mass.: Harvard University Press, 1992.

Ronald Vince. *Ancient and Medieval Theatre*. Westport, Conn.: Greenwood, 1984.

Farley Richmond. *Indian Theatre: Traditions of Performance*. Honolulu: University of Hawaii Press, 1990.

Richard Beadle. *The Cambridge Guide to Medieval Theatre*. Cambridge, England: Cambridge University Press, 1994.

James Crump. *Chinese Theatre in the Days of Kublai Khan*. Tucson: University of Arizona Press, 1980.

Benito Ortolani. *The Japanese Theatre: From Shamanistic Ritual to Contemporary Pluralism*. Princeton, N.J.: Princeton University Press, 1995.

J. R. Mulryne and Margaret Shewring. *Theatre of the English and Italian Renaissance*. New York: St. Martins, 1991.

Gerald E. Bentley. *The Professions of Dramatist and Player in Shakespeare's Time, 1590–1642.* Princeton, N.J.: Princeton University Press, 1984.

Melveena McKendrick. *Theatre in Spain, 1490–1700.* Cambridge, England: Cambridge University Press, 1989.

William D. Howarth. *French Theatre in the Neo-Classical Era, 1550–1789.* West Lafayette, Ind.: Purdue Univesity Press, 1994.

Robert D. Hume. *The London Theatre World, 1660–1800.* Carbondale: Southern Illinois Univesity Press, 1980.

Ronald W. Vince. *Neoclassical Theatre: A Historiographical Handbook.* New York: Greenwood, 1988.

Don Wilmeth and Christopher Bigsby. *The Cambridge History of American Theatre,* 3 vols. Cambridge, England: Cambridge Univesity Press, 1998–2000.

David Grimstead. *Melodrama Unveiled.* Chicago: University of Chicago Press, 1968.

George Rowell. *The Victorian Theatre.* Cambridge, England: Cambridge Univesity Press, 1978.

Oscar Brockett and Robert Findlay. *Century of Innovation,* 2nd edition. Boston: Allyn and Bacon, 1991.

Roger Shattuck. *The Banquet Years: The Origins of the Avant-Garde in France.* New York: Vintage, 1968.

James Roose-Evans. *Experimental Theatre: From Stanislavsky to Peter Brook.* New York: Routledge, 1996.

Erroll Hill and George Woodyard. *The Cambridge Guide to African and Caribbean Theatre.* Cambridge, England: Cambridge University Press, 1994.

Key Theatrical Events

◆◆◆◆◆◆◆◆◆◆◆◆◆◆◆◆

This timeline presents a chronological list of important theatrical events and plays mentioned in this book. The dates for plays are the first known production unless otherwise noted. (For example, we give the early-nineteenth-century composition date for the play *Woyzeck* because it was not produced until the twentieth century.) We also include a series of important historical and cultural events as points of reference for the context of the theatrical chronology.

THEATRICAL EVENTS AND PLAYS

HISTORICAL/CULTURAL EVENTS

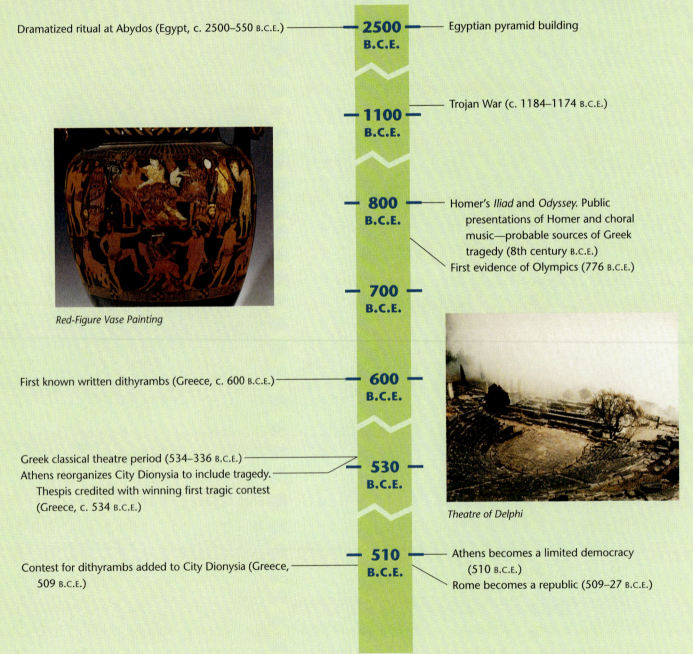

Dramatized ritual at Abydos (Egypt, c. 2500–550 B.C.E.) —— **2500 B.C.E.** —— Egyptian pyramid building

1100 B.C.E. —— Trojan War (c. 1184–1174 B.C.E.)

800 B.C.E. —— Homer's *Iliad* and *Odyssey*. Public presentations of Homer and choral music—probable sources of Greek tragedy (8th century B.C.E.)
First evidence of Olympics (776 B.C.E.)

Red-Figure Vase Painting

700 B.C.E.

First known written dithyrambs (Greece, c. 600 B.C.E.) —— **600 B.C.E.**

Greek classical theatre period (534–336 B.C.E.)
Athens reorganizes City Dionysia to include tragedy.
  Thespis credited with winning first tragic contest
  (Greece, c. 534 B.C.E.) —— **530 B.C.E.**

Theatre of Delphi

Contest for dithyrambs added to City Dionysia (Greece, —— **510 B.C.E.** —— Athens becomes a limited democracy
  509 B.C.E.) (510 B.C.E.)
Rome becomes a republic (509–27 B.C.E.)

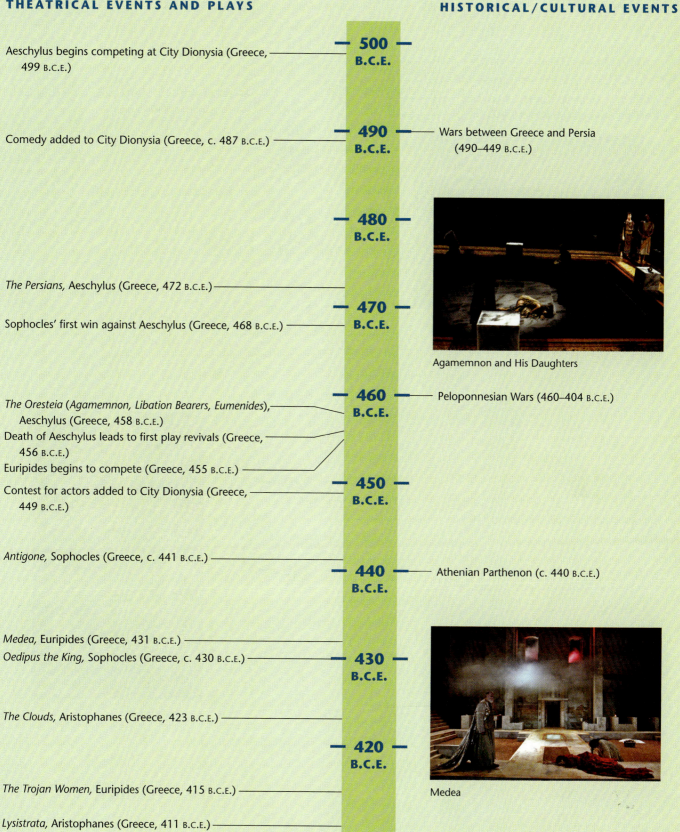

THEATRICAL EVENTS AND PLAYS

HISTORICAL/CULTURAL EVENTS

Aeschylus begins competing at City Dionysia (Greece, 499 B.C.E.)

500 B.C.E.

Comedy added to City Dionysia (Greece, c. 487 B.C.E.)

490 B.C.E. — Wars between Greece and Persia (490–449 B.C.E.)

480 B.C.E.

The Persians, Aeschylus (Greece, 472 B.C.E.)

470 B.C.E.

Sophocles' first win against Aeschylus (Greece, 468 B.C.E.)

Agamemnon and His Daughters

The Oresteia (*Agamemnon, Libation Bearers, Eumenides*), Aeschylus (Greece, 458 B.C.E.)

460 B.C.E. — Peloponnesian Wars (460–404 B.C.E.)

Death of Aeschylus leads to first play revivals (Greece, 456 B.C.E.)

Euripides begins to compete (Greece, 455 B.C.E.)

Contest for actors added to City Dionysia (Greece, 449 B.C.E.)

450 B.C.E.

Antigone, Sophocles (Greece, c. 441 B.C.E.)

440 B.C.E. — Athenian Parthenon (c. 440 B.C.E.)

Medea, Euripides (Greece, 431 B.C.E.)

Oedipus the King, Sophocles (Greece, c. 430 B.C.E.)

430 B.C.E.

The Clouds, Aristophanes (Greece, 423 B.C.E.)

420 B.C.E.

The Trojan Women, Euripides (Greece, 415 B.C.E.)

Medea

Lysistrata, Aristophanes (Greece, 411 B.C.E.)

Key Theatrical Events **249**

Key Theatrical Events

◆◆◆◆◆◆◆◆◆◆◆◆◆◆◆◆◆◆

THEATRICAL EVENTS AND PLAYS

HISTORICAL/CULTURAL EVENTS

Hypsipyle, Euripides (Greece, 408 B.C.E.) ————

Oedipus at Colonus, Sophocles (Greece, 406 B.C.E.)———

The Bacchae, Euripides (Greece, 406 B.C.E.) ————

The Frogs, Aristophanes (Greece, 405 B.C.E.) ————

**— 410 —
B.C.E.**

———— Fall of Athens to Sparta, but play production
continues (404 B.C.E.)

**— 400 —
B.C.E.**

———— Plato's *Republic* (c. 373 B.C.E.)

**— 370 —
B.C.E.**

**— 340 —
B.C.E.**

Aristotle's *Poetics* (Greece, c. 335–323 B.C.E.)————

———— Hellenistic period (336–146 B.C.E.)

**— 330 —
B.C.E.**

Greek Hellenistic Theatre

**— 320 —
B.C.E.**

The Dyskolos, Menander (Greece, c. 316 B.C.E.) ————

Livius Andronicus performs tragedy and comedy ————
at the Ludi Romani in Rome (Rome, 240 B.C.E.)

**— 240 —
B.C.E.**

**— 230 —
B.C.E.**

The Oedipus Plays

**— 220 —
B.C.E.**

———— Great Wall of China (214 B.C.E.)

THEATRICAL EVENTS AND PLAYS

HISTORICAL/CULTURAL EVENTS

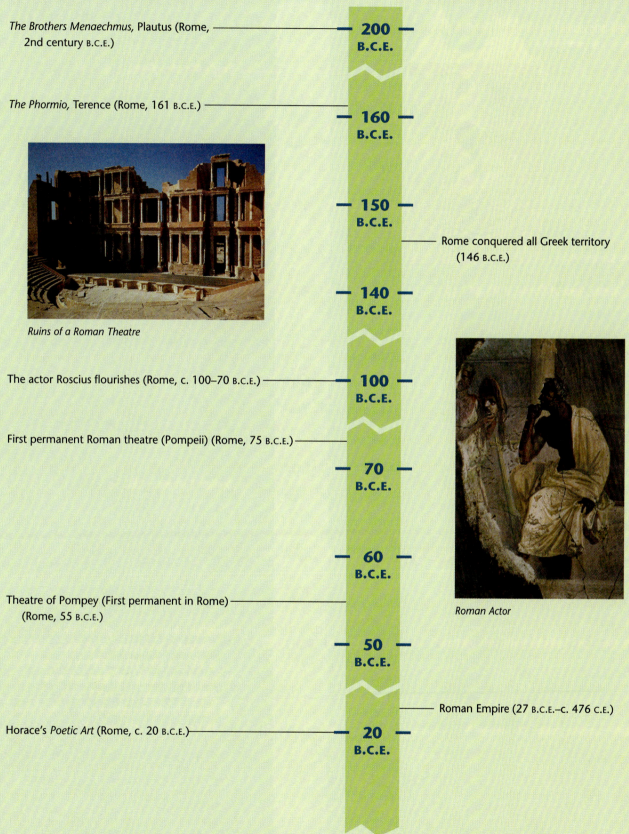

The Brothers Menaechmus, Plautus (Rome, 2nd century B.C.E.) —————— **200 B.C.E.**

The Phormio, Terence (Rome, 161 B.C.E.) —————— **160 B.C.E.**

150 B.C.E.

———— Rome conquered all Greek territory (146 B.C.E.)

140 B.C.E.

Ruins of a Roman Theatre

The actor Roscius flourishes (Rome, c. 100–70 B.C.E.) —————— **100 B.C.E.**

First permanent Roman theatre (Pompeii) (Rome, 75 B.C.E.) ————

70 B.C.E.

60 B.C.E.

Theatre of Pompey (First permanent in Rome) —————— (Rome, 55 B.C.E.)

Roman Actor

50 B.C.E.

———— Roman Empire (27 B.C.E.–c. 476 C.E.)

Horace's *Poetic Art* (Rome, c. 20 B.C.E.) ———— **20 B.C.E.**

Key Theatrical Events

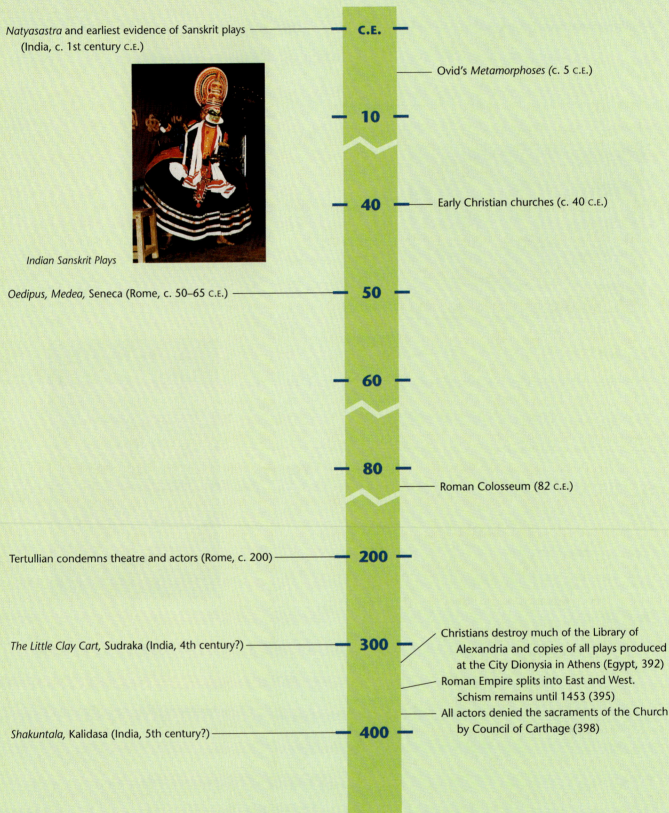

THEATRICAL EVENTS AND PLAYS

HISTORICAL/CULTURAL EVENTS

Natyasastra and earliest evidence of Sanskrit plays (India, c. 1st century C.E.)

C.E.

Ovid's *Metamorphoses* (c. 5 C.E.)

10

40 ——— Early Christian churches (c. 40 C.E.)

Indian Sanskrit Plays

Oedipus, Medea, Seneca (Rome, c. 50–65 C.E.)

50

60

80 ——— Roman Colosseum (82 C.E.)

Tertullian condemns theatre and actors (Rome, c. 200)

200

The Little Clay Cart, Sudraka (India, 4th century?)

300

Christians destroy much of the Library of Alexandria and copies of all plays produced at the City Dionysia in Athens (Egypt, 392)

Roman Empire splits into East and West. Schism remains until 1453 (395)

All actors denied the sacraments of the Church by Council of Carthage (398)

Shakuntala, Kalidasa (India, 5th century?)

400

THEATRICAL EVENTS AND PLAYS

HISTORICAL/CULTURAL EVENTS

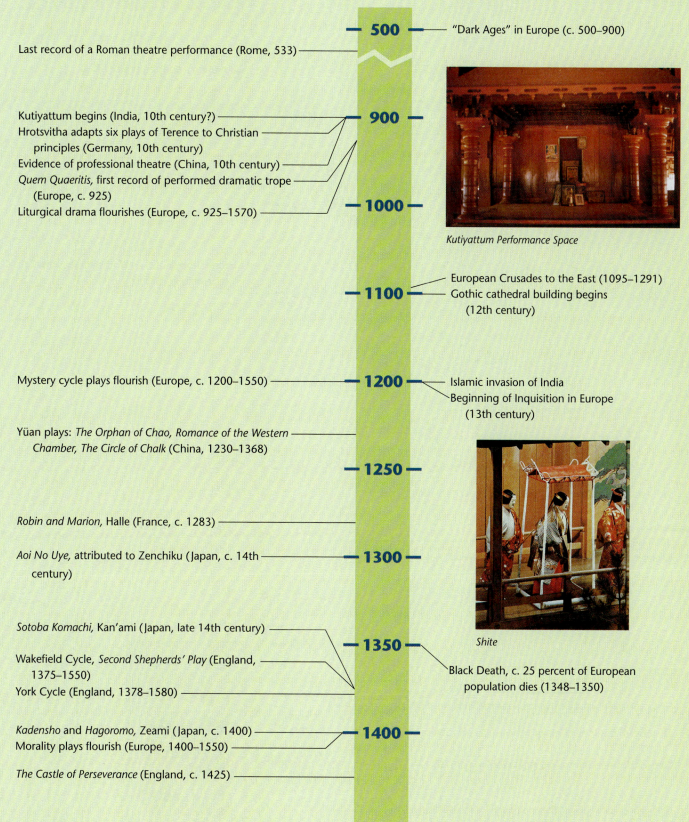

— **500** —

"Dark Ages" in Europe (c. 500–900)

Last record of a Roman theatre performance (Rome, 533)

Kutiyattum begins (India, 10th century?)
Hrotsvitha adapts six plays of Terence to Christian
    principles (Germany, 10th century)
Evidence of professional theatre (China, 10th century)
Quem Quaeritis, first record of performed dramatic trope
    (Europe, c. 925)
Liturgical drama flourishes (Europe, c. 925–1570)

— **900** —

— **1000** —

Kutiyattum Performance Space

— **1100** —

European Crusades to the East (1095–1291)
Gothic cathedral building begins
    (12th century)

Mystery cycle plays flourish (Europe, c. 1200–1550)

— **1200** —

Islamic invasion of India
Beginning of Inquisition in Europe
    (13th century)

Yüan plays: *The Orphan of Chao, Romance of the Western
    Chamber, The Circle of Chalk* (China, 1230–1368)

— **1250** —

Robin and Marion, Halle (France, c. 1283)

Aoi No Uye, attributed to Zenchiku (Japan, c. 14th
    century)

— **1300** —

Shite

Sotoba Komachi, Kan'ami (Japan, late 14th century)

Wakefield Cycle, *Second Shepherds' Play* (England,
    1375–1550)
York Cycle (England, 1378–1580)

— **1350** —

Black Death, c. 25 percent of European
    population dies (1348–1350)

Kadensho and *Hagoromo,* Zeami (Japan, c. 1400)
Morality plays flourish (Europe, 1400–1550)

— **1400** —

The Castle of Perseverance (England, c. 1425)

Key Theatrical Events

◆◆◆◆◆◆◆◆◆◆◆◆◆◆◆◆

THEATRICAL EVENTS AND PLAYS

HISTORICAL/CULTURAL EVENTS

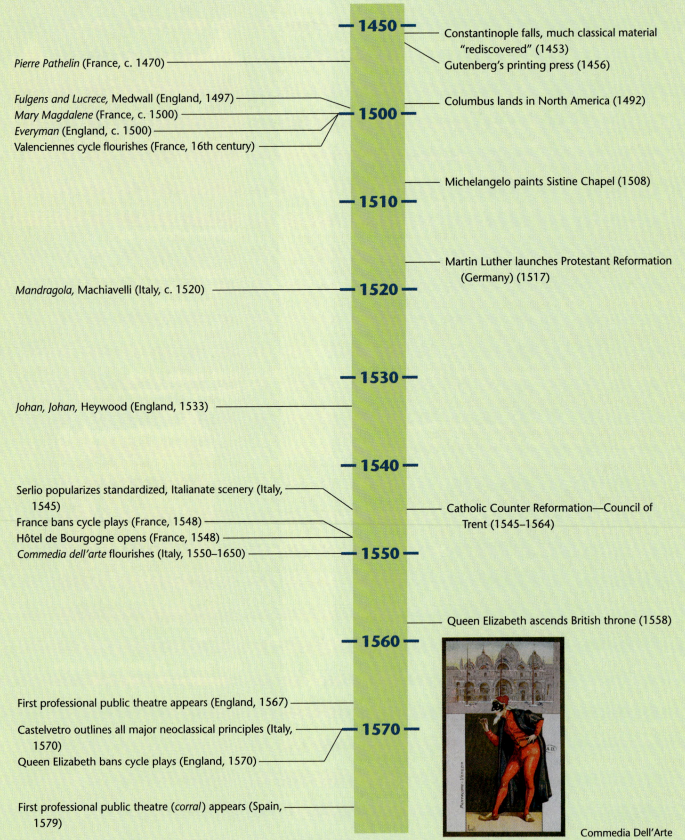

— 1450 — Constantinople falls, much classical material "rediscovered" (1453)

Gutenberg's printing press (1456)

Pierre Pathelin (France, c. 1470)

Fulgens and Lucrece, Medwall (England, 1497)

Columbus lands in North America (1492)

Mary Magdalene (France, c. 1500)

— 1500 —

Everyman (England, c. 1500)

Valenciennes cycle flourishes (France, 16th century)

Michelangelo paints Sistine Chapel (1508)

— 1510 —

Martin Luther launches Protestant Reformation (Germany) (1517)

Mandragola, Machiavelli (Italy, c. 1520)

— 1520 —

— 1530 —

Johan, Johan, Heywood (England, 1533)

— 1540 —

Serlio popularizes standardized, Italianate scenery (Italy, 1545)

Catholic Counter Reformation—Council of Trent (1545–1564)

France bans cycle plays (France, 1548)

Hôtel de Bourgogne opens (France, 1548)

Commedia dell'arte flourishes (Italy, 1550–1650)

— 1550 —

Queen Elizabeth ascends British throne (1558)

— 1560 —

First professional public theatre appears (England, 1567)

Castelvetro outlines all major neoclassical principles (Italy, 1570)

— 1570 —

Queen Elizabeth bans cycle plays (England, 1570)

First professional public theatre (*corral*) appears (Spain, 1579)

Commedia Dell'Arte

THEATRICAL EVENTS AND PLAYS

HISTORICAL/CULTURAL EVENTS

— 1580 —

Cysat's plan of the Lucerne Passion Play (Switzerland, 1583)

— 1585 —

The Spanish Tragedy, Kyd (England, c. 1587)

The Rose Theatre opens (England, c. 1587)

Professional actresses licensed in Spain (Spain, c. 1587)

Doctor Faustus and *Tamburlaine,* Marlowe (England, 1588)

The Spanish Armada defeated by England (1588)

The Faithful Shepherd, Guarini (Italy, 1590)

— 1590 —

Edward II, Marlowe, (England, 1592)

The Comedy of Errors, Shakespeare (England, 1592)

Richard III, Shakespeare (England, c. 1593)

Opera developed (Italy, 1594)

Romeo and Juliet, Shakespeare (England, 1594)

A Midsummer Night's Dream, Shakespeare (England, c. 1595)

— 1595 —

Much Ado about Nothing, Shakespeare (England, c. 1598)

The Globe Theatre opens, (England, 1599)

Henry V, Shakespeare (England, 1599)

Hamlet, Shakespeare (England, c. 1600)

— 1600 —

Twelfth Night, Shakespeare (England, c. 1601)

Okuni's dances develop into Kabuki (Japan, 1603)

Othello, Shakespeare (England, c. 1604)

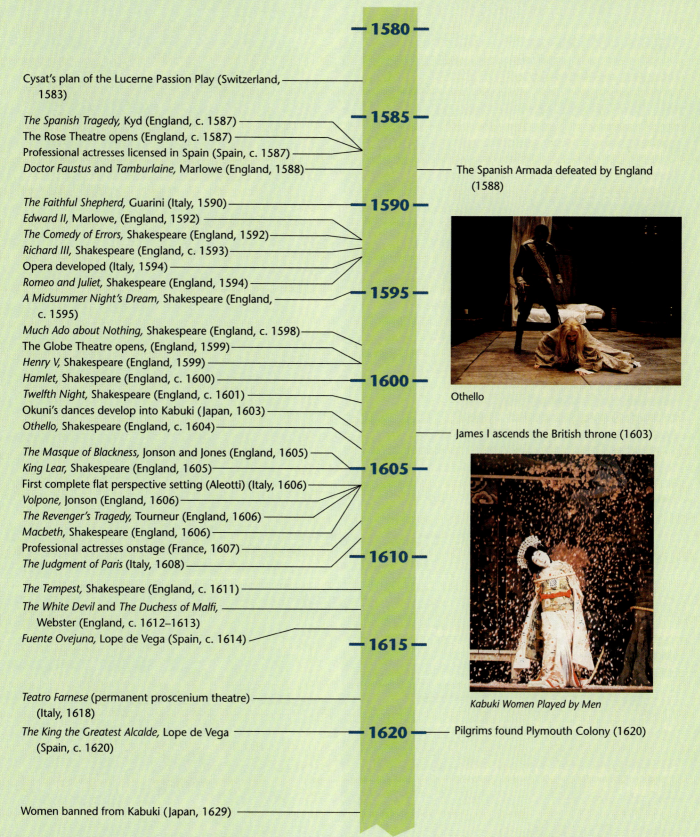

Othello

James I ascends the British throne (1603)

The Masque of Blackness, Jonson and Jones (England, 1605)

King Lear, Shakespeare (England, 1605)

— 1605 —

First complete flat perspective setting (Aleotti) (Italy, 1606)

Volpone, Jonson (England, 1606)

The Revenger's Tragedy, Tourneur (England, 1606)

Macbeth, Shakespeare (England, 1606)

Professional actresses onstage (France, 1607)

The Judgment of Paris (Italy, 1608)

— 1610 —

The Tempest, Shakespeare (England, c. 1611)

The White Devil and *The Duchess of Malfi,* Webster (England, c. 1612–1613)

Fuente Ovejuna, Lope de Vega (Spain, c. 1614)

— 1615 —

Teatro Farnese (permanent proscenium theatre) (Italy, 1618)

Kabuki Women Played by Men

The King the Greatest Alcalde, Lope de Vega (Spain, c. 1620)

— 1620 —

Pilgrims found Plymouth Colony (1620)

Women banned from Kabuki (Japan, 1629)

Key Theatrical Events

◆◆◆◆◆◆◆◆◆◆◆◆◆◆◆◆

THEATRICAL EVENTS AND PLAYS

HISTORICAL/CULTURAL EVENTS

'Tis Pity She's a Whore, Ford (England, c. 1630) — **1630**

The Constant Prince, Calderon de la Barca (Spain, 1635)
The Cid, Corneille (France, c. 1636)
Life Is a Dream, Calderon de la Barca (Spain, c. 1636)

Chariot and pole system (Torelli) (Italy, 1640s) — **1640**
Palais Cardinal (later Royal) opens (Richelieu)
    (France, 1641)
Theatres closed by civil war and Puritan decree (England,
    1642)

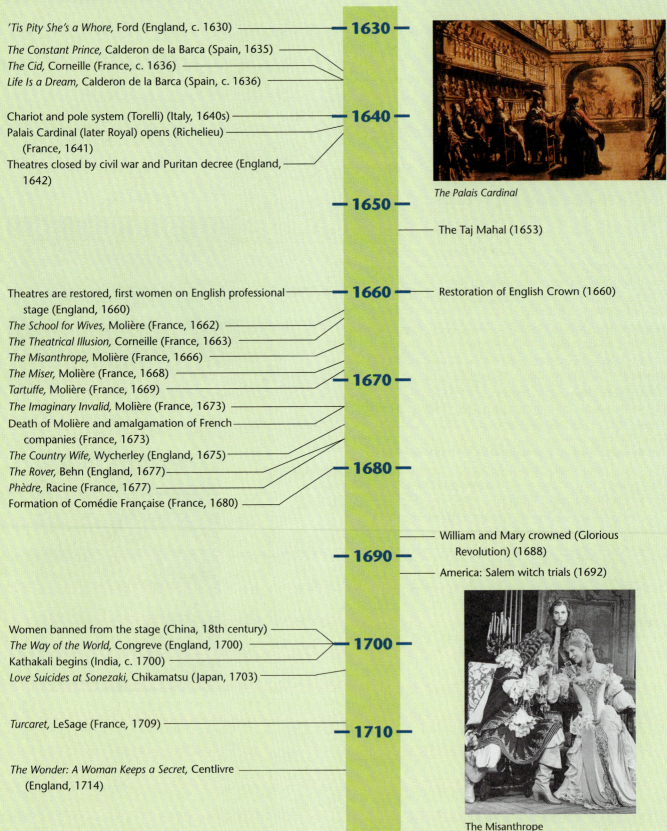

The Palais Cardinal

— **1650**

The Taj Mahal (1653)

Theatres are restored, first women on English professional — **1660** — Restoration of English Crown (1660)
    stage (England, 1660)
The School for Wives, Molière (France, 1662)
The Theatrical Illusion, Corneille (France, 1663)
The Misanthrope, Molière (France, 1666)
The Miser, Molière (France, 1668)
Tartuffe, Molière (France, 1669) — **1670**
The Imaginary Invalid, Molière (France, 1673)
Death of Molière and amalgamation of French
    companies (France, 1673)
The Country Wife, Wycherley (England, 1675)
The Rover, Behn (England, 1677) — **1680**
Phèdre, Racine (France, 1677)
Formation of Comédie Française (France, 1680)

William and Mary crowned (Glorious
    Revolution) (1688)
— **1690** —
America: Salem witch trials (1692)

Women banned from the stage (China, 18th century)
The Way of the World, Congreve (England, 1700) — **1700**
Kathakali begins (India, c. 1700)
Love Suicides at Sonezaki, Chikamatsu (Japan, 1703)

Turcaret, LeSage (France, 1709) — **1710**

The Wonder: A Woman Keeps a Secret, Centlivre
    (England, 1714)

The Misanthrope

— 1720 —

Caroline Neuber, first important woman theatre manager (Germany, 1727)

The Beggar's Opera, Gay (England, 1728)

The London Merchant, Lillo (England, 1731)

— 1730 —

Licensing Act (England, 1737)

— 1740 —

The Servant of Two Masters, first version, Goldoni (Italy, 1743)

Garrick becomes actor-manager of Drury Lane (England, 1747)

The Comic Theatre, Goldoni (Italy, 1750)

Kumagai's Camp (Kabuki) (Japan, 1751)

Hallam company opens in Williamsburg (America, 1752)

Mistress of the Inn, Goldoni (Italy, 1753)

First revolving stage in the world (Kabuki) (Japan, 1758)

"Drame" introduced by Diderot (France, 1758)

— 1750 —

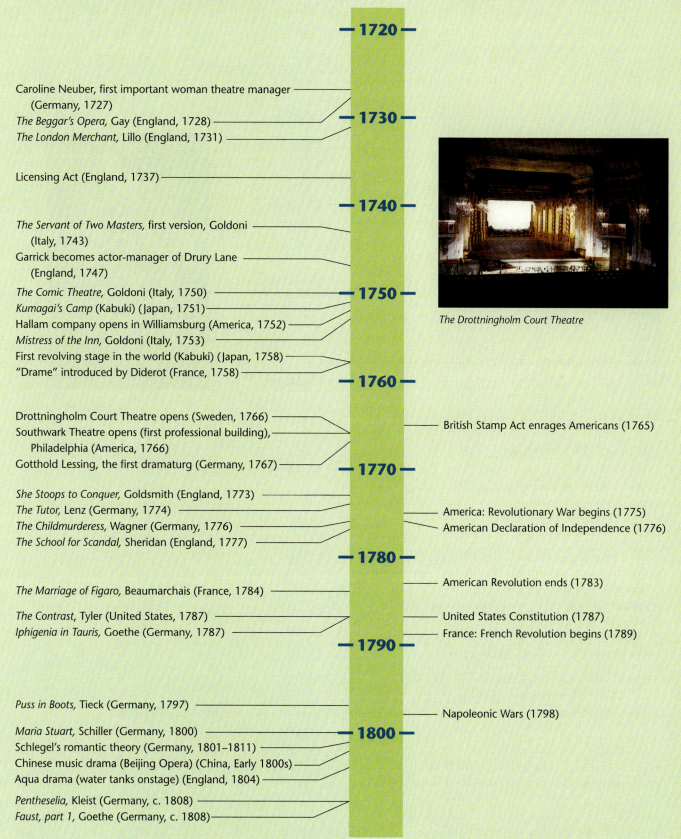

The Drottningholm Court Theatre

— 1760 —

Drottningholm Court Theatre opens (Sweden, 1766)

Southwark Theatre opens (first professional building), Philadelphia (America, 1766)

Gotthold Lessing, the first dramaturg (Germany, 1767)

British Stamp Act enrages Americans (1765)

— 1770 —

She Stoops to Conquer, Goldsmith (England, 1773)

The Tutor, Lenz (Germany, 1774)

The Childmurderess, Wagner (Germany, 1776)

The School for Scandal, Sheridan (England, 1777)

America: Revolutionary War begins (1775)

American Declaration of Independence (1776)

— 1780 —

The Marriage of Figaro, Beaumarchais (France, 1784)

American Revolution ends (1783)

The Contrast, Tyler (United States, 1787)

Iphigenia in Tauris, Goethe (Germany, 1787)

United States Constitution (1787)

France: French Revolution begins (1789)

— 1790 —

Puss in Boots, Tieck (Germany, 1797)

Napoleonic Wars (1798)

Maria Stuart, Schiller (Germany, 1800)

Schlegel's romantic theory (Germany, 1801–1811)

Chinese music drama (Beijing Opera) (China, Early 1800s)

Aqua drama (water tanks onstage) (England, 1804)

Pentheselia, Kleist (Germany, c. 1808)

Faust, part 1, Goethe (Germany, c. 1808)

— 1800 —

Key Theatrical Events   **257**

Key Theatrical Events

◆◆◆◆◆◆◆◆◆◆◆◆◆◆◆◆◆◆◆◆

THEATRICAL EVENTS AND PLAYS   **HISTORICAL/CULTURAL EVENTS**

— **1810** —

Prince Friedrich of Homburg, Kleist (Germany, c. 1811) ————

———— War of 1812

— **1815** —

Gaslight onstage, Chestnut Street Theatre, Philadelphia ————
   (United States, 1816)
The Scarlet Princess of Edo (Kabuki) (Japan, 1817) ————

The Vampire, Planché (England, 1820) ————   — **1820** —
African Company in New York (United States, 1821) ————

Antiquarian productions (Planché) (England, 1823–1824) ————

— **1825** —

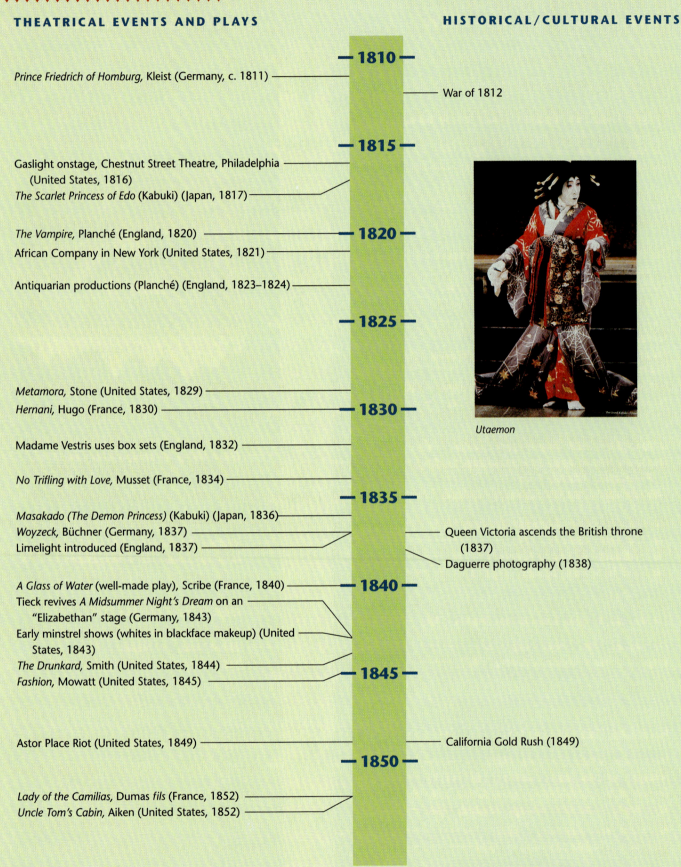

Metamora, Stone (United States, 1829) ————
Hernani, Hugo (France, 1830) ————   — **1830** —

Madame Vestris uses box sets (England, 1832) ————

No Trifling with Love, Musset (France, 1834) ————

— **1835** —

Masakado (The Demon Princess) (Kabuki) (Japan, 1836) ————
Woyzeck, Büchner (Germany, 1837) ————
Limelight introduced (England, 1837) ————

———— Queen Victoria ascends the British throne
   (1837)
———— Daguerre photography (1838)

A Glass of Water (well-made play), Scribe (France, 1840) ————   — **1840** —
Tieck revives *A Midsummer Night's Dream* on an ————
   "Elizabethan" stage (Germany, 1843)
Early minstrel shows (whites in blackface makeup) (United ————
   States, 1843)
The Drunkard, Smith (United States, 1844) ————
Fashion, Mowatt (United States, 1845) ————   — **1845** —

Astor Place Riot (United States, 1849) ————   ———— California Gold Rush (1849)
— **1850** —

Lady of the Camilias, Dumas *fils* (France, 1852) ————
Uncle Tom's Cabin, Aiken (United States, 1852) ————

Utaemon

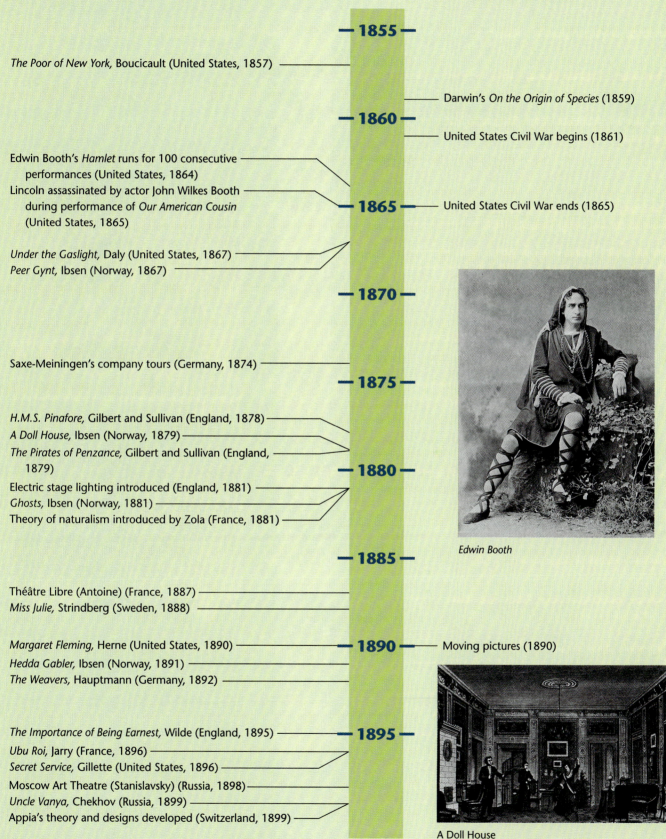

THEATRICAL EVENTS AND PLAYS

HISTORICAL/CULTURAL EVENTS

— 1855 —

The Poor of New York, Boucicault (United States, 1857) ————

———— Darwin's *On the Origin of Species* (1859)

— 1860 —

———— United States Civil War begins (1861)

Edwin Booth's *Hamlet* runs for 100 consecutive
    performances (United States, 1864)
Lincoln assassinated by actor John Wilkes Booth
    during performance of *Our American Cousin*
    (United States, 1865)

— 1865 — ———— United States Civil War ends (1865)

Under the Gaslight, Daly (United States, 1867)
Peer Gynt, Ibsen (Norway, 1867)

— 1870 —

Saxe-Meiningen's company tours (Germany, 1874)

— 1875 —

H.M.S. Pinafore, Gilbert and Sullivan (England, 1878)
A Doll House, Ibsen (Norway, 1879)
The Pirates of Penzance, Gilbert and Sullivan (England,
    1879)

— 1880 —

Electric stage lighting introduced (England, 1881)
Ghosts, Ibsen (Norway, 1881)
Theory of naturalism introduced by Zola (France, 1881)

— 1885 —

Edwin Booth

Théâtre Libre (Antoine) (France, 1887)
Miss Julie, Strindberg (Sweden, 1888)

Margaret Fleming, Herne (United States, 1890) — 1890 — ———— Moving pictures (1890)
Hedda Gabler, Ibsen (Norway, 1891)
The Weavers, Hauptmann (Germany, 1892)

The Importance of Being Earnest, Wilde (England, 1895) — 1895 —
Ubu Roi, Jarry (France, 1896)
Secret Service, Gillette (United States, 1896)
Moscow Art Theatre (Stanislavsky) (Russia, 1898)
Uncle Vanya, Chekhov (Russia, 1899)
Appia's theory and designs developed (Switzerland, 1899)

A Doll House

Key Theatrical Events

THEATRICAL EVENTS AND PLAYS

La Ronde, Schnitzler (Austria, 1900) ———— **1900** —— Sigmund Freud's *Interpretation of Dreams* (1900)

Three Sisters, Chekhov (Russia, 1901) ————

Mrs. Warren's Profession, Shaw (England, 1902) — **1902** —
The Lower Depths, Gorky (Russia, 1902) ————

—— Wright Brothers' flight (1903)

The Cherry Orchard, Chekhov (Russia, 1904) —— **1904** ——
Riders to the Sea, Synge (Ireland, 1904) ————

The Art of the Theatre, Craig (England, 1905) ——
Man and Superman, Shaw (England, 1905) ———

—— **1906** ——

A Dream Play, Strindberg (Sweden, 1907) ————

The Blue Bird, Maeterlinck (Belgium, 1908) —— **1908** ——
The Ghost Sonata, Strindberg (Sweden, 1908) ——

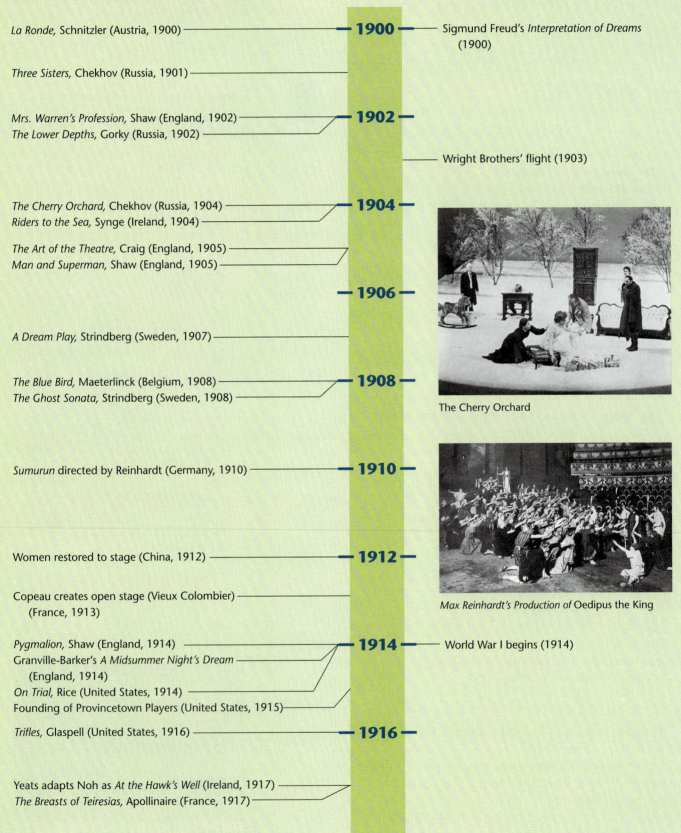

The Cherry Orchard

Sumurun directed by Reinhardt (Germany, 1910) —— **1910** ——

Women restored to stage (China, 1912) ———— **1912** ——

Copeau creates open stage (Vieux Colombier) ——
    (France, 1913)

Max Reinhardt's Production of Oedipus the King

Pygmalion, Shaw (England, 1914) ———— **1914** —— World War I begins (1914)
Granville-Barker's *A Midsummer Night's Dream* ——
    (England, 1914)
On Trial, Rice (United States, 1914) ————
Founding of Provincetown Players (United States, 1915)——

Trifles, Glaspell (United States, 1916) ———— **1916** ——

Yeats adapts Noh as *At the Hawk's Well* (Ireland, 1917) ——
The Breasts of Teiresias, Apollinaire (France, 1917) ——

THEATRICAL EVENTS AND PLAYS

HISTORICAL/CULTURAL EVENTS

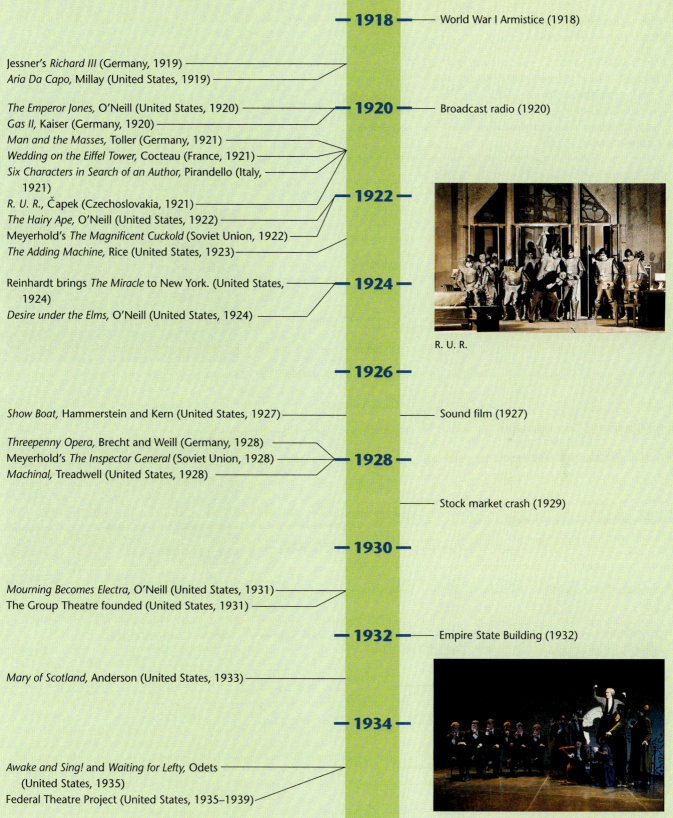

— 1918 — World War I Armistice (1918)

Jessner's *Richard III* (Germany, 1919)
Aria Da Capo, Millay (United States, 1919)

The Emperor Jones, O'Neill (United States, 1920) **— 1920 —** Broadcast radio (1920)
Gas II, Kaiser (Germany, 1920)
Man and the Masses, Toller (Germany, 1921)
Wedding on the Eiffel Tower, Cocteau (France, 1921)
Six Characters in Search of an Author, Pirandello (Italy, 1921)
R. U. R., Čapek (Czechoslovakia, 1921) **— 1922 —**
The Hairy Ape, O'Neill (United States, 1922)
Meyerhold's *The Magnificent Cuckold* (Soviet Union, 1922)
The Adding Machine, Rice (United States, 1923)

Reinhardt brings *The Miracle* to New York. (United States, 1924) **— 1924 —**
Desire under the Elms, O'Neill (United States, 1924)

R. U. R.

— 1926 —

Show Boat, Hammerstein and Kern (United States, 1927) Sound film (1927)

Threepenny Opera, Brecht and Weill (Germany, 1928)
Meyerhold's *The Inspector General* (Soviet Union, 1928) **— 1928 —**
Machinal, Treadwell (United States, 1928)

Stock market crash (1929)

— 1930 —

Mourning Becomes Electra, O'Neill (United States, 1931)
The Group Theatre founded (United States, 1931)

— 1932 — Empire State Building (1932)

Mary of Scotland, Anderson (United States, 1933)

— 1934 —

Awake and Sing! and *Waiting for Lefty,* Odets (United States, 1935)
Federal Theatre Project (United States, 1935–1939)

The Adding Machine

Key Theatrical Events

THEATRICAL EVENTS AND PLAYS | **HISTORICAL/CULTURAL EVENTS**

1936

- *Bury the Dead,* Irwin Shaw (United States, 1936)
- *It Can't Happen Here,* Lewis (United States, 1936)
- *The Cradle Will Rock,* Blitzstein (United States, 1937)

1938

- Theory of Theatre of Cruelty, in *The Theatre and Its Double,* Artaud (France, 1938)
- *Our Town,* Wilder (United States, 1938)
- *The Boys from Syracuse,* Rodgers and Hart (United States, 1938)
- *Mother Courage,* Brecht (Germany, 1939)
- *The Philadelphia Story,* Barry (United States, 1939)
- World War II begins (1939)

1940

- *Good Person of Setzuan,* Brecht (Germany, c. 1940)

Our Town

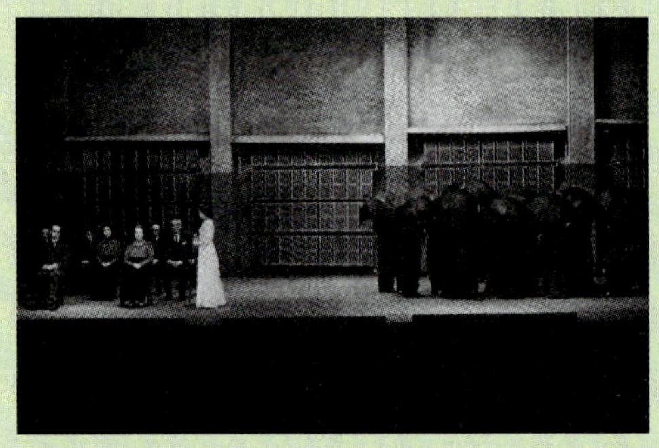

1942

- *Oklahoma!,* Rodgers and Hammerstein (United States, 1943)

1944

- *The Caucasian Chalk Circle,* Brecht (Germany, 1945)
- *The Glass Menagerie,* Williams (United States, 1945)
- World War II ends (1945)

1946

- *The Iceman Cometh,* O'Neill (United States, 1946)
- The Actor's Studio founded (United States, 1947)
- *A Streetcar Named Desire,* Williams (United States, 1947)

Waiting for Godot

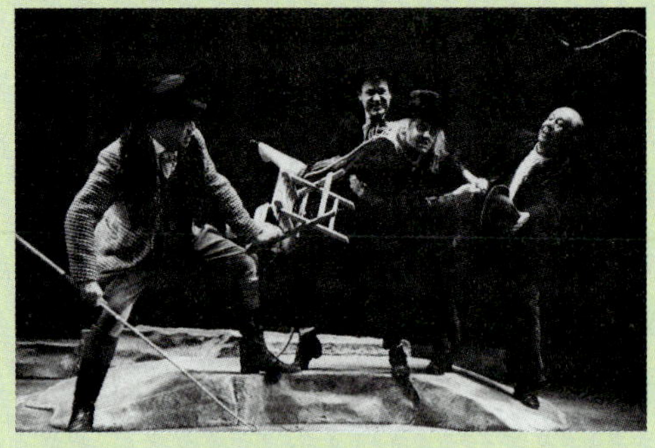

1948

- *Death of a Salesman,* Miller (United States, 1949)

1950

- *The Bald Soprano,* Ionesco (France, 1950)
- Arena Stage (Washington D.C.) founded (United States, 1950)
- Korean War begins (1950)

1952

- *The Chairs,* Ionesco (France, 1952)
- *The Crucible,* Miller (United States, 1953)
- *Waiting for Godot,* Beckett (France, 1953)
- Korean War ends (1953)

— **1954** —

Cat on a Hot Tin Roof, Williams (United States, 1955) ——————

Long Day's Journey into Night, produced posthumously, —— — **1956** —
    O'Neill (United States, 1956)

My Fair Lady, Lerner and Loewe (United States, 1956) —

Endgame, Beckett (France, 1957) ——————————

Permanent Stratford Festival Theatre (Canada, 1957) ——

West Side Story, Bernstein, Sondheim, Laurents —————
    (United States, 1957)

— **1958** —

Sputnik, first satellite (1957)

A Raisin in the Sun, Hansberry (United States, 1959) ——

The Dyskolos (Menander) first published (Greece, 1959) ——

The Fantasticks, Jones and Schmidt (United States, 1960) —— — **1960** —

Cat on a Hot Tin Roof

The Blood Knot, Fugard (South Africa, 1961) ——————

Russian Yuri Gagarin, first person in space
    (1961)

Akropolis, Grotowski (Poland, 1962) ——————

The Tree Climber, Al-Hakim (Egypt, 1962) ———— — **1962** —

A Funny Thing Happened on the Way to the Forum, —
    Sondheim, Shevelove, Gelbart (United States, 1962) —

Who's Afraid of Virginia Woolf?, Albee (United States, 1962) —

The Free Southern Theatre formed (United States, 1963) —

U.S. involvement in Vietnam War. John F.
    Kennedy assassinated (1963)

Dutchman, Baraka (United States, 1964) ———— — **1964** — The Civil Rights Act (1964)

Funnyhouse of a Negro, Kennedy (United States, 1964) —

The Homecoming, Pinter (England, 1965) ————

Day of Absence, Ward (United States, 1965) ————

Teatro Campesino founded (United States, 1965) ————

The Odd Couple, Simon (United States, 1965) ————

Cabaret, Kander, Ebb, Masteroff (United States, 1966) —— — **1966** — Chinese "Cultural Revolution" (1966)

Rosencrantz and Guildenstern Are Dead, Stoppard ——
    (England, 1967)

National Theatre of the Deaf founded (United States, 1967) —

Hair!, McDermot, Ragni, Rado (United States, 1968) —

Paradise Now, Living Theatre (United States, 1968) — — **1968** — Martin Luther King assassinated (1968)

Dionysus in 69, Performance Group (United States, 1968) —

The Serpent, Van Itallie/Open Theatre (United States, 1968) —

Towards a Poor Theatre, Grotowski (Poland, 1968) —

Boesman and Lena, Fugard (South Africa, 1969) —

Apollo 11 (Neil Armstrong), first lunar landing
    (1969)

What the Butler Saw, Orton (England, 1969) ———

A Tempest, Césaire (West Indies, 1969) ———— — **1970** — World Trade Center completed (1970)

Brook's *A Midsummer Night's Dream* (England, 1970) —

Madmen and Specialists, Soyinka (Nigeria, 1971) —

Sticks and Bones, Rabe (United States, 1971) ——

Key Theatrical Events

◆◆◆◆◆◆◆◆◆◆◆◆◆◆◆◆◆◆

THEATRICAL EVENTS AND PLAYS

HISTORICAL/CULTURAL EVENTS

— 1972 —

A Little Night Music, Sondheim (United States, 1973)
The Bacchae of Euripides, Soyinka (Nigeria, 1973)
Equus, Shaffer (England, 1973)

Vietnam War ends. Watergate (1973)

— 1974 —

A Chorus Line, Bennett, Kirkwood, Dante, Hamlisch,
    Kleban (United States, 1975)
Death and the King's Horseman, Soyinka (Nigeria, 1976)
*for colored girls who have considered suicide when the
    rainbow is enuf,* Shange (United States, 1976)

— 1976 —

Miss Margarida's Way, Athayde (Brazil, 1977)
Bedroom Farce, Ayckbourn (England, 1977)
Fefu and Her Friends, Fornes (United States, 1977)
American Buffalo, Mamet (United States, 1977)
Buried Child, Shepard (United States, 1978)
Betrayal, Pinter (England, 1978)
Hamletmachine, Müller (Germany, 1978)

— 1978 —

Equus

Cloud 9, Churchill (England, 1979)
Babes in the Bighouse, Terry (United States, 1979)
Crimes of the Heart, Henley (United States, 1979)

Iran hostage crisis (1979–1981)

True West, Shepard (United States, 1980)
Children of a Lesser God, Medoff (United States, 1980)

— 1980 —

AIDS pandemic identified (1981)

Cats, Eliot, Webber (1981)
Master Harold . . . and the Boys, Fugard (South Africa, 1982)
Top Girls, Churchill (England, 1982)
Noises Off, Frayn (England, 1982)
Glengarry Glen Ross, Mamet (United States, 1983)
L.S.D. (. . . Just the High Points . . .), Wooster
    Group (United States, 1983)
'night, Mother, Norman (United States, 1983)
Tracers, Difusco and cast (United States, 1983)
The CIVIL warS, Wilson (United States, 1983)

— 1982 —

Ma Rainey's Black Bottom, Wilson (United States, 1984)
Sunday in the Park with George, Sondheim, Lapine
    (United States, 1984)

— 1984 —

Master Harold . . .
and the Boys

Largo Desolato, Havel (Czechoslovakia, 1985)
Les Misérables, Boublil, Schönberg (France, 1985)
Fences, Wilson (United States, 1985)
The Conduct of Life, Fornes (United States, 1985)
The Normal Heart, Kramer (United States, 1985)
The Colored Museum, Wolfe (United States, 1986)
Vienna Lusthaus, Clarke and Mee (United States, 1986)
Phantom of the Opera, Webber (England, 1986)

— 1986 —

Challenger space shuttle disaster (1986)

Into the Woods, Sondheim, Lapine (United States, 1987)
The Heidi Chronicles, Wasserstein (United States, 1988)
M. Butterfly, Hwang (United States, 1988)

— 1988 —

Headlights, Terry (United States, 1989)
We Keep Our Victims Ready, Finley (United States, 1989)

Fall of Berlin Wall (1989)
Collapse of Soviet Union (1989–1991)

THEATRICAL EVENTS AND PLAYS

The Piano Lesson, Wilson (United States, 1990)
Body Leaks, Terry, Kimberlain, Schmidman
(United States, 1990)
Assassins, Sondheim, Weidman (United States, 1990)
Mad Forest, Churchill (England, 1990)
Les Atrides, Mnouchkine (France, 1990–1992)
Monster in a Box, Gray (United States, 1991)
Belle Reprieve, Bourne, Shaw, Shaw, Weaver
(United States, 1991)
Angels in America, Kushner (United States, 1991–1993)
Fires in the Mirror, Smith (United States, 1992)

The Balkan Express, Vulović (Canada, 1994)
America Play, Parks (United States, 1994)

Sarajevo: Behind God's Back, Bešo, Yevjhkevich, Wilks
(Canada, 1995)

Rent, Larson (United States, 1996)
Jane Eyre, Caird, Gordon (Canada, 1996)

The Lion King, John, Rice, Allers, Mecchi
(United States, 1997)

Copenhagen, Frayn (England, 1998)
The Blue Room, Hare (England, 1998)

Valparaiso, DeLillo (United States, 1999)

Blast!, Mason, Pinney, Prime, Vanderkolff
(United States, 2000)
Proof, Auburn (United States, 2000)
Aida, John, Rice, Woolverton, Falls, Hwang
(England/United States, 2000)
Homebody/Kabul, Kushner (United States, 2001)
Topdog/Underdog, Parks (United States, 2001)
The Producers, Brooks, Meehan (United States, 2001)
Urinetown, Kotis, Hollman (United States, 2001)
The Guys, Nelson (United States, 2001)
Reconstruction of *Hypsipyle*, Euripides (Greece, 2002)

HISTORICAL/CULTURAL EVENTS

1990 — Gulf War (1990–1991)

1992 — Bosnian War (1992–1995)

1994 — Nelson Mandela elected; apartheid officially
ends (South Africa, 1994)

1996

1998

Angels in America

September 11 attack on World Trade Center
and Pentagon (2001)

2000

2002

The Lion King

Key Theatrical Events **265**

ACT III

Collaboration in Art and Practice

[The] author, director, scene designer and actor must . . . resist every temptation to score personally. Each must make himself a free, transparent medium through which the whole flows freely and without obstruction. No one at any moment can say, "Ah, this moment is mine!"

ARTHUR HOPKINS (DIRECTOR)[1]

A small community is created through work on theatrical production. Artists, craftspeople, and technicians shape the event to be shared with an audience. While each individual may take pride in his or her own creation, the work of each of these practitioners is complete only when combined with the work of all the others. Creating theatre is truly a "co-labor." The work has been divided many ways. The different jobs as we describe them here are based on standard practice in many theatres, but as with the use of space, there are no rules about division of labor in the theatre. In this book we first discuss the director (and some of the director's collaborators), then the actor, playwright, and designers. Even when we talk about a norm, in the following chapters you will also find examples of practitioners who follow a different pattern because that type of collaboration suits them and produces the kind of event that they value. Although a standard division of responsibilities helps to ease the difficulty of diving into the creative process, the nature of collaboration is to some extent created anew with each theatrical venture. The practitioners not only create the art to share but also redefine the nature of the collaborative process.

A MIDSUMMER NIGHT'S DREAM at the Guthrie Theatre.
Photo by Michal Daniel.

METAMORPHOSES, by Mary Zimmerman, produced at Second Stage, New York.
Photo by Joan Marcus.

The Director
Vision and Leadership

The **director** in the theatre has a job similar to that of the conductor of an orchestra or the coach of a basketball team. The director is a leader. Although many individuals contribute to the group effort, the director must galvanize the collection of assorted personalities and temperaments into a functioning whole, must inspire as well as unify. As it exists today, the job of director incorporates a number of different types of activities—textual interpretation and artistic conceptualization, coordination of all visuals, and actor coaching. As we discussed in Chapter 2, it is certainly possible to have theatre without a director, but in current practice a director is usually considered indispensable. How did the director's job come to be? The development of this position in the theatre provides a fascinating study in the shifts of power as the interests and values of cultures change.

◆◆◆◆◆◆◆◆◆◆

Has Someone Always Been in Charge?

At the turn of the twentieth century the director emerged as the most powerful artistic figure in theatrical production. The director's authority was the result of considerable artistic struggle, sweeping technological development, the movements of romanticism and realism, and monumental changes in playwriting and acting techniques that swamped the theatre in the nineteenth

◆ *GETTING OUT, by Marsha Norman. Director Jon Jory, working on stage with actors and crew, prepares for a dress rehearsal for the premiere.*
Courtesy of Actors Theatre of Louisville.

and early twentieth centuries. Some jobs of the modern directors have always been executed by someone, but there are many tasks and responsibilities taken on by modern directors that are unique to the position as it developed after the mid-1800s.

ACTOR-PLAYWRIGHTS AND COMPANY LEADERS

In many periods playwrights or actors were in charge of the production of plays. In the classical Greek theatre (the time of Aeschylus) the playwrights (who at first were also actors) appear to have made various production decisions, selected supporting actors, and coordinated the chorus (although there were also choral trainers). By the time of Sophocles, however, most or all of the playwrights had stopped acting, and contests for actors were added to the Dionysian festival. By the time of Aristotle in the Hellenistic era, guilds of professional actors headed by an artist/priest were in charge of production. There was no separate position of director (other artists, probably the leading actors, filled the bill).

In ancient Rome acting troupes usually had a leading actor or manager, but we know little of this person's responsibilities beyond management of the company and making arrangements with government officials for festival performances. Leaders for acting companies in India that performed Sanskrit plays had some stage management and directorial duties, but the record is vague. Actors, both male and female, appear to have been in charge in ancient China and Japan, but again little detail survives. The openness of the stages and the minimal scenery and properties of Asian classical forms suggest that directing in the modern sense was not necessary or desirable. Most of the extant clues to performance concern acting and dramatic text.

MEDIEVAL PLAY MASTERS

The first indication of the position we today call the director occurred in medieval Europe. In response to the often extravagant, expensive, and crowded productions of the **cycle** plays (biblical dramas), a number of **play masters** (who were sometimes called "prompters" and "ordinaries") appeared. Records still exist regarding play masters from French, Germanic, and English territories. These men coordinated and staged the cycles of their communities. Very good play masters, such as Jean Bouchet in France, found themselves in demand and began traveling to stage the cycles of other communities as well. Does this make the play masters the first touring stars? To organize and document the production process, play masters kept **promptbooks** that might include the play text, drawings of sets, ground plans, stage directions, and various production

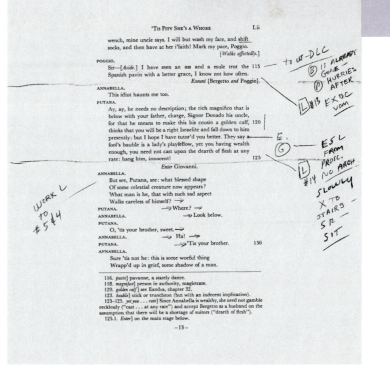

◆ **'TIS PITY SHE'S A WHORE,** by John Ford. A page from a late twentieth-century promptbook early in the play. The handwritten notes indicate additional entrances marked "E," light cues number 13 and 14 marked in a box "L," and the stage direction written on the left side of the page "work L to number 5 & 4." The numbers refer to different levels of platforms. Beginning at line 129, the arrows indicate the continuation of the line by other characters.
Collection of the authors.

Important surviving promptbooks include one from Valenciennes in France dated 1547, and one dated 1583 from Lucerne, in what later became Switzerland. The Passion Play at Lucerne was staged by Renward Cysat, a city government employee.

Many of these medieval "directors" combined some of the duties we now associate with directors, stage managers, technical directors, and house managers. After the extinction of the religious cycle plays due to Reformation and Counter-Reformation edicts, there is no evidence that such directorial control and promptbook work appeared again until the nineteenth century.

ACTOR-MANAGERS

By the seventeenth and eighteenth centuries most Western professional theatre companies were led by actor-managers such as Molière in France and Caroline Neuber (one of the earliest female managers) in Germany. **Actor-managers** made financial decisions, selected the repertory of plays, hired the actors, and performed (some were leads, and some played secondary roles), but they seem to have had little to do with staging. Following traditional patterns, most actors controlled the space themselves. Typically in the West, leading actors took center stage, with others standing left and right of them or in a semicircle downstage on the apron. Stage business for a particular role, such as the handling of props, was often set by popular performers and passed down to actors who followed. Asian actors also followed staging and characterization choices that were inherited. When an actor took over a role made popular by an established company member, he was expected to reproduce the favorite physical moments while adding his own touches to the performance. The lucky actors were the first to do important new roles and thus launch the traditional lines of performance.

In the nineteenth century in the West the rules changed with the coming of **antiquarianism** (historical accuracy), three-dimensional scenery, local color, very detailed stage directions, and complicated scenic effects demanded first by romantic melodrama and then realism. The situation was further complicated by numerous long runs of single plays by the 1850s rather than the traditional rolling repertory system (different plays performed on alternating nights). **Combination companies** (full productions rather than individual stars) began touring throughout Europe and North America. To keep track of complex productions and record their work, some actor-managers created detailed promptbooks complete with historical research. Charles Kean and William Charles Macready in England applied this technique primarily to revivals of Shakespeare's plays in which they starred. Dion Boucicault took similar care with the staging of melodrama in the United States, England, and Ireland and was so successful on both sides of the Atlantic that all three countries claim him. Many nineteenth-century promptbooks survive in rare book collections such as the Folger Shakespeare Library in Washington, D.C., and some have very detailed stage directions. Pro-

♦ **'TIS PITY SHE'S A WHORE,** by John Ford. A page from the same promptbook late in the play. At this point in the play, we have the 14th sound cue and the 87th and 88th light cues. This is the scene in which one of the protagonists, Giovanni, enters with the heart of his sister impaled on his dagger.
Collection of the authors.

ductions following these promptbooks must have required careful attention to staging and ensemble acting. Throughout the twentieth century and up to our own time, most professional directors and their stage managers have continued to work with very detailed promptbooks.

THE EMERGENCE OF THE MODERN DIRECTOR

As long runs of single plays became the norm, scenery, costumes, and acting techniques were developed for specific productions. Artistic power shifted from star actors and managers to people who were masterful at interpreting plays and convincing actors to take direction in order to coordinate the stage effects and acting ensemble. From the ranks of managers, actors, and prompters (who fed actors forgotten lines from offstage) came a number of directors who at first concentrated on coordinating the theatrical event and organizing stage pictures. Over time, however, many directors, most of whom were not actors themselves, took charge of the artistic vision. In the early years especially, such artistic centralization often led to a dictatorial style in working with actors and designers. This stringent control is evident in the directorial work of W. S. Gilbert, the playwright and librettist of the Gilbert and Sullivan comic operettas. Gilbert was all-powerful in staging his productions and preplanned actor movement using a miniature model stage, moving his "actors" about like figures in a dollhouse.

In the late nineteenth and early twentieth centuries producer-directors took total charge of their productions. Augustin Daly and David Belasco in the United States, for example, not only wrote their own plays and rewrote those of others, but also cast and rehearsed the actors, created scenic detail, and oversaw all staging. Belasco gave so much attention to lighting the stage that he is considered an innovator in lighting techniques. Nearly all of Belasco's productions and many of Daly's productions were in service to melodrama.

In the 1870s and 1880s an important shift in power and stage detail came from central Europe in the work of Georg, Duke of Saxe-Meiningen and his staging assistant, Ludwig Chronegk. Saxe-Meiningen was the ruler of a duchy (a small domain) and had a lot of money for production. Because they were running a court theatre that was subsidized by a royal household, Saxe-Meiningen and Chronegk felt no commercial pressures and wielded a great deal of authority. They built a remarkable acting ensemble in which all leading actors were also required to take walk-on roles. With unlimited time for rehearsals Saxe-Meiningen designed sets and costumes exclusively according to historical accuracy, and Chronegk worked out staging in meticulous detail. The resulting productions— especially the innovative crowd scenes—stunned European audiences when the troupe toured with classical and romantic plays. A new standard was set.

Many young directors throughout Europe, especially in France, Germany, Russia, and England, were inspired by the Saxe-Meiningen troupe. As playwrights created realistic scripts, André Antoine in Paris and Konstantin Stanislavsky in Moscow further developed a production style for the new generation of plays.

◆ **THE OLD READING ROOM**
at the Folger Shakespeare Library in Washington, D.C. A first Folio of the plays of Shakespeare appears on the table. This is a wonderful room in which to conduct theatre research when rare, original, and unpublished materials are needed.
By permission of the Folger Shakespeare Library.

◆ **THE MERCHANT OF VENICE,** *by Shakespeare, the Rialto exterior scene. Directed by Augustin Daly in the late nineteenth century. Note the attention to detail in the treatment of the stage floor to imitate a stone plaza, the Venetian canal, sailing craft, buildings, and pillar—all imitating real architecture from Venice.*
By permission of the Folger Shakespeare Library.

Antoine (beginning in 1887) created the model for independent theatres (small theatres run without the intervention of local authorities) that were dedicated to realism and naturalism. Antoine often placed furniture along the curtain line and directed his actors to frequently turn their backs to the audience, thus creating **fourth wall staging**—treating the stage space as if it were an enclosed room. The effect for the audience was that of peering in on an actual event rather than witnessing a theatrical performance. Stanislavsky focused on the acting ensemble and actor training in his remarkable productions of the naturalistic plays of Anton Chekhov and Maxim Gorky. By the twentieth century in the West, directors were fully in charge.

◆◆◆◆◆◆◆◆◆

Interpretation

From a preexisting text, the artists of the theatre (directors, designers, and actors) create a construction from all that they recognize as implied or suggested by the text. **Interpretation** is creating meaning beyond what is literal or obvious in the text. The modern director could be defined as an interpretive artist who attempts to unify the production by coordinating the work of all theatrical artists as they make decisions about possible meaning and signification of dialogue, character action, scenic location—all aspects of the world of the play. The director might endeavor to interpret a script carefully and accurately, trying to champion the intent or perceived intent of the playwright. On the other hand, the director may use the script more as a pretext in order to present the director's own vision or ideas that are inspired or supported by the script. Either approach requires that the text be interpreted through analysis, research, brainstorming, intuition, and experiment. Theoretically, there are many valid interpretations of any play, especially one that is rich in ideas or complicated in dramatic action.

Varying interpretations of ideas and characters result in wildly different audience receptions of a play. Shakespeare's *Hamlet* presents an interesting challenge to interpretation: Is Hamlet's madness real or pretense? If Hamlet is really losing his mind after confronting the ghost of his father, then his deliberations over the nature of suicide and what lies beyond death must be taken very differently than if he is only pretending madness in order to pursue his revenge. The Chinese music drama *The Orphan of Chao* includes a parade of violence—murder, suicide, hanging, and throat cutting—throughout the play. A director who is horrified by the cruelty of these events will interpret the play very differently from a director who sees the violence as clan fighting, only to be expected in the struggle over control of an empire. The former director will be intent on shocking the audience; the latter will be more philosophical about the corruption of power.

Even specific physical action in a text can be interpreted differently. In *Romeo and Juliet*, Mercutio is mortally wounded by Tybalt in a street fight. It is clear from the dialogue that Romeo attempts to stop the young men from fighting and comes between them. In that moment Tybalt stabs Mercutio with his sword. What is not clear is whether the deadly thrust was deliberate or accidental on the part of Tybalt. Directors have interpreted this moment in a variety of ways, most commonly as deliberate (taking advantage of Romeo's intrusion to put an end to Mercutio). But the stabbing might also be interpreted as accidental, caused by confusion resulting from Romeo's good-intentioned inter-

ference. The fight can be staged as adolescent posturing by Mercutio and Tybalt or as a deadly battle with intent to kill. The choice is a critical one. It dynamically alters the emotional import of the scene as well as the nature of Romeo's subsequent challenge and slaying of Tybalt, which results in Romeo's banishment.

Interpretation cannot be avoided. Every director, just like every other reader of a play, interprets either consciously or unconsciously. There is no such thing as doing a play "straight"— of allowing the text to be neutral for whatever interpretation an audience member might wish to give it. Because of the nature of the job, a director should be very conscious of interpretation and find ways to express it to actors and designers as well as receive

◆ *ROMEO AND JULIET*, in 1753. David Garrick and the unusually named Miss George Anne Bellamy in the tomb scene. Garrick's version of the play made many alterations in Shakespeare's text, including this scene, in which the two lovers are both conscious at the same time. Most of Shakespeare's plays were severely restructured and rewritten between 1660 and the 1800s.

By permission of the Folger Shakespeare Library.

interpretations of the collaborators. Because plays must be interpreted, no two productions can be the same.

Critics and historians over the years have placed a high premium on directors who have shared remarkable interpretations of famous plays. In his 1906 staging of Henrik Ibsen's *Hedda Gabler,* for example, Russian director Vsevolod Meyerhold recognized the play's symbolism and emotional framework and discarded the representational setting that is called for in the well-known realistic play. Instead of the traditional box set (representing an enclosed room), a wide, shallow shelf surrounded by draperies thrusts the action into the face of the audience. Rather than sitting in a parlor chair, the self-centered Hedda sat on a symbolic white, furry throne. Instead of a stove for the burning of her would-be lover's manuscript, the audience saw only a red pool of light. The play became an entirely new experience, yet the essence, if not the style, of Ibsen's play still reached an audience.

◆◆◆◆◆◆◆◆◆

Developing Concept

As is suggested by the example of Meyerhold's staging of *Hedda Gabler,* interpretation leads to concrete choices in production. A **concept** is made up of the artistic decisions meant to communicate a specific interpretation to the audi-

◆ *A MIDSUMMER NIGHT'S DREAM,* as directed by Herbert Beerbohm Tree. *Note the large crowd of fairies, many of them children with wings, in a forest of literal-looking, but obviously flat, painted trees.*
Victoria & Albert Picture Library.

♦ *A MIDSUMMER NIGHT'S DREAM*, as directed by Harley Granville-Barker, using open space, low platforms, and translucent draperies. A strong movement away from the literal and toward the simplified and sometimes emblematic stage is reflected here. Victoria & Albert Picture Library.

ence. The development of concept can begin well before a director has assembled an artistic team. As the director reads, studies, and analyzes a play, a **dramaturg**—a literary and historical advisor assigned specifically to the production—might serve as a consultant and conduct research on the play, author, or historical period. As the director makes specific interpretive choices, these choices begin to suggest concrete ways of presenting the play. On the other hand, the director could make no conceptual choices until conferences with the designers. Out of their discussion and sharing of vision, the concept begins to emerge. Concept is created visually and aurally; it is made manifest in scenery, costume, lighting, tempo, line readings, movement, and composition—the very things that a director creates, coordinates, or approves. Although an audience is not always certain of a director's interpretation, the audience can always receive the sensory results of concept.

Different concepts produce radically different productions. Three twentieth-century productions of Shakespeare's *A Midsummer Night's Dream* demonstrate the variety of concepts possible for a given play. When Herbert Beerbohm Tree directed it in 1901, he saw the play through the eyes of a late Victorian enamored of sentimentalized realism. The forest setting was depicted with scenery cut out and painted to resemble real trees. Audience members reported seeing live rabbits and real grass on the stage. The fairy characters sported the gauzy wings and gowns of Victorian children's books. In 1914 Harley Granville-Barker startled viewers with a more austere, simplified world on the stage. On a mostly open stage, scenery was presentational: Scenic designers Norman Wilkinson and Albert Rutherston created stylized hills and valleys painted on green translucent

ARTISTS OF THE THEATRE

PETER BROOK

The 1970 production of *A Midsummer Night's Dream* is only one of the many startling theatrical experiments of British director PETER BROOK (b. 1925). Brook began directing in his teens and achieved a reputation for fine, carefully staged productions remarkably quickly. In the 1950s and early 1960s his reputation for unusual productions grew, primarily because of his interpretations of Shakespeare. His 1962 production of *King Lear* was a significant turning point in his career. He abandoned the set (which he had designed himself) during rehearsals for a spare, nearly empty stage. Brook increasingly turned his attention to developing actor performances and striking, simple designs.

In 1964 Brook participated in an experimental four-week season at the Royal Shakespeare Company. Inspired by the theory of Antonin Artaud, Brook and his fellow artists developed techniques designed to act directly and forcefully on the audience's senses and emotions. The powerful, raw imagery of Brook's production of contemporary German author Peter Weiss's play, *Marat/Sade,* set in an early nineteenth-century insane asylum, shocked and excited the theatre world. The Roman tragedian Seneca is rarely revived in the modern theatre, but Brook's production of

♦ *A MIDSUMMER NIGHT'S DREAM,* as directed by Peter Brook, placing all of the action in or on top of a white box set. The trapezes were used to wonderful effect by the actors playing the fairies dressed simply but in bright colors.
Royal Shakespeare Company.

Seneca's *Oedipus* successfully dealt with the play's horrific violence in a way that seemed to speak particularly strongly to the world in 1968. Brook's book *The Empty Space* was published in 1968 as well. It still serves as an inspiring, provocative examination of the nature and purpose of theatre. (We used a quotation from *The Empty Space* to begin the first part of this book.)

After directing many productions in some of the world's finest theatres, Brook felt the need to push the boundaries of his art even further. In 1971 he founded the Centre for International Theatre Research in Paris (later renamed the Centre for Inter-

draperies. Fairies were given an eerie quality, with skin painted entirely in gold except for brilliant red mouths. Despite Granville-Barker's experiment, traditional productions continued with variations on the more realistic approach through the first half of the twentieth century.

Peter Brook began the conceptual work for his 1970 production of *A Midsummer Night's Dream* by deciding to strip away not only the details of forest and palace, but also much of the sweetness and airiness found in so many previous productions. He placed all of the action in a simple white box designed by

national Theatre Creation). Putting together money from many sources, Brook intended the Centre to be an environment for making theatre free from commercial pressure. He assembled an international company, hoping that the combination of many different backgrounds and theatrical conventions would enhance creativity. The Centre allowed Brook to use extended development and rehearsal periods impossible in most theatre venues. His work focused on preparation of the actor for performance using many techniques: physical, vocal, spiritual exercises, improvisation, and shared cultural experience. An extended trip to many areas of Africa brought the entire company into contact with different cultures and performing traditions. Brook alternated periods of research, rehearsal, and self-discovery with public presentations, often taking theatre to audiences (such as prisoners and hospital patients) who would never attend traditional theatre. Material was developed by writers and actors based on a wide variety of source material. In 1971 the company performed in Persepolis, Iran, as part of an international arts festival. The piece, entitled *Orghast,* was an exploration of ritual and was played in a language developed specifically for that piece by poet Ted Hughes with input from the company.

In 1974 the Centre opened a permanent performance space, Bouffes du Nord in Paris. The building had been constructed as a theatre in 1876 but partially destroyed by fire and abandoned in 1952. The French Ministry of Culture provided money to make the repairs absolutely necessary, but the ruined appearance of the auditorium was maintained, complete with gaping holes, charred walls, and crumbling nineteenth-century decorations—a reminder of the historical richness of the space.

In 1982 Brook directed and headed the development of *The Tragedy of Carmen,* a new work based partially on the famous nineteenth-century opera by Bizet and on the original novel by Merimée. Brook sought to divest the raw, emotional story from the many years of tradition and spectacle associated with the opera. The setting was a simple sand-covered circle suggesting a bullring. Perhaps Brook's most gigantic undertaking to date was an adaptation of *The Mahabharata,* the ancient Sanskrit epic poem central to Hindu religion and culture. The text was adapted by Jean-Claude Carrière, but the production evolved over several years of work.

The adaptation took over nine hours to perform and included an enormous cast from sixteen countries. In 1988 Brook returned to an established classic of the stage with a production of Anton Chekhov's *The Cherry Orchard.* A nearly bare stage with only Persian rugs, a cabinet, and screen served as the family estate about to be sold. Audience members were mesmerized by the emotionally full and dynamic performances of the cast, which included English, American, Swedish, and Czech actors.

Brook's passion for theatre has taken him to many places, both literal and figurative. His art is at once intensely connected to the time in which he lives and deeply personal. The ensemble work of his company is legendary, and although his pieces are often developed collaboratively, the final presentation is often highly focused and breathtaking in its simplicity.

Interested? Check out

David Williams, (compiler). *Peter Brook: A Theatrical Casebook.* London: Methuen, 1988.
Peter Brook. *The Empty Space.* New York: Atheneum, 1987.
Peter Brook. *The Shifting Point: Theatre, Film, Opera 1946–1987.* New York: Theatre Communications Group, 1987.

Sally Jacobs. Trees were suggested by squiggles of plastic tubing, and a catwalk around the top of the set allowed performers who were not on stage to watch the action below in full view of the audience. Inspired by Chinese acrobats, Brook approached the play like a circus with acrobatics and trapezes but without the garishness and glitz. Fairies were suspended in the air on trapezes. The result was a restoration of magic, wonder, and sexuality to the play. The fairies were clad in simple, brightly colored robes; the human lovers wore tie-dyed garments popular in the 1960s. The mischievous Puck delivered a speech while swinging

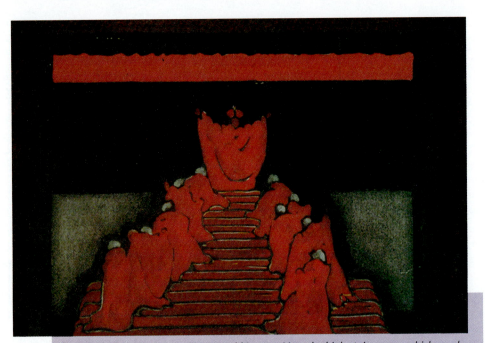

◆ **RICHARD III**, directed by Leopold Jessner. Note the high staircase on which much of the action takes place. The color red was dominant for the power of Richard, who usurped the throne and ruled until the "white" forces overwhelmed him at the end of the play. This image was drawn and painted by the designer Robert Edmond Jones after he saw the production in Germany. It first appeared in the book Continental Stagecraft by Jones and Kenneth Macgowan in 1922.
Continental Stagecraft by Kenneth Macgowan and Robert Edmond Jones (1922).

upside down on a trapeze toward the audience. The differing concepts of Beerbohm Tree, Granville-Barker, and Brook produced memorable but wildly different sensory experiences for their respective audiences.

The most startling or challenging concepts usually arrest the attention of audiences and the notice of historians and critics. Throughout Europe in the 1910s director Max Reinhardt chose cathedrals for the staging of his musical spectacle *The Miracle* to stress the grandeur of the religious experience. When he brought the show to New York in 1924, he and designer Norman Bel Geddes transformed the entire interior of the Century Theatre to look like a cathedral, complete with stained glass windows. In 1919 German director Leopold Jessner staged much of the action of *Richard III* on a large flight of stairs to make concrete Richard's rise to kingship and subsequent fall. Before Jessner, productions of this play had largely focused on interpretation of character. Jessner's production was more about the logistics of power than the seductive actions of the villainous hero. His concept made the audience view the play differently.

Director Sean Mathias defied expectations in a subtler way. In 2001 he successfully revived August Strindberg's *Dance of Death* (1901), a strident, disconcerting play about an awful and dysfunctional marriage. With Ian McKellen and Helen Mirren in the leading roles and a new version of the script by Richard Greenberg, the director found an enormous amount of humor in the play yet still maintained Strindberg's cynical and bitter view of the war between the sexes. Domestic turmoil became fun to watch.

In 1990 French director Ariane Mnouchkine revitalized *The Oresteia* of Aeschylus under the title *Les Atrides* and created one of the most important cross-cultural experiments of the twentieth century. Her exploration of gender strife came to the center in this production, which added dramatic text from Euripides and combined Greek and Indian theatricality, especially Kathakali-style costumes and makeup. Unlike the Greek and Asian sources, Mnouchkine's production used an international cast of both men and women but suppressed gender identification within the costuming. By the late twentieth century innovators such as Brook, Mnouchkine, and others discussed in this chapter had developed international and multicultural concepts associated with poststructural and postmodern theory and practice.

♦ **THE DANCE OF DEATH,**
by August Strindberg, starring Helen Mirren and Ian McKellen. Directed by Sean Mathias; designed by Santo Loquasto.
Photo by Joan Marcus.

♦♦♦♦♦♦♦♦♦

Communicating and Managing the Artistic Vision

If the artistic vision of a production typically rests with the director in the twenty-first century, how is that vision communicated to the show's artistic staff, and how in turn is that vision enriched and modified by the collaborating artists? Most directors strive to communicate clearly with all designers and make certain that the separate contributions result in a unified work of art, but the methods for doing so are dynamically different.

Meyerhold in Russia was an example of the master artist—the creator or "author" of the production—called for by some designers and theorists at the turn of the twentieth century. The word **"auteur"** is sometimes used for directors who operate with almost total control. Although this way of working is often dictatorial, it does not mean that designers or actors are unimportant. Lyubov Popova, the set designer for Meyerhold's *The Magnanimous Cuckold* (1922) created a remarkable **constructivist** set—a set that consisted of exposed beams, supports, and movable parts and was not meant to represent anything from the

world outside the theatre. Meyerhold wanted an abstracted, multilevel space on which the actors could work athletically in a highly choreographed style. Popova's work precisely met the vision of the director.

In a very different vein, German director Peter Stein approached his 1971 production of Ibsen's *Peer Gynt* (1867) in a fully collaborative way. The actors and other members of the company conducted historical research together to create a vision for the production. Stein obviously coordinated the approach, but many discoveries were made by the actors, who functioned somewhat like a collective dramaturg to prepare the remarkable production. *Peer Gynt* is structured like a folk tale, changing location frequently and occurring in vastly different real and imaginary spaces. The company's work resulted in a complete renovation of the theatre (most of the orchestra seats were removed), making the space look more like a warehouse with playing spaces spread throughout the resulting arena on various levels. The title role was shared by a number of actors, and much of the sexual and commercial corruption of the nineteenth century was exposed and explored through the epic wandering of the title character.

Julie Taymor had many talented collaborators for *The Lion King* (1997) but perpetuated her vision not only by directing the production, but also by conceiving and designing puppets combined with actors, masks, and costumes. Consequently, her exploration of the world of the play was very hands-on as she sculpted and built models for the masks and puppets. Her codesigner for

◆ **THE LION KING,** directed by Julie Taymor. A dynamic moment in which giraffes and a cheetah are created by the actors with puppet extensions and stilts. The actor becomes one with the costume but can still be recognized as performer as well as animal.
Photo by Joan Marcus.

masks and puppets, Michael Curry, concentrated especially on technical design and operation. Scenic designer Richard Hudson and lighting designer Donald Holder worked with Taymor to create a sense of the African environment. Taymor asked for a presentational set that did not hide the way the mechanized set pieces or puppets functioned but revealed the ways in which theatrical magic was created. Michael Ward concentrated on hair and makeup design. Tony Meola created the sound design, which included the installation of large speakers under the seats of the New Amsterdam Theatre to create the sound and vibrations of a wildebeest stampede. An account of Taymor's period of conceptualization with her fellow artists is published in *The Lion King: Pride Rock on Broadway* (1997).

Michael Kahn's production of *The Oedipus Plays* (2001), adaptations of Sophocles, at the Shakespeare Theatre in Washington, D.C., was conceptualized as an African rather than Greek trilogy of the Oedipus cycle. Most of the actors played multiple roles. Even Avery Brooks as Oedipus also played a messenger in *Antigone.* Using African music and design as well as full choruses, the plays became a celebration of tribal culture and community action while at the same time exploring the tragic destruction, suffering, and redemption of Oedipus, Antigone, and Creon. The work of Stein, Taymor, and Kahn demonstrates a fully collaborative spirit and working method, but even in the work of a more autocratic director such as Meyerhold it is necessary for the director to unify the vision through inspiration, suggestion, and persuasion, not just authority.

Chapter 10 ◆ *The Director: Vision and Leadership* **283**

Collaborating with the Playwright

A director often prepares and presents a play with no input from the playwright who created the script. The director's job can be quite different when the playwright is present for preproduction preparation and rehearsals, as frequently occurs with the premier production of a play by a living author. A personal relationship with the playwright can be forged that evokes trust and mutual respect for the text, which is the artistic child of the dramatist. American director Elia Kazan certainly understood this and cultivated a close relationship with two of the most important playwrights of his generation: Arthur Miller and Tennessee Williams. He eventually fell out with these artists over both political and artistic conflicts, but for many years he interpreted numerous modern classics such as Miller's *Death of a Salesman* (1949) and Williams's *A Streetcar Named Desire* (1947). Kazan often talked his playwrights into making changes, both major and minor, to lines, action, or structure. Sometimes improvements were made, such as the use of a fluid single space for *Salesman* rather than a series of realistic sets. When directing Williams's play *Cat on a Hot Tin Roof* (1954), Kazan suggested the very positive change of bringing a major character, Big Daddy, back in the last act of the play, but other changes damaged the play's structure. Under Kazan's direction Williams changed a very ambiguous and unsettling conclusion to one of certainty and sentimentality. When Tennessee Williams later published the play, he included both his own version of the last act and "Kazan's version." In 1974 Williams created yet a third version (and probably the best), which combined parts of one and two plus new material. It was directed by Michael Kahn.

When playwrights find a director they trust, they sometimes want to work exclusively with that director. Director Harold Clurman's realistic kitchen sink style with the legendary Group Theatre championed a revolution in American acting and perfectly suited Clifford Odets's working-class, Depression-era plays such as the family drama *Awake and Sing!* (1935) and *Golden Boy* (1937), the story of a young man who gives up his aspirations as a violinist to make it big in the violent world of professional boxing. Both Odets and Clurman sought ensemble acting, in which remarkable levels of unspoken meaning could be revealed through subtle physical changes. On the other hand, the British playwright Harold Pinter and director Peter Hall both reveled in ambiguity of character, event, and meaning. Hall directed the first production of *The Homecoming* (1965), in which Teddy inexplicably leaves his wife Ruth with his father, uncle, and brothers to serve as a surrogate mother and prostitute. By the mid-1980s, however, Pinter (also an actor) was usually directing his own plays.

Sometimes playwrights and directors come to loggerheads, as occurred with JoAnne Akalaitis's 1984 production of Samuel

♦ **THE OEDIPUS PLAYS,** *by Sophocles, as translated by Nicholas Rudall. The chorus in* Oedipus at Colonus, *played by Jonathan Livingstone Rolle, C. C. Campbell, Baraka de Soleil, and Beverley Prentice, must perform most of the time off the stage floor because they are on holy ground. Hence, they often sit or move on posts extending from the walls. Directed by Michael Kahn; scenic design by Charles McClennahan; costume design by Toni-Leslie James.* Photo by Carol Rosegg. Courtesy of The Shakespeare Theatre, Washington, D.C.

♦ **CAT ON A HOT TIN ROOF,** by Tennessee Williams, the original production. The stage is emptied of much detail except for the bed and bar area. Director Elia Kazan and designer Jo Mielziner wanted to focus on the intense action of this family in conflict. Photo courtesy Billy Rose Theatre Collection, the New York Public Library for the Performing Arts, Astor, Lennox and Tilden Foundations.

Beckett's famous *Endgame* (1957). The play had been produced many times with the setting called for in the text—an undecorated, nondescript but stark interior. Akalaitis reset the play in a highly recognizable, rundown subway passage. Beckett was so distressed by the resetting that he not only attacked the production but also tried to have it stopped. Akalaitis had not altered any of the dialogue, but Beckett argued that the production's specificity denied the play's ambiguities and thus undercut its potential for expressing the universality of the human condition. Akalaitis argued for the director's necessary freedom of expression and the right to conceptualize the theatrical event in whatever way the director chooses. The question is not just who owns the rights to a play but whether anyone owns the rights to interpretation. Such controversy over artistic license, concept, and artistic integrity has been very active for several decades now, with directors sometimes under the critical microscope.

On the other hand, Beckett had complete confidence in the interpretations of Alan Schneider from the 1950s until the director's accidental death in 1984. Schneider was dedicated to the texts and intentions of playwrights he admired. Schneider directed at least fifteen different plays by Beckett (some of them several times), including the American premieres of *Waiting for Godot* (1953) and *Endgame* (1957). Schneider had a similar artistic relationship with American playwright Edward Albee and directed most of his work, including *Who's Afraid of Virginia Woolf?* (1962) and *A Delicate Balance* (1966), two domestic dramas that are brutal in their revelation of hidden truth. Because of Schneider's insistence on the primacy of the writer's vision, some critics and historians consider his interpretations of these playwrights' work to be the definitive ones.

Exploring Historical and Cultural Perspectives

When directors make radical changes in a play by a living playwright or use existing texts in ways other than what the author intended, important issues of ownership and interpretation arise. In 1982 the Wooster Group began working on *L.S.D. (. . . Just the High Points . . .)*. Director Elizabeth LeCompte and the company developed the piece collectively. As the work emerged, it became about two decades in the United States and the impossibility of creating definitive history. Material from the 1960s focused on Timothy Leary, the self-proclaimed guru of the sixties drug subculture. The decade of the 1950s was represented by excerpts from *The Crucible*, Arthur Miller's play about the Salem witch trials of the 1600s, first performed in 1953. The play has been widely recognized as an indictment of Joseph McCarthy and the House Committee on Un-American Activities and their persecution of U.S. citizens during the "red scare" of the 1950s.

In the hands of the Wooster Group *The Crucible* was deconstructed. Pieces of Miller's text were integrated into a performance collage that incorporated reading, music, and dance. Period costume pieces from the 1600s were mixed with 1950s dress. The character Tituba (a servant from Barbados) was performed by a white actress in stereotypical blackface makeup. The techniques were designed to

L.S.D. (. . . JUST THE HIGH POINTS . . .), an experimental production created in 1985 by The Wooster Group, directed by Elizabeth LeCompte in the Performing Garage. Most, but not all, of the action takes place at a long table on an elevated platform that stands between the audience and the actors. Performers, left to right, are Willem Dafoe, Nancy Reilly (in motion), Jeff Webster (with guitar), Kate Valk, and Anna Kohler.
Photo by Paula Court.

focus on the specific viewpoint of the play's author—a male Caucasian from the 1950s—rather than the fictional world created by the original play. The juxtaposition with the 1960s material led to the examination of the concepts of rebellion against established sources of power, fear of the

Directors and Absent Playwrights

It is more common for directors to create radical concepts when interpreting plays that are no longer under copyright or under the control of the playwright's estate. Directors Tadashi Suzuki, Anne Bogart, and Giorgio Strehler frequently revive older work with startling, even remarkable results. Italian director Strehler,

unconventional, ecstatic experience and hallucination, and the nature of heroism and leadership.

The Wooster Group sought permission to use excerpts from *The Crucible* when it started working on the piece. After seeing a public performance of *L.S.D.* (still in development) in October 1983, Arthur Miller directed his agent to refuse permission to the Wooster Group. He was concerned that the performance would be viewed as a parody or send-up of his play and that the Wooster Group production might negatively influence future productions of *The Crucible* in New York City. LeCompte sent letters to Miller and his agent trying to explain the group's use of the text, and some adjustments were made in the piece. The group was ultimately threatened with legal action and closed the production in January 1985. In press interviews, Miller stressed that he wanted his play produced only in the way he intended it. The Wooster Group treated the text as a social document, one that could be used as a starting point for raising questions never intended by the author.

An Alternative Viewpoint

Charles L. Mee has created plays produced at theatres such as Steppenwolf (Chicago), New York Public, and Actors Theatre of Louisville. He has collaborated with directors Martha Clarke and Anne Bogart. Mee states, "There is no such thing as an original play." He believes that "whether we mean to or not, the work we do is both received and created, both an adaptation and an original, at the same time. We re-make things as we go." Mee not only provides Internet access to his scripts but also states,

Please feel free to take the plays from this website and use them as a resource for your own work: cut them up, rearrange them, rewrite them, throw things out, put things in, do whatever you like with them—don't just make a few cuts or rewrite a few passages, but pillage the plays and build your own entirely new piece out of the ruins—and then, please, put your own name to the work that results. But, if you would like to perform the plays essentially or substantially as I have composed them, they are protected by copyright in the versions you read here, and you need to clear performance rights. . . ."[3]

Mee's point of view is rather different than Miller's. This controversy over control of artistic material has reached a critical point in the development of contemporary theatre. It may be that resolution of the issue is impossible.

Interested? Check out

David Savran. *Breaking the Rules: The Wooster Group.* New York: Theatre Communications Group, 1988.

Charles L. Mee's web site, "the (re)making project" at www.panix.com/~meejr/html/about.htm for a fuller development of his viewpoint of the play as historical document.

for example, who is often identified as an exponent of poetic or lyrical realism, created an interpretation of Shakespeare's *The Tempest* in the 1980s that was **metatheatrical**—that is, the production used the play to comment on the nature of performance and the world as theatre and ended with a complete collapse of the theatrical scenery.

In 1995 postmodern director Anne Bogart reconceived *The Adding Machine* (1923) at Actors Theatre of Louisville. From this expressionistic play depicting early commercialism and the dehumanization of humanity, Bogart explored the victims of technocracy as seen through the eyes of the computer age. Bogart continues to develop new works as well as adapt old texts. She and director Tadashi Suzuki cofounded the Saratoga International Theatre Institute (now the

SITI Company) in 1992 to facilitate international cultural exchange and collaboration in American theatre. Suzuki has successfully combined traditional Western and Eastern work into a stunning approach to theatricality. As a Japanese director and teacher of acting, he has drawn on classical forms such as Kabuki and Noh, but his casts are international, and he mixes modern images with ancient ones in usually open, austere, but beautiful spaces. He has shared these startling cultural and artistic explorations with audiences throughout the world. Many of his productions are reconceptions of Greek classical plays; *Clytemnestra* (1983) has material from at least four different Greek tragedies, and *Dionysus* (1993) uses the Greek god of ecstatic celebration to investigate the relationship of government and religion.

◆◆◆◆◆◆◆◆◆

Collaborating with Designers

Many directors and designers conceive theatrical space, costumes, lighting, and sound through healthy give-and-take and full collaboration. Typically, the director begins meeting with designers well before casting or rehearsals. The director often brainstorms with designers both separately and together, sharing interpretation, ideas, and images. The director focuses the work of the designers and inspires them to make their own artistic contributions while shaping all of the work into a single, unified concept. The artists may take inspiration from many places, but as a whole, the settings, lighting, costumes, and sound combine to produce a style that is unique to that production.

SUCCESSFUL COLLABORATIONS

Elia Kazan's production of Arthur Miller's *Death of a Salesman* in 1949 was a hybrid of realism and presentationalism. The setting, designed by Jo Mielziner, resembled the skeleton of a small house set against the backdrop of a cityscape. There were few walls and little furniture, and downstage of the floor of Willy's house was an open playing space. Yet the selective pieces of furniture were realistic and usable, the costumes were realistic, and the acting (as in nearly all of Kazan's productions) was realistic, following the system of Stanislavsky and the Group Theatre, of which he had been a founding member (see Chapter 11). The lighting was selective, and in Willy Loman's flashbacks in time the lighting became bizarrely yellowish. This production of *Death of a Salesman* was indicative of much of the work of Kazan and Mielziner together; they were clearly a successful team.

Similar observations could be made of the director/designer team Arthur Hopkins and Robert Edmond Jones before Kazan and of Peter Hall and John Bury or Trevor Nunn and John Napier afterward. For more than ten years, beginning in 1916, Hopkins and Jones led the way in New York with simplified staging often called the **new stagecraft** in plays by Shakespeare such as *Richard III*

Exploring Collaboration

D Metamorphoses

Director-playwright Mary Zimmerman of Lookingglass Theatre Company in Chicago brought back a device that was used by the ancient Romans and was popular in the nineteenth century but used it in a decidedly twenty-first century way. For her adaptation of *Metamorphoses* by Ovid, a rectangular water tank designed by Daniel Ostling filled most of the stage. The tank looked like a shallow swimming pool. It was the primary acting space, and nearly every character had to negotiate the water in reenacting the ancient tales and myths with a decidedly contemporary twist. Confining most of the action to a body of water suggested primordial existence, yet Zimmerman's language and images addressed the experiences and values of contemporary society preoccupied with technology and speed.

Zimmerman's method of developing theatrical material is untraditional and highly collaborative. She begins with an idea for developing a piece from a particular text (such as *The Arabian Nights,* the notebooks of Leonardo daVinci, or in this case, the ancient Greek myths as told by Ovid). She then selects a cast who will help to develop scenes and writes text in between rehearsal periods. Zimmerman works with designers Ostling, Mara Blumenfeld (costumes), T.J. Gerckens (lighting), and Andre Pluess and Ben Sussman (sound) before the script is written or the characters are developed. Because the play is both written and staged within a traditional rehearsal period, the construction of the sets must be underway while the show is rehearsing. In this method of working, the designers influence the entire development of the show. In the case of *Metamorphoses* the presence of the pool of water, a symbol in many cultures of change, influenced the selection of myths to dramatize and images to explore. Zimmerman explains the many ways in which it contributed to the staging of the piece:

> Once you have a pool of water on stage, beauty is easy to produce. The water exaggerates every gesture, it interacts in an endlessly dynamic way with the light, and it changes the clothes and appearance of the actors. We are aware of the reality of the water, and what it is doing to the performers, how difficult it is, how sensual it is: it makes us conscious of the real bodies, the real efforts of the performers. The water is the eleventh performer in the show, and it never has a bad night.[4]

Metamorphoses was originally produced by the Lookingglass Theatre Company, Chicago, was brought to Second Stage in New York City in 2001 and moved to the Circle in the Square Theatre. A photo of this production introduces this chapter.

and *Hamlet* and modern plays such as O'Neill's *Anna Christie.* Hall and Bury, as well as Nunn and Napier, worked together almost exclusively for many years in London at the National Theatre, the Royal Shakespeare Company, the commercial West End theatres, and in the United States on Broadway. Hall and Bury produced many Shakespeare plays and most of Harold Pinter, as well as the landmark *Amadeus* (1979) by Peter Shaffer that combined elaborate eighteenth-century costumes with a sleek, simplified set. Nunn and Napier were comfortable producing both Shakespearean plays and contemporary musicals such as *Cats* (1982)and *Les Misérables* (1985). Once directors and designers find a collaborator in whom they have complete trust and understanding, they are often reluctant to sever that relationship. Such collaborative compatibility is often a key to the long-term success of many of our most well-known directors and designers of the last century.

♦ *THE ADDING MACHINE*, by Elmer Rice, the office scene. The actors mime mechanized office work on an open stage, save the blue façade of doors and windows upstage. Directed by Anne Bogart; scenic design by Neil Patel.
Photo by Richard C. Trigg. Courtesy of Actors Theatre of Louisville.

SEEING IN THREE DIMENSIONS

The ability to see theatrical space three-dimensionally is critical for a director. During the planning stages of a production—whether sitting in a theatre, examining a set model, or studying a two-dimensional ground plan for the set or sketch for a costume design—the director needs to see in three dimensions. Once a set or costume has been constructed, it is usually too late to change it without great expense and loss of valuable time. Directors must be able to see the potential of a design as it will be used in production. They are concerned not only with how a set looks, for example, but also with what kind of entrances and exits and traffic patterns it provides for actor movement. In the planning stages, the director and design team make decisions that will shape the entire audience experience.

Many masterful and innovative directors, with their designers, have found ways to transform space and challenge or delight their audiences with the spatial results. In the 1910s Jacques Copeau and his assistant, Louis Jouvet, created a permanent architectural space that could accommodate any play and place all the focus on the actors and the spoken text without the "distraction" of specific scenery. In Germany in the 1920s Erwin Piscator was the first to combine the new media of film with live actors onstage. The audience for *Sturmflut* (1927) watched actors interacting with film images of battleships attacking them. In both Europe and America since the 1970s Robert Wilson has emerged as a leading director, designer, and auteur. His productions such as *Einstein on the Beach* (1976) and *The Knee Plays* (1984) offered remarkable visual feasts of images; choreographed, repetitive movement; and minimalist music by Philip Glass and David Byrne. In his adaptation of *Crime and Punishment* (1976–84), Russian director Yuri Lyubimov used the shadows of furniture on the stage walls as if they were the objects themselves. In the same production a wooden door became a symbol of oppression and seemed to take on a life of its own as it moved about the stage. The ability to imagine the way a costume, set, or lighting effect will work on stage is critical to the director's work with designers.

◆◆◆◆◆◆◆◆◆
Collaborating with Actors

Despite the importance of interpreting and conceptualizing as well as negotiating the performance space, the director's work with actors is central to making a show work. Ultimately, it is the actor with whom the audience will identify, and the director's job is not only to choose the actors but also to help them achieve a successful characterization while working together effectively.

CASTING THE SHOW

Casting, or selecting the actors for each role, is a crucial responsibility for the director. A **casting director,** or specialist in finding actors for specific roles, assists the director in some professional productions. The standard tool for casting is the **audition.** Auditions vary considerably, but many directors and casting directors want to see unfamiliar actors deliver a prepared audition piece: one or two monologues (speeches from plays), a few bars from a song. In some cases this initial audition may be done via videotape. Directors sometimes have actors do unrehearsed ("cold") readings from the play being auditioned or other material. Other times directors prefer to interview actors or will consider only actors they have seen perform previously. Once the choice of actors has been narrowed, actors may be invited to attend more extensive auditions, or **callbacks,** for the director to make specific casting choices.

In casting a show, the director considers physical and vocal characteristics—not only whether an actor seems to fit a role, but also how the actor looks and sounds in relation to other actors available. If the actor playing Romeo is cast first, for example, there might be three actresses who could perform Juliet well, but one of them might be the best choice for this particular Romeo. Actors are often asked to read together in various combinations. A physical resemblance could be a consideration when actors are to represent a family. The director also must assess more intangible qualities such as talent and range. Will an actor be believable in the specific type of role? Can the actor achieve the intense emotionality, comic timing, or sustained physical activity called for in the script? Finally, the director will consider how the actor works with others. An otherwise talented performer who is not a team player can be devastating to the developmental process. Will the actor take direction or be unwilling (or unable) to implement suggestions? It is often difficult to predict success from a brief acquaintance. Directors often rely on actors they have worked with previously as well as talking to other directors to have the best chance of putting together a cast with the right chemistry to produce an effective working atmosphere as well as exciting relationships on stage.

DEVELOPING CHARACTER AND ENSEMBLE

Most directors help actors to develop characterizations. The challenge is to create a unified style for the production while still allowing each actor to explore a role psychologically and emotionally. Coaching the actors often includes discussion of character background and motivation. Some directors use improvisation to help actors make discoveries about their characters; for example, leaving the text behind, the actors, as characters, might improvise a scene related to but not actually dramatized in the play. Directors may work with masks in rehearsal, even if they will not be used in performance, to explore different qualities of movement and heightened emotion.

As individual characterizations develop, the director modulates the performances in relation to one another. Some directors are very successful at molding an acting **ensemble,** a cast that functions seamlessly together as a unit rather than as individual performers. As the director of many of August Wilson's series of plays on the African American experience in the twentieth century, Lloyd Richards created with his actors a wonderful sense of family and community in plays such as *Fences* (1985), which explores the struggle between a father and son. Ensemble is created not only by intelligent casting decisions, but also by the tone set by the director in rehearsal and the skill with which the director can unify the actors in a common performance style.

Directors have different ways of relating to performers. Some are very hands-on in guiding the actors. David Belasco, for example, early in the twentieth century, would dictate all movement and often act out the roles for the actors. This amount of control may be extreme, but José Quintero, a sensitive director of the mid- to late twentieth century, in directing the plays of Williams and O'Neill often took on the persona of a character as he talked to the actor playing that role. Other directors leave the actors free to make most major discoveries and selections on their own. Arthur Hopkins in the 1920s was masterful at noninterference, giving the actors considerable room and only gently guiding them through very difficult problems. Rather than providing answers, Hopkins preferred to ask questions of the actors regarding character, motivation, and action that inevitably led to appropriate decisions for the production at hand. He believed that his most important responsibility with the actors was in casting brilliantly so that the actors were not only appropriate for the roles, but also able to work together creatively. This model is still followed by many directors.

A sensitive director will deal with different actors in various ways. Some performers need a lot of reinforcement and encouragement; others respond better to a more businesslike approach to criticism. A director may give an experienced actor a freer rein than an apprentice performer. The ability to sense what help the actors need at different stages of character development is an invaluable skill for directors.

◆◆◆◆◆◆◆◆◆◆

Collaborating with Stage Management

Working closely with the director through the entire production process is the **stage manager.** According to the union Actors' Equity (of which stage managers are members), stage managers coordinate a show during rehearsal and performance and keep the director's artistic choices intact during its run.[2] It sounds simple when stated succinctly, but the stage manager is usually the busiest person in the theatre, organizing, setting schedules, enforcing rules, solving problems, and generally making sure everything stays on track. Depending on the show's complexity, the stage manager may bring one or several assistants on board.

A good stage manager takes care of practical matters so that the director can focus on artistic development. If secured early enough in the production process, the stage manager will organize and run auditions. The stage manager is in charge of preparing the rehearsal space, often unlocking and setting up, including taping out the ground plan of the set on the rehearsal floor and acquiring suitable rehearsal props and furniture. The stage manager maintains order and discipline among cast and crew and takes care of the mountain of paperwork generated by a production, including the promptbook. A modern promptbook typically includes a copy of the script marked with all cuts and text changes (these must be minimal if a play is under copyright), blocking notes, and all **cues** (changes in sound, lighting, or set). Professional stage managers are also responsible for keeping records on attendance and health benefits as well as reporting accidents, injuries, and any infraction of the rules to Actors' Equity.

Beginning with the last week or so of rehearsals through final performance, the stage manager serves as the nerve center of the production, calling the show over a headset, giving a warning and "go" cue for lighting, sound, and scene changes as well as warning calls for actors' entrances. When a show runs seamlessly from the audience's perspective, an accomplished stage manager has prepared, rehearsed, and developed a sensitivity for the pace and rhythm of all production elements as they are established by the director. After opening, the stage manager is responsible for keeping the show as the director intended, which might include calling correctional rehearsals and preparing cast replacements. The stage manager is responsible for onstage and backstage activity and must be prepared for any kind of emergency.

Besides having superior organizational skills, a stage manager must be able to work with all kinds of people. The relationship between stage manager and director is often the key to a smoothly functioning production company. Stage managers deal directly with designers, actors, and all technical staff, including **run crews** (workers who maintain and execute cues for props, costumes, set, lighting, and sound during the run of a show). The stage manager must maintain discipline as well as keep up morale, be able to think quickly, stay calm, and act decisively. Because of the wide variety of skills involved, good stage managers, once found, are highly prized. The Stage Managers' Association is a professional organization created as a network for support; for sharing problems, ideas, and stories; and for supporting education.

The responsibilities of the modern stage manager probably developed from the old prompter's position of the nineteenth century and earlier. In the days of rolling repertory, when the actors performed in different shows every night, the **prompter** sat at the side of the stage or in a special box down center to call out any forgotten lines or stage business. The advent of electric lighting and electronic sound as well as long rehearsal periods and long runs helped to create the stage manager's role as it now exists.

Sometimes also called a production stage manager, a **production manager** is usually employed by a theatre company with multiple performance spaces such as a resident theatre company or a large university theatre. The two most important jobs of a production manager are usually scheduling (spaces, rehearsals, and production meetings) and coordinating stage managers for the productions, especially when two or more productions are running and/or rehearsing simultaneously. In an educational environment the production manager is also likely to teach stage management courses and train new stage managers on the job.

Like a good stage manager, a good production manager is highly organized, a good listener, and enabler. Some production managers work out overall production budgets and mediate personnel problems in consultation with the artistic director of the organization. The production manager can provide important frontline responses to the artistic director and alleviate some of the logistical nightmares facing the artistic director of a large theatre company.

The Rehearsal Process

After a show is cast, it goes into **rehearsal**—the period of work in which the show is made ready for the stage. A four- to five-week rehearsal period (six days a week, seven hours a day) is typical for professional productions. Educational and community theatres tend to take four to six weeks (five or six days a week, three to four hours a night). The director decides how to use the rehearsal period and each show may be somewhat different. There are, however, many rehearsal techniques and practices that are customary. For most of the rehearsal period the play is worked in small parts; one day's rehearsal might be spent entirely on one scene or part of a scene.

READ-THROUGH AND ANALYSIS

Many rehearsals begin with the cast reading the play aloud followed by a discussion. In some cases, however, the director or playwright might read the play to the cast. Typically the cast spends at least one or perhaps many days together reading and discussing the play. Other directors prefer to get a play "on its feet" immediately and begin staging right away.

STAGING REHEARSALS

The director is ultimately responsible for **staging**—combining all elements to bring the text alive in three dimensions. As rehearsals progress, the director sets the **blocking,** or actor movement, for the show. Some directors dictate predetermined blocking to the performers; others encourage actors to find appropriate character movement while rehearsing a scene, then adjust or refine that movement. The director looks for blocking that makes sense for the characters and environment but also creates an interesting visual image for the audience. The actors' bodies and all other visual elements combine to create a composition. The director considers the width, height, and depth of the stage or other playing space.

Staging choices can help to create focus on a particular actor or area. If a crowd of people on one side of the stage is turned to face a lone actor on the other side of the stage, the lone actor usually takes focus. An actor standing in an open doorway tends to be in a powerful visual position, since the line of the doorway acts as a kind of frame. The position of actors may also suggest power relationships. If two actors are seated and a third is standing, the standing actor not only tends to take focus but will also seem to dominate the seated actors. Such power relationships can be altered by the actors' body language, however. If the standing actor is staring off into space, for example, and the seated actors are leaning toward each other, it might seem as if the seated actors are conspiring against the standing actor.

Staging can help to tell the story of a play. Even in a wordless scene a character mounting a series of steps and receiving a crown is clearly assuming a royal position. A balanced or symmetrical stage picture tends to suggest harmony. An unbalanced or asymmetrical arrangement can convey the impression of discord or uneasiness. A director also uses staging simply to create interesting compositions. Part of the sensory pleasure of theatre for the audience is the experience of watching shapes in a changing relationship to one another. A triangular composition, for example, is effective in the theatre, the most significant person or thing making up the apex of the triangle. Whether beautiful or desolate, the visual images on the stage should be interesting and evocative. Of course, some directors have little interest in composition and simply develop movement on the stage that seems logical and motivated, choosing to spend rehearsal time on extensive character and ensemble work.

In the musical theatre, staging is closely related to choreography. Some of the most successful directors have served as both director and choreographer, a combination that not only is helpful in achieving unity of production but also enables the director to work with the actors in nearly every aspect of their creative process. Bob Fosse served in both capacities for many productions such as *Chicago* (1975) in which his distinctive seductive style imbued both acting and dance with energy and sexuality. In more recent times director-choreographer Susan Stroman has received accolades, including at least five Tony Awards, for her stylish, inventive ensemble work and staging in productions such as the musical triptych *Contact* (1999), subtitled "three short stories," and the farcical Mel Brooks musical *The Producers* (2001).

DEVELOPMENT REHEARSALS

During the middle weeks of the rehearsal period the director works with the cast on developing characterization and refining movement. Usually, the set and costumes are being built. While still working most of the time on small pieces of the script, directors often schedule periodic run-throughs in which an act or the entire play is performed without stopping. Run-throughs give actors a sense of the play's dramatic development and rhythm and allow designers to see emerging movement patterns on stage.

As the company approaches the end of the development period, the cast begins to run through the entire play consistently so that the actors gain confidence in their work while the director can adjust the pace, rhythm, and continuity of the show. The director must sometimes modify the tempo of scenes and, when appropriate, orchestrate a buildup to the climax of the play. Because a production is rehearsed most of the time in pieces, putting the pieces together at the end is often a daunting task. This period is often the most nerve-wracking portion of rehearsal for all involved and requires both objectivity and sensitivity and sometimes diplomacy on the part of the director.

TECHNICAL AND DRESS REHEARSALS

Near the end of the rehearsal process, light, sound, and set changes are added to the show during **technical rehearsals.** The director, designers, and technical staff experiment with changes and finalize lighting and sound levels as well as timing for all technical elements and communicate these in detail to the stage manager. Costumes are finally added for **dress rehearsals.** Some changes in set, lighting, sound, or costumes may occur up to opening night.

Opening the Production

By the time a production reaches opening night, the director's work is done. The stage manager coordinates the actors and crews as they prepare to do their work in front of the audience. The director (if all has gone well) is left with little to do. Unlike a film director, the director in the theatre has no absolute control over the final live performance. Unlike an orchestra conductor or a sports coach, the director must ultimately let go of the production and trust the actors and stage manager to do their jobs. Once the professional production has officially opened, the director is supposed to step aside and allow the actors to share the play with an audience without any more adjustments, note giving, or changes. If a problem arises, it must be addressed by the stage manager. Directors in educational theatre often look upon the run of the show as a chance to continue the students' learning process and choose to watch performances and continue to give notes to help the actors improve, but the tweaking by this point should be minimal. Letting the production go can be a very difficult but also exciting shift for the director, who has spent so much time with preparation, analysis, and rehearsal.

The Artistic Director

Some directors, typically having worked in the field for a period of time, assume the great responsibility of heading up an entire producing organization. Most professional nonprofit resident theatres (those that have a permanent home and produce a season of plays) are led by an **artistic director** who has primary responsibility for the artistic life of the theatre. In the late 1940s and early 1950s artistic directors founded organizations that are still a vital part of the theatre scene in the United States. Theatre 47 in Dallas was founded by Margo Jones, the Alley Theatre in Houston by Nina Vance, and Arena Stage in Washington, D.C., by Zelda Fichandler.

In a resident theatre the artistic director frequently makes the final decision on plays to be done and directors and designers to be hired. While the director of a production is responsible for the outcome of a particular show, the artistic director must think about the season as a whole. Is there variety? Is the theatre serving its constituency well? Are the productions meeting the artistic goals of the theatre? Artistic directors may work closely with a board of directors—a committee of artists, civic leaders, and businesspeople from the community who are typically generous supporters of the theatre. The artistic director spearheads fund-raising activities with help from the board and support staff. Such activities include grant writing to public and private agencies and foundations as well as direct appeals to theatre patrons for donations. Although most artistic directors have some responsibility for overseeing the business aspects of the organization, these duties may be shared with a **managing director** and/or **executive director** or **company manager.**

Artistic directors usually direct one or more of the productions each season; many artistic directors achieve national and international renown by sharing important productions beyond their home theatres. Robert Falls of the Goodman

Theatre in Chicago, for example, brought his *Death of a Salesman* with Brian Dennehy to New York in 1999. Many artistic directors such as Sharon Ott (at the Seattle Repertory Theatre and earlier the Berkeley Repertory) and Gordon Davidson (at the Mark Taper Forum in Los Angeles) direct in commercial and resident theatres throughout the country. Artistic direction can be very demanding and frustrating over time, and many successful artistic directors such as Daniel Sullivan (formerly of the Seattle Repertory) and Mark Lamos (formerly of the Hartford Stage Company) have returned to freelance directing and sometimes faculty positions in university theatres.

Professional directors are members of the Society of Stage Directors and Choreographers. Successful directing requires many skills: the ability to read and analyze written work, to see in three dimensions, to "read" people and decide how best to help them in their own artistic journey, as well as the ability to lead and organize. It is a demanding and stressful profession, since the director ultimately takes responsibility for the success or failure of any production. Directors are individuals and tend to be strong in a certain area: creating visual images, encouraging ensemble, using space imaginatively. There may be as many directing styles as there are directors, and each one touches the lives of everyone involved in the theatrical experience.

◆◆◆◆◆◆◆◆◆

QUESTIONS AND ACTIVITIES

1. Discuss the respective strengths and weaknesses of the dictatorial approach and the hands-off approach to directing. For the sake of the discussion, assume the extreme of both styles. What advantages and disadvantages can you foresee for each type?

2. The work of a director who creates startling visual images is often more noticeable than that of a director who concentrates most of his or her attention on nurturing believable performances and ensemble work. What criteria would you use to "discover" the work of the latter director? What sort of things would you look for in evaluating the director's work?

3. Because of the importance of leadership in the position, directors must often negotiate delicate issues of power and authority. For example, college students sometimes have a hard time directing their peers. Discuss various situations in which leadership might prove problematic. Brainstorm about ways in which a director might deal with the situations.

◆◆◆◆◆◆◆◆◆

KEY TERMS AND CONCEPTS

FOR FURTHER EXPLORATION

Gabriella Giannachi and Mary Luckhurst, eds. *On Directing: Interviews with Directors.* New York: St. Martin's Griffin, 1999.

Francis Hodge. *Play Directing: Analysis, Communication and Style,* 5th edition. Boston: Allyn and Bacon, 2000.

Brenda Murphy. *Tennessee Williams and Elia Kazan: A Collaboration in the Theatre.* Cambridge, England: Cambridge University Press, 1992.

Harold Clurman. *On Directing.* New York: Collier, 1972.

Lawrence Stern. *Stage Management,* 7th edition. Boston: Allyn and Bacon, 2000.

David Richard Jones. *Great Directors at Work: Stanislavsky, Brecht, Kazan, Brook.* Berkeley: University of California Press, 1986.

Society of Stage Directors and Choreographers web site, www.ssdc.org.

Stage Managers' Association web site, www.stagemanagers.org.

Actors' Equity Association web site, www.actorsequity.org.

Literary Managers and Dramaturgs of the Americas web site, www.lmda.org.

"THE RIVAL ROMEOS," early nineteenth century.
Collection of the authors.

The Actor

From Mask to Contemporary Performance

O nce you're on, nobody can say 'Cut it,'" actor Jason Robards once told an interviewer. "You're out there on your own. And there's always that thrill of a real live audience."[1] Robards, who died in 2000, had a long, successful acting career in both theatre and film. Many critics and fellow actors called him the perfect actor for Eugene O'Neill's realistic plays. His performances in *Long Day's Journey into Night* (1956), *The Iceman Cometh* (1946), and *Moon for the Misbegotten* (1947) among many others were unforgettable for those who witnessed them. Although Robards is celebrated for his acting abilities and remarkable performances, his realistic, introspective style would have been very out of place in any period before the late nineteenth century. His wonderfully rough and gravelly voice (even when young), which made him distinctive to audiences, would probably have kept him off most stages before his time. It is clear that acting styles, tastes, and methods have changed dramatically and altered many times since the Greeks and Asians developed dramatic forms and early techniques for the art of acting. We should avoid the common assumption that performance has somehow evolved to more sophisticated and superior levels of achievement. It has simply changed with the times and cultural shifts, and it will change again. Yet Robards's words speak to acting of all periods. Even if armed with the words of a playwright and the guidance of a director, ultimately the actor is in the performance space on his or her own engaging a living audience that is waiting to be moved and entertained.

♦♦♦♦♦♦♦♦♦♦

Development of the Actor

From its beginning the art of acting has been one of imitating and representing specific or imaginary human beings and their actions through intellectual, psychological, and emotional exploration. Of course, actors don't represent only people. They might play animals as in *The Lion King* or abstract concepts such as Good Deeds in the medieval morality play *Everyman*. Whatever the nature of the character, however, the actor's instrument is only him- or herself—the voice, body, and mind. From our distant vantage point we know more about the early actor's external expression than his emotional work. Most of the historian's clues about performance before the invention of photography and sound recording come from actors' memoirs or written descriptions by audience members or critics regarding powerful voices, unusual movement, and decoration or adornment of the actor's body. Most of this information, however, dates from the late seventeenth century or later. From earlier eras we have surviving images of actors in paintings, drawings, sculpture, mosaics, and various decorations but little information about how the actors approached performance.

MASKS

In the case of the Greeks and many other early performers, historians have given extensive attention to the use of masks. Greek actors played multiple roles by changing masks and costumes; it is assumed that actors also altered voice and gesture when changing roles. The masks and costumes were no doubt especially important when male performers took on roles of females, gods and goddesses, or bizarre manifestations such as birds, frogs, and clouds in the comedies of Aristophanes.

The use of masks and the size of Greek theatres—even the smallest surviving theatres were large by modern standards—suggest a carefully selected system of gestures. Hand and arm movements were perhaps emblematic (communicating a specific idea), as in surviving Asian performance styles (such as Noh, Kabuki, Chinese music drama, and Kathakali). Such gesturing is consistent with the dancing, singing, and stylized movement that surely were part of the masked choral acting in Greece as well. There is also every indication that Roman mask acting was broad to fill the huge theatres and serve the farcical plays. Likewise, the masked actors of *commedia dell'arte* in Renaissance Italy were expansive, grotesque, highly physical, and full of clowning.

Masked acting is not confined to antiquity; actors in many African and Asian cultures have continued to use masks all along. Over the last hundred years or so, Western actors and directors frequently have returned to masks and found that when wearing masks, actors must select larger and more simplified gestures to harmonize movement with the mask. Playwrights such as Luigi Pirandello and Eugene O'Neill experimented with masks as an acting device. In *Six*

◆ *THE CAUCASIAN CHALK CIRCLE,* by Bertolt Brecht. In this production at the University of Nebraska, the wicked character Natalia is represented by the actress with an evil mask as she confronts one of her fearful servants. The mask is large, yet the mouth is free. Much modern mask work has returned to the lessons learned in commedia dell'arte with the mask covering the upper face, leaving the mouth and jaw free to articulate clearly.
Collection of the authors.

Characters in Search of an Author (1921), Pirandello called for masking his six title characters, who are abstractions, but all other characters—the human actors, director, and others—were performed without masks. In *The Great God Brown* (1926), O'Neill used masks to represent social and family roles, but more important, the masks were devices for hiding the characters' psychological anguish from other characters. The action gets more complex, however, when one character dies and another character takes up the dead man's mask, puts it on, and pretends to be his deceased friend.

Contemporary directors have utilized masks to help establish style of production. Peter Hall adapted the Greek convention of masks for his all-male production of *The Oresteia* at the National Theatre in Great Britain in 1981. To create the world of the jungle for her production of *The Lion King* (1997), Julie Taymor combined masks, puppets, and imaginative physical work. Often the masks also revealed the actor's face so that the mask became an extension, like a puppet controlled by the puppeteer. Modern directors have found that when working with masks, casual, offhand movement looks silly or insignificant. Movement with masks therefore becomes dancelike, something more akin to choreography, as we see in Julie Taymor's productions. The mask is powerful, dynamic, and iconographic. It can represent a fixed moment, a psychological motif, or an emblematic emotional state. Even a mask, however, can seem to change depending on the angle of presentation by the actor or the way in which lighting illuminates the mask.

THE ACTOR'S FACE

Historians know little about nonmask acting until the medieval religious cycle performances, and even then masks were used to depict devils. It is clear, however, that many medieval actors used their own faces to portray biblical characters. From about the thirteenth century in the West, the unmasked face became the norm, although masks would periodically return. Performers in Asia and Africa continued to use masks all along.

What new demands or opportunities for the actor accompanied exposing the actor's face? Historians get clues from the surviving plays and occasional private accounts but must still guess at some parts of changing acting styles. One obvious dynamic change is a new focus on the attractiveness of the performer. Renaissance and later accounts frequently laud the beauty of actresses and the charisma of both genders. Although makeup (sometimes very elaborate) became a standard for actors, audiences began to more clearly recognize their favorites on sight, and such recognition might have launched the beginning of fascination with performers in the public social arena. From the eighteenth century onward, evidence for this attraction to performing personalities survives in published biography and autobiography. The cult of personality escalated in the nineteenth century as a part of the movement of romanticism and remains a strong feature of our own cultural landscape.

Today, many audience members respond with strong affirmation to physical beauty and to highly skilled performers whose visage undergoes remarkable transformation. It is easy to see the importance of facial expression in the work of modern **pantomime** artists who rely only on physical expressiveness and do not use their voices in performance. Dynamic facial alteration is used brilliantly by Marcel Marceau, the most famous contemporary pantomime artist. His routine of the mask maker, in particular, demonstrates instantaneous and emotionally charged change of expression as he portrays both the maker and the masks. Facial antics play an important role in the success of film stars such as Jim Carrey and Robin Williams; TV actors Lucille Ball, Dick Van Dyke, and Kelsey Grammer; the master stage comics Nathan Lane and Bill Irwin; and the queen of contemporary musical theatre, Bernadette Peters. Such facial transformation is associated with clowning and farcical plays, but audiences are also mesmerized by the facial power and mutability of Anthony Hopkins, Zoe Caldwell, James Earl Jones, and Judi Dench when they are playing villainous or dramatically intense characters.

◆ **WAITING FOR GODOT.**
Actor Alvin Epstein making up as Lucky. Note the masklike quality of this makeup, which severely transforms the actor's face.
Photo courtesy Billy Rose Theatre Collection, the New York Public Library for the Performing Arts, Astor, Lennox and Tilden Foundations.

◆ **THE LIFE OF AN ACTOR,** *by Pierce Egan. In this comic image of a nineteenth-century theatre, we see a white actor being blacked up as Othello and other last minute backstage action as someone mistakenly raises the curtain too soon.*
Collection of the authors.

THE ACTRESS ENTERS

The actors in institutional theatre in Greece and Rome were strictly male, but women were not always absent from acting. Although we have sketchy information that women might have performed in Greek **mime** (a kind of variety entertainment), actresses certainly acted frequently in Roman mime. This kind of performance was undoubtedly entertaining but was not taken seriously by those who left a record of it. Women in medieval Europe (especially France) performed in the religious cycle plays, but historians know little about them. As professionals women became more prominent in Italy with *commedia dell'arte*, in Spain during the Golden Age, and in Restoration England. In Italy (and to some degree internationally, since some of the *commedia* troupes toured or took up residence in other European countries) some actresses became popular favorites. In the late 1500s Isabella Andreini was celebrated in poetry throughout Europe. She was repeatedly praised euphorically for her skills and beauty as a *prima donna* and young lover in the I Gelosi company, which she led with her husband. We could consider Andreini the first superstar actress.

In Spain, despite repressive social and religious conditions for women, professional actresses abounded after 1587, but they often encountered censure

♦ *A FUNNY THING HAP-*
PENED ON THE WAY TO
THE FORUM. Nathan Lane,
playing Pseudolus, is wonderfully
adept at projecting a large comic
personality through gesture, face,
and voice. Audiences generally
find him not only very funny but
endearing as well.
Photo by Joan Marcus.

♦ *THE GREAT WHITE HOPE, by Howard Sackler, 1967–1968 at Arena*
Stage. The remarkable actor James Earl Jones first broke onto the theatrical
scene with the lead in this play. Jones, as the boxer whose private life and
marriage to a white woman were at the center of a controversy, appears
here with, left to right, Norma Donaldson, Jimmy Pelham, George
Mathews, George Ebeling, Eugene Wood, Jane Alexander, and Lou Gilbert.
Directed by Edwin Sherin.
Courtesy of Arena Stage.

ARTISTS OF THE THEATRE

BERNADETTE PETERS

BERNADETTE PETERS (b. 1948) is arguably the best-known actress on the American stage. Although she has performed successfully in television and film, her natural home seems to be the Broadway theatre. She is small in stature, but her energy on stage is breathtaking.

Her powerful, flexible voice and charismatic stage presence won her the opportunity to create two roles in Stephen Sondheim/James Lapine musicals. In the first act of *Sunday in the Park with George* (1984) she played Dot, the practical yet caring mistress of artist Georges Seurat (played by Mandy Patinkin). Peters brought a down-to-earth quality to the young woman who loves an artist but understands that life must go on and her unborn child must be provided for in a way that Seurat's bohemian lifestyle will not support. In the second act she played Marie, a grandmother who helps a young artist (Patinkin) connect with his past and find renewed energy to create. As the Witch

in *Into the Woods* (1987), Peters was both funny and heartbreaking. The diversity of her vocal talent was showcased in music as diverse as a comic rap song and the achingly beautiful "Stay with Me." Her split-second transformation from hideous crone to sexy bombshell was a delightful stroke of theatricality. (Both musicals are available on VHS and DVD.)

Peters's career began at age 3½ with spots on popular TV game shows. She made her Broadway debut in 1967 in *Johnny No-Trump,* but her career took off with a stellar performance in the off-Broadway musical spoof *Dames at Sea* (1968). Other career highlights include two Tony Awards. The first was for *Song and Dance* (1985), a musical about love and loneliness in New York City by composer Andrew Lloyd Webber. The first act tells the story of Emma (Peters) in song, and the second act tells the story of one of Emma's lovers in dance. Peters's second Tony was awarded in 1999 for

Annie Get Your Gun. This Irving Berlin musical was created in 1946 for the Broadway star Ethel Merman, who has always been strongly linked with the role of Annie Oakley. Peters managed to make the character her own, however, and delighted audiences for two years with well-loved songs such as "You Can't Get a Man with a Gun" and "There's No Business Like Show Business." In the spring of 2003 Peters took on another role made famous by Merman: Mama Rose in *Gypsy.*

Interested? Check out

Bernadette Peters's film performances in *Impromptu* (1991), directed by James Lapine with Mandy Patinkin, Hugh Grant, and Emma Thompson; *It Runs in the Family* (2003); *Pennies from Heaven* (1981) and *The Jerk* (1979), both with Steve Martin.
www.bernadettepeters.com.
The 1999 Broadway revival cast recording (CD) of *Annie Get Your Gun.*
Peters's solo albums, including *Bernadette Peters Loves Rodgers and Hammerstein* (2002).

---

from the authorities. They appear to have been the first actresses to have plays and major roles written specifically for them. During the English Restoration (beginning in 1660) women first became professionals on the English-speaking stage, and their presence undoubtedly led to the creation of very different kinds of female roles for women in comedies of manners and intrigue. Although such shifts were breakthroughs for women in the European performing arts, actresses as a class were still regarded as morally suspect and socially unacceptable. In both Japan and China women as actresses held the stage from the beginnings of performance, but they lost their permission to perform in the seventeenth century (Japan) and eighteenth century (China) and were reinstated only in the late nineteenth and early twentieth centuries. Many of the new Asian actresses, however, were more interested in performing in modern plays than in the classical forms.

THE TRADITION OF CROSS-DRESSING

Before women were allowed to join acting companies in Britain, men and boys performed female roles, as had previously been the case in Greece and Rome. The use of male performers for female roles is still traditional in some Asian

Exploring Historical and Cultural Perspectives

Women as Ancient Mimes

We know more about Roman mimes than Greek ones. It is possible that women sometimes performed as mimes in Greece. The Greek Xenophon, an author and follower of Socrates, writes of witnessing a female actor, dancer, and acrobat performing with a troupe of men at a private performance, but we do not know with certainty that women performed regularly as mimes until the Roman Republic.

In Rome a mime performer was not a silent pantomimist like the ones we see today. The Roman mime was a speaking actor but also a variety performer similar to those of later vaudeville or early TV. The mime often worked improvisationally in short sketches, although eventually scenes and plays were scripted. Accounts suggest that mimes of both genders were usually unmasked and barefoot and performed bawdy, suggestive scenes laced with satirical comments about current life. Numerous accounts survive attesting to women mimes appearing nude on stage, performing simulated and—at least for a short time—actual sex acts onstage at the order of Emperor Heliogabalus. Mimes were very popular by the time of Julius Caesar and throughout the years of the Empire; sometimes they were even subsidized by emperors. Nonetheless, socially and morally, mimes were held in very low regard and were categorized with prostitutes and pimps. Some mimes, however, including women, became popular performers, and a mime actress named Theodora married the Roman Emperor Justinian. As the Roman Empire Christianized, the mimes came under regular attack by the church because they frequently performed sketches that made fun of Christians and their sacraments. Ultimately, all actors, including mimes, were excommunicated.

Interested? Check out

Richard C. Beacham. *The Roman Theatre and Its Audience.* Cambridge, Mass.: Harvard University Press, 1991.
W. Beare. *The Roman Stage.* London: Methuen, 1964.
George Duckworth. *The Nature of Roman Comedy.* Princeton, N.J.: Princeton University Press, 1952.

forms, such as Noh, Kabuki, Chinese music drama, and Kathakali. Although Shakespeare and his contemporaries sometimes used masks for obvious disguises, the actor's own face was the norm, even with cross-gender casting. Shakespeare wrote roles in which boys would portray women who disguised themselves by dressing as boys before having the character's "real" gender revealed at the play's end, as in *As You Like It* (1598–99) and *Twelfth Night* (1600–1601). Historians believe that male actors costumed themselves as women and engaged in vocal changes and movement to present the female persona but that the audience was very aware that it was observing cross-dressing. You can see modern interpretations of such conventions in the film *Shakespeare in Love* (1998) and in many revivals of the farcical-tragical interlude "Pyramus and Thisby" in *A Midsummer Night's Dream* (1595–1596).

Cross-gender performance has never left the stage in fact and has maintained an important role in theatrical entertainment. Even after actresses became a common sight throughout Europe by the seventeenth century, many of these women began to engage in gender-switching roles, and some men continued to play older female roles. In **breeches roles** for women an actress played a male character or a female character disguised as a male. For some audiences this presentation was erotic, but cross-dressing also pointed up the social perceptions of what was appropriate to each gender's sphere.

Exploring Historical and Cultural Perspectives

Contemporary Cross-Dressing

With a rage of cross-dressing plays or older plays reconceived with cross-dressing since the 1970s, the British and U.S. stages have enjoyed a generous helping of feminist as well as gay and lesbian plays that feature cross-dressing characters serving a variety of functions in comedy and tragicomedy especially. One of the most celebrated of such plays is *Cloud Nine* (1979) by Caryl Churchill. In the first act of this play, a Victorian mother is played by a man, and her son is played by a woman to reveal commentary on sexual stereotypes of the period. As Betty, the mother, says of herself, "I am a man's creation as you see / And what men want is what I want to be." Little Edward remarks in his introduction, "What father wants I'd dearly like to be. / I find it rather hard as you can see."[5] Then in the second act, set in 1979, a young girl is played by a grown man to again underscore how stereotyping and the impact of Victorian values lived on in the late twentieth century.

The Ridiculous Theatrical Company, led by Charles Ludlam, not only deconstructed nineteenth-century plays such as *Camille* (1973 and 1990), in which Ludlam took the leading female role himself, but also created new cross-dressing plays such as *The Mystery of Irma Vep* (1984). Two actors (one was Ludlam) played eight roles, doing lightning-quick costume changes in a parody of Victorian melodrama. In hilarious fashion Ludlam attacked our foibles and pretentious silliness in everyday life as well as in our famous theatrical works of the past. Charles Busch has created many cult hits, typically featuring himself in female roles, such as *Vampire Lesbians of Sodom* (1984) and *Psycho Beach Party* (1986), which satirically examine gender roles through absurd parody. Beginning in clubs, Busch's plays reached off-Broadway and alternative theatres nationwide, and in 2000 he had a Broadway hit with *The Tale of the Allergist's Wife*.

Split Britches, a feminist theatre company that explores lesbian lifestyles, received considerable attention beginning in the 1990s with its satirical and political material punctuated by cross-dressing. Led by Peggy Shaw and Lois Weaver,

◆ *CLOUD 9*, by Caryl Churchill. In the second act the role of the smart-aleck little girl, Cathy, is intended to be played by a grown man in a way that suggests a little girl but also reveals the man beneath the character. The resulting image is funny and alarming simultaneously. Produced at Towson State University.
Collection of the authors.

the company has deconstructed famous plays and novels and satirized societal fear of alternative sexuality in *Lesbians Who Kill* (1992), *Belle Reprieve* (1991), and *Salad of the Bad Café* (2000).

Interested? Check out

Laurence Senelick. *The Changing Room: Sex, Drag and Theatre.* New York: Routledge, 2000.
Lesley Ferris. *Crossing the Stage: Controversies of Cross-Dressing.* New York: Routledge, 1993.
Sheila Rabillard, ed. *Essays on Caryl Churchill.* Toronto: Stoddart, 1997.

♦ **TWELFTH NIGHT.** *A typical nineteenth-century approach to cross-dressing for the character of Viola, played by Ada Rehan. The costume of Maria, played by Catherine Lewis (on the left), demonstrates the typical difference in gender suggestion. Viola is exposing her legs in tights while Maria has a floor-length skirt. Yet there is no doubt that Viola is being played by a woman.*
By permission of the Folger Shakespeare Library.

Cross-dressing roles were common in Spain in the late sixteenth to mid-seventeenth centuries. A good surviving example is Rosaura in Calderón's *Life Is a Dream* (c. 1636), in which the character first appears as an intrepid young man searching for his father and intent on restoring the family honor but midway through the play switches to female attire. At the end of the play she takes to a horse again in a hybrid costume reflecting both male and female attributes. English Restoration comedies, such as *The Country Wife* (1675) and *The Rover* (1677), are full of female characters (played by women) who dress as boys to advance an intrigue or to improve their public mobility. If accepted as male, the women could travel nearly anywhere unaccompanied. Thus cross-dressing continued in a new guise even when both sexes could perform on stage.

Nineteenth-century comedy and melodrama perpetuated the practice of cross-dressing, often with women playing roles not as women in disguise but as characters who were meant to be accepted as male yet reveal the femininity of the actress. The opportunity for both sexes to "try on" the behavior of the opposite gender has been recognized as an intriguing device and has been used in a number of ways by contemporary artists. Cross-dressing continues today as a challenge to actors of both genders who must seek to either fool their audience into accepting the transformation or use the gender switch to comment on gender issues while maintaining recognition of their real sex.

♦♦♦♦♦♦♦♦♦♦

Acting Styles and Methods

Today, descriptions and explanations of acting methods fill many volumes; new how-to books on the acting process seem to appear every month or so. For many centuries, however, actors typically guarded their methods like a magician's secrets. Zeami discussed acting for the Japanese Noh theatre in detail but meant his writings to be revealed only to members of his acting family and be kept unavailable to the public. From the early eighteenth through the nineteenth centuries European actors revealed some of their methods and approaches in published "confessions" and "apologies" (as the memoirs of popular actors were often called). The earliest surviving indicators of actors' methods usually focus on vocal delivery. Although acting styles frequently shifted and actors continued to experiment, most periods of history clearly placed a high premium on the actor's voice. Much of what historians know is based on the rhetorical methods of a given era. **Rhetorical delivery** in ancient accounts, and well into the nineteenth century, was the art of oratory and of any public verbal communication, including physical interpretation through gesture, posture, movement, and facial expression.

THE RHETORICAL TRADITION

It is not likely that actors in classical Greece or Republican Rome would have had success in the huge theatres of their era without powerful voices and clear articulation. Most or all of these actors probably had to have effective singing voices as well, since music was an important part of the performance. There is little to be found in the evidence surviving from these periods that suggests any sort of reality-based, psychological approach to acting (even though actors can develop these roles realistically today if they choose). Given what is known about ancient performance conditions, the acting was presumably highly **presentational** (not an attempt to imitate "real life"). The actors delivered poetry across vast spaces to large audiences outdoors, under the sun, wearing masks, in or near a circular orchestra, underscored by music. The male actors switched roles (and sometimes gender) throughout the performance. Although this style might seem artificial today, the approach to performance was obviously successful since the Greeks held on to these performance essentials for centuries and inspired the Romans to do something similar.

European actors in subsequent periods shared a reliance on rhetorical theory that was based on an understanding of how the passions affected the human body.[2] Before the twentieth century, actors and orators adopted a widely understood system of physical attitudes and gestures that were deemed appropriate for any conceivable emotional state. As limiting as such a mechanized system sounds to us, it is clear that the finest actors were capable of transcending such a system to captivate their audience and engender belief through their uncommon talents and charisma.

Audiences of any period come to the theatre with expectations and the need to understand the performance. The most successful actors fulfill most of these expectations, but they give the audience something more, something that separates them from the "uninspired" actor. David Garrick, for example, in the eighteenth century startled and delighted his audiences with his remarkable mimetic abilities that communicated volumes to his audience beyond the language he spoke. Consequently, critics singled him out for his "natural" acting even though he was still a part of the traditional rhetorical approach to performance. The actor's emotional restraint and the need to repeat roles in multiple performances led many actors to rely on craft—repeatable vocal delivery, gestures, movements, and expressions—rather than on emotion.

With the romantic rebellion at the end of the eighteenth century and the first half of the nineteenth century, however, many actors yielded to a flamboyant overflow of emotionality and eccentricity. Onstage sudden physical and emotional transformations became even more pronounced with actresses such as Sarah Siddons in England and Rachel in France. Actors Edmund Kean and Charlotte Cushman stalked the stage menacingly, even when not playing villains, and Edwin Forrest filled the stage with his athleticism and powerful voice, which was once described as "the falls of Niagara."[3] In the age of melodrama and touring stars much of what the actor performed was punctuated by an exclamation point. This emphasis on emotional display does not mean that carefully developed

♦ **CHARLES KEMBLE AS ROMEO** *in the nineteenth century. This image demonstrates the flamboyant style in which actors often presented romantic leading roles, usually in what we would find to be a rhetorical approach.*
By permission of the Folger Shakespeare Library.

craft disappeared, but many actors sought the appearance of unrestrained emotionality and enjoyed arousing their audiences the way many rock and pop stars do today.

CONTEMPORARY REALISTIC PERFORMANCE

The movement of realism was so remarkably successful after the 1870s that it continues to dominate playwriting, screenwriting, and performance for theatre, film, and television. The actor's approach to a character was also profoundly affected by the emergence of psychoanalysis at the turn of the twentieth century. Psychoanalysis inspires actors to study character action not just in dramatic terms but also through close examination of human behavior. Perhaps the most significant watershed for the acting process, however, was the work of Konstantin Stanislavsky at the Moscow Art Theatre beginning in 1898. This actor-director did not invent realistic (or **representational**) acting, but through his experimentation, direction of realistic plays, training of actors, and books describing his methods, he reached out to most of the theatre world in the twentieth century. Stanislavsky created a common language for sharing the acting process and stressed the importance of psychological exploration of character, a detailed study of human behavior, and the use of self in ways that continue to resonate with contemporary actors.

Stanislavsky's methodology has been adopted and adapted over the years and has become the center of most realistic approaches to acting performance. Rather than focusing directly on how to express an emotion vocally and physically, an actor using the realistic method of Stanislavsky concentrates on action: on obtaining what the character wants or needs at any moment in the play. Playing an action rather than a state of being involves the actor mentally and physically, creating an appropriate environment for emotion to evolve, resulting in a natural and subtle physical and vocal expression. Actors analyze the script in detail and, in particular, identify the **given circumstances** that include everything about the character written by the playwright that is not a matter of interpretation or opinion: where the character is from, for example, or the fact that he or she is highly educated, recently divorced, or terminally ill.

Actors seek out the basic action to be played and not only perform it, but also justify it. One of the reigning assumptions is that actors can know more about the characters than the characters do about themselves. Actors play **character objectives** (or goals) that are important, logical, even vital to the character's action, needs, desires, and state of mind (as if the character were a real person). The actor must modify or shift objectives when encountering obstacles created by other characters, when confronted with changing circumstances, or when entering a new stage environment. In *A Streetcar Named Desire* (1947), for example, Blanche DuBois is a stranger to New Orleans and the run-down section of the French Quarter where she is seeking her sister. Her opening objective is to find Stella, but she becomes so terrified of the strange and threatening urban location that her objective shifts to securing a safe haven from a threatening world. Actors may further identify **subtext,** or the actual meaning behind the

♦ **THE CHERRY ORCHARD,** by Anton Chekhov. Konstantin Stanislavsky in costume for the role of Gaev. The Moscow Art Theatre.
Photo courtesy Billy Rose Theatre Collection, the New York Public Library for the Performing Arts, Astor, Lennox and Tilden Foundations.

Exploring Historical and Cultural Perspectives

Shakespeare and Character Objectives

In reviving plays from the past, modern theatre artists may bring their own methods and style to the production. Shakespeare, of course, was unaware of objective-oriented acting as modern actors practice it. Yet his dramatic action is perfectly suited to this acting device.

Creating or discovering character objectives (also called intentions) can be critical to creating a realistically based character for the stage. Simply put, an objective is a goal sought by the character. Placed in the context of the dramatic action, an objective is the purpose motivating the character's actions. The distinguished acting teacher Robert Benedetti puts it this way in his book *The Actor at Work*: "*need* causes *action* directed toward an *objective*." Objectives chosen by an actor should always be action-oriented—something the actor can play. "I want to win economic freedom from my parents," can be played. It can lead to many specific, playable choices such as "I want to steal this diamond necklace." On the other hand, the objective "I want to be happy" cannot be played effectively because it is a state of being, not action-oriented. An actor who is always playing an appropriate objective for any moment of the play is likely to remain engaged, focused, and logical to the audience in performance. Playing a well-chosen objective assists the actor with line readings, movement, and character behavior on the stage. Sometimes objectives change many times in the course of a play, but often one or two objectives recur and become defining objectives for a character. Stanislavsky advised actors to identify a **superobjective** to carry a character through the entire play even though the objective might be interrupted by others along the way. Characters may win the objectives they seek temporarily or permanently, but in most cases outside of romantic comedy, the major objectives are denied.

A character nearly always wants something: something to achieve, to prevent, or to obtain. When *Romeo and Juliet* begins, Romeo appears to want to win the love of Rosaline (a character we never see), and his objective in going to the feast of his enemies is to see Rosaline. At the banquet, however, he sees Juliet, and Rosaline is forgotten. This incident changes everything for both Romeo and Juliet as all of their objectives shift. Romeo's objective shifts to securing the love of Juliet, and this remains with him throughout the play with interruptions. When Mercutio and Tybalt begin a sword fight, for example, Romeo's objective suddenly shifts to stop their fight (Tybalt is a kinsman of the girl Romeo now loves). Once Mercutio dies by the sword of Tybalt, however, Romeo is overcome with hatred and a desire for revenge and pursues his new objective of attacking Tybalt. After killing Tybalt, Romeo is banished by the Prince, which prevents him from seeing Juliet at all. His major objective is undermined. Once Romeo receives the false news that Juliet is dead, he resolves to join her in death despite the banishment. He is willing to do anything to make this objective successful, including breaking the edict of the Prince, killing Paris, breaking into the tomb of his enemies, and taking poison at the side of what he believes is Juliet's corpse.

Interested? Check out

Robert Benedetti. *The Actor at Work*. Boston: Allyn and Bacon, 2001.

Konstantin Stanislavsky. *An Actor Prepares*. New York: Theatre Arts, 1948.

Uta Hagen. *Respect for Acting*. New York: Macmillan, 1973.

words spoken. A character might say, "no," for example, with the subtext of "you're crazy" or "ask me again and I might say yes"—which would produce very different line readings.

Actors explore the physical, social, and psychological aspects of their characters and may draw on their own experience to connect viscerally with the experience of the character. Exercises in **sense memory** help actors to recall sights, sounds, touch, and smells from specific past events, to "remember" what something feels like. **Affective memory,** or the reexperience of past emotion, can be harnessed to solve moment-to-moment problems that arise when interpreting and fleshing out the character. To find the emotional expression for a particular moment, such as coping with the death of a loved one, an actor might

♦ **TRUE WEST,** by Sam Shepard, as produced in Chicago by Steppenwolf Theatre Company. John Malkovich as Lee and Jeff Perry as Austin. This moment on stage is shortly after Malkovich's character Lee has trashed the typewriter with the golf club and is now drinking a beer.
Photo by Lisa Ebright. Courtesy of Steppenwolf Theatre Company.

♦ **PROOF,** by David Auburn. Mary-Louise Parker as the protagonist Catherine. Directed by Daniel Sullivan.
Photo by Joan Marcus.

remember in detail an event from his or her own life that produced a similar emotional reaction. Typically, however, the actor doesn't think, "What did I feel when my uncle passed away?" but "What did I do? What did I see?" When on stage, the actor doesn't play emotion but appropriate action. The actor must listen and respond to what he or she is given by other cast members. If an actor alters the delivery of a line, it is likely that another actor's delivery in response will have to be altered as well. The goal is often to create an organic **ensemble** that pretends to live spontaneously—to act and react—authentically in the stage world as defined by the play.

Another goal of contemporary realistic acting methods is the creation of a "complete" and open actor—one who is highly versatile vocally and physically and not limited by personal habits—to create believable characters that the audience can accept as genuine. An actor working in the mode of realism should be equipped to create an "honest" interpretation of a character as if breathing and interacting in a real world. The illusion of spontaneity should be absolute. A realistic ensemble wants to create believability among the actors in performance as well as to inspire believability in the audience who witnesses the presentation.

One can see many such performances on the American stage. Audiences were particularly struck by a production of Sam Shepard's *True West* (1982 production) as performed by the Steppenwolf Theatre Company in Chicago. Actor John Malkovich as the derelict character of Lee especially appeared spontaneous and threatening. His physical violence when attacking a typewriter with a golf club, very close to the audience, created anxiety in some audience members as if they, not the typewriter, were threatened. By contrast, Mary-Louise Parker as Catherine in *Proof* (2000) by David Auburn gave an unusually quiet, introspective but emotional, and realistic performance, despite the fact that her character carried on conversations with the "ghost" of her deceased father.

CONTEMPORARY PRESENTATIONAL PERFORMANCE

Although realism seems to be the touchstone for most contemporary acting, presentationalism is alive and well in the theatre. The Asian classical forms provide examples of centuries-old techniques emphasizing stylized movement, gestures, facial expression, and use of the voice. Plays in the Western repertory with devices inspired by the Asian forms (such as those by William Butler Yeats and Bertolt Brecht and his followers) call on actors to go beyond the techniques of realism. Contemporary directors and playwrights feel free to draw from many different traditions for any given show, and actors must be ready to meet this challenge.

The most obvious arena for presentational acting in Western theatre is the musical. Although musicals can be of any genre and mood, the musical actor is often a singer and dancer as well and must express character through painstakingly choreographed movement and dance and through rhymed song and recitative as well as dialogue. The resulting performance is very lyrical. The presentational devices of the musical form clearly separate the preparation and performance from reality. (How many of us carry an orchestral accompaniment in life?) Nonetheless, many musical actors include techniques and devices of psychological realism in their rehearsal and character study even though the product must go beyond the conventions of such an approach. An accomplished musical actor can still make his audience believe the moment—especially the emotionality of the character's presentation. Such performances demonstrate vividly that an actor's work need not be realistic to move or engage the audience. Nathan Lane's performances in *A Funny Thing Happened on the Way to the Forum* (1996 production) and *The Producers* (2001) are good examples. Both plays are very exuberant, presentational musicals, full of silliness. Nonetheless, Lane engendered belief. In the musical *Jane Eyre* (2000 production), despite singing, direct audience address, and working in presentational settings that were frequently in motion on a turntable, Marla Schaffel as the title character created a very restrained, almost realistic presence through it all.

Since the 1890s, experiments of the **avant-garde** (cutting-edge theatre) have fascinated and inspired as well as confused audiences throughout the world. Acting performances in some of this work lie far outside typical realistic practices. When performing in symbolist plays in France in the 1890s, for example, actors spoke their

♦ *JANE EYRE, by John Caird and Paul Gordon. Marla Schaffel and James Barbour, as the central characters Jane and Rochester. Scenic design by John Napier; costume design by Andreane Neofitou; directed by John Caird and Scott Schwartz.*
Photo by Joan Marcus.

♦ **THE CAUCASIAN CHALK CIRCLE,** by Bertolt Brecht. Two grotesque characters in half masks. These characters are simultaneously evil and comic. There are times in Brecht's Epic Theatre when he uses evil characters to create good. Produced at the University of Nebraska. Collection of the authors.

lines in a deliberate monotone while performing before draperies. German expressionism in the 1910s called for choruses to speak in a mechanized, robotic fashion. The 1960s experimental theatres were filled with actors taking on generic characters who presented Everyman-like images, specters of the dead, or plant and animal life. Characters shifted through planes of existence and time. In writing for alternative theatres, one playwright, Megan Terry, even calls for "transformational" acting whereby actors instantly shift from one character to another without any exit, costume change, or other realistic device.

Throughout the last 120 years or so, many playwrights and directors have experimented with alternatives to realistic acting. In Russia, a Stanislavsky-trained actor and director, Vsevolod Meyerhold, broke away from the Moscow Art Theatre to pursue his own dreams and led the development of **biomechanics,** a highly energetic, mimetic approach to physicalization that abstracted human movement and created a very athletic actor. Antonin Artaud's **Theatre of Cruelty** (developed in France between the world wars) emphasized a breakdown of causality and stressed emotionality over intellect. German playwright and director Bertolt Brecht developed politicized acting theory (as part of his total concept of **Epic Theatre**) that is still vital to much contemporary acting in nonrealistic productions. He popularized ideas such as the actor observing the character from the outside and commenting on it through performance. For example, a Brechtian character often interrupts the action to sing—not as a character getting so worked up that he or she must burst into song but singing to comment on ideas in the play. The actor can in turn sing the song not as the character in the play but as an outsider. For Brecht the primary argument of a scene and the social action of the characters were far more important than story and psychology. A presentational acting style in today's theatre may call on all the resources of the actor, including movement as strenuous as acrobatics and vocal technique (even for spoken words) akin to singing. Some theatre artists, such as Tadashi Suzuki, have developed rigorous training methods for preparing the voice and body to meet demands beyond those of psychological realism. Drawing on his training in classical Asian forms, Suzuki's goal is to create an integrated and highly expressive actor freed from the mind/body dichotomy that is so familiar in Western cultures.

Many aspects of these presentational theories and practices, once radical and confusing to many audience members, are now accepted with relatively little adjustment. In *Copenhagen* (1998) by Michael Frayn, which was produced on Broadway, three actors played dead characters reenacting controversial moments from their past. Frequently shifting from past event to direct audience address, the characters interrupted the scenes they were replaying to comment or

◆ **COPENHAGEN.** *The three principals, Philip Bosco (as Niels Bohr), Blair Brown (as Margrethe Bohr), and Michael Cumpsty (as Werner Heisenberg). Directed by Michael Blakemore; set and costume design by Peter J. Davison.* Photo by Joan Marcus.

begin the scene again in another way. The nonrealistic acting methods that developed throughout the twentieth century made an appropriate style for the play possible.

◆◆◆◆◆◆◆◆◆◆

The Actor's Work

While a master pianist or violinist searches for a well-made and expressive instrument with which to perform, the actor seeks to develop his or her own body, voice, and mind to the fullest extent. As the needs of the theatre change, the expectations of the actor do as well. In contemporary theatre practice, an actor may be called on to perform in a different style of play and production with each new job.

ACTOR TRAINING

Before the early twentieth century most acting methods were taught within an apprenticeship system (as were many other trades). A young person accepted into a theatre company began playing walk-on roles or roles with few lines and learned by watching other actors perform and receiving instruction on a need-to-know basis. This basic approach is still alive in Asian classical forms such as

Kabuki, in which actors begin training as children, learn a particular type of role, and graduate to increasingly difficult parts as they mature and demonstrate their proficiency.

By the nineteenth century in Europe many state-subsidized theatres had schools attached, but these were basically an extension of the apprenticeship system, with experienced company members instructing and demonstrating for younger performers. In France Françoise Delsarte (1811–1871) created a system for studying plays, observing human behavior, and finding emotional expression through detailed analysis that became enormously popular in actor-training schools throughout Europe. It was brought to the United States by the actor-inventor-playwright-teacher Steele Mackaye in the 1870s. The Delsartian system of learning movement and gesture was ultimately rejected with the coming of realism, since it relied on a standardized scheme for expressing emotion. Delsarte's systematic approach to preparing actors that relied on training the body, voice, and intellect, however, set the standard for actor training programs as they currently exist in universities and conservatories (schools dedicated specifically to development of performance skills).

Today actors develop their bodies by taking movement classes specifically designed for actors as well as dance, stage combat, and martial arts instruction. Excess tension inhibits free expression; breathing and physical relaxation exercises are therefore important in freeing both the body and the voice. Vocal training, integrated with the physical development, focuses on breathing and voice production (the actual making of sound). Voice and breath are connected to the actor's understanding of the body and all of its possibilities, as well as the actor's imagination. Actors are trained in **projection** (making the voice loud enough to be heard but still sounding conversational) and **articulation** (forming all the sounds of words so that an actor can be understood). Learning the **International Phonetic Alphabet**—a system of specific symbols representing individual sounds—helps actors to both analyze their own speech and reproduce different dialects and accents.

Actors usually learn techniques of script analysis and character exploration developed by Stanislavsky and his followers, such as the great acting teachers Stella Adler, Uta Hagen, and Sanford Meisner. They may be taught detailed analysis of text and given practice speaking verse. Students are trained in careful observation of human beings and other animal life. Exercises in improvisation such as the theatre games developed by Viola Spolin help actors learn to respond immediately with their voices and bodies to changing situations. Although many actors today begin their professional lives with training from a college or university theatre program or a conservatory, most actors continue to develop their craft through classes, coaching, and individual work on voice and body throughout their lives.

THE ACTOR IN REHEARSAL

Memorizing lines is only a small part of the acting process. Actors will analyze the script using techniques they have learned and found effective. If the action of the play takes place in an earlier time and will be performed in costumes and a set of that period, the actor might read about social conditions of the time in addition to other background information provided by the director

◆ **HAMLET**, *by William Shakespeare. Combat scene between Hamlet and Laertes in the 2000 Stratford Festival production. Graham Abbey as Laertes and Paul Gross as Hamlet, with members of the Festival company. Directed by Joseph Ziegler; designed by Christina Poddubiuk.*
Photo by Cylla von Tiedemann. Courtesy of the Stratford Festival Archives.

or dramaturg. At early rehearsals actors usually have scripts in hand and record **blocking** or other notes as the work proceeds. Soon, however, at a date set by the director, actors must be "off book," with lines and movement memorized. A movement coach might teach period manners and movement or provide any specialized training necessary for the show as well as watching the actors' work and suggesting ways to enhance physical characterization. Rehearsal clothes that approximate the special challenges posed by period costumes (for example, corsets, hoopskirts, or togas) are often worn throughout the rehearsal period. When stage combat is required, the movement coach or a separate fight master will teach the actor carefully choreographed routines that must then be practiced daily with partners, first in slow motion and gradually working up to performance speed. A vocal coach often assists the actor in finding an appropriate vocal quality for the character, learning dialects, and clarifying speech.

Rehearsals always include many struggles with the play text. Actors experiment, try many different readings and interpretations, and sometimes argue and persuade as the director encourages discovery and guides the actors through the possibilities for realizing the text and its characters. Although actors bring a great deal of themselves to a role, an important quality is the ability to take direction—in other words, to be flexible enough to implement the director's suggestions. Sometimes a great deal of discipline is needed to

Exploring Collaboration

Actors as Collaborators

The interaction that is most visible to an audience is that of the actors. A show can succeed or fail on the basis of whether or not actors truly collaborate with one another. At the most basic level, actors must rely on each other for the show to progress. A moment's lapse could mean a missed entrance, a blown cue line—any number of mistakes that could be catastrophic for the other actors, the technical crews, and the show as a whole. Professional integrity and the knowledge that colleagues are depending on them (as well as an instinct for self-preservation) lead actors to develop intense powers of concentration and a kind of split consciousness. They are focused simultaneously on character material (thinking/responding as the character) and technical considerations, such as whether the audience is able to hear the lines, how to hold an important prop, how to find an exact spot on the stage when entering in the dark, and sometimes whether or not a fellow actor needs help.

Mistakes are inevitable in live performance. Even the most experienced actor may occasionally "go up" (forget a line). An alert actor can often save a fellow performer by altering or repeating a line or ad-libbing stage business. The mistake might even go

♦ *PICASSO AT THE LAPIN AGILE, by Steve Martin. Actors hard at work. Directed by Sullivan Canaday White; scenic design by Tom Burch; costume design by Jessica Byrd Watters and Annelise Beeckman.*
Photo by Richard C. Trigg. Courtesy of Actors Theatre of Louisville.

unnoticed by the audience, particularly if the actor is sensitive to the body language of the partner in a scene and senses distress. This kind of subtle, nonverbal communication flows regularly on stage between performers. Actors

focus concentration on the work to be done. In early rehearsals directors start and stop a scene many times to ask questions, suggest alternatives, explore motivation, adjust positions, or discuss timing. Actors learn to play what they are given by other actors—to respond to new line readings and physical action from others onstage. Much of the rehearsal period is dedicated to learning to trust and depend on the other actors. A strong rapport among performers can add a spark of energy and spontaneity to production, and a character is fully developed only when it seems to live within the same world as the others on stage.

tend to feed off one another's energy. Flat and slow interaction can often be energized by an actor who enters the scene with higher energy.

On the level of artistic decision, actors collaborate in developing characterization. Any choice an actor makes will have an impact on the other performers. If the actress playing Juliet decides that her character is terrified of being caught by her nurse or family during the balcony scene, the actor playing Romeo might need to work all the harder to keep her from fleeing into her bedroom. When an actor gives something new while performing a scene, the partner must respond to that change appropriately for the character. One of the worst situations for an actor is a partner who gives nothing or very little. Finding a way to respond to an expressionless face or line reading is the worst kind of acting challenge.

Some directors even go so far as to send actors away to work on a scene with the vague challenge "Come back and show me something new." A highly imaginative team of actors might return with various ways to play the scene, allowing the director and actors to take the scene to a higher level.

When a show is going well (and sometimes even when it's not), actors forge strong relationships with each other. When they are able to work together repeatedly, actors learn each other's strengths, weaknesses, and preferred methods, making the development process speedier and (sometimes) less painful.

Some actors are so attuned to one another that they make special efforts to perform together. Occasionally, they may even be married, as were Alfred Lunt and Lynn Fontanne, who performed together frequently in the 1920s and then exclusively through the 1930s and beyond. Audiences were fascinated by their onstage/offstage union. Centuries earlier, in seventeenth-century France, fascinated but gossipy responses greeted the performances of Molière and his much younger wife, Armande Béjart. In our own time another inspiring married acting couple, Ruby Dee and Ossie Davis, continue to work together both as actors and social activists.

Interested? Check out

Jared Brown. *The Fabulous Lunts: A Biography of Alfred Lunt and Lynn Fontanne.* New York: Atheneum, 1988.
Autobiographies of actors are usually full of firsthand accounts of performer relationships and anecdotes. For example:

(An eighteenth-century actor) Colley Cibber. *An Apology for the Life of Colley Cibber.* (1740) Mineola, N.Y.: Dover, 2000.

(A nineteenth-century actor) Emma Stebbins, ed. *Charlotte Cushman: Her Letters and Memories of Her Life.* Boston: Houghton, Osgood, and Company, 1878.

(A twentieth-century actor) Alec Guinness. *Blessings in Disguise.* New York: Alfred A. Knopf, 1986.

As rehearsals proceed, the actors find themselves frequently modifying or severely changing choices made early in the process. Every change almost always evokes other changes as the performance approaches completion. As opening approaches, actors use the **run-throughs** to create a sense of continuity and learn the shape of their part—when they have down time, when they need to prepare to go onstage, the energy level needed for emotional or physical high points in the action. Typically, directors give notes to actors after a run-through; it is the actors' responsibility to implement the changes at the next run-through, which might require study or practice outside of rehearsal.

◆ *A MIDSUMMER NIGHT'S DREAM, 1999 production. The four lovers quarrel in the forest. Complicated physical activity like this requires not only careful rehearsal but also mutual trust on the part of the actors. Left to right, Tim Redmond as Demetrius, Gregory Ivan Smith as Lysander, Didi Doolittle as Hermia, and Maren Maclean as Helena.*
Photo by Karl Hugh. Courtesy of Utah Shakespearean Festival.

Frequently, the actors do not rehearse in the theatre in which they will perform for an audience until technical rehearsals or shortly before. The delay is usually due to economic constraints or limitations of available theatre spaces. Once the actors move into the real space, however, there are always adjustments. Acoustics sometimes change dramatically; the performance space is often considerably larger than the rehearsal space. Actors must adjust to the finished sets, which might include some surprises. Except during fittings, the actors rarely wear the costumes until **dress rehearsals** several days before opening, so appropriate rehearsal clothes are important. Despite careful planning, it is sometimes necessary to modify actor movement for the costumes or vice versa. The same is true for hand and set properties and the addition of lighting and sound. Adjusting to the stage lighting, especially if there is abundant movement in the lighting and many blackouts, can be a considerable task.

Problems are worked out in **technical rehearsals** and dress rehearsals (and **previews** if the company uses them). Before going on stage, actors typically go through a warm-up, or series of physical, vocal, and mental exercises. Like athletes and singers, actors depend on their bodies and voices and take care to prepare them before a performance. After all the preparation, collaboration, and rehearsal the actor finally interacts with an audience, not just other actors and the director. With the addition of an audience there is a jump in engagement and energy from the actors, and the collaboration between actors and audience commences.

STAGE VERSUS FILM ACTING

In today's entertainment world, most actors work in film and television as well as in the theatre. There are important differences between acting on stage and acting for the camera. When acting in the theatre, an actor builds a role gradually over the rehearsal period and works up to emotional high points as the show proceeds. Sustaining the performance over several hours is an important consideration. Movies and TV shows are frequently shot out of sequence, so the actor does not build a performance over time. Instead, the actor must be able to reach an emotional high point on cue with little preparation and must be able to repeat the performance for different filmings, or takes. Only one is selected. Lines are usually learned in advance only for the scenes being shot on a particular day, and rehearsal for each scene is often limited.

The level of vocal projection and articulation necessary for the stage would seem highly exaggerated when filmed. Most film work requires a subtle style of acting appropriate to the close-up shot, which can reveal minute changes in facial expression. The slightest whisper can be amplified to an appropriate volume. An important aspect of acting for the stage is the ability to repeat a performance night after night yet still retain the vital sense of spontaneity. Actors who are lucky enough to be engaged in a long-running show constantly look for ways to keep their performance fresh without changing aspects clearly set by the director. Although each kind of acting has its own problems and rewards, acting on stage has the advantage of immediate communication with the audience during the performance.

THE PROFESSIONAL ACTOR

The life of a professional actor can be exciting and precarious, emotionally overwhelming or exhilarating. The professional actor needs to be steeled for the possibility that he or she might always have a "day job." Most actors frequently find themselves unemployed or between gigs—or "at liberty," as actors called it in the 1920s. For example, for the 2000–2001 season, Actors' Equity Association, the labor union that represents professional actors and stage managers in America, reported that 54.1 percent of its members in good standing (20,858 out of 38,566 Equity actors) were unemployed for the entire season. Of the 17,708 who worked, the average actor worked in the theatre for only 16.4 weeks out of 52. The median income from stage acting for all Equity actors that season was only $6,138, a figure lower than those in the two previous seasons.[4] These bleak figures demonstrate how risky the profession can be, since the figures used to calculate the average include the incomes of actors who are doing well financially.

Sometimes the profession seems like endless auditions, callbacks, interviews, and lunches with producers, filled more with promises than with real job offers. Sometimes the actor feels like a commodity rather than a person. In the musical *A Chorus Line* (1975), which was developed from the actual experiences of performers, a character sings a lament, wondering whether his resume is the sum of his identity. Sometimes the acting profession is more about getting an

Equity card (union membership), securing an agent, or trying to get cast than it is about art.

For the actor who is talented and lucky enough to work regularly, however, life beyond rehearsals and performances is filled with travel, adjusting to new locations and working methods, and changing media. Besides the stage, film, and television programs many successfully employed stage actors also work in video, commercials, industrials (live advertising shows for companies and products), modeling, recording voice-overs, books on tape, and radio. Through it all, many actors continue their own training in private studios and teach younger actors. Actors must read (and not just submitted play scripts), engage in observation of people, and go to the theatre when not performing. The actor who has not yet reached the level of consistent employment might ask, "How much time do I give myself to make it?" The question is tricky because most actors expend years trying to get in the proverbial door. Professional acting is a crowded business with many casualties. Only the determined and the talented should apply. As things now stand, there is no shortage of young actors willing to make the sacrifices and take the risks.

◆◆◆◆◆◆◆◆◆

QUESTIONS AND ACTIVITIES

1. Choose a character and scene in a play that you have read. Identify an objective for the character. In other words, what do you think the character is trying to accomplish in the scene? Avoid states of being (such as "I want to be happy") and look for active wants and needs (such as "I must convince my mother to give me the $100"). How would different choices of objective change the way you played the scene?

2. Recall a scene from a play you have seen on stage. Imagine the actors playing the same scene for a film.

Assuming that the dialogue stayed the same, what might change about their performances?

3. Discuss the acting in a show you have seen. Did the cast take a representational or presentational approach? Why do you think this choice was made? Were the performances believable within the world of the production? Did the actors seem to be performing in the same style? Did they function smoothly as an ensemble? Why or why not? How did the actors use body and voice to create specific characters?

◆◆◆◆◆◆◆◆◆

KEY TERMS AND CONCEPTS

FOR FURTHER EXPLORATION

Stella Adler. *The Art of Acting*. New York: Applause, 2000.

Robert Cohen. *Acting Professionally: Raw Facts about Careers in Acting*, 5th edition. Mountain View, Calif.: Mayfield Publishing, 1998.

Toby Cole, ed., et al. *Actors on Acting: The Theories, Techniques, and Practices of the World's Great Actors, Told in Their Own Words*, 4th edition. New York: Random House, 1995.

John Harrop and Sabin R. Epstein. *Acting with Style*, 3rd edition. Boston: Allyn and Bacon, 2000.

Actors' Equity Association web site at www.actorsequity.org/home.html.

ARCADIA, by Tom Stoppard, Huntington Theatre Company.
Photo by Charlie Erickson.

CHAPTER 12

The Playwright

Imagination and Expression

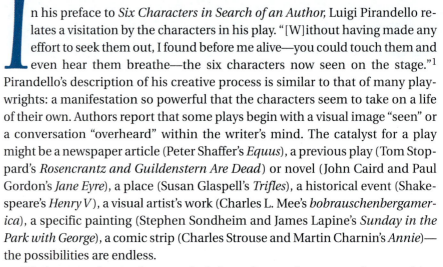

In his preface to *Six Characters in Search of an Author,* Luigi Pirandello relates a visitation by the characters in his play. "[W]ithout having made any effort to seek them out, I found before me alive—you could touch them and even hear them breathe—the six characters now seen on the stage."[1] Pirandello's description of his creative process is similar to that of many playwrights: a manifestation so powerful that the characters seem to take on a life of their own. Authors report that some plays begin with a visual image "seen" or a conversation "overheard" within the writer's mind. The catalyst for a play might be a newspaper article (Peter Shaffer's *Equus*), a previous play (Tom Stoppard's *Rosencrantz and Guildenstern Are Dead*) or novel (John Caird and Paul Gordon's *Jane Eyre*), a place (Susan Glaspell's *Trifles*), a historical event (Shakespeare's *Henry V*), a visual artist's work (Charles L. Mee's *bobrauschenbergamerica*), a specific painting (Stephen Sondheim and James Lapine's *Sunday in the Park with George*), a comic strip (Charles Strouse and Martin Charnin's *Annie*)—the possibilities are endless.

We do not understand a great deal about the creative process, but one thing seems clear: Writers use both the subconscious and conscious mind, dredging up material from a place that is not consciously under their control, then using intellectual, critical faculties to organize, shape, and edit. Playwright David Henry Hwang has noted, "If I felt I knew everything, there'd be no point to writing. You're trying to discover what you know unconsciously but haven't revealed to yourself."[2] Much of what we call "talent" in a writer may be the strength of the original vision, but such inspiration is useless without the ability to transform that raw material into words that can be communicated to other people. Dialogue must be represented precisely on the page to give the performer clues about how to deliver it; a comma in the wrong place or a poorly chosen word can drastically affect the actor's interpretation of a line.

Writing for the stage is quite different from writing a novel, short story, or poem. The playwright must be aware of creating a blueprint—a document that is not complete in itself but is rich and full enough to inspire visual and interpretive artists and artists of the body and voice (actors) to create an aesthetic whole. The odd spelling of the English word "playwright" holds a key to its special meaning. In the medieval period the term "wright" was used for a craftsperson: a shipwright built ships, a wheelwright made wheels and wheeled vehicles. A *playwright,* therefore, is not just a writer, but a *crafter* of plays. The written document is not an end in itself, but the beginning of a three-dimensional aural and visual experience to be built and shaped. In the case of a musical a composer, lyricist, and playwright (or librettist) might collaborate extensively to develop a workable blueprint. For most of theatrical history the most convenient way to communicate such a plan to others or to preserve its essence was through written text, and we are fortunate that documents survive to give us an inkling of our theatrical legacy.

◆ **EQUUS**, *by Peter Shaffer. Tom Hulce as Alan, a disturbed teenager who rides the horse, Nugget, played by Everett McGill in the Broadway production directed by John Dexter. The lighting instruments visible here were mounted low above the stage and created great intensity at center stage while Alan and Nugget took their nocturnal rides on an open square platform that could rotate rapidly during highly emotional moments.*
Photofest.

ARTISTS OF the THEATRE

SUZAN-LORI PARKS

Playwright **SUZAN-LORI PARKS** (b. 1964) revels in the creativity that her colleagues (both on stage and in the house) bring to theatre. When she records the dialogue of her characters on paper, she thinks in terms of music, even putting in the stage direction "rest" (as in a short period of silence). For a moment of silence between two characters just before an important emotional change occurs, she alternates the characters' names on the page with no dialogue indicated; she calls this technique a "spell." Parks understands that she is turning responsibility over to the actors and director to fill these essential silences. A rest, she says, can be a moment of "just standing there" or "a moment filled with action. It's up to the director and the actors, and that's part of the fun; that sometimes, you know, they get to create whatever they want, whatever they need for the moment to work." Parks believes that the characters begin as part of her and then become the work of the actors: "And that's the most exciting thing for me about being a playwright; that when I'm writing, I, you know, control, control, control, you know, every word, every moment, every beat, every sound, everything. But then when I step into rehearsal, I let go."[3]

Once her work is in front of an audience, "it's the role of the audience to divine meaning from the play." Parks believes that good literature "gives the reader or the audience member many meanings, and for every seat in the house, for every audience member, there is a different take on the play."[4]

In 2002 Suzan-Lori Parks became the first African American woman to win the Pulitzer Prize for Drama with her play *Topdog/Underdog,* the story of Lincoln and Booth, two brothers caught in an intensive love/hate relationship. George C. Wolfe, artistic director of the

◆ *TOPDOG/UNDERDOG,* by Suzan-Lori Parks. The brothers Lincoln and Booth, played by Jeffrey Wright and Don Cheadle, plotting. Public Theatre, New York.
Photo by Michal Daniel.

New York Shakespeare Festival and the Public Theatre in New York City, directed *Topdog/Underdog* at the Public and in its subsequent Broadway run. Parks credits Wolfe with championing her work early in her career. Writer James Baldwin had an important influence on Parks when she was a student in his creative writing class and in fact was the first to suggest that her personality as a writer was suited to the theatre.

Parks explores the impact of history on the lives of her characters and examines the effects of racism in plays that are varied in style. *The America Play* (1993) features an African American man who impersonates President Lincoln in a sideshow (also the career of the character Lincoln in *Topdog/Underdog*). *Venus* (1996) is based on the true story of an African woman who was exhibited as a sideshow phenomenon in early nineteenth-century London. The central character of *In the Blood* (1999) is the homeless mother of five children.

As part of an army family, Parks lived in many different places while growing up and attended high school in Germany. She received a B.A. from Mount Holyoke College in 1985 and currently heads the Audrey Skirball Kenis Theater Project's Writing for Performance Program at CalArts. In addition to the Pulitzer Prize, Parks has been honored with two Obie Awards for Best New American Play produced off-Broadway (for *Imperceptible Mutabilities in the Third Kingdom,* 1990, and *Venus,* 1996) and numerous other awards and grants. Her first novel, *Getting Mother's Body,* was published in 2003.

Interested? Check out

"Women of Color Women of Word—African American Female Playwrights" at www.scils.rutgers.edu/~cybers/parks2.html.
Jane T. Peterson and Suzanne Bennett. *Women Playwrights of Diversity: A Bio-Bibliographical Sourcebook.* Westport, Conn.: Greenwood Publishing Group, 1997.
Sydne Mahone, ed. *Moon Marked and Touched by Sun: Plays by African-American Women.* New York: Theatre Communications Group, 1994.

The Changing Position of the Playwright

At times, crafters of plays have been anonymous, their identity consumed by the producing organization; at other times, playwrights have been celebrated as individual artists. The position of the playwright in the complicated web of theatre making changes according to how theatre fits into society as a whole and according to the role of the text in production.

PLAYWRITING AS CIVIC CONTRIBUTION

We are told that the earliest Greek playwrights performed and staged their own plays, thus functioning as what we would now call playwright, actor, and director. Thespis and Aeschylus were actors as well as playwrights. Playwriting was not a profession—people who wrote plays earned their livings in other ways—but theatrical activity was considered a significant civic contribution. It was an honor to be selected to compete and an even greater honor to win a prize for the best set of plays. The theatre became professionalized in the late Greek and Roman periods, but the strong sense of civic connection resurfaced in the Middle Ages. Although a few of the medieval play texts identify the playwright, we do not even know the names of most of the authors of the cycle plays based on biblical stories. Groups of cycle plays are identified by the name of the community that presented them: the York Cycle, for example, or the Wakefield Cycle. Participation in the religious and civic event was apparently more important than individual identification or ownership. Playwrights remained anonymous or nearly so in Asian forms as well. With the notable exceptions of early Noh and the celebrated playwright Chikamatsu in the Bunraku theatre, we know little about the authors of classical Japanese theatre or the creation of remarkable plays of the Yüan period in China or Sanskrit plays in India.

THE PLAY AS COMMODITY

Identity of the writer became more important as professionalism increased during the Renaissance. In Elizabethan England, for example, a script was a potentially valuable commodity. Early Greek plays may have belonged to the state. Cycle plays belonged to the cities, but an Elizabethan writer could sell plays to competing theatrical troupes. In general, a playwright sold a play for a flat fee to a company, which usually chose not to publish the text, since to do so would make it available to competitors. In consequence some of the first publications of Shakespeare and his contemporaries were pirated editions; someone in the audience, or perhaps a disgruntled actor, scribbled out dialogue from memory and sold the copy to a printer. Even though Shakespeare's plays were very popular, they were not revered as great literature until much later. The first collected edition of his work was not published until 1623, seven years after Shakespeare's death. Sometimes an author was attached to or a member of a specific acting troupe and intimately involved in its success; Shakespeare wrote many plays for the Lord Chamberlain's Men, later renamed the King's Men, a company in which he was a shareholder. A profitable production meant more money for the shareholders, so the popularity of a play had important financial consequences.

Until the late nineteenth century most authors received only the flat fee for their plays, with occasional extras added for successful scripts. Playwrights in eighteenth-century England, for example, were given the profits from a "benefit night" on the third, sixth, and twentieth nights of the play's first run of performances (if the show ran that long—a run of twenty nights was rare). On some occasions playwrights received only benefit payments; therefore, a play that closed after the first or second performance night might render a playwright no revenue at all. In 1791 the French National Assembly passed the first law giving **royalties** (a fee for each performance) to playwrights. The writer's heirs were entitled to collect payment up to five years after the author's death. It was some time before other countries followed suit.

SOCIAL POSITION OF THE PLAYWRIGHT

In the seventeenth and eighteenth centuries neoclassicism encouraged a more literary approach to text, setting specific standards for playwrights to follow in composition and honoring those who did so. Such critical praise often meant little at the box office, however, and any involvement with the stage made a writer, particularly a woman writer, morally suspect and socially unacceptable. The notion that the writer's talents were sold to the highest bidder led to a comparison with prostitutes. Despite the popularity of her plays, Aphra Behn, the first professional woman playwright in England, was frequently vilified and dismissed as an immoral and unnatural phenomenon. Writing for the theatre remained a

♦ **HEDDA GABLER,** by Henrik Ibsen. Ibsen's plays were frequently read and regularly produced in Ibsen's lifetime just as in our own. Here, Judith Light plays Hedda and Robin Gammell plays Judge Brack in the Shakespeare Theatre's 2001 production of Doug Hughes's translation. Directed by Michael Kahn; costume design by Murrell Horton. Photo by Carol Rosegg. Courtesy of The Shakespeare Theatre, Washington, D.C.

tenuous means of earning a living for both sexes; the playwrights who did not maintain other jobs in the theatre such as acting or management were novelists, journalists, poets, and editors. The playwright Molière was both an actor and the company manager; similarly, playwright Richard Brinsley Sheridan was a theatrical manager and politician. The coming of romanticism in the late eighteenth century led to a growing emphasis on individual talent and originality. Shakespeare was at that time elevated to near divine status, but such reverence did not usually extend to contemporary playwrights.

In the early nineteenth century dramatists were frequently referred to as "hacks." The rapidly growing middle- and working-class audience called for a great amount of new material, which writers often furnished by translating and loosely adapting preexisting works (often without crediting the original author) and cobbling together highly theatrical but often derivative melodramas and fantasy plays. In the last quarter of the century the social position of the playwright began to improve, along with the rest of the theatrical profession. The work of Henrik Ibsen and the playwrights who followed his example led to an increased emphasis on the theatrical text as literature. Because of the controversy surrounding production of the early plays of realism, such as *A Doll House* and *Ghosts,* the public often was first introduced to those works in printed form. Ibsen's plays were frequently discussed, attacked, and praised by readers long before they were seen in production.

COPYRIGHT REGULATIONS

Late nineteenth- and early twentieth-century international **copyright** laws brought recognition of the play as a writer's intellectual property. England passed its first (rather limited) copyright law in 1833. The first International Copyright agreement was created in 1886, but it took some countries a long time to sign; others never did. Today, in most countries, an author retains all rights to the play except for those specifically sold or assigned to someone else. No theatre may produce a play, no publisher may print it, without first receiving the permission of the writer and (usually) compensating the writer financially. To violate this standard is unethical as well as illegal; a playwright should be paid a royalty each time a play is produced. For work created after January 1978, current U.S. copyright law gives the author ownership of the work for life and to the author's estate for seventy years after the author's death. Most works published between 1964 and 1977 are under copyright (depending on the circumstances of publication); works published between 1923 and 1963 may be under copyright if the original term was renewed. Works published before 1923 are considered in the public domain and can be produced freely, although to be ethical, it is important always to acknowledge the author of the play in all production information. Even when a play is in public domain, however, a translation might well be under copyright.

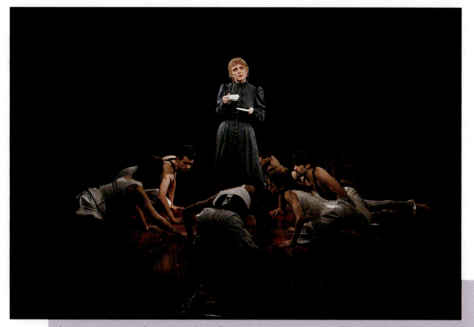

♦ **MISS JULIE,** *by August Strindberg. In a moment created for this production (not written by Strindberg), we see Julie politely drinking tea in nineteenth-century dress while surrounded by a chorus crawling toward her in nineteenth-century underwear. With Ellen Lauren as Julie. Directed by Anne Bogart; costume design by Marcia Dixcy Jory.*
Courtesy of Actors Theatre of Louisville.

Molière's plays may be produced freely, for example, but when an English version created after 1923 is produced, permission must be obtained and a royalty paid to the translator. In 1920 the Dramatists Guild, Inc., was formed as part of the Authors League of America to safeguard writers' interests. The Guild now offers a standard contract to members for both commercial and nonprofit theatres.

Still, only a very few writers today make their entire living writing for the theatre (or even for theatre and film). There are many more scripts in existence than there are production opportunities, and most playwrights spend many hours after the writing is completed in copying, mailing, and otherwise marketing their work to theatres, publishers, agents, and play contests. Publications such as *Dramatists Sourcebook* (Theatre Communications Group) and *The Resource Directory* (Dramatists Guild) list organizations that accept new plays for consideration.

♦ ♦ ♦ ♦ ♦ ♦ ♦ ♦ ♦ ♦

The Playwright and Production

In most traditional models, the playwright is responsible for the initial vision of the play, for crafting the words to be spoken and suggesting important action or visual images. There are many ways in which the relationship between writer and production team can be organized.

WRITING WITH ACTORS IN MIND

When a writer is connected to a company or at least familiar with actors who are likely to perform the roles, a special connection exists between the written text and the first production company. Aristotle complained that Hellenistic playwrights were catering to the whims of actors. Shakespeare and Molière wrote parts for people they worked with on a daily basis and for themselves; Shakespeare was an actor; Molière was a lead, playing Alceste in *The Misanthrope* and Harpagon in *The Miser.* Zeami and Kan'ami were actors as well as leading Noh playwrights, and in the case of Zeami we have not only a body of plays but also a critical text on the acting process. In the nineteenth century it was common for authors to create a work for a specific star. The American actor Edwin Forrest even sponsored contests for the best play with a leading role for him, a process that resulted in some of his most famous characters, such as Metamora in a play by that title by John A. Stone. One successful modern collaboration is the team of writer and director Jane Wagner and actress Lily Tomlin, who have worked together on plays, movies, and comedy albums. In the one-woman show *The Search for Signs of Intelligent Life in the Universe* (1985, revived in 2000), Wagner created a series of characters that called on Tomlin's considerable talents as a comedienne and character actress.

In such cases the playwright can tailor a character to the strengths of particular actors. An actor's appearance, personality, or history can help to shape the fictional character, and a stage-wise playwright would of course take into account the various levels of talent available in the company and any specialties: comedy, tragedy, singing, dancing, acrobatic ability. Shakespeare's characters sometimes changed significantly when an actor joined or left his company; the clown roles, for example, altered dramatically when William Kempe (Dogberry in *Much Ado about Nothing*) was replaced by Robert Armin (Feste in *Twelfth Night*). Mark Hollmann recalls that the casting of actor John Cullum in *Urinetown* ten days before starting rehearsals off-Broadway led to a new song in the musical: "Knowing that we were writing the song for John Cullum was such a kick in the pants—a good kick in the pants. It gave me a specific idea of what kind of song it could be."[5]

Of course, writing for a specific company imposes some limitations as well. It might restrict the number or type of characters to be created; it might dictate the space into which the play must fit. Because of production conventions, playwrights of the seventeenth and eighteenth centuries used settings for their plays based on stock scenery already owned by the theatre. Today, experienced playwrights are keenly aware of theatre production budgets as they consider settings and casting requirements.

WRITING WITH A
THEATRE IN THE HEAD

Many plays are written with no prior knowledge of when, by whom, or even if they will be produced. In such cases the writer's imagination is freer to roam, but there will necessarily be a wider gulf between the initial vision and its concrete manifestation on the stage. For some authors this inevitable transformation is exciting; for others it is problematic. Eugene O'Neill, for example, created detailed physical descriptions of his characters, no doubt based on the vivid pictures in his mind. The possibilities were slim, however, of finding an actor who could perform the role as well as match O'Neill's precise depictions, and he was continually disappointed in the gulf between the scene in his head and the one on the stage. In O'Neill's mind, Anna Christopherson, the lead in the play *Anna Christie*, was tall and blonde. In the first production the actress Pauline Lord was a short redhead, yet her performance was electrifying and considered definitive by her generation. Long after O'Neill's death, the portrayals of Anna by Liv Ullman in 1977 and Natasha Richardson in 1993 were much closer to O'Neill's image.

◆ *ANNA CHRISTIE*, by Eugene O'Neill. Pauline Lord as the original Anna Christopherson. The first act of the play takes place in a bar, and some of Anna's past involvement with prostitution makes itself evident to the audience but not to her father. Photo courtesy of Theatre Collection, Museum of the City of New York.

A basic awareness of the physical aspects of theatre is important for writers who wish to see their work produced. A writer who participates in production in other ways gains the advantage of practical knowledge. Someone who attends and studies the theatre regularly as an audience member can also develop a strong sense of dramatic feasibility. A writer who is completely unconnected to the theatre in any way might have a difficult time satisfying the needs of the stage. Many beginning playwrights, for example, think in filmic terms, imagining visuals that are not possible in live theatre (such as a close-up), or write in a style that is more appropriate for silent reading than oral delivery. Such writers often benefit from involvement as a volunteer in theatrical production. Participating at a theatre that produces new scripts is particularly valuable. Playwrights learn great lessons from hearing their plays read aloud by actors or colleagues. Playwrights themselves can read their dialogue aloud to test the readability and sound of the lines. An understanding of the limitations as well as the imaginative possibilities of the live theatre are essential for someone who is planning the skeletal structure on which many contributing artists will build.

COLLABORATING WITH ACTORS, DIRECTORS, AND DRAMATURGS

In current theatrical practice, it is typical for the playwright to collaborate with the creative team on the first production of a play. This collaboration may range from occasional long-distance consultation by phone, fax, and e-mail to daily on-site participation in building the production. The playwright can serve as a valuable resource for unlocking a play's possibilities and may offer interpretations, explain development, and give opinions of performances and designs. The relationship between the author and a play's first director can be productive and exciting or painful and destructive. The potential for conflict over power is great, since the playwright enters the process with a prior sense of ownership and the director feels responsible for the final production. If actors and designers get different messages from the playwright and director, personal and artistic confusion can be the result. Wise directors often discuss the working relationship and procedures with the writer in advance, before dealing with the entire

♦ **THE THREE SISTERS,** as performed by the City Center Acting Company. Some plays are particularly important for creating an acting ensemble. The plays of Chekhov fall into this category. Here is a famous group celebration in a dining room.
Photo courtesy Billy Rose Theatre Collection, the New York Public Library for the Performing Arts, Astor, Lennox and Tilden Foundations.

company. Some directors prefer that the playwright not speak directly to actors and designers but route all feedback through the director. Others cultivate a more free-wheeling approach to sharing ideas but insist on serving as the clearinghouse for any major conceptual or interpretive discussions.

The way in which playwrights and directors interact varies greatly. Some writers need reinforcement and careful questioning; others thrive on a more adversarial relationship in which conflict with the director pushes them to new creative places. There are as many successful ways of working as there are successful teams; no one approach will work for everyone. The choice of certain directors, playwrights, and actors to work together repeatedly suggests both the difficulty of finding a combination that works and the artistic value of that combination once it is established. At the turn of the twentieth century Stanislavsky was the first director to recognize that a new, more subtle style of acting was necessary to make the plays of Anton Chekhov work. In the early twenty-first century the highly visual, physical style of director Anne Bogart is an appropriate match for the plays of Charles L. Mee, which venture past psychological realism and linear construction.

Often, a **dramaturg**—a specialist in dramatic literature and theatre history—is available to help the playwright. A dramaturg typically reads the script, attends readings, attends rehearsals, and offers suggestions to the playwright and director. A playwright might consult the dramaturg on issues of structure, characterization, or dialogue to get informed advice on solving problems the play may have. As with the director, the playwright's working relationship with

Exploring Collaboration

The Sondheim/Lapine Collaboration

The highly successful collaboration of Stephen Sondheim and James Lapine began when Lapine contacted Sondheim about the possibility of working together. After agreeing on the idea of theme and variations as a starting point, the two artists hit on the Georges Seurat painting "Sunday Afternoon on the Island of La Grande Jatte" as the focus for their musical. *Sunday in the Park with George* (1984) was the result. Lapine wrote the book; Sondheim wrote the music and lyrics. After two years of development, *Sunday in the Park with George* opened officially on Broadway on May 2, 1984, under the direction of Lapine, whose production choices further extended the ideas of the play into the visual realm.

The two men bring different strengths to the partnership. Sondheim's focus is aural; he is attuned to rhythm, language, pitch. Lapine's early career as a graphic artist developed a strong visual sense. Together, they produced an innovative theatrical experience. *Sunday in the Park with George* explores the position of the artist in society and the relationship between art, emotion, and human connection.

Soon after *Sunday in the Park with George* opened on Broadway, Lapine and Sondheim decided to collaborate again, this time focusing on a fairy tale or adventure. Lapine began charting story lines of various tales and reading modern commentary on their meaning. *Into the Woods* (1987) explores the themes of community and responsibility by intertwining familiar folk tales. Whereas the language and music of *Sunday in the Park with George* was inspired by the painter Seurat's technique of pointillism (tiny, self-contained dots of color, which at a distance merge to create a complete image), *Into the Woods* utilized several different styles of song appropriate for the wide variety of characters. Lapine again directed the first production. Bernadette Peters, who had originated the role of Dot in *Sunday in the Park with George*, returned in the important role of the hideous-turned-sexy witch of *Into the Woods*.

The two writers pursued independent projects but came together again for *Passion* (1994), a story of a man's relationship with two women that explores the irrational, consuming nature of love. Lapine wrote the book based on the 1981 movie *Passione d'Amore* and directed the first production. Sondheim created a full romantic score and lyrics to reflect the heightened emotions of the characters.

The history of the Sondheim/Lapine collaboration illustrates the exciting possibilities that can be unlocked when talented artists combine forces to produce an artistic product bolder, more brilliant, and with more depth than either might have achieved on his own.

Interested? Check out

Michiko Kakutani, "How Two Artists Shaped an Innovative Musical," *New York Times on the Web*, June 10, 1984, www.nytimes.com/books/98/07/19/specials/sondheim-innovative.html.
Sunday in the Park with George (1986) available on VHS and DVD.
Into the Woods (1991) available on VHS and DVD.

---

a dramaturg can take many forms, depending on the situation and the personalities involved.

TEXT OR PRETEXT?

One of the thorniest artistic and ethical issues in the theatre of our time is the relationship of the text (and therefore playwright) to the rest of the production. In the first half of the twentieth century the director was frequently looked on as an interpretive artist whose job was to come to as complete an understanding of

♦ *A TOUCH OF THE POET,* by Eugene O'Neill, was produced in 1997–1998 at Arena Stage in a nearly open space defined by furniture pieces, a somber floor, and high angle lighting seeming to emanate from windows hung in the air. Often the characters were kept at great distances from one another, a device that was especially effective when the women were suffering due to the excesses and alcoholism of their husband/father. The mother and daughter appear here played by Tana Hicken and Fiona Gallagher. Directed by Michael Kahn; designed by Ming Cho Lee. Photo by Stan Barouh. Courtesy of Arena Stage.

the playwright's intent as possible and then serve that intent in all aspects of production. The words of the play usually were considered set in stone whether the play was ancient or modern. Judicious cutting of the play was considered acceptable for time considerations, and directors usually did not feel bound to reproduce all stage directions indicated in the script. Any addition or re-arrangement of the text without the playwright's permission, however, was considered inappropriate, since the playwright was the final authority.

As early as the first decade of the twentieth century, however, a different point of view began to surface in theatrical circles. When designers Gordon Craig and Adolphe Appia began to focus attention on the director as the master artist of the theatre, the stage was set for regarding the script as a pretext for production—as one element of equal weight with design and performance. Antonin Artaud declared that there should be "no more masterpieces," discouraging reverence for the text in favor of a visceral, sensual experience. The shift in paradigm had a profound effect on the perceived status of the playwright. Today it is possible to find practitioners who embrace either position, as well as those who fall on a continuum somewhere between the two extremes. Directors Peter Sellars and Anne Bogart are current examples of theatrical **auteurs**—directors who, in building the three-dimensional performance, feel responsible for creating meaning for the audience, and when the play is in public domain, may use or reconstruct the playwright's text to serve the director's purpose in managing

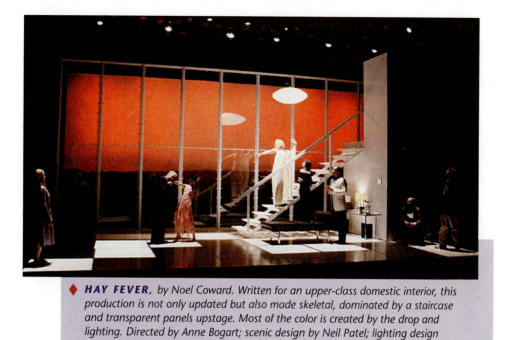

♦ **HAY FEVER,** by Noel Coward. Written for an upper-class domestic interior, this production is not only updated but also made skeletal, dominated by a staircase and transparent panels upstage. Most of the color is created by the drop and lighting. Directed by Anne Bogart; scenic design by Neil Patel; lighting design by Christopher Akerlind.
Photo by Larry Hunt. Courtesy of Actors Theatre of Louisville.

the theatrical whole. Here the director, rather than the author, is the primary creative force. When the playwright is living, a difference in how author and director regard the relationship of text to production can result in artistic and even legal conflict.

REVISION IN REHEARSAL

When the playwright is able to collaborate in the production process, she or he has a valuable opportunity to see and hear the play "on its feet." Some playwrights make few revisions once the play is in rehearsal, but others use the experience to continue shaping the play. Early in the rehearsal process, structural problems may become apparent, and the author may move scenes around, cut, or add material. When dialogue is not working, it can be refined or eliminated. Frequently, during the rehearsal process a playwright may rewrite a scene repeatedly, attempting to fix a problem identified by the director, dramaturg, an actor, or the playwright. Valuable comments from directors and actors can lead to changes or improvements in the script. It is not unusual in a musical for entire songs to be added or cut. A speech was turned into "The Rape Song," a pivotal number in *The Fantasticks,* fairly close to opening to take advantage of the singing talents of Jerry Orbach.[6]

As the rehearsal process continues, actors need a set script to rely on and changes tend to become fewer and less drastic. In the high-stakes world of commercial theatre, however, changes may be made at the last minute, even after the show is in front of an audience. In the first half of the twentieth century, shows bound for Broadway used to be performed "out of town" for a period of

◆ **CAT ON A HOT TIN ROOF,** *by Tennessee Williams. Confrontation between Brick and Maggie. In the 1990 production Kathleen Turner plays Maggie and Daniel Hugh Kelly plays Brick. Directed by Howard Davies.*
Photo by Michael Tighe. Photo courtesy Billy Rose Theatre Collection, the New York Public Library for the Performing Arts, Astor, Lennox and Tilden Foundations.

revisions and adjustments before officially opening in New York City. New plays now are usually developed in small theatres before they are produced on the main stage of a resident theatre or adopted by a commercial producing organization. With the current practice of **previews,** professional productions often play for weeks before a paying audience at a somewhat reduced ticket price before the official opening to which critics are invited. Some established nonprofit theatres offer special programs to showcase new plays.

WHEN THE PLAYWRIGHT IS AN ACTOR OR DIRECTOR

At times the playwright also serves as a member of the production team. The precedent for directing and/or performing in one's own work goes back at least as far as the ancient Greeks in the West and Noh theatre in the East. Modern writers are divided on the advisability of doing such double duty. In the 1910s and 1920s Rachel Crothers both designed and directed some of her own plays. Edward Albee has taken to directing much of his work. After being disappointed by a number of premieres, Sam Shepard began directing the first productions of his plays, feeling it necessary to complete his vision in physical form in the theatre.

The advantage to directing one's own play, of course, is increased control of the final product. When the writer also has the skills to realize the vision on stage, either through staging or performance, the production is most likely to get as close as possible to the original idea of the play. Playwright-director Emily Mann notes that when directing her own work, she can determine whether a problem is caused by the acting, writing, or directing and has the power to fix a

EXPLORING HISTORICAL and CULTURAL PERSPECTIVES

For six weeks in the early spring, producers, directors, critics, playwrights, designers, actors, theatre lovers, and tourists from around the world converge on Louisville, Kentucky. The occasion is the Humana Festival of New American Plays. Actors Theatre of Louisville (ATL), a nonprofit, professional theatre, was founded in 1964 and began presenting a festival of new plays in 1977. The event has grown to include productions of full-length plays as well as a ten-minute play contest and uses all three stages of the ATL complex. Actors Theatre states that approximately 3,000 scripts are received annually for consideration in the New Play Program. Nearly 66,000 plays have been submitted since 1976. A $1,000 cash prize is offered annually to winners of the National Ten-Minute Play Contest. Over three-fourths of plays produced at the Humana have been published in individual acting editions as well as Actors Theatre anthologies, making scripts widely available for reading, study, and production. *Getting Out* (Marsha Norman, 1977), *Crimes of the Heart* (Beth Henley, 1979), *Agnes of God* (John Pielmeier, 1980), and *Keely and Du* (Jane Martin, 1993) are just a few of the plays premiered by ATL that have gone on to be widely produced and highly acclaimed.

Interested? Check out

More about the Humana Festival, Actors Theatre's regular season of plays, and its other innovative programs at the ATL web site: www.actorstheatre.org.

◆ *CABIN PRESSURE,* created by the SITI Company, conceived and directed by Anne Bogart, was performed at the 23rd Annual Humana Festival of New American Plays in 1999. Here, the actors in stylized jurist's wigs confront the audience on a bare stage. Scenic design by Paul Owen; costume design by Walt Spangler; lighting design by Mimi Jordan Sherin.
Photo by Richard C. Trigg. Courtesy of Actors Theatre of Louisville.

◆ *CABIN PRESSURE. In another moment from this play, four actors, Will Bond, Kelly Maurer, Ellen Lauren, and Stephen Webber, suggest a very different era while sitting politely in front a projection of the Eiffel Tower.*
Courtesy of Actors Theatre of Louisville.

341

writing problem immediately.[7] Such intense involvement has its limitations, however; a playwright who is also functioning as an actor cannot listen objectively to the dialogue. A playwright who also directs the show does not have the benefit of a separate director's viewpoint. Playwrights who have had their work directed and acted successfully by others frequently point out that the energy and vision of the artistic team enhanced the production in ways previously unimagined. An insightful director, actor, or designer may discover qualities in the script of which even the playwright was unaware. In an ideal production the company does not just realize the playwright's vision but transcends it.

Development of New Plays

The playwright's collaboration with directors and actors is sometimes extended earlier into the development stage of the script. Play readings offer a chance for the writer to hear the play come alive without the large investment of a production. A reading may be private and very informal, may be presented to the public or an invited audience, may be rehearsed, and may sometimes even be minimally staged but with the actors keeping scripts in hand. Often the audience for a reading is invited to comment and give suggestions to the playwright. New plays sometimes also undergo a workshop process in which a director and actors work with the writer to develop the script using reading, discussion, and improvisation. The playwright then uses the discoveries from workshop in revising the script.

Many theatres currently offer programs dedicated to helping new work along. In addition to its regular season, Center Stage in Baltimore offers First Look, a series in which new scripts are developed in workshop with "in-progress" performances open to the public. Some theatres specialize in developing new work. The New York Theatre Workshop and Chicago Dramatists, for example, exist to develop and produce new plays and foster the development of playwrights. Many musicals are now developed in workshop—*A Chorus Line* and *Rent,* for example. Stephen Sondheim often chooses to develop shows in workshop for a long time prior to public performance. New Tuners (part of Theatre Building Chicago) and the B.M.I. Lehman Engel Theatre Workshop (New York) offer musical theatre development programs for composers, lyricists, and playwrights.

NONTRADITIONAL PLAY DEVELOPMENT

Since the 1960s some theatre artists have chosen to disrupt the boundaries of responsibility between playwright, director, and actor by creating scripts in innovative ways. Some artists prefer to write and perform their own work, which leads to a very personal, complete production. Solo artist Spalding Gray has developed material in front of an audience in a very intuitive way and has mined his own experience to produce monologues such as *Swimming to Cambodia* (1985), *Monster in a Box* (1990), and *It's a Slippery Slope* (1996). Anna Deavere Smith chooses to develop material not from her own life, but from interviews with a wide variety of Americans. For *Twilight: Los Angeles, 1992,* she conducted research in the wake of riots over the beating of Rodney King by

Los Angeles police. Smith, who is African American, performed characters as different as a white Hollywood talent agent, a Korean grocer, and police chief Daryl Gates.

Some companies choose to develop the play from the beginning in a workshop setting. Playwright Moisés Kaufman developed *The Laramie Project* (featured in this book's cover photo) with Tectonic Theater Project and members of the community of Laramie, Wyoming. Through interviews and workshops the collaborators explored the horrific, homophobia-inspired murder of Matthew Shepard in 1998. Sometimes a playwright is involved in the actual scripting process and retains control and copyright. Caryl Churchill wrote *Cloud 9*, for example, after participating in a workshop on sexual politics with the Joint Stock Theatre Company. Although Churchill actually composed the play alone, it was inspired and guided by collaborative exploration in workshop. *Tracers* (1980) by John DiFusco, Vincent Caristi, Richard Chaves, Eric E. Emerson, Rick Gallavan, Merlin Marston, Harry Stephens, and Sheldon Lettich was created by a group of veterans from the Vietnam war—actors, director, and writer. The play's authorship comprises the names of all those who participated.

ISSUES OF OWNERSHIP

The collaborative process of script development as it is currently practiced raises difficult issues of intellectual property. Ultimately, the playwright has control of any play he or she has written—but who "owns" the moment that was developed by actors in a workshop improvisation and later written into the script? If the director comes up with an important piece of action or a major visual image or a dramaturg suggests a successful idea for restructuring, should the contributing artist share in the intellectual ownership (and therefore any monetary rewards)? This volatile issue has been and continues to be debated by individual artists and the guilds or unions that represent them (Dramatists Guild, Actors' Equity, Society of Stage Directors and Choreographers, and Literary Managers and Dramaturgs of the Americas). At times disagreements over artistic ownership end up in court.

FREEDOM AND LIMITATIONS

In today's theatre a "crafter of plays" may choose to write alone, with collaborators, or in workshop and to build a script that is unfettered by questions of personnel and production budgets or specifically tailored to the needs of a company or theatre. There are no artistic rules for playwrights to follow; they are free to choose models from the past, establish new conventions, let their imaginations soar. Ironically, escalating production costs create a different kind of limitation. Given the handcrafted aspect of live theatre, companies can afford to produce only a limited number of scripts. Competition is fierce, and aside from musicals, marketing a large-cast, big-budget play is next to impossible. Theatrical producers tend to look kindly on plays with few characters and minimal set requirements.

The economic restrictions currently placed on playwrights may be of short or long duration. We know, however, that historically, theatrical conditions are not permanent. It is impossible to know but exciting to imagine what new expectations await our future crafters of plays.

The *Rent* Controversy

The collaborative nature of theatre, particularly the methods of script development now in use in many theatres, can have stunning artistic results but can also produce legal confusion. The musical *Rent* went through a long process of development with many people contributing to its growth. Inspired by the story of the opera *La Bohème,* the show began as an idea from Billy Aronson, who worked on it with Jonathan Larson in the early 1990s. The two agreed that Larson would continue alone on the project. In 1992 Larson made contact with the New York Theatre Workshop (NYTW), a nonprofit off-Broadway theatre designed to workshop and present new dramatic material. NYTW encouraged the development of *Rent* and in 1994 mounted a studio production of the script at that stage. Those in charge at NYTW agreed that the musical was promising but needed a lot of work before a full production could be mounted. NYTW hired Lynn Thomson as a dramaturg, and she worked closely with Jonathan Larson on rewriting the script during the summer and fall of 1995. Most of the work took place in Larson's apartment with no one else present. Just before the off-Broadway opening in 1996, playwright and composer Jonathan Larson died suddenly and unexpectedly at the age of 35. *Rent* went on to become a hit, moved to Broadway, won numerous awards, and became the center of a highly controversial lawsuit.

Thomson claimed to have contributed a considerable amount of the writing and asked Larson's heirs for credit as coauthor and 16 percent of the author's share of royalties. She maintained that, had he lived, Larson would have made sure that she received adequate compensation. Of course, Jonathan Larson was not available to substantiate or refute her claim.

The case went to court. During the trial, luminaries of the American theatre testified for both sides. Tony Kushner, author of *Angels in America,* noted that he voluntarily assigned 15 percent of his royalties to two dramaturgs who helped to create the final version of that script. In July 1997

♦ **RENT,** *by Jonathan Larson. The full cast in the Broadway production. Directed by Michael Greif; set design by Paul Clay; costume design by Angela Wendt; lighting design by Blake Burba.*
Photo by Joan Marcus.

Judge Lewis A. Kaplan ruled against Thomson because there was no legal proof that Larson intended Thomson to be a coauthor, but Kaplan noted that there was considerable merit to Thomson's case. An appeal was filed and dismissed. Thomson filed a lawsuit seeking to keep the material that she had created from being used in the musical. In 1998 Thomson settled out of court with the Larson estate, the terms to remain confidential.

The legal battle over *Rent* emphasizes the difficulty of assigning rights to intellectual property when the process of making art is characterized by intensive collaboration. Alisa Solomon wrote in *The Village Voice* that the case "revealed the impossibility of understanding theatrical collaboration through the discourse of copyright law. The latter demands measurable, documented procedures; the former, an energized, free-flow exchange."[8]

Interested? Check out

Transcripts from the court proceedings at www.dramaturgy.net/RENT.

QUESTIONS AND ACTIVITIES

1. Discuss the advantages and disadvantages of playwrights directing their own work. Make a list of all the things that would be easier and all the things that would be harder to accomplish. How are writing and directing different activities?

2. Choose a story from a newspaper, magazine, or the Internet. Discuss how it could be turned into a play. Describe the setting and the major characters. How would the play begin? How would it end? The article is only the inspiration; determine whether there are several different ways in which the play might be developed.

3. Like painters, playwrights construct a fictional reality that is based on how they view the world. Take a picture of a person from a magazine or Internet article. Write a description of the picture as a starting point for a character. Go beyond the description to specify imagined character traits. Compare your version to others' versions.

♦♦♦♦♦♦♦♦♦

KEY TERMS AND CONCEPTS

royalties, p. 331
copyright, p. 332

dramaturg, p. 336
auteur, p. 338

previews, p. 340

♦♦♦♦♦♦♦♦♦

FOR FURTHER EXPLORATION

Toby Cole, ed. *Playwrights on Playwriting.* New York: Cooper Square Publishers, 2001.

Roger A. Hall. *Writing Your First Play,* 2nd edition. Woburn, Mass.: Butterworth-Heinemann, 1998.

David Savran. *In Their Own Words: Contemporary American Playwrights.* New York: Theatre Communications Group, 1988.

W. B. Worthen, ed. *Modern Drama: Plays, Criticism, Theory.* Stamford, Conn.: Thomson Learning, 1995.

Web site for the Dramatists Guild of America at www.dramaguild.com.

Web site for Literary Managers and Dramaturgs of the Americas at www.lmda.org.

GROSS INDECENCY, by Moisés Kaufman, Huntington Theatre Company.
Directed by Michael Bloom.
Photo by Charlie Erickson.

The Designer

Materializing Conception and the World of the Play

One night, after audience members have taken their seats in a theatre, they see a dimly lit stage. The stage floor is **raked** (not flat but set at an angle), and towering structures made of metal pipe surround the playing space. Rays of intense light shoot through the metal structures, creating oddly shaped, ominous shadows and pools of red on the floor. Music fills the space. It is in a minor key with a pronounced, driving rhythm.

On a different night, the audience members enter to the sounds of fast, melodic piano music. The scenery depicts a courtyard. The outside of several stucco buildings can be seen, with stone patio areas filled with tables, chairs, and pots of red geraniums. The colors in the set are warm earth tones—oranges, warm browns, yellows. There are no obvious lighting effects, but the scenery seems to emit a warm glow. The mood is one of happiness and well-being or reassurance.

Before even seeing an actor, perhaps without even knowing what the play is about, the audience members have been prepared for a specific experience. The first night they anticipate something "heavy"—a tragedy or serious play—something that might end unhappily. The second night they are ready for a comedy—something light, fast moving—perhaps with many complications but turning out well in the end.

The designers' job in the theatre is to control environment. Set, lighting, and costume designers contribute effects that the audience sees; sound designers create effects that the audience hears. These sensory impressions not only communicate information to the audience in an efficient way, but also influence the audience's emotional involvement with the play. The designers help to shape the audience experience; their individual contributions become part of the whole and affect the work of the rest of the company. Designers in the theatre today must be both inspired artists and collaborators.

◆ **KABUKI ONNAGATA ACTOR** *in a flying scene as if propelled by a magical parasol, flying over cherry trees.*
Photo by Chiaki Yoshida.

◆◆◆◆◆◆◆◆◆◆

The Development of the Designer

In the long history of the theatre the prominence of designers is somewhat new. Of course, someone has always designed or decorated scenery or the performance environment. Someone has always designed, purchased, made, or selected costumes and masks. Someone has always provided properties. Once theatrical activity moved indoors, someone had to find a way to illuminate it. From the earliest Greek performances someone was writing and performing music and working on offstage sounds (in other words, designing sound). Few names of theatre architects or set designers before the seventeenth century are known to us, but someone had to design and build all of those remarkable theatres in Greece, Rome, and their colonies and territories.

Before the Italian Renaissance and in many cases long after, most of these designers and technicians were invisible—or at least are so to today's students of theatre. While the remains of some of their remarkable work can be appreciated, little is known of their relationship to productions of plays and the ongoing activity of theatre companies. Before the nineteenth century, few designers were publicly credited. Even with the appearance of well-known designers, many designers continued to be anonymous until the twentieth. Creators of sets, costumes, and properties were usually considered an adjunct to the "real" business of the theatre, which was carried out by actors, playwrights, and managers. Now, of course, designers are usually recognized and sometimes well compensated for their contributions to the professional theatre. Designers are usually at the heart of production preparation long before actors begin rehearsing a new production.

What precipitated the change? Perhaps the two biggest factors were the rise of the modern director and the advent of electric light (both in the late nineteenth century).

SCENE DECORATORS, PAINTERS, AND STAGE CARPENTERS

As early as the fifth century B.C.E. in Greece the playwright Aeschylus was credited with providing some kind of "skenographia," or decoration of the **skene** (stage house) upstage of the **orchestra** (circular performance space), at the Theatre of Dionysus. Many translators over the years have interpreted this term to mean scene painting, but the exact reference is uncertain. Aeschylus also supposedly introduced machinery and scenic elements that indicated tombs and altars. If the surviving descriptive passages are true, then the classical Greeks had some interest in designing for particular productions, not just general decoration. A late classical account of theatre architecture in Greece and Rome refers to **pinakes** (flat, painted scenery) and **periaktoi** (prism-shaped, three-sided scenic units) that could be painted and revolved. Exactly how any of these items might have been used or how often is unknown. Actors depicted in vase paintings wear traditional robes and footwear. Masks apparently covered the entire head, but little is known about how they were made. An ancient anecdote from an anonymous biographer included in the marginal notes of early copies of Greek tragedies tells us that the chorus of furies in *The Oresteia* of Aeschylus was terrifying to the audience; the masks and costumes surely had something to do with instigating the fear.

The Romans used curtains and floor traps in some of their theatres, and a few Greek theatres had an underground tunnel extending from the skene to an opening in the orchestra. The possibilities are intriguing. The plays that survive from both Greece and Rome suggest that properties were frequently used, but perhaps some action was mimed rather than executed with properties. In Chinese music drama, for example, characters are often depicted on horseback, but the actor rides without the presence of either real or property horses. Actors use mimetic action and a symbolic system of gestures to replace many properties.

The medieval period created designs for its cycle plays (based on biblical stories) that often incorporated spectacle such as transformations, rainstorms, and fire effects emanating from the mouth of hell. Despite a number of written accounts from the period, not many details remain about methods and designs.

Few helpful medieval paintings or drawings survive, and as intriguing as they are, they raise more questions than answers. Promptbooks and written eyewitness accounts from around 1200 to 1550, however, underscore a popular attraction to and probable expectation of stage spectacle, both literal and symbolic. Some costumes seem to have been symbolic as well. Adam and Eve, for example, were dressed in white leather to indicate nakedness. Devil costumes and masks could be quite imaginative in their expression of evil and the grotesque. Most characters wore medieval dress, even though many characters were biblical; historical accuracy did not become an issue in the theatre until the nineteenth century.

In Japan, China, and India, formalized, generic stage space dominated the theatrical forms. We do not know who is responsible for the standard painted pine tree background for Japanese Noh; the curtained, carpeted space of Chinese music drama; or the columned open space of early Indian theatre, but clearly someone designed remarkable, suggestive theatre spaces for these forms that became the norm for performance in each of these cultures. Costumes for the classical Asian forms were often colorful and splendidly decorated. Over the centuries the spaces and standardized designs continued to be replicated; costumes, masks, and makeup became virtually fixed for particular characters in particular plays, and Kabuki in the eighteenth century adapted the Noh space to serve its own purposes.

An important shift in the West arrived during the Italian Renaissance with innovations in perspective drawing and painting. Flat painted scenery often dynamically recreated detailed and accurate images of palatial buildings, town squares, and sylvan glades. This type of scenery, called **wing, drop, and border scenery,** included flat painted panels on either side of the stage (wings), a large expanse of painted fabric upstage (drop), and strips of cloth or panels hung horizontally across the tops of the wings (borders). Wing, drop, and border scenery became the standard first in Italian court entertainments and opera and then in the professional theatre and was ultimately framed by the proscenium arch. Such pictorial representation became the standard in Europe and the Americas and remained so until well into the nineteenth century. Wings, drops, and borders are still used in variations from time to time, although since the nineteenth century, three-dimensional scenery and properties have been combined with flat scenery. The pictorial, illusionistic, literal depiction of theatrical locale remains one of the standards for scenic design.

Italian designers such as Giacomo Torelli and Giuseppe Bibiena achieved fame throughout Europe for their scenic designs and theatre architecture in the seventeenth and eighteenth centuries, but most of their work was in the service of court entertainments and opera, neither of which followed the strict guidelines of neoclassicism, the ruling system of the theatre. Neoclassicism, the Renaissance interpretation of Greek and Roman models of plays and theory, called for a play to take place in only one location. This restriction was a stumbling block for designers and playwrights working in the theatre because it did not usually allow for changes of settings within a play. Also, because they staged a rolling repertory of plays and did not have long runs of single plays at the time, professional theatres could not afford different settings for every play. The building and painting of new scenery was an extravagant expense.

Consequently, the generic design approach that was popularized by Sebastiano Serlio in the sixteenth century became the standard. Each theatre company had a handful of settings that could serve many different plays: a standard urban exterior or domestic interior for comedy, a generic palatial exterior or interior for tragedy, and a wooded exterior or domestic interior for tragicomedy. Accordingly, few

♦ **DROTTNINGHOLM COURT THEATRE** *in Sweden. Wing, border, and drop street scenery from the eighteenth century. The upstage rake of the stage floor is obvious in this photograph. Note also that the candelabra overhead primarily light the apron (the principal acting area) in pre-electric days. Typically the candelabra were joined by footlights (candles or oil lamps), which provided low-angle illumination for the actors.*
Photo by Rolf Hintze. Courtesy of Sveriges Teatermuseum, Stockholm.

audience members paid attention to the designs and often took them for granted. The sets were usually background indicators for the play. About the only time any excitement for scenery was generated was when a theatre manager announced that his theatre had expended much money to have new scenery painted for a new season of plays. The painters often remained anonymous. No artist made his living solely or primarily as a scene designer. Theatre designs were supplemental, a source for extra money to be made on an occasional basis. Designers in the seventeenth and eighteenth centuries were more like consultants or adjuncts than collaborators. Actors were in charge of acquiring and maintaining their own costumes (a major professional expense), and the focus was on looking attractive rather than the more modern considerations of appropriateness to character and situation.

DESIGNERS AS STARS

By the mid-eighteenth century a few theatre managers had decided it was time for a change. In London actor-manager David Garrick decided to remove the audience members from onstage seating and create a new focus for the stage environment. From France he hired Philippe De Loutherbourg, an innovative designer who created many new settings for the repertory of the Drury Lane Theatre. De Loutherbourg used **ground rows** (low, flat painted scenery at stage level that extended the line of the wing out toward center stage). This development invited the audience to focus on the floor, not just on scenery above the floor. He

also experimented with transparencies for transformation scenes as well as color media for candlelight and oil lamps. Early on, he understood the importance of lighting to the theatre. Convinced that audiences would be fascinated by the latest technology, De Loutherbourg created a miniature theatre for exhibition halls using scenery without an accompanying play. Audiences came to watch his tiny scene shifts and innovative special effects, which suggested what full-size stages would support in the nineteenth century.

Meanwhile, in Italy the family of Bibienna designers, although working in opera and court entertainment, began creating settings that featured multiple vanishing points for perspective drawing and moved toward asymmetrical views of interiors and exteriors. This work, however, confined itself to two-dimensional scenic units. Nearly everything was done with paint.

It was in the nineteenth century that three-dimensional scenery changed audience expectations of the possibilities for scenic design. The **box set,** an enclosed set with walls and sometimes ceiling, became a standard for interiors after 1830. This innovation invited designers to decorate the stage floor as in a house or palace, for example, increased the numbers of set properties (such as furniture) in imitation of contemporary interiors, and coaxed actors to move upstage off the apron and inside the box.

In 1823 James Robinson Planché designed historically accurate costumes for a revival of Shakespeare's *King John.* He followed this design with historically accurate costumes and scenery for another of Shakespeare's plays, *Henry IV, Part I,* in 1824. Called **antiquarianism** at the time, such practice inspired many designers to research authentic styles of dress, architecture, and interior design from the past and incorporate or adapt accurate historical images when producing plays written or set in the past. Within a few decades most stage design in the West favored literal depictions of recognizable locations, often utilizing three-dimensional elements, and historical accuracy has remained a standard practice for some productions up to our own time.

At the turn of the twentieth century another shift occurred that continues to inspire design in our own era. Attracted to Asian theatrical and decorative forms, intrigued by the use of open space as a design element, and troubled by the excesses of realistic and literal detail in popular theatre, designers Adolphe Appia from Switzerland and Gordon Craig from England launched a design movement that returned to simplicity and suggestion rather than detailed evocation of the real. In the first quarter of the twentieth century their designs and those of many followers such as Robert Edmond Jones in the United States and Ernst Stern in Germany swept over stages in Europe and America. In turn, many Asian forms borrowed from the West (Kabuki, for example, adopted the proscenium arch). Such cross-fertilization created many new hybrids in theatrical design, a trend that continues in contemporary production.

Development of the Revolve

The **revolve** (also called revolving stage and turntable) was invented in Osaka, Japan, in 1758 for use in Bunraku (puppet theatre) and soon after, in Kabuki theatre. Its creation is attributed to a Bunraku playwright, Namiki Shozo. Although small in scale for Bunraku and at first resting on top of the stage surface (a temporary measure), the revolve as adapted to Kabuki became a large revolve that was set permanently into the stage near the end of the eighteenth century. By 1827 this scenic device had become very complicated, with the invention of an inner revolve that was somewhat smaller than the larger one (like concentric circles). The inner revolve was capable of moving with the larger one or in the opposite direction, creating the possibility for extraordinary scenic changes. The revolve continues to be a mainstay of Kabuki production and the device often measures about sixty feet across usually set at center stage. Early on, Japanese artists recognized both the practical and spectacular possibilities of revolves, which can hold two entire settings at once or bring tableaux and actors into place while other elements remain stationary.

The revolve was not used in Western theatre until the turn of the twentieth century (in 1896 for opera at Munich, Germany). At about the same time that many European playwrights and practitioners started discovering Asian theatrical forms, German directors and designers recognized the possibilities for revolves and began designing their own versions and incorporating them into the productions of classics, especially Shakespearean plays that have many changes of location. Director Max Reinhardt with his designer Max Ernst made very effective use of the revolve in many revivals of Shakespeare such as *Henry IV* (a chronicle), *Othello* (a tragedy), and *The Merchant of Venice* (a tragicomedy). Their 1905 production of *A Midsummer Night's Dream* featured a central revolve for all of the forest scenes (all but the opening and closing scenes of the play). Most of the large revolve was covered with trees, resulting

♦ **THIS CONSTRUCTIVIST SET** for Candide, *by Leonard Bernstein and Hugh Wheeler, not only filled the stage but also extended well out into the house for this production with many levels, platforms, ramps, and stairs—all of wood. Notice the small revolving stage that was propelled by the actors, not by machinery or electronics. Scenic design by Lori Bush, University of Nebraska.* Collection of the authors.

in myriad entrances and exits and a variety of views effected by simply rotating the revolve a few feet at a time. At midcentury Bertolt Brecht was especially fascinated by the revolve and built its usage into the composition as well as the direction of his plays such as *Mother Courage* and *The Caucasian Chalk Circle,* particularly for journey scenes as well as scenic changes. Of course, revolves in many variations have frequently adorned the productions of multiset plays and musicals such as *Noises Off, The Lion King,* and *Jane Eyre* throughout the twentieth century and up to the present.

Interested? Check out

Earle Ernst. *The Kabuki Theatre.* Honolulu: University of Hawaii Press, 1974.

W. Oren Parker and R. Craig Wolf. *Scene Design and Stage Lighting,* 7th edition. Fort Worth, Tex.: Harcourt Brace, 1996.

Walter Rene Fuerst and Samuel J. Hume. *Twentieth-Century Stage Decoration.* New York: Dover, 1967.

♦ **TWO JOSEF SVOBODA DESIGNS.** *The action for Josef Svoboda's design of* Oedipus the King *(left) was played on a huge staircase that extended from the orchestra pit below the stage and disappeared into the fly space. Actors could enter from many locations—left, right, and below. This "impossible" architecture was not only stunning in the theatre but also suggested the classical origins of the play while locating the theatrical event in the twentieth century. Svoboda's design for* As You Like It *(right) used low platforms suggestive of both architecture and an almost magical scenic environment completed by projected scenery that suggests a forest. Changing the projections could alter the location and mood completely. Only the platforms were constant.*
Photographs by Dr. Jaromir Svoboda. From *The Scenography of Josef Svoboda* by Jarka Burian.

By the second decade of the twentieth century many audience members expected each production to have a unified style that was appropriate for the play. Costumes were designed considering both individual character traits and the total look of the show. Set, lighting, and costumes were carefully coordinated. Perhaps the most dynamic designer of the twentieth century, Josef Svoboda, created remarkable experiments with space and lighting and worked on an international stage. Beginning in 1958 in what was then Czechoslovakia, he combined platforms, three-dimensional scenery, and open space with projection screens; mixed film with still projections; and mastered the art of projected scenery. Sometimes he completely transformed space with lighting alone. In the wake of Svoboda and with the aid of modern computer-generated imaging for both lighting and sets in creating designs as well as executing the designs on stage, the possibilities for theatrical design seem nearly limitless. Such computerized imaging is at its busiest in Las Vegas shows and Broadway musicals such as *Aida* (2000) and *Jane Eyre* (2000), but it adorns small, intimate performances as well. Costumes currently range from the realistic and everyday to highly stylized flights of fancy. In the early twenty-first century theatrical design has reached a very sophisticated level of achievement, yet it is clear that there is much more to come. No doubt, many current designers would say, "You ain't seen nothin' yet."

The Designers' Choices

Designers have a wide variety of styles to choose from in today's theatre. Audiences might see on stage only a few chairs and tables in front of a simple curtain or an elaborate fabrication of an entire room, complete with all walls, ceiling, and decorations. The stage could be cluttered with multicolored plastic cubes that the actors seem to use for furniture, vehicles, and props; or the space might be empty, a highly polished wooden floor with no attempts to hide stage walls or lighting instruments. Audiences might observe abstract images creating a stylized environment for performance, as if witnessing a bizarre dream, or the actors could mime everything as they ask the audience to imagine the presence of objects in their hands. The actors themselves might even pretend to be scenery, suddenly becoming trees blowing in the wind or the doors of a palace swinging open. Thus, the designers face many opportunities and challenges in creating an environment for the play.

REPRESENTATIONAL AND PRESENTATIONAL

Representational scenery, costumes, lighting, and sound imitate precisely the kind of environment and details in which the action of the play would occur in real life. At its most extreme, in the movement of naturalism at the end of the nineteenth century, representational scenery appeared to be a real location in every detail with all the appropriate props and decorations. A domestic interior might include books, magazines, lamps—all three-dimensional objects that could be handled by the actors. If the setting is an exterior one might see dirt, rocks, grass, fallen leaves—every element one would expect to find in a natural environment. Dressed in clothes looking just like those of the period in which the action takes place, the actors probably move and behave in the set as if it were actually the room represented, and they seem to ignore the audience as the actors' behavior suggests an imaginary **fourth wall.** Often audiences are fascinated by how close to reality the scenic pictures seem to come. Occasionally, audience members applaud representational scenery because they recognize its details and approve its authenticity. Such scenery, or simplified versions, most often appears in realistic plays written since the nineteenth century, such as Lillian Hellman's *The Children's Hour* (1934), which is set in a house converted to a school for girls, or *Long Day's Journey into Night* (1956) by Eugene O'Neill, set in an unfriendly living room in 1914. The texts of these plays specify considerable scenic detail in their descriptions of interior settings.

Representational scenery can also be applied to plays of any period if the artists so choose as long as the artists' choices suggest literal reality. Although representational scenery and costuming are often elaborate, this is by no means a necessity. Nonetheless, labor-intensive construction and decoration as well as expensive building materials and set props often provided for complete representational settings and costumes (especially indicating earlier historical periods) are found prohibitive for theatre companies that must economize. Notwithstanding the opinion of some critics and artists that representational

designs are confining and limiting to creativity, representational interpretations often reveal imagination, skill, and extraordinary artistry.

A **presentational** approach to design offers many possibilities. Presentational scenery, costumes, and lighting can suggest, distort, or even abstract reality. The scenery is often deliberately incomplete or presents an environment that would be impossible to find in life. Such designs might rely primarily on mood, color, shapes, or visual symbols implied by the text of a play or born in the imagination of the director or designer. Unfortunately, the presentational setting is sometimes a choice of expediency due to economic and temporal limitations placed on the theatrical artists; but more significantly, it is often an artistic choice that asks the audience to receive the theatrical event in unexpected or challenging ways. The presentational setting might expose the building's permanent architecture or ask us to fill a void with our own imaginings prompted only by scenic suggestions. Presentational costumes can comment on the characters or color-code them or suggest the whole by a mere piece.

Many plays as written call for presentational designs or performance styles. While obvious in some plays from most historical periods, the call for presentational scenery has been particularly evident in stage directions since about 1890, in plays such as *Ubu Roi* (1896) by Alfred Jarry, with its grotesque but childlike approach to space and time, or *Waiting for Godot* (1953) by Samuel Beckett, set in a bleak exterior marked only by a scrawny tree. Presentational settings are also typical of nearly any musical play, for example, *Aida* (2000) by Tim Rice and Elton John. Design aspects of some productions combine the presentational and representational, however. A recurring location in *Urinetown: The Musical* (2001) by Mark Hollmann and Greg Kotis is the exterior of a public toilet that looks very authentic

♦ *URINETOWN,* by Mark Hollman and Greg Kotis. The impoverished inhabitants of this town line up at a public urinal and confront the woman who manages it. Directed by John Rando; scenic design by Scott Pask; costume design by Gregory Gale and Jonathan Bixby.
Photo by Joan Marcus.

but appears in the midst of a void, like an island in an invisible sea. The basic approach to creating the environment of the play will be established early in the design process as designers communicate with the director and with each other.

HISTORICAL VERSUS IMAGINARY

With any new production the designers, collaborating with a director, always confront the decision of whether to create a stage environment or costumes that are abstract or highly stylized or literal in terms of the historical period and precise location of the action of the play. If the production team wants the historical period to be recognizable to the audience, it needs to decide whether to change the location or time period in which the play is set. For example, *A Doll House* by Henrik Ibsen is set in an upstairs multiroom apartment in Norway in the 1870s. The design team might decide to reset the action in 1920s America or 1980s Tokyo with a focus on commercialism or in 2002 South Africa with an all-black cast struggling with the residue from apartheid. In shifting periods or locations, of course, some of the local details would need to be altered.

Alternatively, the desire might be to abstract the space. The famous final moment of *A Doll House* is a slamming door. The play has been produced with symbolic settings that would not exist in a real apartment: a space dominated by a multitude of doors or a gigantic door to symbolize the significance of the final moment. The action could also be set on a large, open, reflective floor surrounded by mirrors; everywhere Nora turns, she is faced with images of herself that might distort or magnify as she increasingly becomes dissatisfied with who she is and how she does not understand her place in society. Perhaps the mirrors are large enough and angled to allow the audience members to also see themselves; when they watch Nora looking at herself in the mirror, they see themselves with her.

ARTISTS *of the* THEATRE

MING CHO LEE

MING CHO LEE (b. 1930) has been an extraordinary influence on American scenic design through both his innovative work and his mentoring of young designers. Born in Shanghai, Lee studied Chinese watercolor landscape painting. Its simplicity and texture would have an effect on his later design work. Lee emigrated to the United States in 1949 and, beginning in 1954, worked as an assistant for Jo Mielziner. Mielziner, the designer for Elia Kazan's productions of *Death of a Salesman* (1949) and *Cat on a Hot Tin Roof* (1955), was well known for his pictorial style featuring selective realistic elements with a poetic or lyrical background. Lee ventured into new territory, creating more abstract, presentational settings that created an architectural environment for the play. Texture became a major concern, and Lee experimented with many materials that were not typically used onstage, including steel pipe, urethane foam, and Mylar.

Lee's design for the 1964 production of Sophocles' *Electra* for the New York Shakespeare Festival is considered pivotal in its combination of elements: A multilevel thrust stage was surrounded by stone (sculpted foam) panels suspended from vertical metal pipes. Lee continued to investigate ways to suggest location without literal reproduction. The design for the Tennessee Williams one-act play, *The Gnadiges Fraulein* (1966) featured a grotesque house in distorted perspective and combined a painted background with architectural elements. His design for the original New York Shakespeare Festival production of the rock musical *Hair* (1967) featured a steel scaffold and a collage of posters.

Lee's designs through the 1970s, 1980s, and 1990s reflect constant stretch and experimentation. His 1972 design for Ntozake Shange's *for colored girls who have considered suicide when the rainbow is enuf* featured a soft-fabric flower. The design for Patrick Meyers's *K2* (1982) depicted the side of a mountain onstage and has been called ultrarealism. First created for Arena Stage in Washington, D.C., the *K2* design won a Tony award when the show moved to Broadway. *Mourning Becomes Electra* (1997) at Arena Stage featured a revolving mansion exterior. Lee has designed for resident theatres across the United States, including the Guthrie Theatre in Minneapolis in 2002 and the Shakespeare Theatre in Washington, D.C., in 2001. He has designed extensively for opera and dance as well as plays. Lee serves as cochair of the design department at the Yale School of Drama and has trained a legion of younger designers by employing them as assistants. He shares his wisdom through frequent lectures and discussions at schools and theatres throughout the United States.

◆ *K–2*, by Patrick Meyers. Ming Cho Lee created one of his most memorable settings for this play, a ledge only eight feet wide, along a wall of ice. Two mountain climbers at 27,000 feet are trapped and facing death. Lee first designed the setting for this play in 1983 at Arena Stage and then transferred it to Broadway. In this image he has recreated it for a revival in 2000–2001. The actors are Craig Wallace and Rick Holmes.
Photo by Scott Suchman. Courtesy of Arena Stage.

Interested? Check out
Arnold Aronson. *American Set Design.* New York: Theatre Communications Group, 1985.

There are no rules limiting the possibilities of designing and staging the play. The only limitations are those of imagination and economics.

INTERPRETING SPACE

Some theatrical spaces, such as the proscenium theatre, are clearly designed for scenery. Nevertheless, many directors and playwrights have deliberately used little or no scenery in the proscenium space—a choice that calls the audience's attention to the permanent features of the theatre, suggests simplicity, and lends a generic sense to the artistic proceedings. Performances under such circumstances are often referred to as **metatheatre,** or productions that self-consciously comment on the play as taking place in a theatre. Sometimes plays are written in this way. In *The Comic Theatre* (1750) by Carlo Goldoni, for example, the action is set in an eighteenth century Italian theatre where a rehearsal is about to begin. The front curtain begins to rise but is stopped by the company manager (a character), and an argument ensues over whether to rehearse with the curtain up or down. More frequently, a director or production team interprets a play metatheatrically even if the playwright never had such a thing in mind.

Designers must give considerable attention to the ways in which theatrical space affects the audience experience. Consider a large auditorium versus a small, intimate arena, for example. Imagine the same play being performed in both. Intricate detail will not be noticed by anyone beyond the first few rows in a large theatre. In the small space, however, there is greater opportunity for subtlety and detail. Many conditions and spatial relationships can manipulate or alter the theatrical event. Is the audience truly sharing the space with the performers, or is there a clear separation? A separation is defined by most theatre architecture, but the production techniques employed may try to break down or minimize that barrier. Designers today might find themselves designing for the audience space as well as the stage space.

COLLABORATING WITH SPACE

Obviously, theatre artists cannot literally collaborate with space, since space cannot negotiate, but the space that is available or deemed "necessary" for a production receives much attention from the director and set designer when they are planning, rehearsing, and performing a play. There are many things about a given space that cannot be altered. Many features, however, can be changed, hidden, eliminated, or adapted. Sometimes practitioners find themselves "lost in space," unable to gain control of it and feeling victimized by what is considered inflexible. The space ends up controlling the production rather than the other way around—a situation that is unfortunate but not uncommon. On the other hand, imaginative, talented, and lucky theatre artists can make remarkable or clever use of what might otherwise seem a limitation or liability. Working with or around an unusual feature sometimes produces a fine theatrical moment that would otherwise have remained undiscovered.

A university production of Brecht's *Threepenny Opera* in Baltimore in 1986 was housed in a theatre that featured an unusual single vomitory that opened from below the audience seating onto the downstage apron of a proscenium stage. This feature often seemed to get in the way of stage action. On this occasion, however, the set designer William J. Pierson found a novel way to use it. He built a bridge from the stage out over the vomitory and concealed it; the bridge functioned as an extended thrust stage, allowing the action to spill out into the audience. The designer also placed a trapdoor at the downstage end of the bridge with access through the hidden vomitory beneath the bridge. When it was time for the antihero Macheath to appear in jail, he suddenly popped up through the trap, only to be incarcerated in the midst of the audience.

Many professional resident theatre companies, university, and community theatres have a home space—one or more theatres that they rent or own and in which they produce many different productions with varied needs and demands. Therefore, when selecting plays to produce in their familiar theatres,

♦ **THREEPENNY OPERA**, *by Bertolt Brecht and Kurt Weil. This set, designed by William J. Pierson, extends out into the house and utilizes the vomitory as a secret entrance. It is a deliberately ugly setting with the orchestra on stage and the actors on a revolve. Towson State University.* Collection of the authors.

they know precisely what many of the problems are likely to be in fitting a play to the available space. The artists in such circumstances often feel as though they have a relationship with the home space. Other production companies have no home. They must plan productions for a space that is new to them or in some cases unknown until near the time of opening.

SEEING BEYOND THE PLAYWRIGHT AND DIRECTOR

When a designer joins the artistic team for a new production, he or she will most likely read the play first and then listen to the ideas or concept of the director, or perhaps director and designer will conceptualize together. Whatever the method, the designer is faced with many clues and directions from the written play and many more from the director. Designs are often at their most exciting and imaginative when the designer can not only be true to the intent or spirit of the playwright's creation and the director's vision, but also see and realize things that verify and enhance, going beyond the scope of playwright and director. If this were not true, then most playwrights and directors could simply dictate exactly what they want to an accurate draftsperson and skilled carpenters, painters, dressmakers, and tailors. Sometimes this has occurred, of course, but the resultant settings and costumes are more craft than art. The talented designer is an artist with whose creative work the production concept takes on evocations of space, or body, or sound that complement and fulfill the play and direction. Design dynamically serves to establish style, emotional tone, and location of the action of the play. Design enables the audience to see what should be seen.

At their best, designs become ideal space, illumination, and character identification serving the movement and action of the play at that time. For director Michael Blakemore's 2000 production of *Copenhagen,* Peter Davison designed both set and costumes. The play recreates real events surrounding the race of the Allies and Germans to develop the atomic bomb, but it does so in a stylized, impossible manner. The three characters are former friends, and two are scientists who ended up working for opposing causes. They are dead yet remember and reenact events. Because memory is not certain and the events dramatized are contested, there are often several variations of the same story. The performance space for *Copenhagen* was essentially empty (two straight-back chairs were sometimes used) but formed as an elliptical shape.

♦ **COPENHAGEN,** *by Michael Frayn. A shot of the three principal actors performing in the ellipse. The image was probably taken from the elevated on-stage seating area.*
Photo by Joan Marcus.

The intent as stated by the designer was for the actors' movement within the space to imitate atomic particles moving about. But the design did more than this. On the upstage side a neutral-colored wall followed the line of the ellipse and incorporated two tiers of seats for audience members. The effect of the high wall was of unfeeling enclosure and governmental or military presence—like expressionless halls of power. The effect was also like a courtroom: The audience members were witnesses to the action; they were not just observing the action but judging it.

With the entire setting a presentational space that was bathed in light, neutral colors, Blakemore put his characters in dark, realistic clothing of the postwar period, lending them authenticity. The lighting by Mark Henderson and Michael Lincoln sometimes flooded the space intensely as if "exposing" the troubled characters but also isolated the character "particles" at times, allowing the audience to zero in on each crisis facing the characters. Just as the characters frequently moved about the space, the lighting also moved.

♦♦♦♦♦♦♦♦♦♦

The Scenic Designer's Work

The scenic designer creates a home for the action. The shape of the acting space and the look of any scenery or set props are the scenic designer's responsibility. While reading and analyzing the play, the scenic designer pays particular attention to any practical considerations (the need for actual doors, for example, or for a certain number of entrances/exits) as well as atmosphere or image that might be reinforced visually.

WHAT DOES THE PLAY DEMAND?

When thinking about space and design for a specific play, many designers strongly consider what the playwright seemed to have in mind (when that is possible). Other designers dismiss that notion and conceive the production almost exclusively in their own terms. In either case a designer must take into consideration a play's **given circumstances** (what the play text specifically calls for).

The Ghost Sonata (1907) by August Strindberg is a fascinating and difficult play about death and decay. It takes place in four locations, but the fourth is visited only briefly; the first three are dealt with extensively. In the first location the action takes place in an exterior setting, just outside a strange apartment house. Through the windows (if the design is literal) the audience can see glimpses of the interior. Throughout the first scene the interior of the house and its inhabitants are discussed extensively. The second scene takes place inside the house (the round room), but through an open door the audience can see a portion of the hyacinth room. The third scene is set in the hyacinth room, which provides a view back into the round room and at the end opens up briefly to the "isle of death." Consequently, most of the play is spatially structured by a journey into and through the house. This play has been produced with representational, highly detailed realistic scenery, but it has also been performed in presentational settings that are more related to mood than location. Some productions have used four separate sets; others have built a single setting that moves and transforms. Some artists see Strindberg as calling for scenery that literally opens up and draws us inside the awful house of death step by step. All of these approaches are valid responses to the play, but the uses of space are remarkably different when experienced in a theatre and elicit very different audience responses.

COMMUNICATING WITH THE PRODUCTION TEAM

After reading and analyzing the play and meeting with either the director or the entire design team, the scenic designer will usually produce a series of quick sketches. These are shown to the director as a way of communicating the ideas that have been developing in the designer's head. Through brainstorming and conferencing, the director and designers move toward acceptance or modification of the designs or sometimes find themselves starting all over. When the designer and director feel that they are on the same wavelength, the designer will execute the following:

♦ A **ground plan**—a drafting of the plan of the stage as seen from overhead. A ground plan shows where any scenic pieces or perhaps set props (such as furniture) are to be placed. The director can see the potential for blocking in the ground plan; the lighting designer can see how the acting area will be shaped and what set pieces need illumination.

♦ A **section**—a drafting showing the vertical elements of the space and their relative positions (for example, the height at which scenery, lighting, and masking are to be hung).

♦ A **rendering**—a picture of the set, drawn in perspective from the audience's point of view. The rendering shows most clearly what the stage will look like from the house. It is usually done in color and depicts the appearance of the set under lights.

♦ A **model**—a three-dimensional miniature version of the set, built to scale (usually one quarter or one half inch to the foot). A model has the advantage of allowing the director to experiment with blocking.

Some designers choose to do both renderings and a model; some choose one or the other.

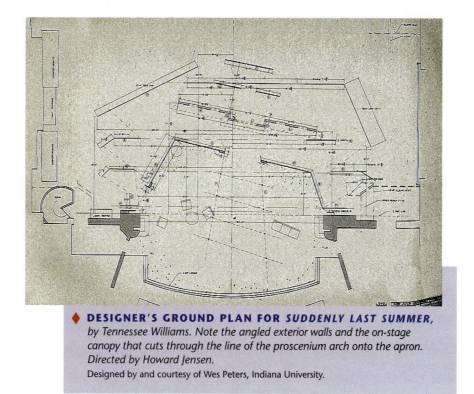

◆ **DESIGNER'S GROUND PLAN FOR** *SUDDENLY LAST SUMMER,*
by Tennessee Williams. Note the angled exterior walls and the on-stage
canopy that cuts through the line of the proscenium arch onto the apron.
Directed by Howard Jensen.
Designed by and courtesy of Wes Peters, Indiana University.

When the design receives final approval from the director, the designer (or
sometimes a designer's assistant) generates a series of working drawings to show
how the scenery is to be built. These draftings may include the following:

◆ A **front elevation**—breaking the set into units to be built and showing each
piece of scenery from the front.

◆ A **painter's elevation**—(in color) showing the plan for painting each piece
of scenery.

◆ A **rear elevation**—showing each piece from the back. Rear elevations are
particularly important in constructing the scenery, since a rear view may
show how each piece of scenery is to be built.

These documents allow the designer to communicate his or her vision to
others on the production staff. Traditionally drafted by hand, the drawings can
now be generated with greater ac-
curacy, efficiency, and flexibility for
changes by using computer imaging.
While creating the draftings, the designer establishes **sight lines**—in other
words, determines what the audience can and cannot see. Anything
that is visible but should not be (the
top of a piece of scenery, for example,
or backstage space) is hidden with
masking—black velour draperies or
flats that can be hung or placed vertically and horizontally across the stage.

◆ **DESIGNER'S RENDERING
FOR** *SUDDENLY LAST
SUMMER,* which matches the
ground plan. Here you can see
the effect of the canopy, angled
walls, and the decorations, which
make it a gardenlike setting.
Designed by and courtesy of Wes
Peters, Indiana University.

Exploring Collaboration

Robert Edmond Jones with Arthur Hopkins

In 1915 young Robert Edmond Jones had a design project for a forgettable one-act play entitled *The Man Who Married a Dumb Wife,* which appeared in an exhibition of new stagecraft designs in New York. Harley Granville-Barker, a visiting British director who was dedicated to principles of the new stagecraft, happened to see Jones's rendering. Granville-Barker was so taken by the set design that he decided to add a production of this play as a curtain-raiser for the season of plays he was bringing from England featuring work by Shakespeare and George Bernard Shaw. He hired the unknown Jones to design the set and costumes he had suggested in his rendering. This unplanned production set in motion a remarkable instant celebrity for the work of Jones, which sometimes outshone the plays he was designing.

Granville-Barker's production caught the attention of another innovative director, Arthur Hopkins, an American who was fascinated with European experiments. Hopkins quickly established a long-term artistic relationship with Jones, beginning later in 1915 with a production of *The Devil's Garden* by Edith Ellis. From this point until 1934 these two masterful theatre artists collaborated on at least forty-one productions. Jones always designed the sets and usually lighting and costumes as well. Although Hopkins and Jones often worked with other people, they clearly had an affinity for one another's methods and complete trust in their artistic collaboration.

The glory years were the 1920s, when they collaborated on realistic plays, fantasies, expressionism, modern comedy, and classical tragedy; they might have set a Broadway record in the period for the number of plays they produced written by women playwrights, such as Sophie Treadwell, whose *Machinal* (1928) was the last important presentation of American expressionism before the decline of that strident style that always featured a chronically disturbed central character on the brink of psychic disaster.

In their presentation of comedy of manners and intrigue they had no equals as they presented glib, character-driven whimsy and social commentary such as *Good Gracious, Annabelle* (1916) by Clare Kummer and *Holiday* (1928) by Philip Barry. They presented these plays realistically, but the realism was always simplified and streamlined, without the more typical approach to extravagant detail for interior scenes. This simplified realism was also used in their interpretations of Ibsen's plays such as *Hedda Gabler* and *The Wild Duck* (both in 1917) starring Alla Nazimova just as this Russian actress was emerging as an American star. The Hopkins/Jones production of Eugene O'Neill's *Anna Christie* (1921) was one of the most successful commercial productions of early selective realism in the history of the American theatre. Although audiences and critics marveled at the perfect evocation of a pre–World War I barroom, many of the details that are so common to realistic staging were simplified and replaced by atmospheric lighting and gritty interior

EXECUTING THE SCENIC DESIGN

The set designer develops plans and makes the artistic choices but relies on technical staff for execution. Throughout the building of the set, the designer communicates frequently with the technical director. The **technical director** is responsible for the safety of the theatre space, for scheduling, for construction and equipment installation, and for making sure designs are executed according to designer's specifications. As someone with a great deal of technical and practical knowledge, the technical director serves as problem solver. The technical director oversees the transfer and setup of scenery and props into the stage space.

When sets are built on site, a **scene shop foreman** oversees their construction by a crew of carpenters, scenic painters, and other craftspeople. Commer-

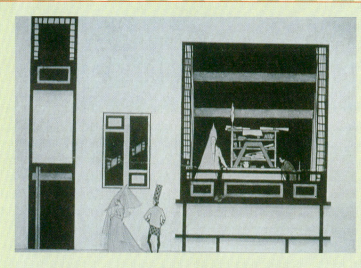

walls and windows. Jones and Hopkins managed to make dirty and grimy space look alluring.

Perhaps their most famous work occurred with their revivals of Shakespeare with the famous Barrymore siblings: John in *Richard III* (1920) and *Hamlet* (1922), Lionel in *Macbeth* (1921), and Ethel in *Romeo and Juliet* (1922). All of the settings for these multilocation plays were variations of a **unit set** (a single scenic unit used to represent many different locations). These productions were inspired by unit-set experiments in Europe, but Jones and Hopkins gave them

personal interpretations that have remained important to the history of American theatre.

Interested? Check out

Ralph Pendleton. *The Theatre of Robert Edmond Jones.* Middletown, Conn.: Wesleyan University Press, 1958.
Ronald H. Wainscott. *Staging O'Neill: The Experimental Years, 1920–1934.* New Haven, Conn.: Yale University Press, 1988.
Arthur Hopkins. *Reference Point.* New York: Samuel French, 1948.
Robert Edmond Jones. *The Dramatic Imagination.* New York: Theatre Arts, 1941.

cial productions without a home theatre send designs to special scene shops for construction and then transfer the items to the performance space just before technical rehearsals. The **props manager** organizes the collection or building of all properties in the show.

The scenic designer keeps in close touch with the technical staff during the building process and participates actively in technical rehearsals—watching how the set functions, taking notes about changes that need to be made, and conferring with the technical director.

The union for professional designers is United Scenic Artists of America. In the professional theatre, technical positions are staffed by members of the International Alliance of Theatrical Stage Employees, Moving Picture Technicians, Artists, and Allied Crafts of the United States, Its Territories and Canada, the labor union representing technicians, artisans, and craftspeople in the entertainment industry. Strict rules about working time and job descriptions protect the livelihood of these professionals. A carpenter, for example, is not allowed to refocus a lighting instrument; an electrician may not hammer a nail. In amateur theatre, where the rules are less stringent, volunteers typically pitch in to do the work, often supervised by a professional. Students working for class credit and experience are directed by faculty and staff in educational theatres. Many people who are not interested in performing find fun and fulfillment in working behind the scenes.

◆◆◆◆◆◆◆◆◆◆

The Lighting Designer's Work

To a casual observer the work of the lighting designer is sometimes the least noticeable in a production, yet all the other visual elements depend on it. Lighting, at its most basic, provides visibility and manipulates that visibility by supporting the moment-to-moment action of the play. Much of the lighting task is about revealing. Lighting the actors is crucial in most productions; audiences can lose interest quickly if they cannot see the faces of the performers. Because lighting can radically change the mood of a production and the look of costumes, set, and properties, lighting designers must work very closely with all of their colleagues.

The installation of gas lighting in the early nineteenth century made systematic control of theatrical lighting possible; a technician could change intensity on the stage or in the house by moving one lever. The open flame of the gas and the possibility of explosion, however, made gas a dangerous addition to theatres. A fireman became a part of the theatre's staff, meant to remain on duty in case of emergency even when the theatre was empty. The invention of the long-lasting incandescent light bulb by Thomas Edison and others by 1879 and its subsequent refinement for the theatre made the concept of actually designing lighting possible. Early electric lighting systems were still dangerous and caused numerous theatre fires, but perfection of the technology led to increased safety and flexibility for the theatre artists. Many early directors took full charge of lighting, as did many set designers in the early days of electric light. By the 1920s directors and set designers often argued over the right to light the production. As technology developed and the many possibilities became evident, lighting became a design component in its own right. Most lighting designers today tend to specialize in lighting alone, and a number of lighting teams have emerged in the last few decades.

CHANGING SPACE WITH LIGHTING

Aesthetic distance and spatial relationships are manipulated by uses of light or the absence of light. The sun was the only light for theatre in classical Greece and Rome, and the sun does not necessarily cooperate with human artistic plans. Indoor theatres of the seventeenth and eighteenth centuries used candles and oil lamps, which established mood and general illumination, but provided little variety despite many attempts by artists to manipulate it. Gaslight generated an enormous amount of heat and discomfort for the audience, especially in the balconies. Through all of these periods, however, until late in the nineteenth century, the audience was always lit. A major shift occurred when theatre practitioners began dimming the house lights, accentuating the separation between performance and viewing space. We are so accustomed now to sitting in the darkened house watching a brightly lit stage that many outdoor theatres are used at night so that the audience can be in darkness and the stage can be lit. This dynamic does as much as any other element of the theatre space in terms of manipulating aesthetic distance.

CREATING MOVEMENT AND MOOD WITH LIGHTING

Lighting designers have many tasks. One of the most important, of course, is lighting the actors and the action so that they can be seen clearly, but this is not a simple matter. Lighting must be used to mold the human face and figure. In a stage flooded with light, it may still be difficult to see the actors clearly unless shadows in some areas make the three dimensions of the face and body apparent. Lighting can make the human form and face look ugly or beautiful, flat or three-dimensional. Low-angle lighting set below the horizon (such as footlights) can create stark, disturbing images or ghostly faces (shadows rise from below). Likewise, high-angle or "down light" can suggest mystery or anonymity in the face with shadows moving downward from an actor or object.

Lighting can create primary and secondary focus. Actors are nearly always lit with more intensity than the scenery. On an otherwise dimly lit stage, an actor in a spotlight will attract the gaze of the audience members. If an empty area is suddenly illuminated, the audience expects something to happen in that space soon. Lighting can set objects and actors in relief—pull them out of the stage picture—or blend them in. Lighting also hides or minimizes some stage elements until they become the focus of the dramatic moment. A particular chair

◆ *A MIDSUMMER NIGHT'S DREAM. Oberon and Puck in pseudo Middle Eastern garb, lit primarily by low-angle light, while an obviously artificial moon hangs overhead like a lantern. Directed by Mary Zimmerman, Huntington Theatre Company.* Photo by Charlie Erickson.

◆ *THE MEDIUM, conceived and directed by Anne Bogart. A dynamic use of side light. The stage is mostly bare except for small pillars. The actors, left to right, are Kelly Maurer, Will Bond, and Stephen Webber. Lighting design by Michitomo Shiohara.* Courtesy of Actors Theatre of Louisville.

might have been visible during an entire scene, but just before a murder takes place at that chair, the lighting could grow brighter on that piece of furniture and dimmer on the rest of the stage. A traditional way of making a performer seem to appear out of nowhere is actually a lighting effect. The performer stands behind a **scrim**—a translucent piece of fabric. When lit from the front, the scrim appears opaque (solid). When the scrim lighting is extinguished and the actor behind it is lit, the scrim seems to disappear, and the performer becomes visible.

Lighting helps to create mood, and the orchestration of lighting can modify, sustain, or eliminate the mood. A dimly lit stage can create a somber atmosphere, while pleasingly bright lighting suggests happiness or stability. If the lighting becomes very intense, however, it can suggest an institutional setting, sterility, or perhaps threat or unseen power.

Sometimes lighting is used as a representational tool that heightens the sense of reality. Stage lighting can imitate sun or moonlight depending on its color. Audiences tend to read blue lighting as moonlight. Even though the light of the moon is not really blue, the color suggests moonlight on stage. Light at noon seems to come from directly overhead. In late afternoon the angle of light is nearly horizontal: Objects can be brightly lit on one side and dark on the other, throwing them into relief. These effects can be suggested on stage by adjusting the angle and intensity of the lighting instruments. Producer-director David Belasco spent much of his production preparation time in the early twentieth century perfecting realistic lighting effects, some of which became famous. In *Madame Butterfly* (the play in 1900, not the opera), Belasco created an extended lighting sequence that imitated the passage of early evening through night to dawn as the protagonist sat on the stage waiting in vain for her lover to return.

Light can be combined with shadow and color to imitate a specific place. It often finishes the job begun by the setting, but lighting alone can alter the set

◆ *ART, by Yasmina Reza. In this and the next photograph the setting hardly changes at all, but different locations are created by radical changes in lighting. Scenic design by Robert M. Koharchik; lighting design by John Philip Martin; directed by Tim Ocel.*
Courtesy of Indiana Repertory Theatre.

in remarkable ways. At the turn of the twentieth century, designer Adolphe Appia was especially influential in describing and rendering possibilities for light and shadow. Utilizing open spaces, especially platforms and elevations, Appia created designs that featured strong contrasts, and he experimented with ways to create shadow dynamically in the theatrical space. Most of his work was on paper, since few theatre producers were ready at the time to pursue and finance Appia's vision, but the Swiss designer had many disciples in the decades after his work.

Like the other designers, lighting designers sometimes study and adapt

♦ **ART,** *by Yasmina Reza. In this image of* Art, *the only change to the setting is the addition of an all-white painting (the source of argument in the play), stage left. All other changes are created by light.*
Courtesy of Indiana Repertory Theatre.

techniques from the past. Footlights were standard equipment throughout the eras of candles, oil lamps, gas, and early electricity. They were positioned on the stage floor at the edge of the apron and were focused upward to light the actors. Early in the twentieth century, many designers started eliminating footlights; they were considered garish by many innovators and tended to cast strange shadows on the actors' faces. Footlights returned (often selectively for low angle effects) late in the twentieth century. Designer Santo Loquasto designed a towering set for Sean Mathias's 2001 production of *Dance of Death* by August Strindberg. Lighting designer Natasha Katz often used low-angle lighting to give the set and actors an eerie effect, underscoring the bizarre marital arguments in the play and sudden (frightening) bouts of unconsciousness of the character Edgar.

THE LIGHTING DESIGNER'S TOOLS

Lighting designers work with four basic elements:

♦ **intensity** (how bright the lighting is),
♦ **color**
♦ **distribution** (how light is spread over the stage: angle and texture) and
♦ **orchestration** or **movement** (changes in any of the first three elements).

Intensity is controlled by the amount of lumens pumped onto the stage, which depends on the number of lighting instruments used. *Color* is created by filtering the light with color media or color filters—translucent sheets of plastic (high heat polyester) or dichroic filters (tempered glass with metal coating) made in a wide range of different colors and placed in front of lighting instruments. *Distribution* of light is determined by where lighting instruments are placed as well as the type of instruments used. Angle is an important part of distribution, since it affects the mood and appearance of the actors as well as suggesting time of day. The location of each instrument (both horizontally and vertically) determines the angle at which its beam hits the stage, actors, or objects illuminated.

♦ **MACBETH**, by William Shakespeare, the banquet scene. The live actors, Kim Martin-Cotten and Mark Mineart, work on each side of the banquet table, but the three central figures are projections, as is the large face, which represents the ghost of Banquo. Directed by Marc Masterson; lighting design by Tony Penna; scene design by Steve O'Hearn; costume design by Connie Furr-Soloman.
Photo by Larry Hunt, courtesy of Actors Theatre of Louisville.

In controlling distribution, today's lighting designers can choose from a wide variety of instruments that are designed to do different jobs. The type of instrument that is used most frequently is a **spotlight.** Glass lenses create a focused and controllable beam of light, and various shaped metal and glass reflectors affect the quality of light and the shape of the beam. A **Fresnel** spotlight, for example, uses a lens adapted from nineteenth-century lighthouses (and takes its name from the man who invented it). This lens creates a beam of light with a soft edge, and the beams from different instruments can be easily blended to create the appearance of an even area of light. An **ellipsoidal** spotlight, in contrast, creates a hard-edged beam and includes four shutters around the circular lens to further control its focus; a shutter can be moved in to keep light away from a set wall, for example. **Par lamps** (parabolic aluminated reflectors) create parallel rays. Newer automated instruments can change all of the elements electronically; a single instrument may be able to change color, distribution, and intensity instantly.

Orchestration of lighting in today's theatre is accomplished by using the **lighting console,** a control board with a memory system. Many instruments can be hung on stage and turned on or off only when they are needed. Intensity can be changed in any area throughout the show by adjusting one or any number of instruments. Color can be changed by intensifying instruments with one particular color filter and dimming others. With the creation of dimmers and lighting consoles in the twentieth century, designers developed complicated **crossfades,** which can be rapid or slow. Lengthy changes transform the space so subtly that the audience often doesn't notice them until the change is nearly complete. A room growing dark near the end of the day, for example, might take twenty minutes. With the advent of lighting consoles it became possible to preprogram all of the **cues** (timed changes) sequentially (there are often hundreds in a busy show) so that mistakes by the console operator are minimized and the cues can be precise each time.

Projections are often included in current lighting designs. A **projection** is an image thrown onto the stage using light. The simplest kind of projection uses a metal cutout like a stencil, called a **gobo** (also called a pattern or template). The gobo is inserted in a gate on an ellipsoidal spotlight, and the solid areas block the light, casting shadows on the stage. In this way, leaf patterns can be thrown on stage creating the image of a forest, bars suggesting a prison, or abstract shapes to create any number of effects. Some gobos are also combined with color filters and provide full-color images, not just shadow patterns. Photographs or abstract images on slides and transparencies can be projected on the stage, screens, and objects. At times projectors have even taken the place of or supplemented painted or three-dimensional scenery. Gobo rotators can create motion effects with the projected light.

Lighting instruments themselves, as well as the consoles, have been improved markedly in the last few decades: more powerful and sophisticated lamps, automated instruments that can be refocused or set in motion while in the air, improvements in projectors enabling additional movement in the light thrown from the instruments, and laser lights (such as Natasha Katz's laser-light pyramid effect in *Aida* that surrounded the three main characters as they sang their laments). New developments appear each year, just like improvements in computer hardware and software.

COMMUNICATING AND EXECUTING THE LIGHTING DESIGN

When analyzing the play, the lighting designer will pay particular attention to the play's structure, mood, and all possibilities for orchestration of lighting. If the design is realistic, he or she will consider how the lighting can contribute to establishing time and place, as well as any practicals needed. A **practical** is a visible light source onstage that is often enhanced by unseen lighting instruments. For example, when a desk lamp or overhead chandelier on stage is turned on, light usually emanates from the practical, but accompanying instruments may punch up the effect and help to imitate and perhaps intensify the light thrown by the practical on the stage.

The lighting design process begins at the same time as other designs; the lighting designer meets with the director and production team regularly, and the lighting design evolves with the costumes, sets, and the director's staging, all of which usually continue to be refined until the production is ready to open.

The lighting designer faces a great challenge in trying to communicate his or her vision to the director and production staff, since lighting is the most ephemeral of the theatrical elements. Computer imaging now gives the designer a chance to preview the effectiveness of the lighting and share the effect with the whole creative team. Though not providing a perfect facsimile of the onstage effect, the computer allows the designer to provide a very good idea of what he or she plans to do. Sometimes lighting instruments are set up in a lighting lab to show actual effects in miniature. A costume designer, for example, could check the look of a fabric under the correct stage lighting.

♦ **OEDIPUS THE KING,** *by Sophocles, computer-generated lighting concept dominated by large shadows and grim mood. This is a moment in the play when the chorus on stage is awaiting the return of Oedipus from the palace since he learned the truth of his birth. Directed by Howard Jensen, Indiana University.*
Lighting design by and courtesy of Robert Shakespeare.

The designer creates a technical drawing or **lighting plot** showing where each instrument is to be hung, along with the type of instrument and color filters to be used. Before technical rehearsals a **master electrician** works closely with the lighting designer and directs a lighting crew to hang, focus, and filter the lighting instruments and to set up circuitry, the lighting console, and sometimes sound equipment also. In the early days of electric light, most designers sought to conceal the lighting instruments from the audience to create realistic effects (most people don't have stage lights in their living room). Throughout the twentieth century, especially when lighting musicals and presentational productions, many designers took to hanging instruments in full view (from the balconies, sides of the house, or, as in Bertolt Brecht's theory, deliberately low above the stage) to call attention to the fact that the audience is in a theatre. Such practice has become so commonplace, however, that it no longer makes a statement. Frequently, a lighting or sound booth is erected in the house rather than using a built-in booth, probably influenced by the practice in touring rock concerts where the operators have an audience view of the stage and can hear better than they could in a glass-fronted booth.

During tech week (the week of technical rehearsals) the director and designer sometimes choose to have a lighting rehearsal, in which the cues (changes

♦ **OEDIPUS THE KING.** *The lighting concept image for a few moments later in the play—the entrance of Oedipus after he has blinded himself—has switched to back and down light, framing him in the doorway. Note that light spills forward onto the stage, picking up the figures of the chorus as all of the actors and the lights focus on Oedipus.*
Lighting design by and courtesy of Robert Shakespeare.

in lighting, sound, or set) are constructed and run with no actors present. The director and designer can then look at the lighting on stage together and make adjustments. Stage management and technical staff often stand in for actors when it is important to see the effect of light on a human body. Actors are present for a **cue-to-cue** technical rehearsal, in which only the parts of the play that include cues are run; any dialogue or action in between is skipped. The stage manager organizes and runs the cue-to-cue. The designer and director then make adjustments, particularly in the timing of the cues, until the desired effect is achieved. A **technical rehearsal** (or tech run) follows, in which the stage manager, actors, and run crews practice putting all elements (except costumes) together in a complete run of the show. The lighting designer continues to work with the director, stage manager, and technical staff through **dress rehearsals,** refining and perfecting the contribution of lighting to the total production.

A successful lighting designer is a sensitive artist with a mastery of lighting technology. He or she must know the fundamentals of electricity but above all must be an artist who sculpts and paints with light and has a thorough understanding of the other design positions. Obviously, a good lighting designer must keep abreast of technological change. Computer skills are an important and fast-growing requirement for technicians in many of today's theatres. When budgets allow, automated lighting instruments, projections, and laser graphics may be added to more traditional technology, and designers must have an understanding of the full range of possibilities to serve the production well.

Although sometimes designing alone or with others, the lighting team of Jules Fisher and Peggy Eisenhauer has been working together for more than seventeen years. For their lighting of *Jane Eyre*, Fisher and Eisenhauer created one of their most complex and interesting designs. It required full mechanical integration with a large revolving stage, flying and gliding scenery, and a circular light bridge that turned with or sometimes independently of the stage revolve. Almost in homage to their predecessor Josef Svoboda, many of the scenic effects were created by projections, sometimes shot through multiple scrims, creating intriguing distortions of window effects. This high-tech approach to scenery and lighting created a curious admixture with the nineteenth-century costumes and the story from Charlotte Brontë's novel, which was the source of the musical.

◆◆◆◆◆◆◆◆◆

The Costume Designer's Work

Designing costumes became important when the theatre embraced historical accuracy and an overall artistic vision for production became the norm. The production team, rather than individual actors, then became responsible for providing costumes that harmonized with the other designs. Costumes can work with lighting and setting to establish the time period and location of the play. The designer must be conversant with various historical styles and forms of dress and have the necessary skills for research. Depending on the concept of the production, period costumes may be altered or abstracted. If

historical accuracy is not a part of concept, the designer is free to create an imaginary style appropriate to the concept.

Beyond expressing concept and establishing the world of the play, costumes become a critical part of the audience's reception and understanding of the characters. A character who first appears in a red satin gown will suggest a different set of associations than one who appears in a ragged homespun dress. In analyzing the play, a costume designer pays particular attention to the physical needs of the character. If one character must dance the night away, the design choices are different from those made for a character who sits rigidly on a wooden stool most of the time. The designer analyzes character as well. Socioeconomic status is an important consideration in how the character dresses, as well as basic personality. An outgoing character might wear bright colors and unusual styles; a retiring character might choose dark colors and conservative styles. Changes in social status or psychological state can be expressed graphically through changes in costume.

THE COSTUME IN SPACE

The costume designer communicates from the beginning with the other designers as well as the director, though costume choices may evolve as other design elements evolve. When it comes to colors, textures, fabric choices, and finishing details, designers and director often negotiate so that the furniture, for example, does not clash with the costumes or, in some cases, does not erase the costumes, since the color and texture nearly match. The costume designer must also be acutely aware of lighting, because the stage lighting could severely alter or destroy the image a costume designer is seeking. It is important that the costume, scenic, and lighting designers communicate frequently about choices.

Distance on the stage is also critical to costume design choices. If the designer is creating a costume that will never be closer to the audience than thirty feet from the front row, the choices will be considerably different than if a costume will be seen mostly on the apron or down center. Directors must communicate such staging to the designer, and most designers periodically attend rehearsals to see such distances as well as the physical action of the actors. If a director has an actor rolling about the floor in an expensive wedding dress, as could occur in the Polish play *Tango* by Slawomir Mrożek, the designer needs to know.

COMMUNICATING AND EXECUTING THE DESIGN

A costume designer begins showing the director quick sketches that are meant to express basic ideas and offer choices. The director may approve, reject, or ask to see additional development. When the designer and director seem to have reached agreement as to basic approach, the designer produces costume **renderings**—pictures of the costumes on the actors. Ideally, a rendering is done for each costume in color, often with appropriate swatches of fabric attached.

♦ **WHIMSICAL COSTUME
RENDERING** *for the character
Feste in* Twelfth Night, *by William
Shakespeare. Produced at Iowa
State University.*
Costume design by and courtesy of
Linda Pisano.

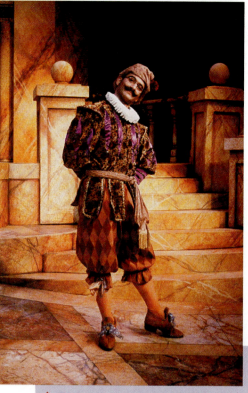

♦ **THE REALIZED COSTUME**
of Feste in Twelfth Night, *on the
completed setting painted to simu-
late marble.*
Design and photo by and courtesy of
Linda Pisano.

In creating each design, the costume designer works with four variables:

♦ **Silhouette** or **line**—the outer shape of the costume. It is easy to understand silhouette if you think of a costume as a shadow on the wall; no
color and no detail are visible, just the basic shape. Silhouette is particularly indicative of time period and culture. The draped and gathered cloth
of the Indian sari creates a particular female silhouette. A tight-fitting
bodice, tight waist, and skirt flaring out, stopping midway between knee
and ankle, make up a typical silhouette from the United States in the
1950s. The profile of an upper-class woman from Europe or the United
States in the 1860s to 1880s would reveal a floor-length skirt with a bustle
(large protrusion) over the rear end.

♦ **Color.** Different colors tend to create different emotional responses
in human beings. The designer thinks not only about the effect that a
particular color will have on the audience, but also about the message
that it sends about the character who chose to wear it. The designer
must also understand that symbolic associations with color are culturally specific; white (symbolizing purity) is traditional for weddings in
the United States, but red (symbolizing good luck) is appropriate for
weddings in China.

◆ **Texture**—the "feel" of the fabric. Even if an audience member never touches the cloth, the sense of sight gives information about how a fabric feels. Fine, smooth fabrics such as thin silk and satin tend to suggest sophistication. Soft, rich fabrics such as brocade and velvet suggest wealth. Rougher fabric—homespun, for example—can suggest low status or hard times. Associations with texture are also culturally specific; in the United States during the 1930s and 1940s denim was considered a working man's fabric and was associated with manual labor; denim is currently fashionable for many people no matter what the activity or social status.

◆ **Accent**—details to finish or set off a costume. Buttons, lace, piping along edges, embroidery, and jewelry are all examples of accent. A woman's dress in a peach color might be accented with large black buttons down the front or a single rhinestone brooch at the shoulder. A single red rose in the lapel of a man's black jacket is a striking accent.

Commercial or touring productions without a home theatre send the designs to a professional costume shop for construction. For productions in an established theatre the costume designer will choose to build costumes from scratch, buy them, or pull them from stock (i.e., choose from items that already exist in the theatre's costume collection). Availability of funds and building time are critical, and the costume designer must consider the expense of fabrics and other materials as well as size and experience of the staff. The costume designer works closely with the **costume shop manager,** who coordinates the efforts of cutters, stitchers, and other costume personnel. Items pulled from stock must be altered to fit specific actors and might be dyed or changed to achieve the appropriate look. Building a costume from scratch is a labor-intensive process that involves taking the actor's measurements, drafting a pattern, cutting, sewing, and fitting the garment on the actor. The designer often works closely with the costume shop personnel to achieve the look reflected in the original rendering.

Costume designers are sometimes responsible for more than clothing. They design makeup and masks unless a separate designer is assigned those duties. Purses, hats, and shoes must be found or created to coordinate with each costume. The craft area of a costume shop is often a busy place, with shop personnel making or trimming hats, constructing masks, making armor, and fashioning jewelry.

Finished costumes are usually the final visual element added to production. The designer creates a **costume plot,** a chart that records items of clothing worn by each actor in each scene of the play. For small shows it is fairly simple, but for large-cast shows with multiple or quick costume changes, the costume plot is especially important for organization. During tech week some directors like to have a costume parade: Actors are dressed in costumes and appear under the appropriate stage lights. The director and designer discuss any changes that need to be made. At the first dress rehearsal the actors wear and use all the items created for them while performing the entire play. Ideally, actors will have used substitutes during rehearsals for any items that would cause major

◆ *AMADEUS, by Peter Shaffer. Mozart and Constanza, although in fancy dress, play erotic games on the floor. The mostly open setting and highly reflective floor underscore the prominence of the actors and the distinctive features of the eighteenth-century costumes. Richard Robichaux plays Mozart and Natalie Griffith plays Constanza. Costume design by David Zinn; scenic design by Michael Ganio; directed by Michael Donald Edwards.*
Courtesy of Indiana Repertory Theatre.

changes in movement. Rehearsal skirts, for example, are frequently used to approximate long skirts of earlier periods; if corsets are to be worn, the actors must work with them early to learn how to adjust breathing and movement. Actors who are unused to wearing shoes with high heels must learn to walk in them. Despite the best planning, there are always some surprises related to costume. The designer, director, actor, and costume shop collaborate to solve problems and ensure costumes that are both appropriate to the concept and workable for the actor before opening night.

MEETING THE CHALLENGE

Costume designers must contribute to concept and sometimes find dynamic ways to either call attention to the costumes or lead the audience to accept them as a natural part of the entire environment and period suggested. For *The Oedipus Plays* (2001), directed by Michael Kahn at the Shakespeare Theatre in Washington, D.C., designer Toni-Leslie James drew on traditional African tribal costume, especially in fabric patterns, and maintained earth tones throughout. The three choruses were distinct as types but included variety among the participants. The design for *The Oedipus Plays* was a remarkably different task from James's design for *Angels in America* (1993) which featured late twentieth-century dress or the funky costumes of *Jelly's Last Jam* (1992). In Sam Mendes's 1997 revival of *Cabaret,* William Ivey Long created ratty, suggestive costumes that almost became scenic in the shabby chic of the Berlin club environment designed by Robert Brill. Frequently, both settings and costumes were dominated by grays and blacks, which prepared the audience for the Holocaust image

♦ **CABARET,** by Fred Ebb, Joe Masteroff, and John Kander, In this dynamic image, actors, musicians, and dancers become one with twisting bodies forming a pyramid effect. Directed by Sam Mendes; choreographed by Rob Marshall; scenic design by Robert Brill; costume design by William Ivey Long; lighting design by Peggy Eisenhauer and Mike Baldassari.
Photo by Joan Marcus.

at production's end. These deliberately ugly costumes are in stark contrast to Long's flashy, stylish costumes in the dance musical *Contact* (1999) and his playful designs for *The Producers* (2001).

Realistic plays or plays evoking periods from long ago often present interesting challenges, especially if the cast is large. Designer Andreane Neofitou is quite adept at both period and large cast challenges, having worked often for the Royal Shakespeare Company and created the costumes for *Les Misérables* (1985) and *Jane Eyre* (2000). Especially when working on these and other productions with set designer John Napier, who often creates high-tech environments with minimal historical detail, Neofitou must suggest the visual sense of period with costumes.

For some shows, costume designers must create a fantasy period—either a futuristic vision, a hybrid of different periods, or a completely fabricated past that never existed. The latter is what designer Bob Crowley created for the musical *Aida* (2000). He wanted to suggest the Egyptian past, yet there was much about the costuming that was contemporary as well as fashion-show chic.

♦♦♦♦♦♦♦♦♦

The Sound Designer's Work

Until just before the Great Depression sound effects or music in the theatre were created live by technicians or musicians. Some well-equipped theatres from the Elizabethans to the nineteenth century featured machines such as thunder runs, wooden troughs in the floor above the stage level or even over the house into which heavy balls could be rolled to create the rumbling effect of thunder. A more traditional approach was the thunder sheet—a large sheet of metal that a stagehand could strike or shake to mimic the rolling and crashing of thunder.

Recorded sound was first used in the production of Elmer Rice's *Street Scene* in 1929, which featured the nearly constant sound of a busy New York street. Obviously, recording and playback methods since that time have become very sophisticated thanks to high-speed techniques, audio mixing and editing, computerized sound consoles and digital recording. Productions still use live music of course, and sometimes sound effects are created live, but aside from musicals, most sound in the theatre is now recorded. Even the dance musical *Contact* used recorded music, though this was unusual for commercial musical theatre.

Many theatre companies used to relegate sound design and sound engineering to the lighting design area, but increasingly, sound design has been emerging as an independent and dynamic part of the design process. When analyzing the script, the sound designer looks particularly for any ambient sound that is suggested (crickets chirping, music from a nearby carnival) as well as effects that are important to the action of the play (an offstage car crash, a train passing, gunfire). The director and designer sometimes decide on effects that are not called for in the script to support mood or suggest action happening offstage. Many prerecorded sound effects have long been available on records, tapes, and compact disks. The designer can choose or adapt one of these or record a newly created sound effect, if appropriate equipment is available, and program the sound cues on a digital console.

Music is frequently called for in scripts that are not considered musicals, and directors sometimes add music as background, underscoring, or as bridges for scene changes or to prepare the audience before the action begins on stage. Music can establish time period and can be a powerful tool in creating atmosphere. The director and designer often work together in selecting appropriate music for a show; the designer finds and records the music. Permission should be obtained for using preexisting recordings.

For many musicals since the 1960s actors wear wireless body mikes (microphones) and sometimes headsets, as in *Rent* (1996). Such a system must be created or adapted by the sound designer. Especially with the advent of rock musicals and the introduction of electronic musical instruments to not only rock but to many styles of music, the electronic control of sound became vital to performance. The theatre's debt to the rock music industry is great in this regard. Accomplished sound designers are in demand for nearly any kind of play. Tony Meola, for example has designed sound for radically different styles of plays such as *The Lion King* (1997) and *Copenhagen* (2000).

◆◆◆◆◆◆◆◆◆◆

Integrating All the Designs

Designers work closely with the director to meld their contributions into an artistic whole. The task becomes increasingly complex yet exciting as technology opens up new possibilities. The pursuit of increased specialization and continued

reading and learning in the field must be balanced with the need for the designers to communicate and negotiate with other production personnel. Besides the give-and-take required with directors, designers must consider the actors; no design choice is successful if it is not functional for those who are walking on the set, dancing in the costumes, or delivering a speech while facing a bright light. Sometimes the lines of design responsibility are blurred; a special lighting effect (such as a neon sign) might form an important element in set design; a property sometimes becomes a costume, or a costume becomes a property. In *Mad Forest* (1990) by Caryl Churchill, for example, a large Romanian flag with the crest cut out is pulled down and worn by a character. In *Long Day's Journey into Night* (1956) by Eugene O'Neill, an old woman enters the room at the climax in a morphine stupor, carrying her faded wedding dress. Such events often lead to interesting discussions in design meetings about whose responsibility it is to create such a costume/prop. The skills necessary to communicate consistently and unambiguously are as important to successful design as are visual or aural sensitivity and talent.

In some cases when integrating the designs, one person might try to do it all. In 1924, for example, one of America's most talented designers, Robert Edmond Jones, not only directed the first production of Eugene O'Neill's *Desire under the Elms,* but also designed the sets, costumes, and lighting. Sound designers had not yet come onto the scene. One could imagine whimsical design conferences at which Jones sat at a table talking to himself.

◆◆◆◆◆◆◆◆◆

QUESTIONS AND ACTIVITIES

1. Discuss the set design for a show you have seen. Was the approach representational or presentational? Did it depict a particular location? How did the set contribute to the mood or atmosphere of the show? What did it tell you about the setting or characters?

2. Discuss the costume designs for a show you have seen. What did the costumes tell you about the individual characters? Did the costumes suggest a time and place? How did they contribute to the mood or atmosphere of the show? Were costumes and makeup representational or presentational?

3. Discuss the lighting design for a show you have seen. What did you notice the most about the lighting on

stage? Did it seem to come from a realistic source? Did it seem to suggest location? Did the lighting change as the action of the play progressed? How did it affect the mood or atmosphere of the show?

4. Discuss the sound design for a show you have seen. Was there preshow music or sound (while the audience was being seated, before the show started)? How did it affect your expectations? Were there sound effects or music in the play? Did it/they serve a realistic purpose? Was sound used to help the flow of the show? Was there music under the actors' curtain call? What mood did it suggest?

KEY TERMS AND CONCEPTS

raked stage, p. 348
skene, p. 349
orchestra, p. 349
pinakes, p. 349
periaktoi, p. 349
wing, drop and border scenery, p. 350
ground rows, p. 350
box set, p. 352
antiquarianism, p. 352
revolve, p. 353
representational, p. 355
fourth wall, p. 355
presentational, p. 356
metatheatre, p. 359
given circumstances, p. 362
ground plan, p. 362
section, p. 362
rendering, p. 362
model, p. 362

front elevation, p. 363
painter's elevation, p. 363
rear elevation, p. 363
sight lines, p. 363
masking, p. 363
technical director, p. 364
scene shop foreman, p. 364
props manager, p. 365
unit set, p. 365
scrim, p. 368
intensity, p. 369
color, p. 369
distribution, p. 369
orchestration or movement, p. 369
spotlight, p. 370
fresnel, p. 370
ellipsoidal, p. 370
par lamp, p. 370
lighting console, p. 370

crossfade, p. 370
cue, p. 371
projection, p. 371
gobo, p. 371
practical, p. 371
lighting plot, p. 372
master electrician, p. 372
cue-to-cue, p. 373
technical rehearsal, p. 373
dress rehearsal, p. 373
rendering, p. 374
silhouette, p. 375
line, p. 375
color, p. 375
texture, p. 376
accent, p. 376
costume shop manager, p. 376
costume plot, p. 376

◆◆◆◆◆◆◆◆◆

FOR FURTHER EXPLORATION

W. Oren Parker and R. Craig Wolf. *Scene Design and Stage Lighting,* 7th edition. Fort Worth, Tex.: Harcourt Brace, 1996.

Arnold Aronson. *American Set Design.* New York: Theatre Communications Group, 1985.

Ronn Smith. *American Set Design 2.* New York: Theatre Communications Group, 1991.

Richard Pilbrow. *Stage Lighting Design.* London: Nick Hern, 1997.

Richard H. Palmer. *The Lighting Art: The Aesthetics of Stage Lighting Design.* Upper Saddle River, N.J.: Prentice Hall, 1993.

Douglas A. Russell. *Costume History and Style.* Boston: Allyn and Bacon, 1983.

Lynn Pecktal. *Costume Design: Techniques of Modern Masters.* New York: Back Stage Books, 1999.

The International Alliance of Theatrical Stage Employees web site at www.iatse.lm.com.

Photo Gallery

Interpreting Space and Design

Learning to see and think about space in three-dimensional terms is critical for designers and directors of the theatre, but it is also useful for playwrights, actors, critics and audience members. Possessing or developing the skill of perceiving and interpreting three-dimensional images enhances remarkably the understanding and appreciation of the visual imagery of theatrical events.

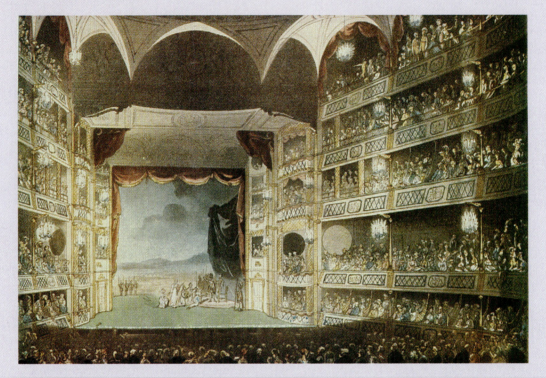

DRURY LANE THEATRE

The Drury Lane Theatre in London, England, was first built in late 1600s and was frequently enlarged and renovated to accommodate growing audiences and changing production needs. This image was first published in 1808–1811 in *Microcosm of London*. We see the proscenium theatre as it appeared after its enlargement of 1794. The features of this theatre were typical of the late eighteenth and early nineteenth centuries: a generous apron below the proscenium arch for the actors, a large scenic space above the arch for changeable wing and drop scenery, a functioning proscenium door on each side of the stage opening onto the apron and used for many exits and entrances, and for the audience five levels of boxes and galleries rising above the pit (orchestra). The house could accommodate more than 3,000 audience members. Note that the audience as well as the stage is fully lit by candles, which remained lit throughout the performances.

Collection of the authors.

ASTLEY'S THEATRE

Astley's Amphitheatre, which opened in 1784, burned several times. This image was probably the third Astley's, built in 1804 and illustrated in *Microcosm of London.* Although the stage was nearly as large as Drury Lane and well equipped, the house of this specialty theatre was much smaller. It is typical of theatre in many historical periods to mix dramatic and variety entertainments. Equestrian shows at Astley's were combined with melodrama and comedy with titles such as *The Blood Red Knight,* in which a castle was attacked and burnt. Even tragedy was produced here using both a performance ring and a proscenium stage with proscenium doors, thus creating split focus like a circus. Note that the audience could nearly surround the ring in the pit, boxes, and galleries; also note the four levels of seating similar to traditional theatres, and the huge candelabra overhead for illumination of both ring and audience. Novelty and variety theatre continues to thrive. We can still see dramatized equestrian shows such as *Dixie Stampede* in Myrtle Beach, South Carolina.

Collection of the authors.

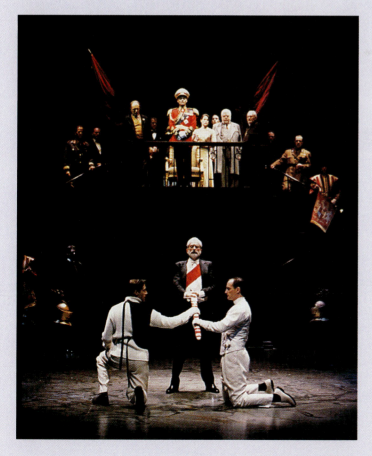

THE UPPER LEVEL IN SHAKESPEARE

Elizabethan theatres such as Shakespeare's Globe featured an upper performance level. Contemporary designers and directors continue to adapt this feature for both thrust and proscenium theatres. Here we see a 2000 production of Shakespeare's *Richard II* using an upper level to stage a duel that King Richard interrupts and cancels, much to the frustration of the fighters. Richard stands high above the field and Lord Marshal, who is instructing the knights as they prepare for battle. The upper level allows pageantry, consolidates the crowd of onlookers from court, and underscores the monarch's power early in the play. Later the height can be used for castle walls as the king encounters Bollingbroke (one of the duelists), who ultimately overthrows Richard and usurps the crown. Directed by Gerald Freedman; set designed by John Ezell; costumes designed by Lawrence Casey; lighting designed by Mary Jo Dondlinger.

Photo by Carol Rosegg. Courtesy of the Shakespeare Theatre, Washington, D.C.

IMPOSSIBLE SPACE

This scenic rendering by Wes Peters for a production of *Tango* by Polish playwright Slawomir Mrożek demonstrates a whimsical and "impossible" approach to proscenium space as a location with elements that seem to float and defy logical construction. What is called for in the play is a disordered interior crowded by the experiments of avant-garde artists who find themselves in conflict with their surprisingly conservative son, who rebels against his rebellious parents by trying to restore order. The conflict is humorous but leads to deadly consequences.

The second image shows the design as realized on the stage. The doors and windows are close to the original rendering, and much of the suspended scenery is virtually the same. A floating baby carriage, however, has been added, and the addition of stage lighting gives a different quality to color and intensity. Nonetheless, on the whole the design and executed setting are very close and reflect a cartoonlike effect. "Impossible" architecture is made concrete. This show was produced at Indiana University and directed by Sergei Ponomarov.

Designs and photographs courtesy of Wes Peters.

FORMALITY

This setting for *Romeo and Juliet* was designed by Ming Cho Lee for a production directed by Jon Jory in 1994. Note the extended apron with steps down to vomitoria on each downstage corner of the apron used as entrances and exits. The setting's symmetrical façade also has five upstage doorways, which are matched by open windows with balconies—playable spaces. The façade appears as solid architecture, but it is painted with human figures to suggest an antique style. This is an open playing space with a variety of levels and access. The result is a strong suggestion of a formalized place in keeping with the severity of the world in which the two lovers reside. The casket at center is for the death scene.

Photo by Richard C. Trigg. Courtesy of Actors Theatre of Louisville.

REALITY-BASED STAGING

Realistic approaches to space abound in the contemporary theatre. Although British Restoration comedies (1660–1700) were not originally produced realistically, they easily lend themselves to such an approach as in this 2000 revival of *The Country Wife* by William Wycherley. Both setting and costumes indicate the historical period of the play. The play was first performed in 1673, and the costume designer Robert Perdziola selected a style from the 1650s.

In the Restoration period the scenery would have been two-dimensional, all painted, wing and drop designs. Here, however, the setting designed by Simon Higlett has an architectural approach. The result is an authentic, functional look. The staircase and its long landing above provide variety in playing levels, and the minimal presence of furniture and highly polished floor accentuate open space and allow freedom of movement. The actors are given prominence and the detailed costumes are set off to advantage. The large window and its lighting suggest a natural light source for the space. Directed by Keith Baxter; lighting designed by Peter West.

Photo by Carol Rosegg. Courtesy of the Shakespeare Theatre, Washington, D.C.

REVOLVING STAGE

Since the early twentieth century the revolving stage has found many uses in Western theatre. A typical application is to accommodate multiple settings, changing one offstage while another is used for performance onstage. In these two photographs we see Eugene O'Neill's *Ah, Wilderness!* as produced in 2002. O'Neill calls for two interiors of a house in 1906, one interior of a bar, and one exterior of a beach. The scenic designs by Russell Metheny combined both the domestic interiors as an exterior façade of the house with generous porch and furniture on the "lawn," but all is placed on the revolving stage. When the barroom is called for, the set revolved to reveal the bar before returning to the house (where most of the action takes place). Then the bar offstage is replaced by the beach scene, which here becomes a pier. This system effectively simplified the complete box set changes utilized in the original 1933 production—a process that might seem cumbersome now. Directed by Janet Allen; lighting designed by Michael Lincoln.

Photos courtesy of Indiana Repertory Theatre.

THE DYNAMICS OF BACKLIGHT

These two photographs demonstrate different effects of backlight in production. The first is from a production of *The Great God Brown* by Eugene O'Neill at Towson State University. It looks as though it could be a dance, but it is an image of four of the principal characters lit exclusively by backlight on an all black set. We can see the silhouettes and a few details of costumes and positions of the actors' bodies, but no faces. Because all is surrounded by darkness, the characters are isolated, not only from their surroundings but also from one another. Form is more important here than character. Lighting designed by Scott Rosenfeld; costumes designed by Georgia Baker.

The second photo is of *Cloud Nine* by Caryl Churchill, interpreted in an all-white box set designed by William J. Pierson at Towson State University. A soldier (actually a ghost) has just burst through the door backlit by a bright spot so that we see no details of his face or costume (mostly the silhouette). Because the set is white, however, and unlike the first photo, light streams down the raked stage as considerable light bounces back to reveal portions of the walls. Low-intensity amber lighting on the two actors downstage gives them secondary focus and allows the audience to witness character reactions to the ghost.

Collection of the authors.

CONCEPT IMAGING FOR LIGHTING

Lighting design made an important advance with the creation of computer rendering. This image is a part of the lighting conception for *Oedipus the King* by Sophocles. The computer rendering is by lighting designer Robert Shakespeare for a production directed by Howard Jensen at Indiana University. This is the preset (what the audience sees on stage before the play begins) revealing the dank atmosphere of Thebes. We see the large door of the palace, but the action is set in the twentieth century—an Eastern European look with elements reminiscent of run-down classical architecture. Smoke periodically emanates from the ground downstage of the palace. When a preset is used, portions of the setting are typically illuminated in a fashion that is meant to intrigue the audience and suggest mood without fully revealing the scenery. Computer rendering also allows the lighting designer to share his or her ideas with the rest of the production team before any lighting instruments are hung in the theatre.

Image courtesy of Robert Shakespeare.

ICON AS SCENERY

In this whimsical setting for *bobrauschenbergamerica* by Charles L. Mee, the performance space becomes a U.S. flag. Because the flag holds important distinctions for people likely to see the production, the audience could keep commentary of the imagery in mind. The characters are performing on and inside a symbol because the flag is not merely a background; rather it is the room for the staged action. One can see the characters trapped by the flag, walking on the flag, emerging from the flag (through its doors), or even escaping the flag. The play is about the American artist Robert Rauschenberg, whose work was often developed as collage of everyday objects and advertising. The designed space celebrates the collecting nature of Rauschenberg's approach to art. Directed by Anne Bogart and created by the SITI Company for the Humana Festival of New American Plays at Actors Theatre of Louisville (2001); scenic and costume design by James Schuette; lighting design by Brian Scott.

Photo by Richard C. Trigg. Courtesy of Actors Theatre of Louisville.

PROJECTED SCENERY

Projected scenery has become common since the 1970s. In this production of Shakespeare's *Macbeth* the screens and surfaces upstage of the actors changed frequently in color, pattern, texture, angle, and intensity. Because this was a high-tech production in which three actors played all of the roles, the effect was one of frequent transformation—almost as if the characters were generated cybernetically. This effect was of course enhanced by the use of masks and dynamic, Asian-inspired costumes that made the human form seem larger than life. Actors: Kim Martin-Cotten and Will Bond. Directed by Marc Masterson; scenic design by Steve O'Hearn; lighting design by Tony Penna; costume design by Connie Furr-Solomon.

Photo by Larry Hunt. Courtesy of Actors Theatre of Louisville.

APPLICATIONS OF THE SCRIM

Aida (2000) by Elton John, Tim Rice, Linda Woolverton, Robert Falls, and David Henry Hwang calls for a swimming pool scene. The result in the Broadway production created a stunning moment when the audience saw the pool appear vertically (as

though the audience is hovering above it). Such an image, so common in film, can surprise us in the theatre. The pool is painted on the downstage side of a scrim (translucent fabric) and lit from the front while actors are also lit upstage of the scrim to make them appear to be swimming in the pool. The actors were flown to give them full body movement. Uses of the scrim are as old as the late eighteenth century and are popular for sudden appearances, disappearances, transformations, visions, and dreams. Scenic design by Bob Crowley; lighting design by Natasha Katz; directed by Robert Falls.

Photo by Joan Marcus.

Glossary

above. Stage direction indicating upstage or away from the audience.

accent. The details of a costume. Buttons, lace, piping along edges, embroidery, jewelry, are all examples of accent.

active participation. In theatre, the audience involvement in the live event. Unlike in film and television, the audience members choose where to direct their attention, and their reactions are shared with the performers on stage.

actor. A person who embodies a character on the stage. The Latin word *actor* meant "doer" and became the word of choice for performers in most Western traditions.

actor choices. How the performer embodies the character physically, vocally, and emotionally, including such things as gesture, facial expression, movement, and vocal quality, and emotional expression.

actor-manager. An actor who served as leader of a theatrical company in Europe during the seventeenth through nineteenth centuries. Actor-managers made financial decisions, selected the repertory of plays, and hired the actors.

Actors' Equity Association. The professional union of theatrical actors and stage managers in the United States.

aesthetic distance. Psychological separation, or a sense of detachment; the recognition that what happens on stage is not reality; literally, "the distance of art."

affective memory. A technique for developing a character in which the actor reexperiences a moment from his or her life that stimulated an emotion similar to the one that the actor's character is feeling at a certain point in the play.

allusion. A reference to previous art, literature, historical event, geography, or culture in a play; allusion contributes to the creation of thought.

antiquarianism. In nineteenth-century Europe, the practice of researching and recreating authentic styles of dress, architecture, and interior design when producing plays written or set in the past. This term was later replaced by "historical accuracy."

apron. In a proscenium theatre an extension of the stage that continues toward the audience below the proscenium arch.

arena space/theatre. An actor/audience configuration in which the audience completely surrounds the performance area.

articulation. The actor's shaping of the sounds of words (especially consonants) in order to be understood by the audience.

artistic director. In most professional nonprofit resident theatres (those that produce a season of plays) the staff member with primary responsibility for the artistic life of the theatre. The artistic director typically hires the season's directors and designers.

artistic intent. The purpose of a production, such as to entertain, to shock, to persuade, to comfort. In establishing the intent of the artists, an audience member can more effectively evaluate how well the production achieved its goals.

aside. Words spoken by a character that are intended to be heard by the audience but not by other characters. Traditionally delivered directly to the audience. Most asides are brief.

audition. The standard tool for casting a production. Auditions may include prepared audition pieces, interviews, or unrehearsed ("cold") readings from the play or other material.

auteur. A director who operates with almost total control and, in building the three-dimensional performance, feels responsible for creating meaning for the audience. The director, rather than the playwright, is the primary creative force.

***autos sacramentales*.** Religious plays performed in Spain during the Golden Age (c. 1580–1680) and well into the eighteenth century.

avant-garde. Art that pushes recognized boundaries. Originally a French military term meaning *vanguard* (the front line of troops who are the first to engage the enemy), the term was appropriated by artists to signify those who venture into new, unknown territory in the arts. The term is often used synonymously with the term *experiment*.

balcony. Audience seating areas suspended above the orchestra from the back of the house.

Beijing Opera. See **Chinese music drama.**

believability. Audience acceptance of the authenticity of character and action.

below. Stage direction indicating downstage or toward the audience.

biological traits. First level of characterization, including the species, sex, age, and race of the character.

biomechanics. A highly energetic, mimetic approach to acting that abstracted human movement and created a very athletic actor, first developed by Russian director Vsevolod Meyerhold.

black box. A flexible performance space (usually small) in which the actor/audience configuration can be easily changed for each production.

blank verse. Poetry that does not use rhyme but has a specific, set rhythm (iambic pentameter with occasional variations). Blank verse was used extensively by Elizabethan playwrights.

blocking. Planned actor movement usually recorded in a promptbook.

book musical. A musical play that tells a story and has spoken text as well as songs.

booth stage. A portable thrust stage, probably used by ancient Greek and Roman mime performers and definitely used by actors in the Middle Ages and well beyond.

box. A partially enclosed audience seating area popular from the Renaissance through the nineteenth century. Boxes were the most expensive form of seating.

box-office manager. Theatre staff member responsible for organizing and overseeing ticket sales, including supervising the staff members who deal directly with the public.

box set. Scenery that imitates the interior of a room with walls, sometimes ceiling, furniture, and visual detail, standard in Europe and North America after 1830.

breeches role. From sixteenth- to nineteenth-century Europe, a male character performed by a woman or a female character who disguises herself as a man.

Broadway. Both a particular area of New York (the theatre district bordered by 41st to 53rd Streets and Sixth to Ninth Avenues) and the size of the house in New York commercial theatre (some Broadway theatres seat as many as 1,900 patrons).

Bunraku. Traditional form of Japanese theatre using large puppets (three fifths the size of a human). The operators remain visible to the audience.

callbacks. A second or later round of auditions to which specific actors are invited.

casting. The selection of actors to play each character in the show; casting is usually the responsibility of the director.

casting director. A specialist in finding actors for specific roles who assists the director in some professional productions.

catharsis. A term used by the Greek philosopher Aristotle (384–322 B.C.E.) to describe the audience's emotional release at the end of a tragedy; a performance was designed to engage the audience's feelings and build in intensity so that the spectator felt cleansed or purged of strong emotion by the end of the play.

causal plot. Structure of a script organized by a cause-to-effect relationship of events; event A leads to event B, which leads to event C, and so forth. Without A and B there is no C. Most thrillers and comedies on film and television have a linear and causal structure.

cazuela. In the Spanish Golden Age, a segregated area for unmarried or unaccompanied women at the back of the house on the second level facing the stage.

center. In stage directions the space in the middle of the stage. Abbreviated C.

character. The fictional person created to perform the action of the play; one of the six elements of a play identified by Aristotle.

character objective. Goal or intention of a character as defined by the actor; what the actor decides the character is trying to accomplish at any given moment of the play. Actors play character objectives that are important or logical to the character's action, needs, desires, and state of mind.

Chinese music drama. A form of classical Chinese theatre that is highly stylized with movement, dance, chant, and music. In the early 1800s Chinese artists combined forms of theatre that had developed in many different regions to create what is now known as Chinese music drama, also called Beijing Opera.

choreographer. Artist who stages dancing or stylized movement. A choreographer must work closely with the production's director; sometimes one person serves as both director and choreographer.

chorus. A group of performers working together vocally and physically. A chorus of approximately twelve to fifteen singer-dancers who interacted with and responded to the actors was an important element of ancient Greek theatre.

chronicle. A dramatic adaptation of historical events dealing with kings and frequent struggles for the crown, especially popular in Elizabethan England. Also called a *history play.*

cliff-hanger. A play with a causal plot that does not have falling action; the play stops at the climax and the outcome of the conflict is not shown.

climax. The emotional highpoint of the action in a causal plot; the conflict has reached a critical stage, and the outcome is finally decided.

collective hero. A group of characters serving together as the protagonist of a play.

color. An important design element in the theatre. Different colors tend to create different responses in human beings; designers think not only about the effect that a particular color will have on the audience, but also about the message that it sends about the world of the play. In lighting, color is created by filtering the light with color media or color filters.

combination company. Full touring productions (all actors, scenery, costumes, etc.) that toured throughout

Europe and North America. The term was used in the nineteenth century, but the concept is applicable for touring companies today that transport all elements of production with them as they perform throughout the country or world.

comedia. A secular (not religious) play during the Golden Age in Spain.

comedy. A dramatic genre emphasizing humor, typically taking an objective (rather than emotional) approach to life.

comedy of character. A subgenre of comedy in which the action is driven by the eccentricities of its major figure.

comedy of idea. A subgenre of comedy organized around thought.

comedy of manners. A subgenre of comedy that explores the behavior of a particular segment of society; characters frequently find their own desires are at odds with social expectations.

comic relief. Action that is created to ease emotional tension or contrast with a major event at strategic points within a tragedy, melodrama, or other genre that is not principally comic.

commedia dell'arte. Improvisational comedy that originated in Italy sometime before 1568. *Commedia* actors played conventional characters (some of which were masked) and planned the scenario and comic business ahead of time but developed specific dialogue and action as the show progressed in front of an audience.

commercial theatre. Shows that are produced to earn a profit for investors.

community theatre. Amateur theatre in which shows are created by residents of a particular area who come together without being part of a professional or academic institution.

company manager. See **managing director.**

composer. An artist who creates original music for a theatrical production.

concept. Artistic decisions meant to communicate a specific interpretation of a play to the audience. Concept is created visually and aurally with scenery, costume, lighting, tempo, line readings, movement, and composition. Development or the coordination of development of concept is a responsibility of the director.

conceptual director. Typically, a director who creates a production without an existing text or who chooses a text that then becomes a pretext for the director's conception. Such creative work is often dominated by dynamic visual images, music, dance, and carefully choreographed movement.

conflict. The central element of causal plot, two forces working against each other: two or more characters (generally) want the same thing (money, power, a kingdom, love) or want different things to happen (escape or justice, revolution or consolidation of power).

constructivist scenery. A scenic unit that consists of exposed beams, supports, and sometimes movable parts.

context of performance. The place of performance that suggests audience expectations for a particular production; an audience member has a different set of expectations when attending a Broadway show with a high ticket price than a community theatre production, for example.

continental seating. Arrangement of audience seating that does not include aisles except at extreme left and right; the orchestra seats are unbroken in one long horizontal arc, and rows of seats are placed a good distance apart to facilitate audience passage.

convention. An agreement between the production personnel and the audience. A widely used convention in the twenty-first century is the dimming of the house lights, which tells the audience that the performance is about to begin.

corral. A type of theatre that was popular during the Golden Age in Spain and featured a raised, roofed stage backed by a façade with doors and a discovery space, a second balcony level, three levels of galleries and boxes for the audience, and a pit (*patio*) for standees open to the sky.

costume plot. A chart that records items of clothing worn by each actor in each scene of a play.

costume shop manager. Staff member who coordinates the efforts of cutters, stitchers, and other personnel in building costumes.

critical research paper. A paper examining how a play or production works that includes the ideas of other critics or historians as well as those of the writer.

criticism. Analysis, interpretation, or evaluation of a play or production.

cross. Actor movement of any length across the stage. Abbreviated as X.

crossfade. Two or more simultaneous changes in lighting made possible by the creation of dimmers and lighting consoles in the twentieth century.

cue. (1) A signal for a change in a technical element (light, set, or sound). (2) A signal for an actor to speak or move.

cue-to-cue. A technical rehearsal in which only the parts of the play including cues are run; most dialogue or action in between is skipped. The stage manager organizes and runs the cue-to-cue.

cycle. A series of religious plays (often called mystery plays) popular throughout Europe during the Middle Ages. Cycles (or cycle plays) were based on biblical stories ranging from the creation of the world to the last judgment and were performed outdoors in the vernacular (local language).

deconstruction (or **deconstructed production).** A radically reinterpreted famous play in which the original play may still be recognized. The new production, however, uses the written play as only a pretext and frequently comments on or negates the apparent intent of the original play.

decorum. The neoclassical concept of universality in morality and characterization, which led to characters drawn by playwrights according to current notions of what was most appropriate for behavior, values, and language in terms of characters' age, sex, social class, occupation, and economic condition.

dialogue. Words spoken by the characters in a play.

director. The person in charge of the artistic aspects of theatrical production. It is the director's job to guide the transformation of the play to live production. The director interprets the play and heads the artistic team, providing a focus and organization for the creative work.

discovery. Something important is found, learned, or realized during the action of a play; an element of causal plot.

distribution. An element of lighting design determined by where lighting instruments are placed as well as the type of instruments used. Angle is an important part of distribution since it affects the mood and appearance of the actors as well as suggesting time of day.

dithyramb. In ancient Greece, a choric presentation sung and danced in homage to the god Dionysus.

downstage. The stage area closest to the audience; on the raked stage of Renaissance theatres, the stage literally sloped downward as it got closer to the audience. Abbreviated D.

dramaturg. A specialist in dramatic literature and theatre history who serves as a consultant for production. For a revival the dramaturg conducts research on the play, author, or historical period. When collaborating on an original play (a script produced for the first time), a dramaturg reads the script, attends readings, attends rehearsals, and offers suggestions to the playwright and director. Such a specialist who coordinates a season of plays is often referred to as a *literary manager.*

Dramatists Guild, Inc. Professional organization of playwrights in the United States.

dress rehearsal. Rehearsal at which the costumes are worn by the actors. Several dress rehearsals usually end the period of rehearsal before the show is performed for an audience.

educational theatre. Production of plays in schools at primary, secondary, undergraduate, and graduate levels. Production activity may be extracurricular or carefully integrated into classroom structure and preprofessional training.

elements of a play. Plot, character, thought, language, music, and spectacle, identified by Aristotle in the *Poetics* (fourth century B.C.E.).

ellipsoidal. Spotlight that creates a hard-edged beam and includes four shutters around the circular lens to further control its focus.

empathy. Emotional identification. In the theatre empathy refers to a sense of participation—an identification with character. Empathy occurs when you feel along *with* the characters.

ensemble. Actors who function seamlessly together as a unit rather than as individual performers

environmental theatre. A performance in which audience and actors share the same space. There is little or no separation of acting and observing areas, with the result that the audience members are physically part of the performance.

Epic Theatre. Anti-illusionist theatre featuring emotional detachment, narration, songs, and obvious theatricality that was developed by German playwright, director, and theorist Bertolt Brecht.

episodic. A structural term describing a play with an early point of attack; selected dramatized moments in the story are separated by breaks in the action. The playwright may indicate a passage of time between scenes through dialogue.

ethical choice. A choice that a character must face about a moral issue; an ethical choice is often a defining moment for a protagonist, particularly in a tragedy.

ethical traits. A level of characterization that includes the moral standards held by a character.

executive director. See **managing director.**

exposition. Information that is needed to understand the play but is not a part of the dramatized action. Although exposition may be introduced throughout the play, a great deal of information is typically conveyed in the first few scenes.

expressionism. A nonrealistic approach to production in which the subjective experience of the character is depicted on stage. Visual and aural aspects of production often suggest anxiety and the mental breakdown of the central character. German and American expressionism in the 1910s and 1920s dramatized the dehumanization or destruction of humanity at the hands of commercialism, industry, and war.

façade. An architectural background for the action of a play; a generalized standing or hanging structure, often multilevel, that may be neutral or decorated but always resides upstage of the action, creating a background that can suggest nearly any location, inside or out.

falling action. An element of causal plot; the events from the climax to the end of the play in which emotional intensity drops. Typically, loose ends are tied up for the audience and balance is restored, although something clearly is different than at the play's beginning. Falling action is also sometimes called the play's *resolution* or *dénouement.*

farce. A type of situation comedy that emphasizes broad physical action.

flashback. A scene that dramatizes an event that occurred prior to the play's beginning (point of attack) or at least earlier than the scene which precedes the flashback scene in performance.

flat. A scenic unit typically framed with 1 × 3 lumber and covered with canvas, muslin, plywood, or other material. Flats often represent a solid surface such as a wall but are actually lightweight and easy to move.

found space. A place that is used for production, indoors or out, that was never intended as a theatrical space when created or designed.

fourth wall. An approach to staging in which actors move and behave in the set as if it were actually the room represented and act as if an audience is not present; the proscenium arch if present is treated as the fourth wall of an enclosed room.

fresnel. A spotlight that is used to create a soft beam of light that blends with others to create the appearance of an even area of light.

front elevation. Drafting of the set, breaking it into units to be built and showing each piece of scenery from the front.

front-of-house. Theatre operations that deal directly with the audience (such as ticket sales and assistance in finding seats).

gallery. Raised area of audience seating above the orchestra level in proscenium and thrust theatres since the Renaissance.

genre. A classification of drama related to the kind of emotional response a play creates in the audience. The four major genres in the Western tradition are tragedy, comedy, tragicomedy, and melodrama.

given circumstances. Anything established by the playwright that distinguishes location, historical period, onstage properties, time of day, and details about character that is not a matter of interpretation or opinion: where the character is from, for example, or the fact that he or she is highly educated, recently divorced, or terminally ill.

gobo. A lighting projection using a metal cutout like a stencil in front of the light source to block solid areas of light, casting shadows on the stage to suggest leaf patterns, prison bars, and so on.

grand drape. Front curtain in a proscenium theatre sometimes used to hide scene changes or to indicate the beginnings and conclusions of acts or scenes.

ground plan. A drafting of the plan of the set as seen from overhead. A ground plan shows where any scenic pieces or set props (such as furniture) are to be placed.

ground row. Low, flat, painted scenery at stage level. When combined with wing, drop, and border scenery, ground rows extended the line of the wing out toward center stage.

hanamichi. In Japanese Kabuki theatre, a stage-level ramp that passes directly from the stage apron down right center to the back of the house. This narrow path, which places the actor in the midst of the audience, is used for many important entrances and exits. Sometimes a secondary *hanamichi* is used down left as well.

happening. An event, planned or spontaneous, in which the audience watched or participated in the production of temporary art; popular in the 1960s and a precursor of today's performance art.

historical accuracy. Scenery and costumes representing the past and designed according to authentic designs or images from the period suggested.

histrio. A Latin term for actor; the root of our word "histrionic," by which we usually mean exaggerated human responses.

house. The audience area of any theatrical space.

house manager. The staff member who is responsible for the safety and comfort of the audience members during their time in the theatre. House managers coordinate ushers, make sure the audience areas of the theatre are clean and safe, resolve any seating problems, and deal with any emergencies.

hybrid theatre. Many theatres do not fit neatly into either the professional or the amateur category. The designation "semiprofessional" is sometimes used for companies that aspire to professional status but currently are not well established enough to maintain the payroll of a professional theatre.

hyperbole. Use of overstatement as figurative language; for example, "I'm so hungry I could eat a horse."

hypokrites. Greek word for actor; the root of our words *hypocrisy* and *hypocrite.*

iambic pentameter. Set rhythm of verse in which there is a stress on each second syllable and five stresses per line (see also **blank verse**).

improvisation. A type of performance in which dialogue and action are not planned ahead of time and written down but are made up on the spot by the actors.

inamorata/inamorato. Female/male young lover. Stock characters in *commedia dell'arte*. Actors playing the young lovers were not masked and were cast in part for their physical attractiveness.

inciting incident. In a causal plot, an event that destroys the uneasy balance of the play's beginning and sets off the major conflict of forces.

intensity. Brightness of lighting on the stage; intensity is controlled by the amount of lumens pumped onto the stage, which depends on the number of lighting instruments used.

interludes. Secular plays (nonreligious dramas) in the medieval period, many of which were presented between the courses of banquets. Interludes began to be written and performed by the 1200s. Most surviving interludes are farces from France and England.

intermezzi. Spectacular Italian pageants full of symbolism and allegory that were frequently performed at court between other entertainments or during the intervals between acts of a play or opera, popular from the 1400s to the 1600s.

International Alliance of Theatrical Stage Employees. Union for technical positions in the professional theatre.

International Phonetic Alphabet (IPA). A system of specific symbols representing individual sounds that helps actors to both analyze their own speech and reproduce a host of dialects and accents.

interpretation. (1) An audience member's intuitive response or subjective experience of physical action or setting; the meaning that the audience member assigns to what he or she has observed. (2) An artist's creation of meaning beyond what is literal or obvious in the text.

Kabuki. The most popular classical Japanese form of theatre, tragic, comic, and melodramatic in genre, featuring magnificent spectacle, colorful costumes, and the performance of female roles by men (see *onnagata*).

Kadensho. Japanese treatise on the theory of performance and composition for Noh theatre written by Zeami (1363–1444), which presents *yugen* as the central image of Noh.

Kathakali. A form of Indian dance-drama that is rooted in Hindu mythology, featuring dance and stylized gesture performed by men in elaborate, colorful, costumes and makeup. Kathakali originated in the seventeenth century in Southern India.

Kutiyattum. A religious theatrical form from India based on ancient epics using music, open space, male and female performers, and colorful costumes.

language. The playwright's choice of words in a play; one of the six elements of a play identified by Aristotle. Language written for the stage must be capable of being spoken aloud. It is usually a heightened version of human speech.

lazzi. In *commedia dell'arte*, the often complex comic physical routines created by the clowns. Many were described in detail, and the written accounts allow us to duplicate or approximate their performance.

League of American Theatres and Producers. An organization made up of theatre owners and operators, producers, presenters, and general managers. It is the national trade association for the commercial theatre industry. The organization provides support for its members and aims to further the interests of Broadway theatre across North America.

League of Resident Theatres (LORT). An organization of professional resident theatres that provides support for its members, particularly in communicating with the federal government and by serving as a collective bargaining agent with the various employee unions. The analogous organization for English-speaking theatre in Canada is the Professional Association of Canadian Theatres.

levels of characterization. Qualities and traits assigned to a character by the playwright: biological, physical, psychological/emotional, social, and ethical. A minor character might be developed only through the first two levels; a full and complex character will draw on all five.

lighting console. A lighting control board with a memory system.

lighting designer. An artist who designs or affects all visual elements by controlling focus and mood with color, placement, and intensity of light.

lighting plot. A technical drawing created by the lighting designer showing where each instrument is to be hung, along with the type of instrument and color filters to be used.

line. See **silhouette.**

linear plot. Organization of a play in which the action progresses forward and sequentially in time.

Literary Managers and Dramaturgs of the Americas. An organization that supports dramaturgs and literary managers in professional and academic theatre.

liturgical drama. Plays performed by the clergy in Latin as part of the worship service in Christian monasteries and cathedrals during the Middle Ages.

lyricist. An artist who writes the words (lyrics) for songs.

magnitude. The sense of importance typical of tragedy as identified by Aristotle.

makeup designer. An artist specializing in the design of realistic or stylized makeup for the characters; makeup is typically designed by the costume designer or the actors themselves if there is not a particular makeup designer assigned to a production.

managing director. The staff member filling the job of producer in nonprofit theatres. The managing director works closely with the artistic director to ensure the continuity and mission of the organization. The titles *executive director* and *company manager* are also used for staff members who hold producing duties.

mansion. A symbolic scenic unit indicating place in staging during the Middle Ages.

masking. Black velour draperies or flats hung or placed vertically and horizontally across the stage to cut off audience view of backstage areas.

masque. A poetic, extravagant court entertainment with dancing, often celebrating the monarch or a royal visitor to the English court in the sixteenth and seventeenth centuries.

master electrician. A staff member who works closely with the lighting designer and directs a lighting crew to hang, focus, and filter the lighting instruments and to set up circuitry, the lighting console, and sometimes sound equipment also.

melodrama. A dramatic genre featuring a conflict between good and bad characters, fast-paced action, a spectacular climax, and poetic justice.

metaphor. Figurative language equating two unlike objects to suggest a similarity between them; for example, "She was a rock during that difficult time."

metatheatre. A production or play that self-consciously comments on the play as taking place in a theatre.

mie. In Japanese Kabuki, an actor's showy pose and facial expression suggesting sustained emotion.

mime. (1) In ancient Greece and Rome, a "pass the hat" street performer; a kind of variety entertainment. (2) Today used interchangeably with "pantomime" and "pantomime artist."

mimesis. As defined by Aristotle, the artist's process of imitating character and action.

miracle play. European play from the fifteenth or sixteenth centuries that recounted the real or apocryphal lives of saints. Also called *saint's play.*

model. A three-dimensional miniature version of the set, built to scale (usually one quarter or one half inch to the foot).

modernism. The shift in theatre beginning with realism; throughout the twentieth century scholars noted that modern theatre and drama began with Ibsen. Many late-twentieth-century scholars associated modernism with the type of theatre that rebelled against realism and naturalism. In this book we use the term "modernism" to refer to both realistic and much non-realistic theatre from the late nineteenth century to the present day.

monologue. (1) An extended speech heard by other characters in the play. (2) An extended speech used as an audition piece.

morality play. A play depicting humanity's struggle with good and evil using allegorical characters such as Good Deeds and Death, popular during the Middle Ages in Europe.

movement. See **orchestration**.

music. One of the six elements of drama as defined by Aristotle; music has been very important in the theatre of most cultures, and in many cases it has been vital.

music director. An artist who works with singers and orchestra in learning and performing the music for a play.

mystery play. See **cycles**.

National Endowment for the Arts (NEA). A federally endowed program that supports the fine and performing arts throughout the United States.

naturalism. A style of drama called for in 1880 by Émile Zola in which playwrights were to present a "slice of life" on the stage, following the actual pace of everyday life and avoiding well-made play structure.

Natyasastra. Sometimes translated as "Doctrine of Dramatic Art," a detailed Indian document by Bharata that appears to predate the most important surviving Sanskrit plays and outlines the principles of performance, staging, and dramatic form as practiced in India and applied to Sanskrit plays.

neoclassicism. A systematic approach to playwriting and production based on interpretations of classical Greek and Roman models of plays and theory. Neoclassical principles were developed in Renaissance Italy and popularized in seventeenth-century France.

new stagecraft. A term used for an approach to scenic design featuring simplicity, avoidance of detail, and reduction of a location to its most significant elements. New stagecraft was based on the innovative designs of Adolphe Appia and Gordon Craig with their images of platforms, stairs, and open spaces.

Noh. The first great classical theatre of Japan, developed in the court of the shogun in the feudal samurai system of the late fourteenth century. Noh features music, slow, choreographed movement, use of carefully carved masks, and all male performers.

nonprofit theatre. Productions from which no individual or organization realizes a profit from the investment in production; any money taken in at the box office or earned from other sources is funneled back into the arts organization to support other shows and programs. Nonprofit theatre may be amateur or professional.

nontraditional casting. The practice of casting actors of a race different from that of the character as written.

objectives. See **character objectives**.

observation. Audience recognition of what is physically happening on stage: a change in the color of light, for example, or the sudden cross by an actor. The next step for an audience member is interpretation.

off-Broadway. Commercial theatre in New York City with fewer than 500 seats in Manhattan, not located in the "Broadway District." The term dates from 1955.

off-off-Broadway. In the 1960s, theatre in New York City that occurred outside the traditional theatre spaces of Broadway and Off-Broadway. Such work was typically experimental in nature and often occurred in alternative spaces—coffeehouses, church basements, warehouses, and private homes. Today, the term "Off-off-Broadway" is used to refer to professional or semi-professional performances that are not Equity. While the term "Off-off-Broadway" originated in New York, this kind of theatre may exist anywhere. Such theatres in Chicago are known as "off-Loop" and in Los Angeles as "Equity waiver."

onnagata. An actor who is a female impersonator in Kabuki theatre. The male performer attempts to create as complete and literal a transformation as possible through makeup, costume, movement, and gesture. In speech, however, the actor uses a falsetto voice that ultimately stylizes the presentation.

orchestra. (1) in a modern proscenium theatre the audience seating area at floor level immediately in front of the stage. (2) in ancient Greece a typically circular performance space, literally, "dancing place."

orchestra pit. In a proscenium theatre a sunken area between the apron and the audience that was traditionally used to seat musicians.

orchestration. In lighting design, a change of intensity, color, or distribution of light on the stage. Also called *movement.*

original play. A common term for a play in its first production.

pageant. In the Middle Ages, wagons with scenery used in processional staging.

painter's elevation. A color picture showing the plan for painting each piece of scenery.

pantomime. A modern theatrical form in which a silent actor creates a scenario without words, relying only on physical expressiveness.

par lamps. Parabolic aluminated reflectors; a type of lighting instrument used to create parallel rays.

parados. In Greek theatre, an open space between the skene and the theatron that served as entrance and exit for the chorus and sometimes actors.

patio. The pit in the Spanish *corral* or public theatre in the Golden Age.

performance art. Usually one-person or first-person shows that purport to make the artist the subject of the performance.

periaktoi. Prism-shaped, three-sided scenic units that could be painted and revolved, referred to in a late classical account of theatre architecture of Greece and Rome.

physical traits. A level of characterization that includes the character's stature, weight, hair and eye color, and facial hair. In the theatre such traits are filled in automatically by the actor playing the role and by changes made with costume and makeup.

pinakes. Flat, painted scenery, referred to in a late classical account of theatre architecture in Greece and Rome.

pit. The audience standing area in Renaissance public theatres. Also known as *patio, yard* and *parterre.* Later the pit was seating area that we now call the orchestra.

platea. In the Middle Ages in Europe, an open playing space in front of a symbolic scenic unit (mansion).

play. A written text indicating the dialogue the characters speak and some of the physical action, also called a *script.*

play master. A man who coordinated and staged the cycles in Europe during the Middle ages; a precursor of the modern director. Also called *prompter* and *ordinary.*

playwright. The author, or crafter, of the play.

plot. As defined by Aristotle, the organization of the action of a play. Plot is not a story or list of events, but an organizing principle: Plot is what gives a play its unity. Another term for plot is *structure.*

Poetic Art. A critical document by the Roman Horace (65–8 B.C.E.) that influenced the Italian Renaissance as much as Seneca and perhaps more than Aristotle.

poetic justice. A device typical of the end of melodrama: good is rewarded; evil is punished.

Poetics. The first important examination of the tragic form, written by the Greek philosopher Aristotle in c. 335–323 B.C.E.

point of attack. In a linear plot, the point in the story at which the playwright chooses to start dramatizing the action. The story of the play may stretch far into the past, but the playwright selects one moment in that story to begin actually showing (rather than telling about) the progress of events.

postmodern. In the theatre, work that is no longer "modern" (in the sense that Tennessee Williams and Bertolt Brecht were modern). The postmodern comments on, satirizes, or reinterprets the modern. The postmodern artist is sometimes identified as artist and critic simultaneously. Some critics see it as an artistic style, hence postmodern*ism.* Others claim that it is a mind-set, a point of view that looks back on the previous century of artistic work with cynicism or futility—and sometimes despair. In visual terms it is dominated by simultaneous action and electronic or cybernetic technology, and structurally by repetition and deconstruction of masterpieces of the past.

poststructuralism. Dramatic work created after World War II that breaks down traditional causal structure. It may be impossible to figure out a logical story, since none is presented.

practical. A visible light source on stage that is often enhanced by unseen lighting instruments. For example, when a desk lamp or overhead chandelier on stage is turned on, light usually emanates from the practical, but accompanying instruments may "punch" the effect and help to imitate and perhaps intensify the light thrown by the practical on the stage.

presentational. A style of production that acknowledges theatricality and does not attempt to create the impression of "real life" on the stage. Presentational scenery, costumes, and lighting may suggest, distort, or even abstract reality. Presentational acting may include lines directed to the audience or other recognition of its presence.

preview. A performance of a show for a paying audience at a somewhat reduced ticket price before the official opening to which critics are invited.

processional staging. In the Middle Ages, the practice of moving wagons or pageants through the streets carrying actors and scenery to perform in various locations.

prima donna. The leading female role (performed without a mask) in *commedia dell'arte.*

producer. The person in charge of the financial and business aspects of a production. The producer usually negotiates the rights to a play and hires a director, who is in charge of the artistic aspects of production. In nonprofit theatres the job title is often managing director. One person may take on producing responsibilities, or they may be shared by a group.

production. The actual concrete performance of a play with actors, sets, costumes, lighting, and props.

production manager. A staff member usually employed by a theatre company with multiple performance spaces who is in charge of scheduling (spaces, rehearsals, and production meetings) and coordinating stage managers for the productions, especially when two or more productions are running and/or rehearsing simultaneously; also called a *production stage manager.*

professional theatre. Productions created by individuals who make a living (or at least attempt to do so) in the theatre. The professional venue may be commercial or **nonprofit,** and many theatre artists and technicians work in both.

projection. (1) In acting, the process of making the voice loud enough to be heard by the audience in the back of the house yet still sounding conversational. (2) In lighting, an image thrown onto the stage using light.

promptbook. A notebook kept by the director and stage manager of a production containing the text of the play, detailed stage directions, lighting and sound cues, and notes on production practices.

prompter. In the days of rolling repertory, a staff member who sat at the side of the stage or in a special box down center to call out any forgotten lines or stage business to the actors.

propaganda. Material specifically designed to advocate a particular ideology or point of view.

props manager. A staff member who organizes the collection or building of all properties in a show.

proscenium arch. A large open arch that marks the primary division between audience and performance space in a proscenium space. The proscenium arch frames the action of the play for the audience and limits the view of backstage areas.

proscenium space/theatre. An actor/audience configuration in which the audience is on only one side of the performance area; all audience members face the same direction.

prose. Language similar to everyday speech; not verse.

protagonist. The central character of a play.

psychological/emotional traits. A level of characterization developing the character's basic internal makeup. A character's psychological and emotional life provides the motivation for the action of the play.

public theatre. Professional playhouses in England and Spain in the Renaissance. In Elizabethan England, a three-story polygonal building featuring roofed galleries and a central pit (yard) open to the sky. Actors performed on a thrust stage backed by a façade with probably two doors and sometimes a curtained discovery space between them.

raked. Set at an angle. Early proscenium theatres featured a raked stage: The stage was elevated much higher at the back of the stage (upstage) than closer to the audience (downstage). Modern designers sometimes build a raked stage for a particular production as part of the design concept. When the audience area is raked, the seating is elevated toward the back of the house to facilitate seeing over the rows in front.

rasa. Mood; the organizing principle of Indian Sanskrit plays.

realism. A movement of the late nineteenth century championing the depiction of everyday life on the stage and the frank treatment of social problems in the theatre. The plays of Henrik Ibsen of the 1870s were important in establishing a dramatic style for realism. "Realism" continues to be used as a term for representational plays and production style.

rear elevation. A drafting showing each scenic piece from the back. Rear elevations are particularly important in constructing the scenery, since a rear view may show how each piece of scenery is to be built.

regional theatre. See **resident theatre.**

rehearsal. The period of work in which the show is made ready for the stage. A four- to five-week rehearsal period (six days a week, seven hours a day) is typical for professional productions. Educational and community theatres tend to take four to six weeks (five or six days a week, three to four hours a night).

rendering. A picture created by a designer to communicate with other production personnel. In costume design, a picture of each costume on an actor, ideally done in color often with appropriate swatches of fabric attached; in scenic design, a picture of the set, drawn in perspective from the audience point of view. The rendering shows what the stage will look like from the house. It is usually done in color and depicts the appearance of the set under lights.

representational. A style of production that attempts to represent reality on the stage. Representational scenery, costumes, lighting, and sound imitate precisely the kind of environment and details in which the action of the play would occur in real life. A representational acting style does not acknowledge the presence of the audience and uses techniques that result in a subtle, authentic style of performance.

resident theatre. A professional, nonprofit organization that maintains a constant presence in a community and produces an entire season of plays; sometimes called *regional theatre.* See also **League of Resident Theatres.**

reversal. In a causal plot, a line of action veers around suddenly to its opposite. The prime suspect in a murder investigation turns up dead, for example, and the detective must look for another solution to the crime.

review. A published account of a production giving information regarding where, what, when, and how to get tickets. An effective review gives the consumer enough information about the show to make an intelligent decision given personal tastes and priorities.

revival. Any production of a play that occurrs after the original production.

revolve. A circular portion of the stage floor that can rotate, first developed for the Bunraku and Kabuki theatre in Japan in 1758 and adopted in the West in the late nineteenth century.

rhetorical acting. A style of acting that was popular prior to the coming of realism in the late nineteenth century. Actors often attempted to make very direct contact with the audience rather than interact directly with other actors (at least as the norm). A big voice and grand gestures were intended to capture the attention and admiration of a fully lit and social audience.

rhetorical delivery. In ancient accounts and well into the nineteenth century, the art of oratory and of any public verbal communication, including physical interpretation through gesture, posture, movement, and facial expression.

rising action. In a causal plot, small units of action following the inciting incident that build in emotional intensity to the climax of the play.

rolling repertory. A system of daily changes of plays. Maintaining many plays in the company's production season—any play can be performed at any time.

romantic comedy. A subgenre of comedy that follows the attempts of lovers to get together. It shares this basic structure with many situation comedies, but romantic comedies more often produce a feeling of well being and sympathy at the end, rather than strong laughs.

romanticism. A movement of the late eighteenth and early nineteenth centuries that rejected nearly every aspect of neoclassicism, celebrated the natural world, and valued intense emotion and individuality.

royalty. A payment to the playwright made by the producing organization each time a play is produced.

run crew. Workers who maintain and execute cues for props, costumes, set, lighting, and sound during the run of a show.

run-through. A rehearsal in which an entire act or play is performed without stopping except at intermission breaks.

saint's play. See **miracle play.**

Sanskrit play. A play from ancient Hindu culture organized by mood, or *rasa*. Sanskrit drama suggested directions that later Asian theatre would take.

scene shop foreman. A staff member who oversees construction of the set by a crew of carpenters, scenic painters, and other craftspeople.

scenic (or **set) designer.** An artist who creates a visual home for the play on stage. Many people may help build scenery, but the designer envisions and controls the visual effect.

scrim. A translucent piece of fabric. When lit from the front, the scrim appears opaque (solid). When the scrim lighting is extinguished and an object behind it is lit, the scrim seems to disappear, and the object becomes visible.

script. See **play.**

section. A drafting showing the vertical elements of the set and permanent theatrical elements and their relative positions (for example, the heights at which scenery, lighting, and masking are to be hung).

sense memory. The actor's recall of sights, sounds, touch, and smells from specific past events.

sensory imagery. The use of concrete language appealing to the five senses to bring the physical world of the play alive for the audience and help convey the character's experience of environment.

set properties. Large actor-usable additions to the setting, such as furniture.

sharing system. Financial organization of a theatre company that splits any profits after the day's expenses based on how many shares each had invested in the venture or had been granted by the manager depending on his or her duties and importance to the company.

sight lines. The set designer's determination of what the audience can and cannot see.

silhouette. The outer shape of a costume. Silhouette is particularly indicative of time period and culture. Also called *line*.

simile. Figurative language comparing two unlike things using *like* or *as*; for example, "Her cheeks were as red as roses."

site-specific performance. A production developed for and closely linked to a particular location.

situation comedy (or **sitcom**): A subgenre of comedy based on the humorous qualities of the situation in which the characters find themselves.

skene. In ancient Greece, a stage house upstage of the circular orchestra (our source for the words *scene* and *scenery*).

slapstick. Broad comic action; the term originated with *commedia dell'arte* actors and their use of a long, flat paddle with a flap that literally made a loud slapping sound when used for comic beatings.

social traits. A level of characterization that may include a character's job or profession, socioeconomic status, and/or religious or political affiliation.

Society of Stage Directors and Choreographers. An organization that supports directors and choreographers in the professional theatre.

soliloquy. A solo extensive speech that is intended for the audience but not other characters in the play. Often it is meant to convey the private thoughts of a character.

sound designer. An artist who creates acoustic and recorded sound for a production.

space and design choices. Choices made by the director and designers to create a specific effect for the audience.

spectacle. The visual elements called for in a play and added in production, including scenery, costumes, props, lighting, actor physicality, and movement; one of the six elements of a play identified by Aristotle.

spotlight. A type of lighting instrument that is used frequently in the theatre. Glass lenses create a focused and controllable beam of light and various shaped metal and glass reflectors affect the quality of light and shape of the beam.

stage directions. Written descriptions of physical or emotional action or physical appearance.

stage left. The actors' left as they face the audience. Abbreviated SL or L.

stage manager. A staff member who ensures that things run smoothly on and back stage. Stage managers coordinate a show during rehearsal and performance and keep the director's artistic choices intact during its run.

stage right. The actors' right as they face the audience. Abbreviated SR or R.

staging. Combining all elements of production to bring the text alive in three dimensions. Staging is ultimately the responsibility of the director.

structure. See **plot.**

Sturm und Drang ("storm and stress"). A preromantic movement that deliberately broke all the rules of neoclassicism. The *Sturm und Drang* playwrights shocked their audiences with plays full of violence and forbidden topics such as teen pregnancy, rape, self-mutilation, and infanticide.

style. The manner of expression and methods of onstage behavior as they affect composition and performance. Style is dictated by language—poetry, prose, and dialects. Style is identified by character movement and social manners and by changes and fashions in architecture, clothes, furniture, and decoration (on both low and high economic scales).

subplot. A secondary line of action in a causal plot. Conflict different than that of the major line of action is developed. Subplots may be entwined with the major line of action and reach a climax in the same scene, or they may develop independently and reach a climax at another time.

subtext. The actual meaning of dialogue behind the words spoken.

superobjective. The major goal of a character through an entire play, suggested as a realistic acting technique by Stanislavsky.

surrealism. Originating in France beginning in 1917, an avant-garde movement in which the dream world and the real world are intertwined and difficult or impossible to distinguish.

symbolism. Beginning in the 1890s in France, this avant-garde movement was the first major challenge to realism. Its plays were dominated by obvious symbolism and were often played in simple spaces with antirealistic scenery and acting styles. The legacy of symbolism is very much alive in theatre for children, Disney films, and many romantic musicals.

taste. The personal inclination and preferences of the beholder of an aesthetic experience.

technical director. A staff member who is responsible for the safety of the theatre space, for scheduling, for construction and equipment installation, and for making sure designs are executed according to designers' specifications.

technical rehearsal. A rehearsal in which light, sound, and set changes are added to a show. The term is also used for the specific rehearsal in which the stage manager, actors, and run crews practice putting all elements (except costumes) together in a complete run of the show (also called a *tech run*).

technitae. An actor during the Hellenistic period; the term is probably related to the professional status of Greek actors in the fourth century and beyond.

texture. An element of costume; the feel of the fabric (fine, smooth, soft, rough).

theatre or **theater.** The ongoing institution and practice of the theatre as well as the theatre building; both spellings are correct.

theatre critic. A writer who specializes in evaluating production and sharing that viewpoint with the public.

Theatre of the Absurd. Post–World War II plays centered on characters who are strangers to each other, trapped in a violent, meaningless world seemingly without design or purpose.

Theatre of Cruelty. An approach to theatre developed by Antonin Artaud between the world wars emphasizing a breakdown of causality and stressing emotion over intellect. Artaud hoped to work on emotions by assaulting the senses of the audience.

theatron. The audience seating area (literally "seeing place") in the theatre of ancient Greece. At first temporary seating on a hillside, seats were set in stone permanently by the fourth century B.C.E.

thought. The ideas in a play; one of the six elements of a play identified by Aristotle.

three unities. Neoclassical guidelines for writing plays. These were unity of time (the action of the play should take place in twenty-four hours or less), unity of place (action should occur in one location), and unity of action (no subplots unless fully integrated with the central conflict).

thrust space/theatre. An actor/audience configuration in which the audience is on three sides of the performance area.

tragedy. A dramatic genre of plays that is serious and ends unhappily. Aristotle identified magnitude (importance) as a chief attribute of tragedy and noted that it evoked the emotions of pity and fear in the audience.

tragicomedy. A dramatic genre in which tragic and comic tendencies seem equally mixed.

trap. An opening in the stage floor for ascents and descents.

trilogy. Three related plays; ancient Greek playwrights submitted three tragedies—sometimes a trilogy—for the contest in honor of Dionysus in Athens.

trope. An exchange of dialogue in musical form in which the singers or chanters represented characters from the Bible, presented as early as c. 925 in the European Christian monasteries and cathedrals. The first recorded type of liturgical drama.

United Scenic Artists of America. The union of set, costume, lighting, and sound designers in the United States.

upstage. The area farthest from the audience. Abbreviated U.

unit set. A single scenic unit that is used to represent many different locations.

verisimilitude. A neoclassical concept that established that theatrical events as written and staged should be reality-based (events that could really occur in life).

verse. Poetry; heightened language that may have a rhyme scheme or just a specific rhythm. For many centuries stage dialogue was written in verse.

vomitory. An entrance to elevated seating for the audience that runs underneath the audience and comes up to empty out into the seating area.

well-made play. A category of drama in which a meticulous and involved plot takes precedence over all other elements. As perfected by French playwright Eugène Scribe (1791–1861), the well-made play featured an intricate pattern of causality, carefully controlled suspense, and misunderstandings and reversals, leading to an emotionally satisfying climax followed by rapidly falling action.

wheel of fortune. The notion that fortunes change if we wait long enough. In medieval and Renaissance art and literature, it is a literal wheel that carries a person to the top of good fortune before dropping him or her to bad fortune.

wing, drop, and border scenery. Flat pieces of scenery painted to look three-dimensional including flat painted panels on either side of the stage (wings), a large expanse of painted fabric upstage (drop or shutters), and strips of cloth or panels hung horizontally across the tops of the wings (borders). This type of scenery was typical in Europe and beyond from the Renaissance to the late nineteenth century.

wings. (1) In a proscenium theatre, spaces offstage left and right for actors, crew, and scenery not yet in the visible performance space. (2) Changeable flats that could be pulled quickly on and offstage in grooves on the floor and at the top of the tall wings (in wing, drop, and border scenery).

yard. See **pit.**

yugen. In the performance of Noh, the creation of temporary beauty. The beauty of performance is compared to a flower: elegant, lovely, transitory.

zanni. Masked servant clowns such as Arlecchino and Brighella in *commedia dell'arte.*

References

Chapter 1

1. Reprinted from "Questions for a Feminist Methodology in Theatre History," in *Interpreting the Theatrical Past,* edited by Thomas Postlewait and Bruce A. McConachie, published by the University of Iowa Press, 1989. Reprinted by permission.
2. "About the Healing Power of the Arts," http://www.artslynx.org/heal/about.htm (August 12, 2002). Reprinted by permission.
3. National Association for Drama Therapy, "Welcome," http://www.nadt.org/html/About.htm (September 6, 2001).

Chapter 2

1. Peter Brook, *The Empty Space* (New York: Simon & Schuster), 9. Reprinted with the permission of Scribner, an imprint of Simon & Schuster Adult Publishing Group from *The Empty Space* by Peter Brook. Copyright © 1968 Peter Brook.
2. William Hooker Gillette, *Secret Service* in *Staging the Nation: Plays from the American Theater, 1787–1909,* ed. Don B. Wilmeth (Boston: Bedford, 1998), 455.

Chapter 3

1. For detailed analysis of audience reception and perception theory, various approaches to theatre as a system of communication and case studies of the nature of performance and audience, see the Swedish historian and theorist Willmar Sauter, *The Theatrical Event: Dynamics of Performance and Perception* (Iowa City: Iowa University Press, 2000).
2. William Hooker Gillette, "The Illusion of the First Time in Acting," *Actors on Acting,* ed. Toby Cole and Helen Krich Chinoy (New York: Crown, 1970), 564.

Chapter 4

1. The term "crisis" is another term that is often used in discussions of dramatic structure. This contested term is used to suggest several different devices. Some use "crisis" to suggest a period of time after the conflict is defined leading up to the climax (which we call rising action). Some use "crisis" to mean the same thing as "climax" but also an identification of a series of secondary climaxes leading up to the big one. Some use "crisis" instead of "climax," reserving the latter term to heightened audience response in causal drama. Some dramatic analysts prefer to avoid the term altogether.
2. Burns Mantle and Garrison P. Sherwood, *The Best Plays of 1909–1919* (New York: Dodd, Mead, 1933), 202–238.
3. Harold Pinter, *Betrayal* in *Complete Works: Four* (New York: Grove Press, 1981), 180. Reprinted by permission.
4. Susan Glaspell, *Trifles* in *Plays by American Women 1900–1930,* ed. Judith Barlow (New York: Applause, 1985).

Chapter 5

1. Shakespeare, *The Winter's Tale,* IIIiii.57.
2. From *Salesman in Beijing* by Arthur Miller, copyright © 1983, 1984 by Arthur Miller, p. 254. Used by permission of Viking Penguin, a division of Penguin Putnam Inc.

Chapter 6

1. The League of American Theatres and Producers, Inc. "The Audience for Touring Broadway: A Demographic Study 1998," April 2001, www.broadway.org/audience.html.
2. The League of American Theatres and Producers, Inc. "Live Broadway: About the League," 1998–2001, www.livebroadway.com/about.html.
3. League of Resident Theatres, "LORT Objectives," July 27, 2001, www.lort.org/mission.htm.
4. Professional Association for Canadian Theatres web site, May 15, 2002, www.pact.ca/files/homepage.htm.
5. Theatre Communications Group web site, http://www.tcg.org.
6. Educational Theatre Association, "Member Services," 2002, www.edta.org/member_services/how_to_join.asp.
7. Association for Theatre in Higher Education, "About ATHE," February 2, 2001, www.athe.org/about/index.html.
8. American Association of Community Theatre, "Who We Are—and Why," www.aact.org/aactorg.html.

9. Steppenwolf Theatre Company, "About Us/History," www.steppenwolf.org/about/history.html.

10. Ronald Wainscott, *Staging O'Neill* (New Haven, Conn: Yale University Press, 1988), 98.

11. Jesse McKinley, "$100 a Ticket for *The Iceman Cometh*," April 8, 1999, www.aisle-7.com/Hollywood/3048/a7icerwb02.html.

12. "Theatre Facts 2001," Theatre Communications Group web site, www.tcg.org.

13. Joal Ryan, "*Cats*: Broadway's Longest-Lived Show" *E!online*, June 19, 1997, www.eonline.com/News/Items/0,1,1311,00.html.

14 *Les Misérables* web site, www.lesmis.com, October 2, 2002.

15. National Endowment for the Arts, "NEA Fact Sheet—NEA at a Glance: 2001," www.arts.gov/learn/Facts/NEA.html. Reprinted by permission.

16. Stuart W. Little, "TKTS in Perspective," *tdf sightlines online*, Spring 1997, www.tdf.org/publications/sightlines/spring-97/sightlines=spring=97.html/TKTS.

17. Ryan, "*Cats*," www.eonline.com/News/Items/0,1,1311,00.html.

18. Americans for the Arts, "Arts and Economic Prosperity: The Economic Impact of Nonprofit Arts Organizations and Their Audiences." Released June 10, 2002. See www.artsusa.org/EconomicImpact. "The $134 billion total includes $53.2 billion in spending by arts organizations and $80.8 billion in events-related spending by audiences."

19. "Governor Pataki Showcases 42nd Street Success Stories" (June 14, 2001), www.state.ny.us/governor/press/year01/june14_7_01.htm.

20. National Endowment for the Arts, "Reassessment of Support for the Arts: Facilities Development" National Endowment for the Arts EXPLORE, June 15, 1999, http://arts.endow.gov/explore/Colloquia/facilities.html.

21. Conserrat Vendrell. "Attack-Art (Scheduled) Uncertainty Plagues Show Business and Art Following Attack" EFE News Service, Lexis-Nexis Academic Universe, Sept 21, 2001, http://web.lexis-nexis.com/universe/document?_m=87bf97c4395e828419fb8c7588b7b8b8&_docnum=53&wchp=dGLSzV-lSlzV&_md5=69103cd1e1f373206ba3323922e70893.

22. "On with the Show? Don't Bet on It." *BusinessWeek* online, September 28, 2001, www.businessweek.com/bwdaily/dnflash/sep2001/nf20010928_5901.htm.

23. "NY Loves America Tour," January 28, 2002, www.broadwayacrossamerica.com.

Chapter 7

1. Copyright 1941. From *The Dramatic Imagination* by Robert Edmond Jones. Reproduced by permission of Routledge, Inc., part of the Taylor & Francis Group, p. 45.

2. In medieval literature and practice, terms such as "mystery," "miracle," and "interlude" are often used interchangeably. Also the terms often mean different kinds of plays depending on the country in which they occur. We have made choices here to avoid the overlaps and confusion.

Chapter 9

1. Anne Nelson, *The Guys* (New York: Random House, 2002), 5.

Chapter 10

1. Arthur Hopkins, *How's Your Second Act?* (New York: Philip Goodman, 1918), p. 26.

2. Actors' Equity Association Web Site, www.actorsequity.org (July 10, 2002).

3. Charles L. Mee, "the (re)making project," www.panix.com/~meejr/html=about.htm (July 10, 2002). Reprinted by permission.

4. Meredith Kasten, "Interview with Mary Zimmerman," Second Stage Theatre web site, www.secondstagetheatre.com/meta_interviews.html. July 23, 2002. Reprinted by permission.

Chapter 11

1. Jason Robards in "Talk with the Players," *Newsweek* (Dec. 15, 1958), 63.

2. See Joseph Roach, *The Player's Passion: Studies in the Science of Acting* (Ann Arbor: University of Michigan Press, 1985).

3. Richard Moody, *Dramas from the American Theatre, 1762–1909* (Boston: Houghton Mifflin, 1966), 201.

4. Guy Pace, "Actors' Equity Annual Report 2001," (December 3, 2001), 3. www.actorsequity.org/AboutEquity/annual_report.html, accessed November 12, 2002.

5. Copyright 1985. From *Cloud 9*, in *Plays: One* by Caryl Churchill, pp. 251–252. Reproduced by permission of Routledge, Inc., part of The Taylor & Francis Group.

Chapter 12

1. Luigi Pirandello, Preface, *Six Characters in Search of an Author*, translated by Eric Bentley, *Naked Masks* (New York: E. P. Dutton & Co., 1952), 364.

2. David Henry Hwang, quoted in Joel Hirschhorn, "Hearing a Different Drum Song: David Henry Hwang," *The Dramatist* (March/April 2002), 9. Reprinted by permission.

3. © Copyright NPR® 2002. The news report by NPR's Neal Conan was originally broadcast on National Public Radio's "Talk of the Nation®" on April 25, 2002, and is used with the permission of National Public Radio, Inc. Any unauthorized duplication is strictly prohibited.

4. Ibid.

5. "The Making of *Urinetown*," moderated by Gregory Bossler, *The Dramatist* (May/June 2002), 13. Reprinted by permission.

6. Harvey Schmidt, "*The Fantasticks*," moderated by Richard Maltby, Jr., *The Dramatist* (May/June 2002), 27.

7. David Savran, *In Their Own Words* (New York: Theatre Communications Group, 1988), 157.

8. Alisa Solomon, "*Rent* Destabilized," *The Village Voice* (Aug. 12, 1997), p. 83.

Index

Allen, Woody, 63
Alley Theatre (Houston), 44, 297
Alleyn, Edward, 207
Alliance of Theatrical Stage Employees, 365–366
Alliance Theatre Company (Atlanta), 147
Allusion, 109–110
Amadeus (Shaffer), 49, 289, 376
Amateur theatre, 147–149, 154–155
Amen Corner, The (Baldwin), 240
American Conservatory Theater, 171
America Play, The (Parks), 100, 329
Analysis, 29, 32, 57–84, 102–103, 120, 133–140, 295, 318
Anderson, Maxwell, 12, 122
Andreini, Isabella, 306
Andronicus, Livius, 182
Angels in America (Kushner), 69, 105, 169, 243–244, 344, 377
Anna Christie (O'Neill), 289, 335, 364
Anne of a Thousand Days (Anderson), 122
Annie (Strauss et al.), 127, 328
Annie Get Your Gun (Berlin), 307
Another Person Is a Foreign Country (Mee), 49
Antigone (Sophocles), 121, 164, 180
Antiquarianism, 227, 231, 272, 352
Antoine, André, 232, 273–274
Aoi No Uye (Zenchiku), 98
Appia, Adolphe, 40, 235, 338, 352, 369
Apron, stage, 41, 43, 194, 217, 382
Arcadia (Stoppard), 326
Arena space, 45–47, 49, 52, 65, 190
Arena Stage, The (Washington, D.C.), 46, 65, 67, 146, 297, 306, 331, 338, 358
Aria da Capo (Millay), 12, 238
Aristophanes, 81–82, 127, 181, 208, 303
Aristotle, 32–34, 88, 94, 113, 120, 182, 184, 203, 271, 334
Armen, Richard, 334
Arms and the Man (Shaw), 127
Aronson, Billy, 344
Aronson, Boris, 78, 152
Artaud, Antonin, 236, 278, 316, 338
Artistic director, 154, 297–298
Assassins (Sondheim), 101
Association for Theatre in Higher Education, 149
Astley's Amphitheatre (London), 383
Astor Place Riot, 224
As You Like It (Shakespeare), 138, 308, 354
Athayde, Roberto, 31
Atrides, Les (Mnouchkine), 244, 281
Auburn, David, 314–315
Audience, 1, 4, 6–7, 14, 16, 26–34, 37–42, 44–53, 58–66, 68–84, 90–92, 95–96, 100–103, 109–110, 135–136,

159–162, 165–166, 193–194, 224–225, 320–323, 380, 382–383
Audio description, 14
Audition (*see* Actor; Director)
Auteur (*see* Director)
Autos sacramentales, 208–209, 218
Avant-garde, 233–240, 243–245, 315–316
Awake and Sing! (Odets), 240, 284
Ayckbourn, Alan, 126
Azenberg, Emanuel, 155

Babes in the Big House (Terry), 151
Bacchae, The (Euripides), 48, 180,
Bacchae of Euripides, The (Soyinka), 241
Bald Soprano, The (Ionesco), 237
Baldwin, James, 240, 329
Balkan Express, The (Vulović), 11
Ball, William, 292
Bancroft, Squire, 229
Baraka, Imamu, 237
Barefoot in the Park (Simon), 125
Barry, Elizabeth, 213–214
Barry, Philip, 128, 354
Barrymore, Ethel, 365
Barrymore, John, 68, 365
Barrymore, Lionel, 365
Beaumarchais, 215
Beck, Julian, 239
Beckett, Samuel, 99, 102, 115, 131, 134, 237, 284–285, 356
Bedroom Farce (Ayckbourn), 126
Beggar's Opera, The (Gay), 72, 216
Behn, Aphra, 9, 214, 331
Beijing opera (*see* Chinese music drama)
Béjart, Armande, 321
Belasco, David, 151, 273, 293, 368
Bel Geddes, Norman, 48, 280
Belle Reprieve (P. Shaw et al.), 243, 309
Bells, The, 132
Benedetti, Robert, 313
Bennett, Michael, 152, 242
Bérénice (Racine), 70
Bergman, Ingmar, 43, 66, 152
Berkeley Repertory Theatre, 298
Berlin, Irving, 307
Bernhardt, Sarah, 226
Bernstein, Leonard, 22, 50, 242, 353
Betrayal (Pinter), 97, 111
Betterton, Thomas, 213–214
Beyond the Horizon (O'Neill), 79
Bibiena, Giuseppe, 350, 352

Indiana Repertory Theatre, 29, 49, 97, 107, 127–128, 368–369, 371, 376–377, 386
Interact Center for the Visual and Performing Arts, 14
Interlude, 190
Intermezzi, 202
Interpretation, 38, 48, 60–61, 95, 102–103, 119–140, 133–140, 164, 184 (*see also* Design; Director)
In the Blood (Parks), 329
Into the Woods (Sondheim and Lapine), 104, 307, 337
Ionesco, Eugène, 65, 68–70, 237
Iphigenia in Taurus (Goethe), 223
Irving, Henry, 132
Irwin, Bill, 305
It Can't Happen Here (Lewis), 158
It's a Slippery Slope (Gray), 342
Italian Renaissance, 200–204

Jacobs, Sally, 279
James, Toni-Leslie, 6, 164, 284, 377
Jane Eyre (Caird and Gordon), 315, 328, 353, 354, 373, 378
Jarry, Alfred, 234, 356
Jelly's Last Jam, 377
Jessner, Leopold, 280
Jesus Christ Superstar (Webber), 149
Jitney (Wilson), 241–242
Johan, Johan (Heywood), 189–190
John, Elton, 27, 242, 356, 389
Joint Stock Theatre Company, 343
Jones, James Earl, 305–306
Jones, Margo, 297
Jones, Robert Edmond, 79, 122, 172, 280, 288–289, 352, 364–365, 380
Jones, Tom, 4, 129
Jonson, Ben, 124, 206
Jouvet, Louis, 290

Kabuki, 19, 44, 59, 72, 115, 122, 125–126, 137, 152, 166, 193–196, 228, 235, 288, 303, 318, 348, 350, 352–353
Kadensho (Zeami), 193
Kahn, Michael, 6, 164, 283–284, 332, 338, 377
Kaiser, Georg, 235
Kalidasa, 98–99
Kan'ami, 193, 334
Kander, John, 168, 378
Kaplan, Lewis A., 344
Kathakali, 8, 36–37, 115, 165, 185–186, 244, 281, 303
Katz, Natasha, 369, 371, 389
Kaufman, Moisés, 343, 346
Kazan, Elia, 97, 123, 241, 284–285, 288, 358
Kean, Charles, 272

Kean, Edmund, 226, 311
Keely and Du (Martin), 341
Keene, Laura, 229
Kemble, Charles, 311
Kemble, John Philip, 215, 224
Kempe, William, 334
Kennedy, Adrienne, 100, 237
Kern, Jerome, 242
Kerr, Walter, 78
King John (Shakespeare), 352
King Lear (Shakespeare), 207, 226, 278
King, the Greatest Alcalde, The (Lope de Vega), 209
Kinney, Terry, 150, 154
Kiss of the Spider Woman, 153
Kleist, Heinrich von, 130, 223
Kline, Kevin, 62
Klugman, Jack, 5
Knee Plays, The (Wilson), 290
Knott, Frederick, 132
Kotis, Greg, 29–30, 242, 356
Kramer, Larry, 11, 243
Krumlov Castle Court Theatre, 43
K2 (Meyers), 358
Kumagai's Camp (Sosuke), 194, 196
Kushner, Tony, 11, 34, 69, 105, 243–244, 344
Kutiyattum, 185–186
Kyd, Thomas, 206–207
Kyōgen, 125

Labiche, Eugène, 89
Lady of the Camelias, The (Dumas *fils*), 226
Lady Windermere's Fan (Wilde), 128
La Jolla Playhouse, 147, 166, 170
Lamos, Mark, 298
Lane, Nathan, 126, 167, 305–306, 315
Lane, Sarah, 229
Language, 71–72, 81, 88, 102, 108, 110–113, 115
    aside, 111
    blank verse, 110, 206
    dialogue, 37, 59, 62–63, 88, 90–91, 100, 108, 110–113, 134–135, 139, 231, 237, 245, 285
    hyperbole, 111
    metaphor, 110
    monologue, 111, 245
    prose, 110
    sensory imagery, 111
    simile, 110
    soliloquy, 111
    translation, 110
    verse, 110, 137, 171, 180, 311
Lapine, James, 104, 307, 328, 337